The Faces
of Existence

The Faces of Existence

An Essay in Nonreductive Metaphysics

by JOHN F. POST

Cornell University Press

ITHACA AND LONDON

CORNELL UNIVERSITY PRESS GRATEFULLY ACKNOWLEDGES
A GRANT FROM THE ANDREW W. MELLON FOUNDATION THAT
AIDED IN BRINGING THIS BOOK TO PUBLICATION.

First published 1987 by Cornell University Press.

International Standard Book Number 0-8014-1968-9
Library of Congress Catalog Card Number 86-19894

Printed in the United States of America

*Librarians: Library of Congress cataloging information
appears on the last page of the book.*

*The paper in this book is acid-free and meets the guidelines for
permanence and durability of the Committee on Production Guidelines
for Book Longevity of the Council on Library Resources.*

For all those who know what it meant,
if not entirely what it means,
and especially for Pat, Gavin, 'n Gaines.

Contents

Acknowledgments

Basically right in outline, if occasionally wrong in detail—that, I like to think, is true of what follows. Whatever the shortcomings, there would have been fewer had a whole team been at work, each the authority on a particular subject, each in touch with others around the world. I am glad, however, to acknowledge here the invaluable comments, criticisms, and encouragement by a number of philosophers, at various times and in various ways, including above all Andrew Cling, Norman Dahl, Geoffrey Hellman, Terry Horgan, William Lycan, Alasdair MacIntyre, John Pollock, W. V. Quine, Geoffrey Sayre-McCord, Ernest Sosa, Paul Teller, Jeffrey Tlumak, and an anonymous referee for Cornell University Press. Naturally, none is thereby implicated in the final outcome. I am indebted also to Vanderbilt University for a timely sabbatical and to the Vanderbilt University Research Council for supplemental aid. John Ackerman, Editor-in-Chief of Cornell University Press, made a number of helpful comments on the Introduction.

For permission to incorporate portions of "Infinite Regresses of Justification and of Explanation" (copyright © 1980, D. Reidel Publishing Co.) into §§2.3–2.4, and portions of "On the Determinacy of Valuation" (copyright © 1984, D. Reidel Publishing Co.) into §§6.0–6.3, thanks to to *Philosophical Studies* and its publisher, D. Reidel Publishing Company. For permission to incorporate portions of "On the Determinacy of Truth and Translation" into §1.1, thanks go to the *Southern Journal of Philosophy*. The book's dedication was stimulated by Marcus Singer's for his *Generalization in Ethics*.

11

Credit goes to Gaines Post, Jr., brother, friend, dean, and fine schol-ar of twentieth-century European military and diplomatic history, for the first line of §4.6. My wife, Patricia Trueblood Post, who knows not only what it meant but very much what it means, painstakingly read various drafts and frequently saved me from my worst excesses. Finally, thanks perhaps above all both to my father, Gaines Post, Sr., dis-tinguished historian of medieval legal and political thought, for setting the example in so much, from scholarship to the home, and to my mother, Katherine Rike Post, for her unfailing wisdom.

JOHN F. POST

Nashville, Tennessee

The Faces
of Existence

Introduction

Explaining metaphysics to the nation—I wish he would explain his explanation.

—Byron

The real drama in metaphysics remains where it has always been, in balancing the rage for order with delight in near chaotic variety. Order prevails from time to time, in the form of theories about some underlying unity, only to break down when unruly aspects of things disrupt our schemes of the world. What seemed a fine drama can even end as farce. Metaphysicians need therefore to combine their traditional high seriousness with a sense of irony and a capacity for self-satire.

In this spirit I offer one more scheme, if we may call it that. For even as it defends a particular unity-in-variety, it celebrates the variety of unities. Just as there are many faces of existence, there are many ways of unifying them. None represents *the* way things are, some ultimate visage with respect to which the rest are but masks; for there is no such ultimate. Yet this tolerant pluralism is conjoined with ideas often deemed incompatible with it, including a realist notion of objective truth, plus the idea that there is one particular domain of such truth that determines all else, values and meaning not excluded.

This seemingly paradoxical conjunction is but one of several to come, including above all the conjunction of a materialist unification with much that is generally supposed to be incompatible with it. Thus on one level the book endorses physicalist materialism, the thesis roughly that everything whatever is some collection of entities of the kind that mathematical physics is about, and that all truth is determined at bottom by mathematical-physical truth. Yet on another level the book repudiates virtually everything traditionally associated with such physicalism, including the idea that everything is nothing but a physical thing. Not everything real can be brought under some physical or other objective

15

description, and physically irreducible talk is far from automatically false or meaningless. Hence we need not disparage subjective consciousness, or what it is like to be the persons we are, experiencing time and death as we do, and conscience and mystery. Nor need we belittle emotions and secondary qualities; the former can correspond with the facts, and the latter, suitably construed, are among the important ways things are.

Indeed the basic nature of reality is not physical in the first place, if only because there is no such thing as *the* nature of reality. There is even a sense in which value is prior to fact, physical fact included, and a sense in which we may objectively condemn a descriptive world-view if its moral implications are unacceptable. Such reordering of priorities runs counter not only to the usual materialisms but to much modern philosophy. For according to the modern mind, we ought first to establish a satisfactory world-view, then read off its moral implications, if any; we should attend first to neutral fact, then to values, lest we commit wishful thinking. Within materialism this attitude is part of the recurring Democritean slogan, "Only atoms and the void exist; therefore our values are mere conventions." Or as a leading ethicist would have it, "Materialistic . . . philosophers deny that the objective world of matter in motion has any place for moral goods. . . . Good and evil . . . are rather [our] internal and variable reactions to the ways in which [we] are stimulated by the world."[1]

By contrast we see in Chapter 6 that the purely objective, descriptive facts determine which of our value judgments are correct, first principles included. True, no *ought* can be derived from any *is,* or be reduced to or defined by it; or so I assume, if only for the sake of argument. Even so, the world determines one and only one distribution of truth and falsity over our value judgments, whether or not we could ever know just what that distribution is, and whatever our subjective responses to the stimuli might be. Thanks to this determinacy of valuation, the facts are not neutral but laden with value, objectively, whatever may be our interpretations of or projections onto them. And if all fact is determined by physical fact, as physicalist materialism contends, then the objective world of matter in motion is likewise laden with value.

In these and other ways, then, do the chapters ahead reject traditional materialist theses. Yet they also accept three principles characteristic of physicalist materialism: (i) only physical entities exist; (ii) there can be no difference between things without some physical dif-

---

[1]Gewirth, 979.

ference between them; and (iii) all truth whatever, whether in the sciences or beyond, is determined by truths at the level of physics. Principles (i)–(iii), together with a possibly implied realism as regards truth, are the distinctive minimal theses of any physicalism properly so-called. Possibly they are also maximal, in the sense that a physicalism that claims more—universal physical reducibility, for instance—is false.

The minimal physicalist theses do not all appear until Chapter 4, and even there they are accepted mainly for the sake of argument, in order to explain just what physicalism is and to explore how far it might nonreductively account for all the aspects of existence. Gradually, in subsequent chapters, our confidence in the minimal theses will grow, as we learn how they are compatible after all with so much that physicalism traditionally is supposed to contradict. Few things if any are only physical entities, yet only physical entities exist. What precisely this seeming paradox comes to and how we can get away with asserting it are first explained in §4.5 and developed further in Chapters 5–8. What lies ahead is an extended exercise in having our cake and eating it too—an enviable position always, which is why compatibilism is so attractive when the evidence is not totally against it.

A quarter-century has gone by since Wilfrid Sellars first urged the problem of how the scientific and the manifest images of human-being-in-the-world are related, and J. J. C. Smart in effect weighed in on the side of the scientific with his sweeping materialist vision of things.[2] Meanwhile, physicalism has undergone what amounts to a revolution, especially in the last decade. Philosophers in growing numbers have begun to realize that physicalism need not be reductive—that nonphysical properties need not be identical with physical properties, and that terms from disciplines beyond physics need not be definable by terms from physics. A few philosophers have gone on to supply the needed positive account of a nonreductive relation between physical truth and other truth. The needed relation is determination, also called "supervenience" (or a variety of it), which we encounter first in §1.1 and in more detail in §4.3.

These somewhat technical developments deserve to be much more widely known. Not only do they render Smart's and many other materialisms nearly obsolete; they suggest that Sellars' two-image problem is badly conceived in ways that would not otherwise occur to his readers. Thus one of my aims is to make a number of technical ideas accessible to a wider audience. Another is to do so in a way that combines the ideas in a large and largely original unifying scheme. Attempting both at once

[2]Sellars; Smart (1963).

requires more pages than does addressing an audience only of specialists. So yes, the book could be shorter, but then it would be understood by many fewer. And yes, those interested only or mainly in, say, how best to formulate the determination relation could do without the rest. But the result would be a monograph, not a philosophy.

Furthermore, the insight that physicalism can be nonreductive, and that its key relation is determination, suggests new approaches to a variety of topics well beyond the philosophy of mind, where for the most part nonreductive physicalism has so far been explored. Here too I claim originality, in applying the determination relation to problems about truth, objectivity of values, metaphor, pluralism, subjectivity, secondary qualities, the so-called absurdity of existence, and more. Yet the novelty is a mixed blessing. On the one hand, stock objections to objectivism and physicalism are blocked. On the other, because the whole is hard to classify, it risks appearing unintelligible to those who see everything in traditional terms. Where they see either-or, I tend to see both-and, and to stress a compatibilism that must seem paradoxical to those whose categories allow too few distinctions and therefore no middle ground. The resulting philosophy, despite adhering to the minimal physicalist principles, is not happily called physicalism, in view of its inclusion of so much generally supposed to be anathema to the physicalist. A far happier name, surely, would be 'post-physicalism'.

Even theism can be accommodated within a nonreductive physicalism, if we may believe the final chapter. Not that the minimal physicalist theses imply some version of theism (so that if theism is absurd, as some think, then the final chapter represents a reduction to absurdity of what has gone before). Nor is the point merely that physicalism is logically consistent with theism, though there are those who will resist even this much (as I do myself, when the theism is of a certain form). Instead, I sketch a theory or synthesis of physicalism and theism within which each enriches the other while correcting the other's occasional extremes. What emerges is the possibility—admittedly speculative—of a new natural theology, objective and rational, in which an austere naturalism provides a framework within whose confines one could interpret and support the central theistic claims without having to identify God with any physical entity, or indeed with any entity, hence with any mere God of the philosophers. In a sense we shall be entertaining the possibility that a theologian could do in the twentieth century roughly what Aquinas did in the thirteenth, but without either the Aristotelianism or the Thomism.

The only metaphysical or ontological theses theologians would need to assume are the physicalist's minimal ones. Theism thus construed would be not a matter of what there objectively is but an equally objective matter of how we ought to experience and talk about what there is—equally objective thanks to the earlier argued determinacy of valuation. What theologians would need to add to the physicalist's metaphysics is a *normative* argument to the effect that one ought to see and talk as theists do. Such an argument doubtless would be complex and controversial, yet no less objective in principle for all that.

I do not know whether theologians could finally construct and successfully defend some such normative argument, and indeed I raise a number of possibly insuperable objections to it. But at least it would be compatible with physicalism, and even though theologians would still have work to do, it would be work in value theory, or axiology, rather than in metaphysics, or ontology. They would not need to multiply entities beyond what there objectively is in order to defend theism. Thus freed of worries on the score of what there is, they could concentrate instead on persuading us what objectively there ought to be.

These Delphic remarks about theism demand explanation, of course. The intervening chapters supply some of it, cumulatively, though that is not at all their main purpose. This is true even of Chapter 3, which reaches the Aristotelian-Thomistic conclusion that, suitably defined, the First Cause does exist and indeed is eternal, metaphysically necessary, and self-existent. But even though the conclusion sounds thus traditionally theistic, the assumptions and inferences are not. Principles of Sufficient Reason, for instance, are repudiated earlier, as are the usual notions of necessary being. Furthermore, the First Cause as defined in §3.3 proves identical with the whole of spacetime plus its contents—that is, with the Universe. Pantheists and monists might therefore rejoice, but not theists. Missing, according to them, would be God the loving Creator, utterly transcendent, who yet acts and is revealed in history. No mere philosopher's abstraction, much less the Universe, could ever be the living God of faith. Or so we are told.

A certain concept of truth underlies much of what I've said and yet may seem incompatible with it. The concept is a realist one, according to which truth depends on how things are in the world, not on human or other consciousness or understanding, and not on what is verifiable, or warrantedly assertible, even in the long run by ideal inquirers. According to a realist concept, truth may be said to be "invariant," or objective, roughly in the sense that the truth-value of a true sentence does not vary with the time or place in which it is uttered, or with the persons who utter it, or with their evidence, or even with the totality of the (humanly) accessible evidence. Realist truth is not perspectival but truth *period*.

How then can objective truths possibly express, let alone determine, perspectival or subjective matters such as, say, what it is like to be a bat? Let us assume, if only for the sake of argument, that what it is like cannot be expressed in any objective idiom, and probably not in any human language at all, even though there is a fact of the matter as to what it is like to be a bat. This "irreducibility of experience" would obtain anywhere an experience involves the subject's point of view. What it is like to be the persons we are, experiencing time and death as we do, plus intentionality, valuing, and more, would elude objective description precisely because such description omits the subjective point of view. But even granting this irreducibility of experience, objective truths nevertheless determine these objectively inexpressible facts about what it is like to be the subject. The subjective point of view is irreducible and sometimes inexpressible, yet even such perspectival matters are determined by nonperspectival truth, as we see in §5.4. Thanks to the relation of determination, a realist notion of objective truth need filter neither us nor our experience out of existence.

Nor is a realist notion of truth incompatible with the insight that understanding often enjoys a kind of priority over objective truth, or that what Heidegger calls "truth as disclosure" is more basic, on occasion, than propositional truth. Things appear to us, or are disclosed, under certain of their aspects rather than others, in virtue partly of our prior choices of vocabulary and metaphor. Thus we bear some responsibility for the ways things become part of our world or worlds; for us, things never have their being or their properties by themselves but only through the combined activity of our understanding and some undisclosed ground beyond. At the same time, realism is right that propositional truth depends on how things objectively are. In a sense explained in Chapter 7, we are the measure of all things, yet reality takes our measure.

Realist concepts of truth have also seemed incompatible with various theories of metaphor and with certain notions of metaphorical truth. That they are not is the lesson of §§5.2–5.3, even though metaphorical truth will prove to be determined by literal truth. Nor does an austere realism force truth-seekers to abstain from vagueness or from the novel, poetic, sometimes tortured usage that so often precedes new ways of seeing things. Reduction to the literal, let alone to aseptic precision, is nowhere envisaged. Yet there will prove to be a sense in which the poetry that so often precedes even physics is itself also grounded in physics.

Despite all these reassuring compatibilities, there remains a grinning skeleton in the realist's closet. For there is still the question of what exactly is the relation between words and the world, in virtue of which a true sentence is true. Realists have been far less successful in saying what the relation is than in criticizing their opponents. Classical relations of correspondence, obviously flawed, have long since yielded to Tarskian notions of satisfaction, or to notions of causal or other objective reference. These in turn have fared little better, according to many, in view of Quine's arguments against determinate reference, Putnam's model-theoretic argument against the very idea of the *intended* interpretation of our words, and so on. The relation between words and the world in virtue of which a true sentence is true appears as elusive as ever, especially if, as everyone seems to have supposed, it must involve some relation of objective reference between terms and the world. The realist account in §1.1 overcomes these difficulties by explaining how truth is determined by the world even if reference is not, and even if no sense can be made of the idea of the intended interpretation. This relation of truth-determination by the world then enables us to define a suitable relation of correspondence.

Some philosophers, perhaps especially some philosophers of science, worry that a realist notion of truth must be so transcendent as to have no implications for the actual practice of inquirers. But we shall see that it has crucial implications for practice, even if there should happen to be no criteria for truth or even for probable truth. There would remain prerequisites for truth—logically necessary conditions for the truth of a belief. At least seven such prerequisites may be derived, and they apply no matter what the domain of discourse. Thus to the extent that we are interested in truth—meaning truth *period*—there is a unity of method common to all the domains, religion and values included. We are not free to departmentalize by claiming that reason applies only so far, leaving the rest to the passions or to faith. That way lies bureaucratization of the mind.

I have been introducing some of the seemingly paradoxical conjunctions asserted in the chapters ahead: monism yet pluralism; objectivity yet subjectivity; value determined by fact yet irreducible to the facts; determinate truth yet possibly indeterminate reference; physicalism yet possibly theism; and more. Even if some of these conclusions should some day prove untenable, the arguments for them contain ideas and methods that philosophers of any persuasion might use. Metaphysicians of any stripe, not just physicalists, might use the idea of nonreductive determination to good effect if challenged to explain the relation between *their* unifying existents and the aspects of life we are supposed to account for. Philosophers could also profit from a distinction so far unmentioned: between a philosophy that is completely comprehensive or unifying and one that is monopolizing, totalizing, or Procrustean. And many could usefully emphasize, against their opponents, that the priority so often claimed by metaphysicians on behalf of certain existents is, like all such primacy, always priority only in a respect; and that partly as a consequence, many a metaphysical dispute is really a value dispute in disguise.

So I shall not be very perturbed if many of my conclusions end some day as just one more moth circling the flame. That, after all, is the fate of every philosophy. And beyond all particular doctrines and methods, I am animated anyway by the conviction that metaphysics is much more closely related to our everyday lives than is often realized. If here and there the chapters ahead help to clarify this closeness, I shall be content.

Life's good things are possible only if we do or become certain things. We have long since begun to learn this art of the possible when philosophy challenges us to learn it still better, through disciplined reflection on how best to attain as many of our ends as realistically we can. Typically, such reflection reveals what most of us already sense: the ends often conflict and must be modified, or replaced by others, in a lifelong pursuit of some sort of balance, however provisional. And instead of lurching from crisis to crisis, we are enabled by such reflection to anticipate. We look beyond the horizon of immediate troubles; we unfold our maps of the larger world; strategy informs tactics; and we perceive our individual fate tied to the fate of others and to the lay of the land. The balance we pursue proves sensitive after all to what we think about how our little worlds fit into the larger one, and to what we think of its ways, its meanings, its explanations and origin. In the long run, and for practical reasons, we cannot afford indifference to the larger questions, even if we totally lack the gift of wonder. The faces of existence seem to frown upon it.

1 Truth

Pilate sayeth unto him, "What is truth?"
— JOHN 18:38

We attribute to truth a superhuman objectivity . . . though we cannot say what it means.

— ALBERT EINSTEIN

1.0. Introduction

Philosophy begins in wonder, and we hope it ends in truth. This is not the only aim of philosophy, and not always the most urgent, but surely one of the things the lover of wisdom pursues is truth. And yet what is it we pursue, when we pursue truth? Without some clear idea it could be a chimera, though not necessarily—prey vaguely glimpsed through the forest still is prey. But the more we know about the creature—its size, habits, and tracks—the better we can tell how to capture it, and the better we can tell when we have captured that kind rather than what biologists call its mimic. We need to know something about what we are looking for when we are looking for the truth about something.

Unfortunately, 'truth' has many senses. Sometimes it names meditative awareness of an alleged "beyond that is within." Sometimes it names a less quiet state of inwardness or subjectivity. Or it may denote what mystics claim to see, perhaps a universal oneness, ecstatic and ineffable, in which subject and object completely fuse: "Those who know don't say, and those who say don't know," in the Taoist epigram. Sometimes 'truth' is supposed to name an equally unutterable union with God. Or it may be used to name various modes of secular insight and understanding held to be incompletely expressible.

More often, truth is attributed to particular beliefs. So far from being ineffable, such truth is spoken, routinely, whenever we utter a sentence that expresses some particular true belief. It is this, the truth of beliefs, that we consider here. Later we see how the realist account sketched in §1.1 is compatible after all with notions of truth as disclosure, with the occasional priority of such truth and of understanding and metaphor, and with the irreducibility of perspectival matters such as what it is like to be the subject (§§5.3, 5.4, 7.1). We also see how religious and mystical vision might conceivably be construed on occasion as invaluable and correct, even within the frame of an astringent physicalism (§8.2). So let us suppress the urge to stereotype the present account as just another victim of discursive, analytical, rational, Western modes of thought, oblivious to opposite insights. Truth can be discursive—the truth of beliefs—while heightened states of insight and being are not. To call the former true is not to belittle the latter. They are neither true nor untrue but authentic or not, according to standards appropriate perhaps to them alone.

Is there a concept of truth that applies to beliefs regardless of their subject matter? Indeed there is. The concept applies whether the discourse is from science, religion, or the marketplace. The concept is neutral in a further sense. It does not imply that one of the domains—physics, say—is unconditionally more fundamental than the others. Nor does its use beg any question in favor of physicalism or other "scientific philosophies." Their opponents can and often do use the same concept to good effect: Bishop Berkeley, for example, as we see in §1.5(iv). Indeed the concept is neutral with respect to most philosophies. The only exceptions are those few that reject any such notion of truth, though with what merit we shall soon see.

Of course, truth is not the only virtue of beliefs. On occasion we want them to be and do much more, or even much instead. Sometimes we want a belief to be comforting, and rightly. Often we want it to be inspiring, to move us to action or to tears, and rightly. Some beliefs govern our relations with each other. Others are treasured for their simplicity and comprehensiveness. Still others are valued as generally reliable guides to practical action. These virtues of beliefs, plus many others, do not require the beliefs to be true in the strict sense. It is only when we want our beliefs to be strictly true as well that we are bound by the prerequisites spelled out in §1.5. The pursuit of truth enjoys no unconditional priority over the pursuit of other virtues of beliefs, but once we claim truth for a belief we subject ourselves to relentless imperatives.

1.1. Realism

> *Minimally . . . there has to* be *a determinate relation of*
> reference *between terms and pieces . . . of the world, on the*
> *metaphysical realist model.*
>
> —HILARY PUTNAM

Putnam is wrong, as we shall see.[1] Yet so far as Tarski's theory of truth goes, all we really know is that 'true' satisfies the schema

    T. ϕ is true iff S,

where 'ϕ' is replaced by a name or description of the sentence that replaces 'S' (and 'iff' abbreviates 'if and only if'). That is, truth is a property of a truth-bearer or semantic vehicle ϕ, and a property such that ϕ is a truth iff S. On this all the parties can agree. Differences emerge when we inquire how we should construe the sentence that replaces 'S' in the right-hand limb of this biconditional.

Verificationists, for example, can happily agree that 'The dinosaurs existed' is true iff the dinosaurs existed—provided the right-hand limb here is construed as standing for something like 'So far as would be verified by ideal inquirers in light of their long-run evidence, the dinosaurs existed'. Idealists can also agree, provided 'The dinosaurs existed' stands for something like 'Only as presented to (or constituted by) some human or other consciousness, the dinosaurs existed'. These are distinct concepts of truth, even though their defenders can agree on T so far as it goes. Thus we may begin to understand why Tarski's theory of truth is not, by itself, the vindication of realism it sometimes is thought to be.[2]

What we need is a relation between *whole sentences* and the world, whereby their truth is determined by the world even if reference is not.[3] §1.1.1 clarifies the relevant notion of determination, then presents an argument for the determinacy of truth. The argument is not meant to be a non-question-begging proof of realism. Indeed most of it could be accepted by many nonrealists. The point rather is to show the *intelligibility* of a realist relation between words and the world, in virtue of which relation the world would determine truth even if it were not to determine reference, and even if the very idea of an intended interpretation were to make no sense.

---

[1]Putnam (1977), 484. The present section is a revised and expanded version of Post (1984b).

[2]Cf. Sober, 378–379.

[3]Including "partial reference," proposed by Field (1974).

§§1.1.2 and 1.1.3 further explain this realism by defining suitable relations of correspondence and aboutness between whole sentences and pieces of the world, in virtue of which there is a fact of the matter as regards what objects a sentence is about, even if there should happen to be no fact of the matter as regards the reference of its terms. Thus we have determinacy of translation at the level of what whole sentences are about, even if we should happen not to have it at the level of terms. §1.1.4 explains why even a physicalistically inclined realist need not adopt a causal theory of reference with all its difficulties, and why a causal or naturalized theory of knowledge, though probably needed, can be irreducibly normative yet fully acceptable to the naturalist. §1.1.5 distinguishes 'true' from any (other) value terms for which the determination by the world might also obtain.

1.1.1. The Determinacy of Truth

Determination is a familiar relation and basically a simple one. When we say one thing determines another, we mean merely that given the way the first is, there is one and only one way the second can be. A special case obtains between states of a deterministic physical system, according to which, given the system's state at one time, there is one and only one state it can assume at a later time. Equivalently, given the system and given any other system in the same relevant state, then at a later time the states the two are in must also be the same. Such determin*ism,* however, is not presupposed by the idea of determin*ation* we wish to capture.[4] According to that idea, roughly, given the state (at a time) of the things of one kind (e.g., the physical), and given any things of another kind (biological, semantic, mental), there is one and only one state the latter can be in (at that same time). It would follow, for example, that given the state of the (sub)molecular phenomena in and around a cell, there is one and only one state the biological behavior of the cell can be in. This determin*ation* of one kind of thing by another obviously is compatible with complete *in*determin*ism* as regards the temporally successive states of them both.

To say the world determines truth, then, is to say roughly that given the way(s) the world is, there is one and only one way truth-values can be distributed over our whole sentences (whether or not we could ever know what this distribution is). But only interpreted sentences can have a truth-value. So we should say

---

[4]Along the lines of Hellman and Thompson (1975), who were the first to explicate the idea. But see further §4.3.

WDT1. The world determines truth iff, given the way(s) the world is, for each interpretation of our language there is one and only one way that truth-values can be distributed over our whole sentences as thus interpreted.

This may sound trivially true. For it may seem trivially true that for each interpretation $\Im$ of a language $\mathfrak{L}$, there is one and only one way truth-values can be distributed over the sentences of $\mathfrak{L}$. Thus in the case of an atomic sentence ϕ, ϕ will be true under $\Im$ iff what $\Im$ assigns to ϕ's individual terms are related by what $\Im$ assigns to ϕ's predicate; and either they are so related or not, so that for each $\Im$, each atomic sentence is true or false, its truth (falsity) being settled by whether or not the things are so related, so that there is one and only one way truth-values can be distributed over the atomics.

According to certain antirealist theories of truth, however, not every interpreted sentence is true or false. Some are neither—say, those for which there is no discoverable evidence that would be sufficient to confirm or to disconfirm their truth. It follows that in the absence of some further consideration, there is not one and only one way truth-values can be distributed over the interpreted sentences. In a realist's distribution the sentences would all be true or false; in a verificationist's, some would be neither true nor false. So if WDT1 is true, it is hardly trivially true.

How are we to unpack the modal word 'can' in WDT1? Saying of a physical system that there is one and only one state that it can assume is equivalent, as we saw, to saying that given the system and given any hypothetical other that is relevantly similar, the states the two are in are the same. Thus WDT1 is equivalent to

WDT2. The world determines truth iff, given the world and given any other world that is relevantly similar, under each interpretation the same sentences have the same truth-values in both,

where to say the same sentences have the same truth-values in both is to say that for every sentence ϕ, ϕ is true (false, neuter) in one iff ϕ is true (false, neuter) in the other. There remain two notions in need of further explanation. One is of a pair of relevantly similar possible worlds; the other is of a sentence's having a truth-value under an interpretation in a world, hence being true (false, neuter) under $\Im$ in a world.

As regards the first, the key concept, so far as the argument for the determinacy of truth is concerned, is that of a world. We may construe a world W as a structured domain, namely a triple $<D, P, R>$, where D is the set of W's entities, P is the set of their genuine properties, and R is the set of their genuine relations.[5] And two worlds are relevantly similar iff their respective D's, P's and R's are. The reason we need say nothing here about what counts as a relevant similarity is that the argument for the determinacy of truth will nowhere require us to specify the criteria of relevant similarity in virtue of which two worlds have the same sentences true in them. Let the criteria be any we like—verificationist, coherentist, realist, whatever. Then assume W_1 and W_2 are relevantly similar, however relevance is thus specified. No matter what this relevance comes to, W_1 and W_2 will be relevantly similar by hypothesis. But then, as we shall see, the premises of the argument for the determinacy of truth will automatically apply to W_1 and W_2.

As regards the notion of truth under $\Im$ in W, start with the union $\cup D_i$ of all the domains of all the worlds W_i (plus also $\cup P_i$ and $\cup R_i$). Then let an interpretation $\Im$ be a function that assigns things from $\cup D_i$, $\cup P_i$, and $\cup R_i$ to the terms of our language $\mathfrak{L}$. For the atomic sentences of $\mathfrak{L}$, truth under $\Im$ in W may be defined by

> TW. An atomic ϕ is true under $\Im$ in $W = <D, P, R>$ iff the elements of $\cup D_i$ that $\Im$ assigns to ϕ's individual terms are (a) in D, and (b) related by what $\Im$ assigns from $\cup P_i$ or $\cup R_i$ to ϕ's predicate.

In the normal recursive way, one then defines 'true under $\Im$ in W' for ever more complex sentences. Hence Tarski's theory of truth enters the present account as the machinery for defining 'true under $\Im$ in W'.[6] Note that TW allows us to speak of truth under the same interpretation even in two worlds so different as to contain no individuals in common. Also, TW allows us to say either that ϕ is false or that ϕ is neuter, in case the elements $\Im$ assigns to ϕ's individual terms are not all in D.

So much by way of preliminaries. What now is the argument for the determinacy of truth? It has two major premises. Opposing theorists of truth can and typically do accept them both. The first is the principle that if a couple of interpreted sentences ϕ and ψ differ in truth-value, then there must be some further, relevant difference between ϕ and ψ that accounts for this. Where the theorists disagree is mostly in what

---

[5]Following Merrill, though this is not essential. The properties and relations are to be construed extensionally. On this and on domesticating the modal notion of a world, see §4.1.

[6]Also, other ways of neutralizing the paradoxes may be inserted here as, say, in Kripke (1975) or (perhaps better) Burge. Cf. Tarski; Soames.

counts as a relevant difference. For verificationists and pragmatists, the difference has something to do with verifiability or warranted assertibility by ideal inquirers in the long run; if there is no difference inquirers could ever discover in the evidence for ϕ and ψ, then there can be no difference in their truth-value. For coherentists, the relevant difference is a matter of coherence or incoherence with some comprehensive system of sentences. For realists, the crucial difference normally involves how things are, independently of inquirers, evidence, coherence, consciousness, and so on. (We must say *normally,* since if a certain sentence is itself about inquirers, evidence, consciousness, or whatever, then obviously its truth-value cannot be totally independent of these things it is about.)

In slogan form, what the different theorists can thus agree to is "No difference in truth-value without some further, relevant difference," or "Treat like sentences alike." In the case of a single sentence ϕ, this is equivalent to saying that, if, under a given interpretation $\Im$, ϕ has a certain truth-value in one circumstance or possible world, then ϕ has that same value under $\Im$ in any other relevantly similar circumstance or world. This in turn is equivalent to the following universalizability or Equity Principle for Truth:

> EPT. Given any two relevantly similar circumstances or worlds and any interpretation $\Im$, ϕ is true (false, neuter) under $\Im$ in one iff ϕ is true (false, neuter) under $\Im$ in the other.

EPT echoes universalizability principles in morals, according to which (among other things) an act that is morally right (wrong) in one circumstance is morally right (wrong) in any relevantly similar circumstance (a kind of supervenience of the moral on the descriptive; cf. §4.2). If and to the extent that 'true' (or 'true under $\Im$') is itself a normative value term, we should always have expected it to behave in accord with EPT.

Indeed my strategy will be to exploit this recognition that 'true', if not a full-fledged value term, at least resembles a value term to the extent of satisfying the Equity Principle.[7] Thus the strategy is compatible with the denial[8] that truth is evaluative, while at the same time it can accommodate the "normativity" of meaning.[9] We may then apply to truth an analogue of the argument in §6.1 for the determinacy of valuation generally. In fact the determinacy of truth is just a corollary of the determinacy of valuation, as is the determinacy of such epistemic no-

---

[7]Cf. Ellis.
[8]Say by Field (1982), 563.
[9]As Kripke (1982), 37, calls it.

tions as knowledge and justification (§1.1.4), provided only that truth satisfies both EPT and one further meta-ethical principle. Irony there will be, but no cart before the horse, in using an argument from meta-ethics to illuminate problems about truth.

This further meta-ethical principle is our second major premise. It is an analogue of meta-ethical antirelativism, and emerges in the course of the following sort of reflection. In principle, at least, the different theories of truth can accord the same interpreted sentence different truth-values, in light of the theories' differing ideas about what count as the relevant factors in virtue of which a true sentence is true. For example, an interpreted sentence ϕ might be true according to a verificationist or pragmatist concept of truth, in the sense that ϕ is ideal from the point of view of operational utility, inner beauty and elegance, simplicity, and so on. Yet notoriously this same ϕ could be false, according to the realist's concept of truth; some further factor is relevant. In this sort of case, the differing theories of truth would yield genuinely conflicting (value) judgments about the truth-value of ϕ (not because they disagree about the evidence for ϕ—the dispute is not thus epistemic—but because they disagree about the concept of truth, or truth's "first principles").

Now the analogue of meta-ethical antirelativism is this: no two such conflicting (value) judgments are both correct (where 'correct' need not mean true but can mean rationally warranted or justified); one and only one of the possible assignments of a truth-value to ϕ (including neuter) is correct, and one of these two conflicting theories' assignments may or may not be it. (Why this is not question-begging emerges in the next few paragraphs.)

More generally, consider all the sentences of our language, and consider various distributions of truth and falsity over them (allowing that some may be neither). Each theory or concept of truth will yield its own distribution over all the sentences, as a function of its idea of what the relevant factors are in virtue of which a true sentence is true. No one need know just what the distribution is. Even verificationists allow that we do not know everything; they require only knowability. But at the ideal limit, the verificationist's concept of truth would yield its one and only one distribution of truth-values over the sentences, in which sentences with no appropriate method of verification would be neither true nor false. In a realist distribution, at least some of those sentences would be true or false. So the analogue of meta-ethical antirelativism here is

MEA. One and only one of the possible distributions of truth-values (including neuter) over all the sentences of our language is correct, and one of the competing theories' distributions may or may not be it, the realist's included.

This last remark shows that MEA does not entail realism. Verificationists, for example, can happily accept MEA, confident that the evidence will verify that their theory or concept of truth is the correct one, along with its distribution. Hence accepting MEA does not beg the question in favor of a realist theory of truth. Nor does accepting MEA amount to assuming the determinacy of truth. MEA means that one and only one distribution is correct, whether or not its being correct is determined by anything further. But determinacy means that which one is correct *is* determined by something further, and in particular by the world. MEA no more entails determinacy than EPT does; their conjunction is necessary.

The argument for the determinacy begins by assuming that we are given an interpretation $\Im$ and two relevantly similar worlds, say W and the actual world W_a. But then by EPT, for every interpretation $\Im$ and sentence ϕ, ϕ is true (false, neuter) under $\Im$ in W iff ϕ is true (false, neuter) under $\Im$ in W_a. That is, the same sentences have the same truth-values under $\Im$ in W and W_a. But (as we saw in connection with the equivalence of WDT1 and WDT2) saying that the same sentences have the same truth-values under $\Im$ in W_a and in every relevantly similar W is just another way of saying that given $\Im$ and the actual world W_α, there is one and only one way truth-values can be distributed over the whole sentences. Hence under each interpretation, W_a allows just one distribution. And the Tarski-style recursive definition of 'true under $\Im$ in W' imposes the usual very powerful compatibility-constraints on any distribution; for example, it cannot happen that every sentence is true in the one distribution, or every sentence false, or 'Fa' false when '$(x)Fx$' is true, and so on. The distribution is Tarskian, in the sense that the values have to be distributed in a way that is consistent with the recursive definition of 'true under $\Im$ in W'.

Furthermore, because we have assumed MEA, the sense in which the actual world W_a allows just one such distribution under $\Im$ is a *strong* sense, not weak. In the *weak* sense there could be a Tarskian distribution *TD* of truth-values in accordance with one theorist's idea of what count as the relevant factors in virtue of which a true sentence is true, where *TD* would be the one and only one distribution induced by W_a in conjunction with this theorist's idea; and all the while there could be a very different *TD'* induced by W_α in conjunction with some *other* theorist's idea. The weak sense is all we are entitled to if we are given only EPT. In the strong sense there is only one Tarskian distribution allowed, and one of these theorists' distributions may or may not be it.

We are entitled to conclude the strong sense because we have assumed that truth, whatever else it is, is governed by MEA.

This assumption, to repeat, does not amount to assuming the determinacy of truth, nor does it beg the question in favor of realism. Indeed, as we see in a moment, antirealists could happily accept the determinacy of truth just now argued. Note also that the argument nowhere relies on a notion of objective or determinate reference or satisfaction, or on the notion of an *intended* interpretation. So we may conclude that truth is determined by the world, whether or not reference and satisfaction are, and whether or not we can make sense of the idea of an intended interpretation.

In determining truth, the world also determines which sentences have a truth-value, as perusal of the determinacy argument confirms. This is a desired result; "truth-valuedness can depend on *anything*."[10] There need be nothing intrinsic to the sentence, so to speak, which determines whether it has a truth-value (though for some sentences this might be so). A sentence can fail to have a truth-value for remote and even completely unexpected empirical reasons, as in certain sorts of presupposition-failure, or certain paradoxes that involve chains of indirect or deferred self-reference.[11] The determinacy of truth is compatible with all this, as is the realism that emerges below.

Why can antirealists accept the conclusion that the world determines truth? Because they can argue that while the world does determine truth, only a piece of the world does the real work—say, the piece (or pieces) we call consciousness, or else what we call rational inquirers engaged in warrantedly asserting things in light of their long-run evidence, or whatever. For some idealists, of course, the piece we call consciousness is actually the whole.

What separates realism from these views, therefore, is not (or not necessarily) the determinacy of truth but rather *what* determines truth. Realists have long been on record as holding that by no means does all truth depend on consciousness, on warranted assertibility even at some ideal limit, on perspective, or whatever. This is their "declaration of independence," so-called. In light of the above, it seems obvious and natural to interpret this relation of independence as the relation of non- or in-determination.[12] Thus suppose realists assert that the truth of 'The

---

[10]Sober, 373.

[11]Cf. Kripke (1975), 691; and Post (1979), which reinforces Kripke's point that many of our ordinary assertions of truth and falsity are likely to be paradoxical, if the empirical facts are extremely unfavorable, and that therefore (in Kripke's words) "it would be fruitless to look for an *intrinsic* criterion that will enable us to sieve out . . . those sentences which lead to paradox."

[12]Following Hellman (1983).

dinosaurs existed' is independent of long-run warranted assertibility. Their assertion should be construed as meaning that truth in this case is not determined by long-run warranted assertibility. Truth here suffers indeterminacy with respect to such assertibility, though it remains determinate with respect to the world.

At a stroke realists are freed of the burden of explaining the counterfactuals so often used to express their idea of independence. It may well be true that had there been no human or other perceivers or inquirers, still 'The dinosaurs existed' would have been true. But realists are committed to no such relation of counterfactual independence, nor to the difficulties in providing an account of the relevant counterfactuals. They may say instead that the truth of 'The dinosaurs existed' is indeterminate with respect to (the properties of) inquirers or perceivers, meaning that given a world consisting only of inquirers or perceivers, and given any other such world that is relevantly similar, then the sentence 'The dinosaurs existed' need not have the same truth-value in both. Such a world does not suffice to induce one and only one distribution of truth-values over this sentence.

1.1.2. Correspondence

According to realists, then, the truth-values of most sentences are indeterminate with respect to consciousness, linguistic convention, our ability to discover their truth-values, and so on. But realists must stop short of *global* realism, according to which the truth of *every* sentence is indeterminate with respect to all such matters. The reason is that each of these matters is itself a subject matter, so that we can and do frame sentences about them; and the truth-value of a sentence obviously cannot be independent of what it is about, whether it is about consciousness, convention, knowability, or whatever.[13] Thus the truth-values of some sentences are determined at least in part by such matters. Nor can we be sure even that there is *something or other* with respect to which every sentence's truth-value is indeterminate. For again the something would itself be a subject matter about which we might frame various assertions, whose truth-value would then be determinate at least in part with respect to that matter.

Thus realism must be antiglobal or antiholistic. This contrasts with some antirealisms, such as most if not all versions of verificationism, according to which the truth-value of every sentence is determined by the same sort of thing—namely, by verifiability in the long run by ideal inquirers. In this sense, such versions of verificationism can only be global. Much the same seems true of existing versions of pragmatism,

---

[13]As Sober points out.

idealism, conventionalism, coherentism, and more, though nonglobal versions are perhaps conceivable. It is tempting to express antiholistic realism in some such thesis as

> AH. For every sentence there is something on which its truth-value does not depend.

AH entails that there is no true sentence that is true in virtue of everything. But there might be some truths that *are* true in virtue of everything.[14] If so, one place to look for them is in metaphysics, which by tradition is supposed to be about all of what there is.

In any event, realists obviously must explain their relation of being-true-in-virtue-of, and they must do so in such a way that the relation can hold between whole sentences and pieces of the world. Otherwise their realism cannot be anti-global, or local, as we have seen it must be. Realists must explain what relation they have in mind when they say that a certain sentence is true in virtue of, or is made true by, or corresponds with some piece of the world. The determination relation by itself will not do. Granted the determinacy of truth, *every* true sentence is determined true by the world (that is, every true sentence is true in the one and only one distribution of truth-values allowed by the world). Hence every true sentence bears this relation to the same thing—namely, to the whole world, rather than to different pieces of it. The situation resembles that in Tarski's theory, according to which every true sentence bears the same relation to the world—namely, the relation of being satisfied by every sequence whatever of objects in the world.

Instead, the needed relation is between a true sentence ϕ and those entities, properties, and relations that *just suffice* to determine ϕ's truth-value as true, where to say that they *just* suffice is to say that they but no proper subset of them will suffice, which in turn is to say that they form a *smallest* set that suffices. Then suppose we could assume, in addition to EPT and MEA, that

> NMO. No more than one set of things just suffices to determine a sentence's truth-value.

Then we could say that a true sentence ϕ *corresponds* with *the* smallest set of things in the world that suffices to determine ϕ's truth-value as true. For EPT and MEA jointly entail there is *a* set of things in the world that suffices to determine ϕ's truth-value, and unproblematic notions from

---

[14]Again see Sober.

set theory allow us to form the idea of a *smallest* set that suffices and thus to formulate assumption NMO. And from NMO (given EPT and MEA) it follows that for each sentence there is exactly one set that just suffices to determine its truth-value. The world determines ϕ's truth-value by EPT and MEA, and successive partitions of the world, via the subset relation, converge on a single piece of it that is the smallest to determine ϕ's value—provided, of course, we are entitled to NMO.

One objection is easily dismissed. An existentially quantified sentence like 'Something wicked this way comes', the objection goes, is a counterexample to NMO. For on the one hand, a set containing more than one such thing would not *just* suffice to determine the truth-value of this sentence, since any one-membered subset of the set would suffice to do so. On the other, any set containing only one such thing just suffices, and occasionally there is more than one such set. But the objection presupposes that a one-membered set of wicked things that this way come suffices to determine the truth-value of 'Something wicked this way comes'. In fact it does not. Granted, that one such thing this way comes (Macbeth, say) entails that the sentence is true, meaning it is true in any world in which wicked Macbeth this way comes. Yet his coming this way does not determine the truth-value of this sentence. For to say that it does is to say that 'Something wicked this way comes' has the same truth-value in any two worlds which are the same as regards Macbeth's coming this way or not (cf. WDT2); and obviously, a couple of worlds could be the same as regards his not coming this way, while the sentence is true in one (where something else this way comes) yet false in the other (where nothing at all this way comes). Parallel remarks apply to disjunctions and dual remarks to universal generalizations. This and other seeming counterexamples to NMO depend on inferring erroneously from something's entailing that ϕ is true to its determining ϕ's truth-value.

In the immediate context, where the point is not to prove realism but to defend its intelligibility, we are indeed entitled to NMO. For if the objection against realism is that, failing some plausible account of determinate reference and of the very idea of an intended interpretation, the notion of correspondence is unintelligible, then realists need not argue that NMO is *true,* only that it is intelligible. And obviously it *is* intelligible to assume that no more than one set of things just suffices to determine ϕ's truth-value, even if the various notions of determinate reference, intended interpretations, mirroring, and so on, should themselves happen to be unintelligible. The reason is that the assumption involves only some unproblematic ideas from set theory, plus the determinacy of truth, which, as seen, nowhere relies on notions of objective or determinate reference, the intended interpretation, or whatever, but only on EPT and MEA.

Still, one wonders whether there is some argument for the *truth* of NMO. There is, to appear in a moment, in §1.1.3. But first we need a more precise rendering of the concept of correspondence:

> C. Where ϕ is true in the one distribution allowed by the actual world $W_a = <D_a, P_a, R_a>$ but is not a necessary truth, ϕ *corresponds* with the smallest piece of W_a to determine ϕ's truth-value.

A *piece* or *subworld* W_ϕ of W_a consists of subsets D_ϕ, P_ϕ, and R_ϕ of D_a, P_a, and R_a, respectively. W_ϕ is a *smallest* piece (or a least, or just suffices) to determine ϕ's truth-value iff W_ϕ, but no proper piece of W_ϕ, determines ϕ's truth-value. W_ϕ determines ϕ's truth-value iff given any W relevantly similar to W_ϕ, ϕ is true (false, neuter) in W iff ϕ is true (false, neuter) in W_ϕ. When ϕ is not true in the one distribution allowed by W_a, we say ϕ corresponds with nothing. Finally, as regards the requirement that ϕ not be a necessary truth: if ϕ were a necessary truth, then ϕ would be true in *every* world W, hence true in every subworld W of any W_ϕ. But then the only subworld that would just suffice to determine ϕ's truth-value would be the empty subworld, and presumably we would have to say that ϕ corresponds with nothing. Hence C does not apply when ϕ is a necessary truth (not that there need be any). In that case we may stipulate either that ϕ corresponds with everything, or that the notion of correspondence simply is inapplicable.

Note that if for some reason there were more than one piece of W that just suffices to determine ϕ's truth-value, we could always revise C to say that ϕ corresponds with the union of these separately just-sufficient pieces. Thus ϕ could correspond with the union of, say, the separate sets of rabbits, their stages, undetached parts, and so on, together with their respective properties and relations. But this would be a watered-down correspondence. The realist wants more.

Just as antirealists can cheerfully accept the determinacy of truth, so can some of them accept this notion of correspondence: namely, those who also assume NMO (or are persuaded by the argument for it in §1.1.3). The reason, basically, is that (NMO aside) this notion rests only on the determinacy of truth, plus some unproblematic apparatus from set theory. Pragmatists, for example, can agree that each truth corresponds with a piece of the world, in the sense of C, while insisting that in each case the piece consists of the long-run evidence that warrants the assertion of ϕ. For idealists, each truth corresponds with some aspect of consciousness. For coherentists, each truth corresponds with the same systematic whole of coherent propositions.

The realist differs from these theorists, then, not as regards correspondence (in the sense of C) but as regards *what* the various truths correspond with. The point of C is not to define realism or realist truth. Rather, C defines a word-world relation that true sentences can bear to what there is but which is such that not every true sentence need bear the relation to the same things or even the same sort of things. Yet to the extent that realism has been rejected on the ground that no one can make sense of such a relation, C is of far greater use to realists than to anti-realists. In this sense, C is realist in spirit. It enables realists to formulate their necessarily antiglobal or antiholistic theory of truth without having to rely on problematic notions of mirroring, isomorphism, determinate reference, determinate satisfaction, the intended interpretation, or whatever.

1.1.3. The Determinacy of Aboutness

What of the assumption that no more than one set of things just suffices to determine ϕ's truth-value? So far as I can see, there is no argument for the truth of NMO that relies only on such properties of truth as EPT and MEA. Instead, we must detour through aboutness. Part of the realist's theory must be about 'about' in any case. It is tempting to follow generations of realists in adopting the Fregean Counterfactual Test: sentence ϕ is about o only if ϕ would not have had the truth-value it has, had o been different in some respect.[15] But this counterfactual expresses only a necessary condition for aboutness. The realist would still need a complete, positive account of such aboutness, and it too would seem to require counterfactuals. Worse, the counterfactuals break down whenever o is such that o could not have had properties other than those it has (as for example when o is a number). For in that case, the antecedent is necessarily false in 'If o had been different, ϕ would have had a different truth-value'. And no current theory of subjunctives in general, or counterfactuals in particular, has a satisfactory account of such conditionals when their antecedents are necessarily false. The reason is that according to such theories, all subjunctive conditionals with necessarily false antecedents are automatically true, whereas some presumably ought to be false.

We do better to begin by asking what conditions any responsible notion of sentence aboutness should satisfy. One such condition, surely, is that if there is some difference in what a couple of sentences are about,

[15]Cf. Sober, 375–377.

then there ought to be some further, relevant difference between them. This we may call the Equity Principle for Aboutness (EPA). Even Quine agrees with it, in effect; his only point is that what counts as a relevant difference must be a matter of the speaker's behavioral dispositions, or at least of some difference or other at the level ultimately of microphysics. Quine believes that traditional notions of aboutness violate EPA, since there can be a difference in what two sentences are traditionally about without any relevant behavioral or (other) physical difference between them or whoever utters them. Hence traditional aboutness suffers indeterminacy, according to Quine, from which he concludes that there is no fact of the matter as regards what entities a sentence is traditionally about.

Quine and everyone else would further require of any responsible notion of aboutness that in any exhaustive set of genuinely conflicting judgments as to what a sentence is about, exactly one is correct. This of course is Meta-Ethical Antirelativism for aboutness, and it is satisfied by Quine's notion of stimulus synonymy, evidently by design. EPA and MEA for aboutness jointly entail the determinacy of aboutness, just as EPT and MEA for truth jointly entail the determinacy of truth. What a sentence is about is determined by the world. Yet this leaves open the possibility that what the sentence is about is equally either rabbits, their stages, undetached parts, or whatever. Hence it leaves open the possibility that there is more than one set of things that just suffices to determine the sentence's truth-value. Important as the determinacy of aboutness is, it still does not close this gap.

To do so, we need to consider a connection between aboutness and truth.[16] According to Quine (at least implicitly), what a sentence is about, so far as the notion makes any sense, is to be understood via Tarski's theory of truth. A true sentence is about the objects that do the real work in the sequences that satisfy the sentence (namely, all the sequences, in the case of a true sentence).[17] Analysis of the theory further shows that it takes *all* the objects that do the real work in the relevant sequences to determine a sentence's truth-value. That is, it takes the whole of what a sentence is about to determine its truth-value, as opposed merely to entailing that it is true or that it is false.

For example, ϕ entails $\phi \lor \psi$, meaning that $\phi \lor \psi$ is true in any world in which ϕ is. But ϕ does not determine the truth-value of $\phi \lor \psi$. To say that it does is to say that $\phi \lor \psi$ has the same truth-value in any

---

[16]I am indebted to Horgan, in conversation, for getting me to be clearer about the connection.

[17]Quine (1970a), 37–42.

two worlds in which ϕ has the same truth-value; and obviously, ϕ could have the same truth-value in both W_1 and W_2—namely, falsity—while $\phi \lor \psi$ is true in W_1 but not in W_2. Thus if we assume (perhaps erroneously) that $\phi \lor \psi$ is about the union of what ϕ and ψ are separately about, then it takes the whole of the union to determine truth-value here, not just what ϕ (or ψ) is about, even though ϕ entails $\phi \lor \psi$. As before, parallel remarks apply to existential generalizations, and dual remarks to universal.

This feature of Tarski's theory reflects a general intuition, or rather a consequence of the way we use 'true' and 'about' together. According to such usage, ϕ's truth-value is determined at bottom only by something to do with those pieces of the world that include all of what ϕ is about. Any set of things that suffices to determine ϕ's truth-value will include the whole of what ϕ is about. And this principle is accepted at least implicitly by all parties. For example, if what determines the truth-value of 'The dinosaurs existed' is long-run warranted assertibility, this must nevertheless at bottom be long-run warranted assertibility *about the dinosaurs,* so that according to warranted-assertibility theorists, the whole of what the sentence is about—namely, the dinosaurs, so far as talk about them could be warranted—will be included in whatever determines its truth-value. The principle also is assumed by those who infer from the alleged indeterminacy or inscrutability of what a sentence is about to the conclusion that truth itself is not determined by the world—an inference at the heart of their attack on the idea that truth can be some sort of determinate correspondence. In this way each theory of truth arrives at its characteristic idea of what sorts of things sentences ultimately are about: they must be about things of the sort that according to the theory figure in determining truth-value. Otherwise, these things could not be included, as they must be, among the things that determine the sentence's truth-value.

Thus does each theory pay homage to the principle that whatever determines truth-value includes what the sentence is about, or more precisely to

AT. The truth-value of ϕ is determined at bottom only by all the things ϕ is about (or by their properties and relations), so that a set of things determines ϕ's truth-value only if all of what ϕ is about forms a subset of them.[18]

---

[18]Again, seeming counterexamples depend on inferring erroneously from 'ψ entails that ϕ is true' to 'ψ determines ϕ's truth-value'.

Unexpectedly, perhaps, AT entails that no more than one set of things just suffices to determine ϕ's truth-value. For suppose otherwise. That is, suppose there are two distinct nonempty sets S and S^* that separately just suffice (meaning each suffices to determine ϕ's value, but no proper subset of either one does). Let A be the set of things ϕ is about. By AT, A also determines ϕ's value and is a subset of both S and S^*, so that any o in A is in both S and S^*. But then A is a proper subset either of S or of S^*. For suppose not. Then there is nothing in S or in S^* that is not in A; that is, every o in S is in A and so is every o in S^*. But because any o in A is in both S and S^*, it follows that every o in S is in S^* and conversely, hence that $S = S^*$, contrary to the supposition that they are distinct. So A is a proper subset either of S or of S^*. But because A determines ϕ's truth-value, either S or S^* therefore has a proper subset that determines ϕ's value, contrary to the supposition that they both just suffice.

It follows that for each sentence no more than one set of things just suffices to determine its truth-value. Not only is NMO intelligible; it is true. For each sentence there is *the* smallest piece of the world to determine its truth-value. This clears the way for a definition of sentence-aboutness:

> AB. Where ϕ is not a necessary truth (falsehood, neutrality), ϕ is *about* those entities which, together with their properties and relations, form the smallest piece of the world to determine ϕ's truth-value.

If ϕ has the truth-value it has as a matter of necessity, then we may stipulate either that ϕ is about everything or that this notion of aboutness is inapplicable. AB captures the idea that ϕ is about whatever it is in the world whose properties and relations make ϕ have the truth-value it has. And just as antirealists can accept the notion of correspondence in C, they can accept the notion of aboutness in AB. Realists differ from them as regards what sorts of things various sentences are about, just as they differ as regards what it is that true sentences correspond with.

According to AB, what ϕ is about need not be coextensive with the set of objects that play the crucial role in constructing the Tarskian truth-conditions for ϕ. This is especially clear if ϕ is quantified: if ϕ is true in virtue of, hence about, things other than those within the scope of ϕ's quantifiers, then ϕ's Tarskian truth-conditions are one thing, and what ϕ is about is another. For example, Dretske and Tooley have separately argued that empirical laws of nature are about properties and theoretical magnitudes, not the physical objects the laws quantify over.[19] If so, a Tarskian truth-conditional account of aboutness, or of what makes a sentence have the truth-value it has, must fail. No such problem afflicts AB; properties and theoretical magnitudes can easily be among the things in the smallest piece of the world to determine ϕ's truth-value, whatever the range of ϕ's quantifiers.

Note also that what AB defines is a kind of *absolute* aboutness: an interpreted sentence is about various objects or not, irrespective of what the speaker may have in mind, or intend, and irrespective of some frame of reference or background theory. The reason is that, irrespective of any such things, there is one and only one piece of the world that is the smallest to determine the sentence's truth-value. And neither this fact nor the argument for it presupposes that we may speak of speakers' intentions or of determinate reference, as seen. Quine might be right that "reference is nonsense except relative to a coordinate system," yet he is wrong if he thinks (as he does) that it is also "meaningless to ask . . . absolutely" what objects a sentence is about. For AB allows us to ask just that. Contrary to Quine, it "makes sense . . . to say . . . what the objects of a theory are, absolutely speaking," since we may identify a theory's objects with what the theory is about, hence with the objects whose properties and relations just suffice to determine the theory's truth-value. We are not confined to saying merely "how one theory of objects is interpretable or reinterpretable in another."[20] This by itself sharply distinguishes the present approach from Davidson's, and there are other fundamental differences, despite agreement that "reference drops out."[21] In the language of the special theory of relativity, of which Quine is so fond, what AB characterizes is an invariant (indeed Einstein at first called his theory "*Invariantentheorie*").

Further, AB invokes no "myth of the museum," insofar as the myth requires us to "regard a man's semantics as somehow determinate in his mind."[22] For AB nowhere presupposes any such mentalism. Instead, like the definition C of correspondence, it characterizes a direct word-world relation that bypasses intentions and the rest of the mental. It also bypasses dispositions to overt behavior. Nevertheless, the relation is entirely congenial to naturalistic and even physicalistic semantics. For even if the relation is not definable by or reducible to behavioral dispositions—or indeed to any purely natural or physical traits or relations, including the causal—nevertheless, the crucial matter of what objects a given sentence is about is determined by the world, in view of EPA and

---

[19] As Sober, 380, reminds us. See Dretske; Tooley; and Hetherington.
[20] Quine (1969), 48, 50.
[21] Davidson (1977). See also Wallace.
[22] Quine (1969), 27.

MEA, hence ultimately by whatever determines how things are in the world and thus by the microphysical realm, if physicalists are right that how things are in the world is determined ultimately by the microphysical. Only reductive varieties of physicalism and naturalism need worry about AB, and they have looked increasingly implausible for years anyway.

According to Quine, "if the museum myth were true, there would be a right and wrong of the matter"[23] as regards what someone's theory is about. But the relevant question is whether there would be a right and wrong of the matter *only* if the museum myth were true, as Quine often seems to believe. The answer is "No." The reason is that even though AB nowhere involves the myth, still AB implies that there is a fact of the matter as regards what a sentence is about. For we now know that for each sentence there is one and only one smallest piece of the world to determine its truth-value. For example, suppose that what just determines ϕ's truth-value is the set of rabbits plus their genuine properties and relations (in the sense that no proper subset of the rabbits and relations will also suffice). Then ϕ's truth-value is not also just determined by rabbit-stages plus their properties and relations, or by undetached rabbit-parts plus theirs, and so on. In view of AB, therefore, ϕ is about rabbits, not about their stages, their fusion, their undetached parts, or whatever, irrespective of some frame of reference or background theory.

Here Quine might complain that AB allows a difference in what a couple of sentences are about without any difference in their speaker's dispositions to overt behavior, hence that AB violates EPA ("No difference in aboutness without some further, relevant difference"). But AB does not violate EPA, even though AB does not require any difference in the speaker's dispositions. The relevant difference, according to AB, need not be in the dispositions but can instead be somewhere else—say, in the properties and relations of the entities in the two pieces of the world that respectively are the smallest to determine the two sentences' truth-values. The relevant difference need be neither in the dispositions, as Quine thinks, nor in the speaker's mind, nor in any alleged propositions the speaker succeeds in expressing. Contrary both to Quine and to what he calls traditional semantics, the difference could be elsewhere, out there in the world, say, in the pieces of it that are what ultimately determine the truth-values. We need posit nothing not already in Quine's ontology.[24]

[23]Quine (1969), 29–30, 50.

[24]On construing possible worlds as entities safely within Quine's ontology, see §§4.1–4.3.

Of course, our *evidence* may not always suffice to settle *which* piece of the world is the smallest to determine a given sentence's value, hence which things it is about. But such undetermination of hypothesis by evidence is to be expected and is expressly not Quine's point. His point is that there is not even an objective matter for the evidence to settle. And this is just what we are now in a position to see is wrong: there *is* an objective matter here, in virtue of there being one and only one set of things a sentence is about, absolutely speaking. A translation manual is true, as regards what entities the foreigner's sentences are about, to the extent that it correctly identifies for each such sentence which one piece of the world just suffices to determine its truth-value, and thereby which entities (together with their properties and relations) just suffice. For by AB these are just the entities the sentence is about. Insofar as indeterminacy of translation is supposed to entail that there is no fact of the matter here, it follows that translation is determinate at least as regards what whole sentences are about, even if it should happen to be indeterminate as regards the reference of terms.

Unlike other arguments for determinacy, this one relies only on assumptions Quine himself does or would accept. Clearly, he would not allow there to be a difference in truth-value or in aboutness between a couple of sentences without some further, relevant difference in the circumstances of their utterance (say, at the level of microphysics). Thus in effect he accepts the Equity Principle for Truth and Aboutness. In addition, his discussions of conflicting theories or concepts of truth presuppose that no two such theories can both be correct (for example, his is correct while Peirce's is not).[25] In effect this is to presuppose Meta-Ethical Antirelativism for truth. Obviously, he would likewise require of any responsible notion of aboutness that it too satisfy MEA (just as stimulus synonymy satisfies it, by design). Further, Quine accepts AT, though in terms of truth and satisfaction: the truth-value of a sentence is determined at bottom by the entities that do the real work in the sequences that satisfy the sentence, so that whatever determines its truth-value includes these entities (which are the ones the sentence is about).[26] Finally, Quine is committed to possible worlds of the only sort needed here (as we see in §§4.1–4.3) and regards the physical world as a structured domain, as a set D of entities together with their genuine or natural (or projectible) traits P and their genuine or natural relations R. Much of his discussion of natural kinds[27] aims in effect at distinguishing

[25]Quine (1960), 23; see also 75.
[26]Quine (1970a), 37–42.
[27]Quine (1969), 114–138, esp. 117–118.

genuine traits from artificial ones induced by the set-generating principles of set theory.[28]

These assumptions—EP, MEA, and AT (plus worlds as structured domains)—entail determinacy of translation as regards what whole sentences are about. For EP and MEA entail the determinacy of truth and aboutness, which, conjoined with AT and therefore with NMO, allows us to define appropriate correspondence and aboutness relations in C and AB, as seen. Thus there is a deep inconsistency in Quine's philosophy, not merely a tension, between his ideas about translation and his requirements for any responsible notions of truth and aboutness.

How might this have come to pass? Part of the explanation is that according to Quine, meanings mentalistically construed *can* differ *without* there being some further, relevant difference between them (the relevant ones being primarily the behavioral, for him). Thus 'Gavagai', taken as a sentence, can be about rabbits, their stages, undetached parts, or whatever. Yet the circumstances on each occasion of its utterance can be exactly the same (behaviorally). It follows for Quine that meanings mentalistically construed fail to satisfy the Equity Principle—or his slogan, "No difference without a physical difference." It follows further that meaning cannot be determinate, since there can be a difference in meaning without any difference at the level where there *is* determinacy or a fact of the matter.

What Quine did not see is that while this sort of argument might work for meaning as reference, it does not work for meaning at the level of what whole sentences are about. At that level we can characterize a nonmentalistic aboutness relation such that if a couple of sentences differ in meaning, in the sense of differing in what they are about, then there must at least be some difference in the two smallest pieces of the world to determine their truth-values. There was no way Quine could have seen this so long as he believed, as he still does, that aboutness for whole sentences can only be understood (à la Tarski) via reference. But we have been learning that no such relation of reference between terms and pieces of the world is needed.

There may be a deeper reason why Quine could not have seen any argument for determinacy even as regards what whole sentences are about. The present argument was stimulated by an argument for the determinacy of valuation generally (§6.1), plus the further reflection that 'true' and 'about' resemble value terms to the extent of obeying EPT and MEA. The argument construes the (value) terms 'true' and 'about' as objective in the sense that no two genuinely conflicting (value) judg-

---

[28]As Merrill, 78, points out.

ments about the truth or aboutness of a sentence can both be correct. But Quine's Humean and positivist heritage, though transcended in so many respects, leads him to regard values as finally subjective and not a promising subject for philosophy, or "science about science." Quine clearly accepts Meta-Ethical Relativism in morals.[29] Even though he rejects such relativism with respect to truth and aboutness, as seen, his general attitude toward values would discourage the idea that an argument from meta-ethics could possibly illuminate a problem about truth and translation.[30]

1.1.4. Reference, Causality, Knowledge

Could the strategy used here to argue for the determinacy of translation at the level of what whole sentences are about be used to argue for it at the level of terms? Obviously it could, *if* reference could be assumed to satisfy suitable analogues of EPA, MEA, and AT. That is, one would need to assume, first, that we use (or ought to use) the notion of reference in such a way that there can be no difference in what two terms refer to without some further, relevant difference between them; and, second, that in any exhaustive set of genuinely conflicting (value) judgments about what a term refers to, only one is correct. Of the three assumptions, these two are or ought to be conceded by everyone. They jointly entail that the world determines reference (just as EPA and MEA entail that it determines aboutness), so that if we achieve more or less determinate reference, this must be so in virtue of constraints not established by our own stipulations.[31] But they leave open whether for each term there can be more than one thing in the world the term refers to. The contrary assumption, that there is not more than one, is intelligible (just as NMO is). How to argue for its truth is another matter. Hence we need a further assumption, either an analogue of AT or something else, in order to show that there is never more than one thing the term refers to.

As a step in this direction, consider the assumption that what a sentence's terms refer to must be among the things the sentence is about. For example, if a sentence is about rabbits, then its individual terms refer to, and the values of its individual variables are rabbits (and its predicates denote or express traits or relations of rabbits). Even those who insist that reference is inscrutable accept this principle, as when

---

[29]Quine (1978c), esp. 43.

[30]The same attitude may underlie Field's insistence (1982), 563, that "truth is factual, not evaluative."

[31]In accord with Lewis (1984).

they argue that because reference is inscrutable, so therefore is what a sentence is about (since what it is about includes its terms' referents, so that inscrutability as regards the latter entails inscrutability as regards the former). By the same token, because what a term refers to is thus included in what its containing sentence is about, it follows that *the term's reference is determinate to within what its containing sentence is about.* Since what the sentence is about is determinate, as seen, we may conclude that there is a fact of the matter, as regards reference, to within what the containing sentence is about. Obviously, this is a big step in the right direction. If the sentence is about rabbits, then its terms cannot refer to rabbit stages, undetached rabbit parts, or whatever. But what more could be shown, if anything, is best left for another day, as is the question of whether, as I suspect, the present account could be expanded into a complete physicalist theory of meaning immune to the objection that no such theory can accommodate the normativity of meaning.[32]

In any event, since "reference drops out," the realist is not committed to any particular theory of reference, including above all a causal theory with its attendant difficulties.[33] No doubt causal theories often appeal to physicalists because such theories can appear to be the only ones in which the key relation, namely causation, is a physicalistically respectable one. Theories that involve relations of intentionality can appear correspondingly mysterious. Thus it is worth emphasizing again that the present account involves only the nonintentional relation of determination. And this relation is perfectly respectable from a physicalist point of view, as we see further in Chapter 4.

But isn't determination really a kind of causal relation, so that even if the present account involves no causal theory of reference, strictly speaking, it nevertheless involves a causal relation between whole sentences and the world? No. True, some causal relations are determination relations, as when we use 'cause' of an event or situation that completely settles what the outcome that we call the effect will be ("deterministic causation"). But not every instance of determination is an instance of causation. If numbers are either abstract sets or properties of sets,[34] then how things are with sets or their properties will determine how things are with numbers, though one is hardly the cause of the other. And even though the predicate 'true-in-arithmetic' cannot be defined in terms of how things are with numbers as those things are expressed in a given arithmetic theory T (as in effect Tarski showed), nevertheless, how

---

[32]An objection found in Kripke (1982).

[33]Unger presents some of the more urgent difficulties. Cf. N. Salmon, Part I, passim.

[34]Benacerraf argues against the former, Maddy for the latter.

these things are with numbers determines which sentences that contain 'true-in-arithmetic' predicates are true in the appropriate extension of T.[35] Again it would be odd to call this an instance of causation. Likewise, conventions or stipulations regarding the meanings of certain logical particles evidently suffice to determine which sentences are logically valid (that is, true in all possible structures),[36] but again we would refrain from claiming that one is the cause of the other.

Thus there need be no causal signal, and no historical chain of such signals, stretching from some piece of the world to us or our terms when a sentence is determined true by or corresponds with a piece of the world. And just as there need be no such causal relation, there need be no counterfactual relation. It is true that had some piece of the world been different in some relevant respect, then the truth-value of a sentence that corresponds with that piece would have been different. But even though this is true, realists need not say so. Instead, they are committed only to saying, in line with C, that given the piece W_ϕ with which ϕ corresponds, and given any W relevantly similar to W_ϕ, then ϕ is true in W iff ϕ is true in W_ϕ. And this is equivalent not to the foregoing counterfactual but rather to its converse (nearly enough), namely, to 'If the truth-value of ϕ is different in W and W_ϕ, then W and W_ϕ are relevantly different'.

Hence the relation between words and the world in virtue of which a true sentence is true is neither causal nor counterfactual. What, then, are we to say of the widespread idea that it must be, if there is to be some reliable regulation of our beliefs by the world? Here we must distinguish between a relation that is partly constitutive of a given concept, by way of entering our very definition of it, and one that is or might be involved in the *epistemic* matter of how to tell whether some particular item falls under the concept. What I have just been arguing is that neither a causal nor a counterfactual relation of the relevant sort enters the definition of correspondence or of truth-determination. Thus neither sort of relation is even partly constitutive of the concept of truth. This of course is closely related to the point that truth can be understood without invoking a causal theory of reference, indeed without invoking reference at all.

When we turn to the epistemic problem of how to tell whether a given belief is true, matters may well be otherwise. It may well turn out that in order to be justified in claiming that a given belief is true, we

---

[35]Hellman and Thompson (1977), 312, which contains what in effect are further examples of non-causal determination of one thing by another.
[36]Hellman (1985).

must always be in some appropriate causal or at least counterfactual relation to what the belief is about. For it may be that there is no other way in which there can be reliable regulation of any given belief by the world. Thus even though we have no need of a causal theory of reference with its attendant difficulties, we may well need a causal theory of knowledge or at least of justification.

Of course such theories have their problems, but none so severe, I think, as for causal theories of reference. Indeed one of the most nagging problems for causal and other naturalistic theories of knowledge and justification may now have a ready solution. The problem is how to accommodate the normativity of knowledge and justification. According to certain opponents of naturalized epistemology, these epistemic concepts are not only normative but *sui generis,* in the sense that they are not reducible to purely natural terms, nor are claims of knowledge or justification derivable from purely natural facts. This view is a kind of intuitionism in meta-epistemology.[37] It contrasts with a view according to which the normative concepts are really factual in character because reducible to a kind of causal or causal-reliability relation that supposedly obtains between justified beliefs and the world. This view is an analogue of naturalism in meta-ethics, and is held by theorists like Armstrong, Dretske, and Goldman.[38] Such a view seems less to accommodate the normative elements than to deny or eliminate them.

Is there a meta-epistemology, somewhere between these two extremes, according to which the normative concepts are not reducible to or derivable from natural facts, and yet according to which the world determines whether the normative terms 'known' and 'justified' apply to a given belief? Alston evidently thinks there is no such alternative.[39] But clearly there is one according to which the concepts are (or could be) irreducibly normative, yet their relation to the world is neither unacceptable to the naturalist nor otherwise mysterious, since the relation is the familiar one of determination (cf. §§6.1–6.3). The result is a naturalized epistemology free of dubious claims of reducibility. Like remarks obviously apply to naturalized philosophy of science.

Thus our standing in some appropriate causal relation to what a belief is about could well be necessary for us to count the belief either as justified or as known, and yet our standing in that relation need not be all there is to knowledge or justification. Not only need they not be

[37]As Alston (1978) points out in connection with his analysis of Chisholm as an intuitionist in this sense. Cf. Sosa (1983).

[38]As Alston (1978) points out, 277. Nozick, ch. 3, holds a variation on the same theme, or so I interpret the tracking relation.

[39]Alston (1978), 278–279; likewise Nozick, ch. 3.

reducible to any such circumstance; our standing in that relation need not even be the whole of what in the world determines whether the belief is justified or known. Instead, the piece of the world that just suffices to determine whether a certain belief is justified for or known by person P could well include more than P, what P's belief is about, and P's standing in the appropriate causal relation to what it is about. What more should be included is a matter to be specified by the substantive principles of one's normative epistemology (cf. §6.3).

Of course this approach to meta-epistemology presupposes that the world determines the normative matter of whether our beliefs are known or justified. What assurance is there that it does? The argument parallels the argument for the determinacy of truth. To begin with, we would be very reluctant to allow that a couple of items could differ in their epistemic properties without also differing in some relevant natural property. If a belief is justified for P but not for $P*$, there must be some difference in their epistemically relevant natural circumstances. This of course is an analogue of EPT. Further, we would be reluctant to allow that a couple of conflicting epistemic judgments (say as to whether a given belief is justified for P) could be equally correct. Instead, we would adopt MEA for epistemic judgments. By the argument of §1.1.1 (with minor adjustments), these two principles entail that the world determines epistemic truth.

If we add that an epistemic sentence is about something or other, and that like all sentences its truth-value is determined at bottom only by all of what it is about, the way is open to characterizing truth for epistemic sentences as correspondence. The restriction in C to nonnecessary truths is no real limitation, certainly not for naturalistically inclined epistemologists, who tend to insist on the (radical) contingency of epistemic sentences.[40] Realists as regards the truth of epistemic sentences can thus explicate and defend their position against those who would be pragmatists, coherentists, or idealists as regards such truth. So too for realists as regards methodological sentences about science.

1.1.5. Truth and (Other) Norms

What then is truth, according to the realist? Truth is a (partly normative) notion that satisfies EPT and MEA, which jointly entail that the world determines truth. This determinacy, conjoined with AT (whatever determines ϕ's truth-value includes all of what ϕ is about), entails that no more than one piece of the world just suffices to determine ϕ's truth-value (NMO). This in turn enables realists to define a suitable

[40]E.g., Boyd (1982); Boyd (forthcoming), §3.3.

making-true relation of correspondence in C, and a suitable aboutness relation in AB.

Up to this point antirealists can agree, as seen. What distinguishes realism is its insistence that by no means are all true sentences made true by, or correspondent with, or about aspects of consciousness, understanding, linguistic convention, coherence, discoverability, evidence, justification, or whatever. This is just the realist's characteristic declaration of independence in another form.

If we were to demand a completely general positive account of just what in the world it *is* that makes a true sentence true, if not aspects of consciousness or whatever, the realist will reply that no such global or holistic account is possible or desirable, as seen (§1.1.2). Realism must be antiglobal, or local and piecemeal; indeed this too distinguishes it from its rivals, which tend to be global. For they all tend to reduce what makes a sentence true to some one kind of thing—aspects of consciousness, or coherence, or warranted assertibility, or whatever. In this sense, *realism properly construed is inherently nonreductive.* In answer to the question, "What makes a true sentence true?" it answers, "No one sort of thing, for it depends on the sentence. In Wittgenstein's phrase, one must look and see."

What if truth is indeed a normative notion? Then the problem is that very many normative terms are used in accordance with EP and MEA (§6.1). Unless realists can distinguish the supposedly normative term 'true' from them, they risk not having said anything distinctive about truth. But there are at least two distinctions. First, there is typically a difference between the sorts of things that satisfy 'true' (and 'about') and those that satisfy other normative terms. Sentences, propositions, statements—the usual candidates for the truth-bearers—are what satisfy 'true' (plus 'false', 'neuter', and 'about'). By contrast, moral terms like 'right', 'wrong', 'good', 'bad', 'obligated', and so on, typically are satisfied by persons, institutions, acts, and the like. The fact that 'true' can also be applied to a class of acts—certain speech acts—does not affect this basic contrast.

For, second, suppose that one and the same thing—a speech act, say—should happen to satisfy both 'true' and some moral or esthetic term like 'offensive' (or some term of normative cognitive appraisal like 'rationally justified'). Even so, the factors which just suffice to determine that it is true will normally differ from those which determine that it is offensive (or that it is justified). Thus consider 'The dinosaurs existed 70 million B.C.' Shouting this in a church full of creationists would be offensive. The factors which just suffice to determine that it is offensive, whatever exactly they are, obviously differ greatly from those which just suffice to determine that it is true. Indeed there may be no overlap at all between them. This is so despite the fact that they could coincide for a self-referential sentence like 'What I'm now saying is offensive' (depending on the context). The crucial fact here is that it *would* be coincidence: what makes something offensive does not generally make it true, and vice versa.

Thus we may incorporate 'true' and other value terms (if it is one) into a single, unified treatment via EP, MEA, and the consequent non-reductive determinacy of valuation without collapsing the distinctions between truth and other types of valuation. But further argument for the unification, in the form of an argument for the determinacy of valuation generally, must await §§6.0–6.2.

1.2. Domains of Truth, Faces of Existence

> . . . *Leaving one still with the intolerable wrestle / with words and meanings.*
>
> —T. S. Eliot

By building on earlier definitions we can easily construct a few more. The whole truth, Truth with a capital 'T', may be defined as the set or class of all and only the truths. When sentences are the truth-bearers, as here, there is no conflict with the argument that there can be no set of all truths, meaning all true propositions.[41] The whole truth about a particular subject matter is simply the set of sentences about the subject matter that are true. And a domain of truth is the set of all the true sentences couched in the vocabulary of a given domain—law, medicine, the arts, religion, the marketplace, or anywhere some sufficiently distinctive vocabulary arises that both expresses and creates or sustains an image of ourselves and the world.[42]

In addition, sentences often are said to express a way the world is. We need not find or construct some entity that counts as a way of the world. Instead it suffices to have a schema for eliminating the phrase 'expresses a way the world is' whenever it is applied to a sentence we can produce at the time. The schema is

$$\phi \text{ expresses a way the world is iff } S,$$

where again 'ϕ' is to be replaced by a name or description of the sentence that replaces 'S'. It follows that ϕ expresses a way the world is iff

---

[41]Given in Grim.

[42]On the problem of how to individuate domains, see §5.3.

ϕ is true. So it looks as though there could be such a thing as *the* way the world is only if there is exactly one true sentence, or, since this seems absurd, only if there is exactly one domain of true sentences—some one vocabulary that alone is privileged to be used in stating truths. It may seem obvious that no vocabulary is so privileged and that therefore there cannot be such a thing as *the* way the world is. But even though this is true, the matter requires deeper reflection, as we see in Chapter 7.

It is tempting to think of a face of existence as no more than what a domain of truth expresses. We should resist the temptation, as we see in a moment. But there is no reason not to say that every domain of truth expresses a face of existence, even if not every face is thus expressible. The key notion then is

> FE. A set of sentences expresses a face of existence iff the set is a domain of truth.

FE defines the phrase 'expresses a face of existence' by showing how to eliminate it, even though we do not yet know what, if anything, a face of existence is. Now are there more faces of existence than our discourse can express? Intuitively we believe that it should at least be possible for there to be more to existence than we could ever say in our language, perhaps in any conceivable human language.[43] It should at least be possible for there to be more aspects of existence than our present vocabulary can manage, even if we string present vocabulary together forever to form more and more complex expressions. Indeed in §5.4 we see how this could happen.

If it is possible for there to be inexpressible faces of existence, what are they? Roughly speaking, they are aspects or attributes or properties of existence. And what are these? Suppose we use the term 'existence' to denote the sum total, or whole, of whatever there is, including—provided they all are—galaxies, ghosts, and gods, plus numbers, propositions, and other abstracta. An aspect of existence, then, might be some property or perhaps some subclass or part of this whole. And the whole would have the property, whether or not it could ever be expressed.

One trouble with this approach is that we have no tolerably clear idea of what it means for such diverse entities to form a "whole," especially when some of them evidently would be outside space and time altogether. If they were all in spacetime, we could define their whole in terms of a spatiotemporal part-whole relation (§3.1). But they

[43]Cf. A. W. Moore.

are not. Even if each entity of a given kind entered into some appropriate sort of part-whole relation with other entities of that kind, there is no reason to believe that the different sorts of part-whole relations would have enough in common for us to construct from them some grand summation over all the kinds.

A tempting way out is to speak not of the whole but, even more abstractly, of the class or set of whatever there is. Then an aspect of existence would be some property of the set. Unfortunately, there are metaphysicians, including some leading physicalists, who deny that there are any abstract entities such as sets. Talk of sets, according to some, is just a convenient way of talking about certain wholes. So we would be thrown back into the troubles of the preceding paragraph. Even if there are sets, there could not be a set of *everything* there is. Such a set would have to contain all the sets as members, including itself, something prohibited by set theory.

Even if we identified existence with the set of all the entities *other* than sets, there would be a problem. An aspect of existence, we said, would have to be a property of the set. But the only kinds of properties sets can have, strictly, are those allowed by set theory, such as certain cardinalities, orderings, members, subsets, and so on. Do we really wish to identify the faces of existence with such bloodless categories? Perhaps we do, ultimately, but only if there is no alternative.

We can make no further headway in explicating 'face of existence' until we have sorted through some more metaphysics, particularly through physicalism. Happily for the program of the chapters ahead, the term can be defined within a physicalist framework in such a way as to do justice to our intuitions about faces of existence (§§4.6, 5.3). Meanwhile, we may safely think of them roughly as properties of the whole of what there is. The key terms of this rough characterization eventually will be refined, partly to take account of the crucial role metaphor plays in individuating and disclosing faces of existence, and partly to allow for the possibility of inexpressible aspects of existence, such as what it is like to be a bat.

1.3. Problems with Criteria

There is not an idea of which I am certain. I am not even sure that I am on the right road.
—ALBERT EINSTEIN

Certainty, could we but achieve it, would be that lucky state in which a belief is guaranteed true by the evidence we have. Does the evidence ever guarantee truth? A guarantee, or a guaranteeing criterion, would be a criterion the satisfaction of which logically entails that the belief is true. Warranting criteria, on the other hand, merely provide a warrant for claiming that some item satisfies the definition of whatever they are criteria for.[44] In the case of gold, discovering that a very old coin has a certain density and color, and a certain softness, is a warrant—and not a bad one—for claiming that the coin is gold. But it is not a guarantee, since the logical possibility remains that the coin is not gold. It could be electrum—an alloy of mostly gold and a little silver—as were coins in the Merovingian dynasty and much earlier in Lydia before Croesus.

Are there any warranting criteria for truth? Over the ages many have been proposed, some in the spirit even of guarantees. They include scriptural assurance or other authority; mystical assurance; clarity and distinctness; intuitive obviousness; sensory obviousness; impossibility of conceiving otherwise; coherence with the best evidence; and high inductive probability, among many others. All fail to explain adequately either what the connection is between the alleged criterion and truth, or why, in light of the connection, beliefs that satisfy the criterion are more likely to be true than false. The most basic reason for the latter failure lies in the following classic difficulty. Among the certified beliefs—that is, among those that satisfy the criterion—many turn out later to be wrong, so far as we can tell, according to an expanded body of evidence and experience; hence we have little or no reason to think that other beliefs which satisfy the criterion are any better off, as we shall see.

Examples abound of certified beliefs that turned out to be wrong. For centuries people had all the assurances they could want, and excellent authority, for believing that the sun revolves around the earth. The same is true of the belief that light travels in straight lines; that Euclid's geometry is true of physical space; that the brain is an organ for cooling the blood; that eyes see by sending out beams; that slavery is permissible; that the earth's resources and capacity for absorbing wastes are unlimited; and that everywhere on earth the sun rises and sets every 24 hours. That people once held the latter belief is shown by the incredulity and derision with which they greeted explorers' reports of the midnight sun.

Lest we feel complacent about our own beliefs, remember that the same general forces are at work that led to the overthrow of those earlier

44Cf. Rescher, ch. 1.

beliefs by continually expanding our experience and evidence. To take just one dramatic example, it is possible that *all* our commonsense beliefs about the motion and energy of everyday objects are untrue.[45] Such beliefs are expressed by means of ordinary predicates like 'is over there moving that way', 'is big and fast and coming this way', 'contains the energy-equivalent of a barrel of oil', 'is red hot', 'is red' (assuming that the color depends on an energy-state of the surface), and so on. Our use of such predicates evolved, as did all natural language, in the course of millennia of experience with everyday objects in the environment, from stones to arrows to musketballs. In our experience, especially as refined by geometry and classical physics, the object always enjoyed simultaneously a definite position, velocity, and mass—in other words, a determinate position and momentum. The predicates reflect this experience, and they may well presuppose that the objects they apply to all have simultaneous determinate position and momentum. But according to quantum theory (under its usual interpretation), *no* object has either simultaneous determinate position and momentum, or simultaneous determinate position and energy, or any other pair of conjugate quantities. So if our ordinary predicates of motion and energy presuppose the contrary, then all our commonsense beliefs that contain them are untrue.

If they are not true, how can they be the basis—as they surely are—for successful practical action? If it is not true that food is over there moving this way, how did our ancestors eat? They ate well enough for the species to survive, thanks to the fact that a belief need not be true in order to serve as the basis for successful practical action. It need only be true to a high degree of probability. The probability that the running deer now over there in the trees will next be in the open need only be very high, as indeed it is in quantum theory. According to the theory, the likelihood that the deer will not appear where we expect it to is, as one says, negligible for all practical purposes. It is about as likely that the randomly moving air molecules in a room would suddenly all rush out the door.

So there is not much to the idea that our beliefs must be strictly true for the purposes of practical action. Often, even, we commit lives and fortunes to action based on hypotheses known to be false. Navigation for supertankers and other ships is based on earth-centered astronomy, for simplicity. Spacecraft trajectories are plotted using Newtonian equations, which are false, strictly speaking, in light of the general theory of

[45]Post (1978).

relativity but true to a sufficiently high degree of approximation for the practical purposes at hand.

Truth is one thing; truth to a high degree of approximation is another, as is truth to a high degree of probability. It is truth that we seek, truth *period,* when we map the faces of existence. Not that truth somehow enjoys priority over approximate truth. On the contrary, when practical action impends, fussiness over truth *period* rightly takes a lower priority. The fussiness is entirely in order, however, when we wonder whether there are any warranting criteria for truth that meet the challenge posed by historical examples of certified beliefs that later proved wrong. There may be such criteria, though the fate of those proposed to date hardly inspires optimism. The problem is *not* that each such proposed criterion fails to *guarantee* truth, not even that it fails to guarantee that a given belief is more likely to be true than untrue. Rather it may fail even to *warrant* our holding that the belief is more likely to be true than untrue. Any realist theory of truth properly so-called must concede this possibility to the skeptic.

The reason is that among the beliefs certified by the criteria so far proposed, some have turned out to be wrong, as best we can tell. Unless we can specify some relevant difference between the present belief and those others, we have no reason to suppose it will not go the way of the others. Finding rotten apples in a barrel does not mean all are rotten. But unless we know that the proportion of rotten apples to the rest is relatively small, we have no warrant for supposing that the next apple from the barrel is much less likely to be rotten than crisp.

Could we show, in the case of a truth-criterion, that the proportion of untruths to truths certified by it is relatively small? Perhaps, but only by appeal to another criterion, in light of which we decide which of the beliefs certified by the first one we are warranted in calling true. Historically, the many proposals for some such further criterion have merely raised the same problems all over again. Either they fail to explain just what the connection is between the criterion and truth or else they fail to explain why, in light of the connection, beliefs that satisfy the criterion are more likely to be true than untrue. The latter failure is far more typical than is often realized, since the proposed criterion typically is satisfied by beliefs that later proved wrong. Some philosophers nevertheless claim that we do have warranting criteria for truth that are invulnerable to such challenges. Others, especially skeptics, are dubious. Is there some way to avoid this controversy, given the largely metaphysical purposes of the chapters ahead? The burden of the next two sections is to show that there is.

1.4. Criteria versus Prerequisites for Truth

> *A very popular error: having the courage of one's convictions;*
> *rather it is a matter of having the courage for an attack on*
> *one's convictions.*
> —FRIEDRICH NIETZSCHE

> *He who feels punctured must once have been a bubble.*
> —*Tao Te Ching*

The distinction between guaranteeing and warranting criteria of truth is sound and important. But it neglects prerequisites for truth, conditions that are *necessary* for a belief to be true. Guarantees and warrants, by contrast, are sufficient either for its truth or for its being more likely to be true than not. We must therefore ask what good prerequisites for truth are if they are not warranting criteria. What good are they, unless some conjunction of them would be a warrant? And what conjunction is that? Much depends on what kind of connection holds between the proposed prerequisites and our concept of truth. Suppose the prerequisites are logically entailed by the concept. Clearly, we are guaranteed that any belief which fails to satisfy some such logical prerequisite is untrue. That is, flunking a logical prerequisite for truth is a guaranteeing criterion of falsity, provided the belief in question is true or false. (Of course it follows that the negation of the belief is then guaranteed true. But we are entitled only to so much confidence in the truth of the negation as we have in the belief's actually flunking the prerequisite.)

Now suppose we are confronted with a number of conflicting beliefs. Our first step should normally be to check whether they satisfy the logical prerequisites for truth. A belief that flunks even one such prerequisite must be ruled untrue. Any hesitation in ruling it untrue is justified only to the extent that we are unsure whether it flunks a prerequisite. Once we are sure, though, we have no choice but to replace the offending belief. Of course, rather than abandon the belief entirely, we may revise it so as to satisfy the prerequisite; the revision might even prove so solid as to survive all subsequent attempts to eliminate it on grounds of flunking a prerequisite.

Yet even so solid a revision need not be true. Nor need it be more likely to be true than untrue. One reason is the ever-present possibility of a mistake in checking whether a belief satisfies each prerequisite. We might feel sure that it does, yet be mistaken. A more important reason is that the true belief about an issue might not be among the competing beliefs we happen to entertain. Unless it is, the process of eliminating the rest makes the survivor no more likely to be true than its failed competitors. Frequently, we have little or no assurance that the truth of the matter is among the competing theories we happen to consider—no assurance that not all the apples in this barrel are rotten—if only because the range of relevant theories may be indefinitely large. Frequently, then, we have no warrant for supposing the survivor is more likely to be true than not. Moreover, there are cases in which not just one belief but two or more conflicting beliefs satisfy equally well such prerequisites for truth as we happen to possess.

Still, we *can* say of the survivors that at least they are not known to be false on the evidence to date. If nevertheless we suspect they are false, we can say that at least until now they have survived where their competitors have failed. In that respect they are superior, the lesser of evils, by virtue of so far satisfying prerequisites for truth that their competitors have failed to satisfy. When in their turn the survivors fail, we revise or replace them so as to coin new beliefs that survive better.

The new beliefs may not be true either, but the ongoing process introduces some order into our adjudication of beliefs. It allows us to sort them into those known to be untrue, so far as we can tell on the evidence to date, and those not known to be untrue. This may not be all we want, but it is better by far than a chaotic "anything goes," or "so many people, so many opinions," in which cynicism flourishes. The prerequisites are impartial standards by which our appeals beyond temporal authority can be adjudicated, not as definitely true but as superior to the narrow-minded sanctions to which we are occasionally subjected by various institutions, superior by virtue of satisfying the prerequisites where the sanctions fail. Thus even if there should prove to be no successful criteria of truth, we are not stuck with a relativism of so many people, so many opinions. For not many opinions long survive the trial by prerequisites.

We therefore have a response to a question Pilate probably had in mind when he asked, "What is truth?" The question is tendentious, often put with cynical intent: "Who can tell me what is true or false, right or wrong? Why shouldn't I just choose the expedient? Who, after all, can prove what is right or wrong, especially in religion, statecraft, and morality?" The answer is that one should not just choose the expedient unless, minimally, the expedient belief is among the beliefs not known to be false on the evidence to date. Frequently, the merely expedient belief flunks a prerequisite for truth, as we see in the next section. In such cases choosing the expedient is a mistake, so far as we can tell from our evidence, whether or not we have any criteria for its truth, hence whether or not we can prove what is the truth of the matter. Proof is beside the point. We must not be tricked by Pilate's question into supposing that the only alternatives are proofs or anything goes; certainty or so many men, so many opinions.

We noted that frequently we have no warrant, in the absence of criteria, for supposing a new or revised belief any more likely to be true than false, even when it succeeds where its predecessors fail. If so, why bother with the replacement? Because at least it represents an improvement over its predecessors—not necessarily in the sense of being closer to the truth, even assuming we know what that would mean, but in the sense of surviving better in an expanded body of evidence and experience.[46] It has survived, so far, where its predecessors have failed. The replacement may be only the lesser of evils, a Hobson's choice, but we would be foolish to reject it for that reason alone.

We would be just as foolish to refrain from acting on such well-honed belief. As seen in §1.3, beliefs need not be true in order to serve as the basis for successful action. They need only be reliable to the extent required for the purposes at hand. But a belief that has survived so well in an expanded body of experience clearly *is* reliable, so far as our experience goes, or we would have flunked it along with its predecessors. It is hard to see what practical action could require beyond success to date in circumstances of the sort in which we now contemplate acting. Does it require in addition some assurance that the belief we act on is true? To suppose so is to forget that often we knowingly base successful action on false beliefs. Does it require some assurance that the future will resemble the past, that like circumstances produce like results? I doubt it; life is full of occasions when we must act with no such expectations. But even supposing that practical action does require such expectations, where could we look, except to our experience so far, for some assurance that they will be fulfilled? Even if we did look elsewhere, we would need to remember that our experience so far is not of a perfectly regular, predictable universe but often of like circumstances' producing *un*like results, as in quantum physics and probably human history. I see no reason why lack of successful criteria should inhibit us from acting on beliefs that surpass their competitors in surviving our most determined, honest efforts to eliminate them for failing to satisfy a prerequisite for truth.

Indeed we are entitled to hold such beliefs with deep conviction. We are rightly convinced not of their truth, but of their superiority over

---

[46]On the evidently insuperable difficulties in the way of Popperian notions of getting closer to the truth, cf. Tichy; D. Miller (1974a), (1974b); Harris; Keuth.

their failed competitors. Occasionally, we are obligated to defend them with our lives. The clearest cases arise perhaps in connection with beliefs in certain freedoms and rights. We might have no guarantees that such beliefs are true, or even any warranting criteria for their truth or for their being more likely to be true than untrue. Nevertheless, if they continue to survive in an ever-expanding body of experience and evidence despite our best efforts to eliminate them, then they deserve our deepest loyalty. For in the absence of undisputed criteria of truth, what else would we have to go on, besides surpassing satisfaction to date of such prerequisites for truth as we happen to possess?

We may well begin to wonder whether we even *need* criteria of truth. Would prerequisites suffice? Granted, they would not suffice to assure us that the survivor beliefs are more likely to be true than untrue. But we have just been learning that the beliefs need not be true, strictly, for us justifiably to live by them and to die for them, nor need they even be more likely to be true than untrue. They need only have survived where their competitors have failed. So prerequisites for truth might be all we need for adjudicating the beliefs by which we live and die. Philosophical skeptics might be right that there are no successful criteria and that nothing is known, a possibility realism must concede, but they are wrong when they conclude that we must therefore suspend judgment.

A complaint sometimes lodged against certain philosophers is that they place a higher value on avoiding falsehood than on seeking truth. It might be thought that similar priorities afflict the process of elimination contemplated here, the trial by prerequisites. But the trial does not devalue truth-seeking. It assumes that someone may yet propose, indeed may already have proposed, successful warranting criteria of truth, and urges us to use such criteria should they appear. In the meantime we are counseled to do the best we can. We are to replace or revise any belief that flunks a prerequisite precisely because we *are* interested in having true beliefs. For if we seek truth, then minimally, if an untruth is revealed, we should give it up. But in addition, trial by prerequisites tells us to replace the untruth with something better, something that survives where others fail. If we sought only to avoid falsity, we would not bother with this further, constructive step, above all when we know that the replacement might prove as likely to be false, so far as we can tell, as its discredited predecessors.

Prerequisites for truth, even though they are not criteria, are valuable in another respect. They represent essential standards of truth shared by different domains of discourse. The concept of truth presented in §1.1 is topic-neutral, having no favorites among the domains. Difference of domain is a matter of different vocabulary (§§1.2, 5.3); the truth-concept is the same. But then so is anything logically entailed by the concept, such as the logical prerequisites. By virtue of the commonality of the definition from which they spring, they are shared by all the domains of discourse, hence by all the domains of truth (as we see further in Chapters 5–8).

It follows that different domains share a certain unity of method when it comes to judging, as best we can, whether a given belief is true. Those who would exempt their belief from a logical prerequisite for truth, whatever the domain, either do not know what they are talking about or are talking about truth in another sense. That is, they can change the subject. Historically, this is precisely what has been done by those who would completely departmentalize the domains, especially science and religion, arguing that they share no standards of truth.

1.5. Seven Prerequisites for Truth

> *The whole structure of reason . . . is no longer adequate. It begins to be seen for what it really is—emotionally hollow, esthetically meaningless and spiritually empty.*
>
> —ROBERT PIRSIG

> *To enjoy to the full the conquests of daring, we must demand that it operate in a pitiless light.*
>
> —IGOR STRAVINSKY

> *The against comes before the for.*
> —PABLO PICASSO

Creativity and criticism mean little without each other. Even in the arts, insight and imagination often must satisfy pitiless prerequisites, the artist's own, though not completely discontinuous with the standards of other artists and laymen. Conversely, hard criticism—that flinty "against"—fires us to create something that will survive, something we can be for. Let no one object to the present emphasis on prerequisites for truth that they are the Procrustean instruments of dull nay-sayers. Their role is to shock us into finding better things to which we may say "Yes!" The structure of reason, properly viewed and properly practiced, is the opposite of "emotionally hollow, esthetically meaningless and spiritually empty." Criticism and creativity are equal forces in the same generative process, *yin* and *yang* blending one into the other, as the critics of reason ought to have known.

To this end, at least seven logical prerequisites for truth can be teased out of our truth-concept. They are (i) well-formedness, (ii) nonemptiness, (iii) successful presupposition, (iv) self-consistency, (v) consistency with all other truths, (vi) truth of all the logical consequences, and (vii) objectivity. Few in number, the seven are powerful in effect, individually and collectively. This is not to say that cherished beliefs are or ought to be replaced overnight, as soon as we begin to think they flunk a prerequisite. Much depends on whether we know of a replacement that does any better. Also, further investigation often reveals that they do not flunk after all, that the trouble lies elsewhere. Evidence we had relied on may turn out itself to flunk a prerequisite. And even where cherished beliefs do flunk, frequently it is only long after the fact that, with the gift of hindsight, we can best judge that they do. The connection between the prerequisites and our concept of truth is simple, but judging whether our systems of belief satisfy them is often not.

(i) *Well-formedness.* In §1.1.1 we defined truth for sentences—for grammatically well-formed bursts of talk that can be true or false. Therefore, a logically necessary condition for the truth of something is that it be syntactically and semantically well formed, according to the conventions of English or some other language. Gibberish is out, along with other kinds of linguistic nonsense.

This prerequisite might seem trivial. Who would ever attribute truth to babble? But people have and do, as for example when they ascribe truth to speaking in tongues and struggle to divine its message. The research shows that glossolalia produces no well-formed sentences of English or any other language.[47] Tapes of the rhythmic outbursts are interpreted very differently even by members of the same small religious group.[48] As for the many (other) forms of divination, few seem to satisfy this prerequisite. People once ascribed truth to the wild mouthings of Sybils in states of trance. The ululations of entranced priestesses, seers, shamans, and the like were treated the same way. In some corners of the world they still are. In addition, there are people who still "read" tea leaves, oracle-bones, flights of birds, entrails. It was not so long ago that the educated sought to read the book of nature and find truth there. They took quite literally what we regard as a charming metaphor. Astrology perhaps still does. Examples there are, even, of philosophies reputed to be semantically or even syntactically ill formed, in part, according to any plausible stretch of the rules even of their own language. But I will name no names.

(ii) *Nonemptiness.* Even if a burst of talk is well formed, it may convey no information, nothing that can be true or false. It may be empty. Politicians are especially good at seeming to say a great deal when actually they have committed themselves to nothing. But empty

[47]Cf. F. Goodman.
[48]Kildahl; cf. Samarin.

talk occurs elsewhere as well. Perhaps its surest sign is that nothing is denied, no state of affairs whatever. Some think this was the eventual fate of talk of the ether, a diaphanous medium pervading everything, postulated as what light waves are waves in. The hypothesis was so often qualified, in order to deflect awkward evidence, that in its waning days it may well have become compatible with any facts whatever. But a belief that excludes nothing cannot be true (unless it is a mere tautology). It cannot even be false. For if it is true or false, it must at least exclude whatever its negation expresses. It must be incompatible also with the negations of its logical consequences. So a belief congenial with any state of affairs whatever cannot be true or false (tautologies aside). It can only be empty.

Although several factors contributed to its demise, emptiness was the eventual fate of the phlogiston theory. Combustible things were supposed to contain phlogiston, the principle of fire, regarded as a material substance given off when things burn, leaving only the residual ash. Like the ether idea, this was not a bad theory in the beginning, and it served the old chemistry quite well until trapped by rising experience and new ways of thinking and seeing. The awkward evidence included the fact that the residue weighed *more* than the unburned combustible, contrary to what one would expect if phlogiston were released. To get around this problem, some theorists went so far as to ascribe *negative weight* to this wonderful material substance, thereby taking a big step in the direction of rendering the theory compatible with anything at all. When a promising alternative theory became available, the growing emptiness became intolerable. Other attempts to defend the theory, which might once have seemed plausible, now only contributed further to the impression of emptiness.

(iii) *Successful presupposition.* Another way beliefs can fail to be true or false is to suffer presupposition-failure. If there is no Loch Ness monster, then the belief that it is a survivor of a species thought long extinct is neither true nor false. The belief would be based on a false presupposition, like the question 'When did you stop robbing banks?' But how does this prerequisite follow from our concept of truth? According to Schema T, ϕ is true iff S. The schema makes sense only if we first fix on a particular interpretation $\Im$ of the terms in the sentence ϕ (as in TW, §1.1.1). For example, suppose 'Snow is white' is used to mean that Bill Snow is playing the white pieces at chess. Then $\Im$ assigns Bill to 'Snow'. But if there is no such player, not all the terms in 'Snow is white' receive an interpretation, strictly, and the schema cannot apply. The sentence therefore is neither true nor false, though on other interpretations it is true or false.

(iv) *Self-consistency.* Though it can be made to sound trivial, this prerequisite historically has had profound, widespread effect. People sometimes sneer at mere consistency, and of course it is not much if one is looking for criteria. But the same people are rarely indifferent to *in*consistency, even though they may not fully realize why, and even though they may not realize how often it has spurred creative second thoughts—sometimes revolutionary—after which it is impossible ever to see the world in the old ways.

The usual way to show that a belief is inconsistent is to deduce a contradiction from it. When successful, such reduction to absurdity is dramatic, and there is no appeal. Suppose I regard it as known that nothing is known, as did an ancient school of skeptics. It takes no genius of a logician to see the self-inconsistency here. I must retract or revise. The favored revision in the successor school of skeptics was "Nothing at all is known, not even this." This second thought has instructed skepticism ever since.

Typically reduction to absurdity is more complicated. The Pythagoreans originally believed that in some sense everything is made of numbers—roughly what we would call integers and ratios of integers, though not quite; to them, numbers were at once units, geometrical points, and physical atoms. Their religion rested heavily on this bit of metaphysics, this number mysticism, and took for granted that every magnitude could be expressed as a ratio of integers. Someone then derived a contradiction from the assumption that the length of a diagonal on a square could be so expressed, when the square's sides are a unit long: the length is not a ratio; it is an irrational. Today the derivation is routinely presented in elementary textbooks, as part of a demonstration of the existence of irrational numbers. But the person who first dreamed it up must have been ingenious. Legend has it that the miscreant was himself one of the Pythagoreans, and that they suppressed his result and threw him into the sea. If so, what may have been the first recorded conflict between science and religion ended all too prophetically.

Other Pythagoreans responded more constructively, contributing to what eventually became a general theory of the irrationals. In effect the theory was a revision and enrichment of the earlier theory. Pythagoreans could continue to regard number as the key to what they perceived as the order and harmony of the universe, but the notion of number would have to change and their number myticism with it.

In an eighteenth-century conflict, Bishop Berkeley argued correctly that there were inconsistencies in the notion of an infinitesimal, then at the heart of the new mathematical physics. Berkeley thus embarrassed a scientific orthodoxy, showing in effect that it flunked a prerequisite for truth. His aim was to discredit the new mechanical picture of the world.

He would have succeeded had there been no constructive response to the inconsistencies. But there was, culminating in the theory of limits early in the nineteenth century.

Likewise, certain of today's theories of justification and rationality may have to change, to the extent that they are committed to the view that every theory whatever (including itself) is falsifiable or at least criticizable. For it looks as though a wide range of such theories, hence a wide range of empiricist and pragmatist epistemologies, are self-referentially inconsistent—or if consistent, then inherently incomplete.[49]

Finally, consider the orthodox Christian belief that there is real, undeniable evil in this world, a world created by an all-powerful, all-knowing, perfectly loving God—evils aplenty, many not originating with us but with the world. If the terms here are taken in anything like their normal meaning, the belief appears inconsistent: surely such a God, so willing and able, would have created a world without so much evil. To wonder whether the belief *is* inconsistent is to raise the problem of evil. Christians try to preserve consistency typically by denying that the key terms in the belief have their normal meaning. They may say that God's love is to be understood in a special way, or that what *we* take to be evil needn't be, in God's plan. In effect, this is to revise the belief, to elaborate and perhaps to enrich it, depending on how we are to interpret evil and God's love. Unfortunately, there is considerable danger in thus attempting to elaborate the belief so as to satisfy the consistency prerequisite. Qualification piled on qualification can lead to emptiness. A love so qualified that it tolerates, when it could prevent, the bayoneting of infants and lingering death for millions in the tropics by parasitic worms reminds one of a material that has negative weight. It is religious phlogiston.

(v) *Consistency with all other truths.* If two or more beliefs are inconsistent with each other, at least one of them is untrue. Part of the point of this prerequisite is that even if a cherished theory is self-consistent, it may not be consistent with other beliefs of which we are as fond. We may not know which belief to change, but something has to give. If the other fond beliefs stubbornly survive trial by prerequisites, the theory should at least be revised, though not in the direction of emptiness. The revision may well represent a great improvement over our earlier version of the theory. "A clash of doctrines is not a disaster, it is an opportunity."[50]

Every example of self-consistency that involves a conjunction is, in

---

[49]Post (1971), (1983).
[50]Whitehead (1925), 185.

effect, an example also of consistency with other beliefs. The conjunctive belief that (a) all human beings are created equal and (b) blacks may be enslaved and Indians shot on sight may be regarded as two beliefs, (a) and (b). Then, instead of wondering whether the conjunctive belief is self-consistent, we may wonder equivalently whether (a) is consistent with (b). And of course it goes the other way: wondering whether two or more beliefs are consistent with each other is equivalent to wondering whether their conjunction is self-consistent. It follows that all the examples lately given to show the importance of self-consistency show the importance also of the present prerequisite. But even though the two prerequisites are equivalent in this respect, still it is wise to separate them. Calling them by different names reminds us that in the trial by prerequisites, tunnel vision is intolerable. The crucial trouble for a belief may lie just beyond the periphery. The belief may be self-consistent, and even consistent with some others, but not with all those that strike us if we open our eyes wide.

Suppose we deem it expedient to exhaust the fossil fuels for purposes of transportation and heating. Suppose that this policy is both self-consistent and (what is less clear) consistent also with the belief that we will not release so much CO_2 into the atmosphere as to trigger a runaway greenhouse effect by triggering the release of colossal amounts of the CO_2 stored in the oceans. Suppose further that we are justifiably confident that alternative energy sources will be available by the time the fossil fuels are gone. So far so good. But if we open our eyes wider, there is trouble. When the fossil hydrocarbons are gone, where will we get adequate feedstocks for making drugs, synthetic fibers, pesticides, and—above all—essential fertilizers? Our belief that there will continue to be enough of these things, cheap enough, may well be inconsistent with the expedient of exhausting the hydrocarbons for other purposes, even if the expedient should happen ever so conveniently to be consistent with our beliefs about a greenhouse effect and about eventual alternative energy sources.

(vi) *The truth of all logical consequences.* If ϕ is a consequence of a set of sentences, and ϕ is untrue, not everything in the set is true. We are not told which sentence or sentences in the set might be at fault, but we do know we had better start looking. Kant evidently thought his moral theory had the consequence that I must in no circumstance tell a lie, even when a would-be murderer, weapon in hand, asks whether his intended victim is hiding in my house. We may update the example by imagining a terrorist who would hurl a satchel charge into a schoolroom if told who the children are. In such cases our considered judgment is that the lie is not only permissible but obligatory. Assuming that this judgment continues to survive trial by prerequisites, Kant's theory must be revised, unless it can be shown not to have this consequence after all.

Moral beliefs can flunk this prerequisite in another way, by having consequences that are empirically false. Suppose I believe that without exception adults ought to work rather than live on welfare. But "ought" implies "can," so that adults for whom work is physically impossible have no obligation to work. Empirical facts about them—paralysis, blindness, functional idiocy, extreme malnutrition, total lack of transportation—all cancel the alleged obligation. The political expedient of indiscriminately cutting welfare therefore typically flunks this prerequisite. It survives by ignoring inconvenient fact. So does equally indiscriminate funding of welfare, though it is preached less often than wholesale cutting.

(vii) *Objectivity*. An object is something that persists through different perspectives. "Do you see what I see?" If not, I hesitate to claim that an object is there. Something that is there for me but not for anyone else may be of great value to me, perhaps rightly. But it is not an object in the full sense unless I can show that everyone else is mistaken, as Galileo showed with his theory and telescope that there are moons around Jupiter, and biologists that there are microbes. Otherwise the claim that the object is there would be true for me and false for you. Its truth-value would vary with the person who makes it. But our truth-concept from §1.1 is of truth *period,* not truth-for-me, truth-for-you, truth-from-some-perspective. One way to capture this invariance is to think of the truth-bearers as eternal sentences (sentences all the tokens of which have the same truth-value). The truth-value of an eternal sentence cannot vary with person, place, or time of utterance. *Objectivity* is a consequence of this invariance; indeed it is another name for it.

An oil drum has a round top. Most of the time the top appears elliptical, since we see it from an angle. Seen edge-on, it appears straight as a board. Only when viewed from a point on the perpendicular to its center does the top appear circular. And only because we already know the top is circular do we know to view it from some such point if we wish appearance to coincide with reality. How, then, did we first learn that the top is round? Roughly, by realizing that a round thing would project exactly the sequence of shapes we observe, the ellipses that vary from thin to fat, from a minimum (straight as a board) to a maximum (circular). We accord objective existence to the shape that would most simply account for all these varying projections. Such a property is said to be an invariant.[51] Sentences that fail to be eternal cannot ascribe

---

[51]On this use of the term, and on the idea, see Born; Taylor and Wheeler, §5; Grünbaum (1968), 298. Strictly, we should speak only of an invariant under or with respect to certain transformations. For brevity I omit this phrase, letting the context indicate what transformations are intended.

invariants, or object properties, to things (which is not to say that every eternal sentence ascribes an invariant, nor is it to deny that sentence-tokens can). Let us see why.

Often what we take to be an objective property is only a property of a projection, an accident of perspective. Ordinary temporal order, oddly enough, is one such. Blink both eyes at the same time. One eyeblink has the property of being simultaneous with the other, and the sentence that says so looks to be invariantly true, or eternal ('The one eyeblink is simultaneous with the other'). But we now know, thanks to Einstein, that the two eyeblinks are *not* simultaneous according to certain other frames of reference, such as that of a spacecraft hurtling inbound from the moon on a course at an angle to your line of sight. Thus the truth-value of this seemingly eternal sentence does vary after all with the time and place of its utterance. The sentence is not *true,* but true only with respect to particular frames.

Ordinary simultaneity, therefore, and ordinary before-and-after are not objective properties or relations of events.[52] The sentences that express them are not eternal after all. This is one of the lessons of Einstein's special theory of relativity. STR shows also that ordinary length and mass, long thought to be invariants, are not. Instead, they are properties of projections onto various coordinate systems. It is as though we had mistaken a feature of a map for a feature of the terrain.

What *are* objectively there, according to STR, are certain spatiotemporal invariants—the same for every system—of which the ordinary properties and relations are mere projections. Thus the theory of relativity is primarily a theory of objectivity, ironically—a theory of how certain invariants account for varying appearances of objects and events to different observers in motion relative to them and to each other. Indeed as remarked in §1.1.3, Einstein at first called it "*Invarianten-theorie.*" STR provides a set of rules, or transformations, for describing the precise connections among the various projections of the same object on different systems of reference. In like manner certain rules enable us to anticipate what the oil drum will look like when viewed from ten feet above where we are now standing.

We learn about our world rather as the blind men learned about the elephant, or tried to. But we keep groping and probing and comparing notes until we have substantially more to go on than they. Then we look for invariants in our notes and posit an object with just such properties in order to explain what we experience. We call it an elephant. Other experiences would prompt us instead to speak of a mouse; still others, a human, a gene, an atom, a quark, a galaxy, a universe.

[52]Cf. Smart (1972); D. C. Williams.

According to many, the sciences have no peer in ascertaining what objectively exists, what is real. If so, the reason lies in the organized, systematic way they hunt for the invariants in our perspectives. In this regard, as in others, science is merely an extension of common sense. Common sense asks, "Do you see what I see?" Science amplifies the question, asking, "What are the invariants in what anyone would observe anywhere anywhen?" Its objectivity is "superhuman," in Einstein's word, only in the sense of transcending, or aiming to transcend, the perspectives of particular persons, times, and places. Much of the much-maligned, increasingly depersonalized view of existence found in science grows from this deep taproot in common sense. Occasionally it conflicts, or seems to conflict, with other things rooted in common sense.

For example, common sense tends to be highly anthropocentric, with good reason. Its human-centeredness is indispensable for certain purposes and for most action, like earth-centered astronomy for navigation at sea. By mapping everything in polar coordinates centered on us, anthropocentrism reflects the high value we rightly place on ourselves as subjectively conscious actors and originators of so much, including science itself plus the very idea of objectivity. The trouble is that exclusive use of such maps can lead us finally to view everything in relation to ourselves. We may come to believe that everything exists for consciousness—to bring it about and to sustain it—or even that all things depend on subjective consciousness for their very existence. We may thus mistake a feature of our map for a feature of existence by neglecting different maps and by neglecting to inquire what invariants persist through their various coordinate systems. Something in all of us—some constituent of consciousness or of common sense—tries to relate all things to the present in which we are acting, the "now" with which the other present contents of our consciousness are simultaneous (§5.4). Indeed subjective consciousness is widely supposed to consist of a succession of such nows. But no such now or present can be an invariant, because of the noninvariance of ordinary simultaneity. Thus the invaluable present—that fleeting moment in which we live and to which something in us tries to relate everything—lacks the transcendence we expect of an objective existent. If we care about truth, we cannot view everything in terms of the succession of nows that reputedly make up our consciousness. This is but one way in which "philosophy is the self-correction by consciousness of its own initial excess of subjectivity."[53]

Other things go by the name of objectivity, including the capacity of certain claims to attract substantial intersubjective agreement about

---

[53]There is some irony that it is Whitehead (1929), 22, who says this.

them. Such agreement can be reassuring, but it is neither necessary nor sufficient for a claim to be invariantly true or invariantly false, or for it to have satisfied the other prerequisites for truth. Thus the presence of, say, moral disagreement, even widespread, does not imply that there are no moral truths for us to disagree about, or that moral claims are not objective in the sense of being true or false.[54] If they are objective in this sense, then even if there are no criteria of moral truth, we are stuck with a relativism neither of anything goes nor of so many people, so many opinions. Few of our glib opinions about morals satisfy well-formedness *and* nonemptiness *and* successful presupposition *and* self-consistency *and* consistency with all other truths *and* the truth of all consequences *and* objectivity. Nor do many even of our considered opinions long survive unchanged in the ongoing trial by prerequisites.

There remain the troublesome cases in which two or more conflicting opinions satisfy the seven equally well. How are we to choose? Often we need not. We may suspend belief and intensify our efforts to narrow the field to one, by subjecting the competitors to further trial by prerequisites in light of experience that we enlarge precisely in order to narrow the field. But sometimes the field cannot be narrowed this way, or at least not until long after we finally must choose. Fortunately, we can narrow the field still further by requiring our beliefs to be not merely true but also some other equally virtuous things. By adding virtues for beliefs we can multiply prerequisites—prerequisites not for truth but for *acceptability* in light of *all* we want a belief to be and do.

1.6. Additional Virtues for Beliefs

> *The injunction to seek truth regardless . . . has the self-righteous ring of a commandment not to put other gods before truth.*
>
> —Nelson Goodman

Truths are a dime a dozen. A run through the multiplication tables or on a calculator will generate as many as we like. Obviously, we want much more than truth alone. What else we want depends heavily on the context. In one situation the valuable belief may be one that inspires. In another a routine guide to practical action may suffice. In still another we may seek comprehensiveness and simplicity. The latter two virtues are what we concentrate on in this section, all too briefly. When we speak henceforth about prerequisites for acceptability in light of all we

---

[54]Even according to Mackie, ch. 1, who nevertheless believes there are no objective values. Cf. §§6.0–6.2.

want a belief to be and do, it is primarily comprehensiveness and simplicity that we have in mind, plus some related cognitive virtues not explicitly discussed here.

One virtue we almost always want for our beliefs is relevant truth, truth that answers a question we have, or helps to answer it. In the beginning is the question, partly for the very good reason that it is our questions, often tacit, that determine what is relevant. If you ask whether I walk to work and I reply that I fix my own lunch, something has gone wrong. My reply may be true, but ordinarily it is utterly irrelevant. Likewise, philosophy begins in wonder, and we hope that it ends not only in truth but in relevant truth—truth that answers some question, or helps to answer it, perhaps by showing that it is not a genuine or well-formed question in the first place.

In addition to relevant truth, frequently we want comprehensive truth, truth that connects a variety of things so as to enhance understanding. Comprehensiveness—or scope, as it sometimes is called—is a matter roughly of the richness of logical consequences of a belief. The belief that *all* people deserve equal consideration has greater scope than the belief that all *white* people do. Provided the two beliefs satisfy all other prerequisites equally well, the one with greater scope is to be preferred: it connects more. Physics plays its special role in the sciences largely because its theories connect all physical entities whatever, not just those of interest to chemistry, biology, or psychology, to name a few. And a philosophy is to be preferred that relates several faces of existence rather than focusing narrowly on one, especially if the face is alleged to be the only one.

Another prerequisite for acceptability is simplicity. A standard illustration is that of fitting a curve to data-points on a graph. There are infinitely many complicated curves that go exactly through every datum. Typically we ignore them, concentrating instead on the simplest curves and choosing the one that comes nearest to fitting the data. Those data that lie off the curve are blamed on extraneous effects of the experimental situation—dirty test tubes, shaky hands, tired eyes.

Just what simplicity is and why it is a prerequisite are controversial. Some believe that simplicity is related to comprehensiveness: the simpler hypothesis is the one with greater scope, and vice versa. Some believe instead that simplicity is related to objectivity: data-points, like the projections of the oil drum, are the varying effects on our apparatus of the single object or process that would most simply account for them all. This does not define simplicity so much as remind us that simplicity evidently enters our very conception of an object. Nevertheless, even if simplicity is not thereby defined, the fact that it enters our conception of an object shows how deeply simplicity is ingrained into our ways of accepting beliefs. Thus, whether it is related to scope or to objectivity, simplicity is not some peripheral esthetic feature it would merely be nice to have. Its rationale is deeper, connected with comprehensiveness or objectivity or both.

A crucial consequence of the simplicity prerequisite, and perhaps thereby of comprehensiveness or even objectivity, is Occam's razor: do not multiply entities beyond necessity. Instead of positing several objects to account for the elliptical shapes that vary from thin to fat, we posit one—the round top of the oil drum. It is far simpler than supposing that we are presented with a sequence of different elliptical objects as we move about. Likewise, before the age of about five months, an infant has not one mother but several: the one in the nursery, the one in the kitchen, and so on. Then somehow the infant puts them together, eliminating extra entities in favor of one. The fact that this occurs in all normal infants at about the same age suggests that we are dealing with an inborn trait. This suggests in turn that the trait has some survival value for the species, leading to the further speculation that simplicity of hypothesis favors successful prediction, and hence that the simpler hypothesis is more likely to be true. Speculation aside, we see again how close is the connection between simplicity and our very concept of an object as the simplest way to unify otherwise disparate experiences. Our search for invariants begins in infancy, when it results in our positing one mother in place of several. All of us wield Occam's razor well before any of us can shave.

We continue to wield it in a variety of ways, amplified by science and philosophy. For example, the various sciences repeatedly have been able to account for various phenomena without reference to any divinity. Repeatedly, theism has been seen to be a bad explanatory hypothesis, when it is meant as one, however good it may once have been in that regard. It posits a superfluous entity—superfluous, that is, for the purposes of scientific explanation, however crucial it may be in other respects. This suggests that such rational justification as theism may have is not rooted in explanatory power—at any rate not in the sort of explanatory power valued by the sciences, a value they inherit from the infant, cutting extra entities in favor of one. The justification of theism, if any, and its point, must lie elsewhere.

2 Mystery and Ultimate Explanation

*At first people wondered about the more obvious problems
that demanded explanation; gradually their inquiries spread
farther afield, and they asked questions upon such larger
topics as changes in the sun and moon and stars, and the
origin of the world.*

—ARISTOTLE

*How comes the world to be here at all instead of the
nonentity which might be imagined in its place? . . . The
question of being . . . [is] the darkest in all philosophy. All
of us are beggars here, and no school can speak disdainfully of
another or give itself superior airs.*

—WILLIAM JAMES

2.0. Introduction

Who has not wondered, from time to time, why we exist, and
ultimately why there is anything at all? Are we and the rest of the
universe nothing but some brute happening, utterly without explanation? And what of the properties of our universe—why does it have
them and not others? Why, for example, are the stars and the life they
may harbor so far away? Why must there be so much loneliness and
horror? These and other questions well up in us as we reflect on our
little worlds and how they might fit into the larger one. We look for
larger meanings to illuminate the daily round. The possibility that there
are none can be unsettling, even a cause for despair. If there is no reason
for the existence of the universe, how can there ultimately be any reason

for mine? Is the reason for my existence—or are the reasons—to be found in myself and not out there? If so, how can the reasons have the force of truth? Mustn't they be grounded somehow in the world and thereby in some explanation of why the world is here at all, in some ultimate visage of existence? And what could that be? What if it should prove to be some sort of reptilian indifference to us and our hopes?

Most of us have neither the time nor the training to deal with such questions. So we shrug, go about our business, and get along as best we can with the fragmentary answers we absorb from our culture. Besides, we have often been told that such cosmic questions express mysteries unfathomable by human beings, and we may thereby feel relieved of any responsibility to inquire. Equally often we have been told that while such questions are answerable, the answers are not to be found by science or reason. Instead, these are matters of faith, perhaps of mystical insight, completely beyond the reach of reason. Again we may feel relieved of the responsibility to inquire, since inquiry generally proceeds in accordance with the trial by prerequisites.

The unity of method represented by the prerequisites should put us on guard against thus departmentalizing the cosmic questions. If we seek truth about them, the logical prerequisites apply, inexorably. Not that there can be no mysteries, here or anywhere else. The trial by prerequisites nowhere presupposes that we can answer *all* our questions, or even very many of them.

Indeed the possibility of mystery, in the sense of truths we do not know and perhaps can never know, is guaranteed by any remotely realist notion of truth, according to which the true answers to our questions, even if they occur to us, need not be recognized as true. Our criteria, such as they are, may lead us instead to accept a false answer. For certain questions our criteria may be so obviously inadequate that we refrain from accepting any answer at all, even though we know there is a truth of the matter which we may or may not someday be able to ascertain. For certain other questions imagination may fail even to suggest any answers at all—or at least any answers that we have some chance of adjudicating in light of the prerequisites for truth, plus any reliable criteria we might have. The question 'Why does the universe exist at all?' could be one for which imagination fails us. If so and if it has a true answer, it expresses a mystery, perhaps unfathomable. But if it has no true answer, perhaps because it is based on a false presupposition, then whatever our initial intuitive response to this seemingly profound metaphysical question, it expresses no mystery, and we must adjust our philosophies accordingly.

2.1. Mystery

> *There is no unfathomable mystery.*
>
> —Moritz Schlick

> *A philosophy unaware of mystery would not be a philosophy.*
>
> —Jacques Maritain

> *In the deepest heart of all of us there is a corner in which the ultimate mystery of things works sadly.*
>
> —William James

We begin with the question 'Why does the universe exist at all?' Later in the chapter we take up such other cosmic questions as whether the universe is some inexplicable, brute happening; whether it has any larger meaning or meanings; and so on. We take them up, but we do not put them down. We can make further progress on some of them only in light of chapters to come.

Whether a question expresses a mystery depends not only on the question but on what we mean by 'mystery'.[1] The word comes from a Greek root, applied originally to lips or eyes, meaning "closed" or "shut." The root then was applied to those initiated into mysteries, those who vowed to keep silence about what they were allowed to see or hear. Hence deep in the origins of the word there is the presupposition that *there is* something hidden from us, about which initiates are to keep their mouths shut. The silence does not mask nothing; the poke has a pig in it.

This presupposition carries over into Jewish and Christian borrowings of the Greek for 'mystery'. There *are* secrets, there *are* truths hidden from all of us, kept now by almighty God, not by the hierophants or priests of some cult, or so we are told. Such truths are supposed to relate primarily to a divine plan for human salvation. That there is such a plan is said to be revealed to us, plus something of its content. But ultimately, it cannot be completely known by human beings. Not only are there mysteries; some are unfathomable.

Contemporary usage of the word, though broader, generally remains faithful to its origins. In line with them, therefore, let us characterize a mystery as what is expressed by a question to which we do not know the answer, though *there is* a true answer to be known. Characterized this way, mysteries range from the trivial to the profound. If I lose my keys, then it is a mystery as to where they are. There is mystery

---

[1]On the following etymology, cf. Munitz, ch. 1.

also as to why Mayan civilizations collapsed repeatedly, their people dissolving back into the jungle, though several explanations have been offered. Another mystery is whether the expanding physical universe will someday contract. And provided there is some true answer to the question 'Why does the universe exist at all?' then it expresses a mystery, unless we know the answer.

Some mysteries we expect to solve, or to be able to solve. Mostly they are toward the trivial end of the scale. Are there any that human beings are *unable* to solve? In particular, are there any that could not be solved no matter how hard and how long we tried? Consider Fermat's Last Conjecture. It is thought to be true, yet no proof has been found either of it or its negation. Is there a formal proof of either one to be found? This question may well express a mystery that we are unable to solve. If there *is* a proof of the conjecture, we might eventually stumble across it. But if there is none, and if, further, there is no proof of its negation, we could search forever and never know. The mystery would be unsolvable. Is the question 'Why does the universe exist?' like that?

Or is it instead like the question 'What is the best way to trisect an angle using only compass and straightedge?' This question presupposes there is a way to trisect an angle using only the equipment specified. Since there is none, the presupposition is false, and any answer therefore flunks the successful-presupposition prerequisite. Thus there is properly no answer to the question, let alone a true one, any more than there is properly an answer to the question 'When did you stop beating your spouse?' Such a question cannot even arise, let alone express a mystery, not even for an infinite intellect. It is unfathomable in about the same way as an ocean without depth. The problem is not with our depthfinders, or with us and our finitude, but with the question. There simply is nothing to fathom.

Questions based on false presuppositions are not meaningless or unintelligible.[2] We understand perfectly well what is meant by 'When did you stop beating your spouse?' or by 'What is the best way to trisect an angle using only compass and straightedge?' Indeed it is only because we understand them that we can isolate some of their presuppositions and point to their falsity. Note also that even though there is properly no *answer* to such questions, there *is* a proper *response*.[3] Instead of answering, or trying to answer, we respond: "Your question is based on a false presupposition and therefore is out of order." In parliamentary debate the motion to divide the question is privileged, mainly in order

[2]Cf. Belnap; Bromberger.
[3]Cf. van Fraassen (1977), 149.

to prevent the confusion caused by questions based on erroneous presuppositions.

Is the question 'Why does the universe exist at. all?' based on a false presupposition? That depends in part on how the word 'universe' is being used. 'Universe' can have the sense, among other things, either of 'physical universe' or of 'sum total of what there is, physical or otherwise'. Those who are asking the question of being, as William James called it, are not just asking why the *physical* universe exists. They are asking of the sum total of what there is why *it* exists, rather than nothing. When they express their question by means of 'Why does the universe exist at all?' they are using the word 'universe' in the sense of 'sum total of what there is' or 'whole of existence'. Hence all the troubles we noted in §1.2, about the word 'whole', recur here. But the essential features of the question of being can be explained without dredging up those particular troubles. In the next chapter we consider the question 'Why does the *physical* universe exist?' In particular, we consider whether this question is based on a false presupposition and, if not, whether we know the answer or could ever know. The present chapter concentrates on the more radical question of why there is anything at all.

Whether this more radical question is based on a false presupposition depends in part on how the word 'why' is being used. When we ask 'Why?' about something, typically we are seeking some sort of explanation. But even though this is the typical use of 'Why?' it is by no means the only use. Suppose I ask, "Why does the United Nations exist at all?" Instead of seeking an explanation, I may be expressing exasperation, or even suggesting that the U.N. be abolished. I may already understand perfectly well why the U.N. exists, in terms of conditions at the end of World War II, plus the intentions of its founders and the somewhat different motives of its present members. Or suppose I ask, "Why was I ever born?" An account of my parents and their motives for mating may be the last thing called for. I may be expressing regret that I was ever born, or anger, or helplessness, or the wish to be dead.

In asking the question 'Why does the universe exist at all?' are we seeking some sort of explanation? Or are we expressing an emotion? Often it is the latter; we may be expressing anxiety, estrangement, helplessness, regret, astonishment, awe, affirmation, or even joy and exuberance at the fact of existence.[4] Or we could be wishing there had been no universe, much as we sometimes wish we had never been born. Perhaps instead we are denying that existence is necessarily any better

[4]Cf. Munitz, 6.

than nonexistence. For we may have been disturbed by Voltaire's question: "Why, as we are so miserable, have we imagined that not to be is a great ill, when it becomes clear that it was not an ill not to be before we were born?"[5]

If I am expressing an emotion in asking the question of being—or a wish, denial, or affirmation—then the question expresses no mystery unless I am at the same time also seeking an explanation. Asked by someone else, the same question may seek an explanation and thereby express a mystery if we do not know the explanation. Thus it is absolutely crucial to determine whether we are seeking an explanation when we ask, "Why does the universe exist at all?" If not, our question expresses no mystery in the sense of the term we lately defined in the spirit of its origins. Our question might express mystery in some *other* sense of the term, perhaps a feeling that *something* is strange, uncanny, eerie, weird, full of wonder.

Most things *are* a wonder in some respect, and we must never lose the gift of wonder. Indeed the "question of being" is used by some philosophers to symbolize the importance of wonder, a holy seeking prepared to transcend received categories of thought and feeling, if need be, in order to satisfy our hunger to understand.[6] But if I express the feeling that the existence of the universe is a wonder, it is hard to see how I would not also thereby be expressing the feeling that its existence is mysterious. For ordinarily, to say something is strange, uncanny, eerie, weird, or a wonder is to imply that there is something mysterious about it—some question about it to which we do not know the answer. And the only question in the neighborhood that might express mysteriousness in this deep sense is 'Why does the universe exist at all?' But it expresses a mystery only if it seeks an explanation.

Of course the question 'Why does the universe exist at all?' might be a misleading way of asking 'What are the origins of the universe?' or 'How did the universe come to be?' The first of these two other questions presupposes that the universe has an origin, perhaps in time. The second presupposes that the universe came to be, apparently at a time or even over a period of time. But the question 'Why does the universe exist?' shares neither presupposition. So the questions are distinct in at least these ways, and it is wise to keep them separate. We can best do so by assuming that if we wanted to ask these other two questions, we would ask them in words less misleading as to our intent than 'Why does the universe exist at all?' These other questions might express

[5]Cf. Edwards (1967a), 301.
[6]As Heidegger (1959) seems to, ch. 1.

mysteries, or they might not; we can say something about that in the next chapter. Here we can already say that any mystery they might express is distinct from the one allegedly expressed by 'Why does the universe exist at all?' This question, the so-called question of being, is meant to be rather more profound than the other two, though they are hardly trivial.

A question that begins with 'why' and seeks an explanation is called, in the dazzling jargon of the trade, an explanation-seeking why-question. The trend of the argument so far can be summarized by saying that either the question of being is an explanation-seeking why-question; or it expresses no mystery but rather some emotion, attitude, or symbol; or it is a misleading way of expressing separate and somewhat less profound questions. In this last case, a mystery might be expressed, but it would be different from the one intended by those who believe that the question of being expresses an ultimate mystery. So if the question is to express a mystery of the profound sort intended, it must be construed as an explanation-seeking why-question. One who asks the question in this spirit, therefore, is asking '*What is the explanation* of the existence of the universe?' Hence the question 'Why does the universe exist at all?' presupposes that *there is* some explanation. The mystery, if there is one, is *what* the explanation is.

Is there an explanation, known or unknown, knowable or unknowable, of why the universe exists? If not, the question is based on a false presupposition. The question of being would be perfectly meaningful or well-formed but out of order. It would be unfathomable only in the sense that there is nothing to fathom. The poke would have no pig in it. But if there is some explanation, the question is proper and expresses a mystery, unless we know what the explanation is.

Someone might object that all this is irrelevant because it neglects the question 'Why does *some universe or other* exist?' in favor of the easier question 'Why does *this* universe exist?'[7] It neglects 'Why is there something or other, rather than nothing?' in favor of 'Why is there *this* something, rather than nothing?' There might be no mystery, given that some universe had to exist, as to why this one did, yet profound mystery as to why one or another had to exist in the first place.

However, in the case of universes one and only one can exist, given the all-inclusive sense of 'universe' relevant here. For if more than one existed, then the entire collection they form would be the actual universe (however scattered and discontinuous). Let us call the only existing universe Ω. Given that Ω can be the one and only existing universe,

[7]This was called to my attention by Phil Oliver, in conversation.

the statement that some universe or other exists is equivalent to the statement that Ω exists (just as 'Something is F' is equivalent to 'a is F' when necessarily a is the only F). Therefore, any explanation of why some universe or other exists would also be an explanation of why Ω exists, and vice versa. So if there is no explanation of why Ω (*this* universe) exists rather than some other, then there is also no explanation (known or unknown or unknowable) of why some universe or other exists rather than nothing, and hence no mystery. The two questions, seemingly so different, are on a par when they are construed as explanation-seeking why-questions and 'universe' has its all-inclusive sense.

Whether there is an explanation of why this universe exists is a question that might itself express a mystery, perhaps unsolvable. If so, we could not know whether the question of being is based on a false presupposition, hence whether it expresses a mystery. Only by answering the prior question of whether there is some explanation can we learn whether there is anything to fathom about the question of being. Obviously, we can make no headway with the prior question until we know something about explanations and their ways.

2.2. Explanations

> *We could not obtain an explanation for the existence of the world by including that which is to serve as the explanation, as part of that which is to be explained.*
>
> —MILTON MUNITZ
>
> *The explanation of one thing is another thing.*
>
> —BERTRAND RUSSELL

Even without knowing much at all about the nature of explanation, we can at least agree that either the existence of the universe has an explanation in terms of something outside the universe or it does not. When as here the universe is the sum total of what there is, there can be nothing outside, nothing not included. For by definition, anything there is—anything at all—is included in the sum total of what there is. Since there is nothing outside, the existence of the universe cannot have an explanation in terms of something outside.

So we are forced to accept the second alternative: there is no explanation in terms of anything outside; either there is no explanation at all, or there is one in terms of something not outside the universe, possibly the whole universe itself. And if there is no explanation at all, then the question of why the universe exists is based on a false presupposition and can express no mystery. It follows that either there is no mystery of existence or else there is an explanation in terms of something included in the sum total of what there is. Is there any such internal explanation?

Such an explanation could be in terms either of (i) the whole of existence or of (ii) some part of the whole. In case (i), we would have to say that something about existence as a whole explains why the whole of existence exists. We would have to say that something about the nature of the whole explains why the whole exists, that the reason for its existence somehow is contained within its very nature. In case (ii), we would have to say that something about one of the existents explains why everything that exists does exist, including itself. We would have to say that the reason for the existence of everything in the universe, including this special existent, somehow is contained within the very nature of this special existent.

In either case, unfortunately, it sounds odd to say that the very nature of a thing explains its existence. It sounds rather like saying that the U.N. exists because to exist is part of its nature, or that it is of the essence of the U.N. to exist. Ordinarily, the existence of a thing is explained by reference to the nature and powers of some other thing or things. Do we really know what we mean when we speak of an explanation by reference solely to the nature or essence of the thing? Does such "explanation" really explain, or does it mask the absence, strictly, of any explanation properly so-called?

Traditionally, the being said to be explained by the necessity of its own nature is God. God's essence is said to include God's existence; God is said to be a necessary being. The existence of everything else in the universe then is supposed to be explained by reference to God. This tradition may have the comforting ring of familiarity, but to some it also rings hollow. Their objections are manifold. First, there may be no God. Second, even if God exists, it is not at all clear that God is literally a necessary being, that the properties that constitute God's nature explain God's existence. For, third, the idea that some entity x could exist by the necessity of its own nature turns out to treat x's existence as if it were a property of x when, instead, x's existing implies only that x instantiates the properties x does have. Fourth, the idea turns out also to be based on an erroneous inference from our idea or concept of the entity to the entity's existence. Fifth, the notion or notions of necessity presupposed apply not to extralinguistic things but to our statements about them; moreover, there are no necessary truths of the sort required, either because there are no statements made true solely by the meanings of their terms, or because other accounts of necessity also are defective and fail to distinguish allegedly necessary truths from the rest. Sixth, the third point shows, as do the fourth and fifth, that "explanation" of the existence of a thing solely in terms of the necessity of its nature is no explanation at all; and besides, seventh, explanation properly so-called always makes reference to some other thing or things, so that even if there were a "necessary being" in the sense of a being that exists and has the same properties in every logically possible world, still there would be no necessary being in the sense that the explanation of its existence lies solely in its own nature.

Of course there are rejoinders to these objections, and some of the objections are weaker than the others.[8] The rejoinders mostly reject the largely empiricist assumptions that underlie the objections. Because physicalists are among the most insistent empiricists, our program in the chapters ahead requires that we grant the truth of such assumptions, if only for the sake of argument, in order to see how far physicalism is compatible after all with so much we hold dear. Given the purposes of those chapters, therefore, we are forced to abandon necessary beings and the "explanation" of something's existence in terms of the necessity of its own nature. But even aside from this program, the notion of a necessary being—one whose explanation lies solely in its own nature or essence, as opposed to one that exists in every possible world—is in deep trouble, and philosophers of whatever persuasion would be unwise to rely on it.

If there is no explanation, known or unknown, of the existence of a thing solely in terms of its own nature, then there is no such explanation of the existence either of God or of the whole of existence. But then there is no explanation at all, known or unknown, of why the universe exists. For as we saw, there is also no explanation in terms of anything outside the universe, since by definition there is nothing outside. It follows that there is no mystery of existence—not just according to physicalists but according to anyone who objects, for whatever reason, to the very idea of a necessary being or to the idea that the existence of a thing, even of a very special thing, can properly be explained without reference to some other thing or things.[9]

There would be no mystery of existence, probably, even if the existence of a thing *could* be explained by the necessity of its own nature. For there would be a mystery, in that case, only if we did not know .the explanation. But those who champion the idea of a necessary being usually do so precisely in order to argue that anyone who grasps the relevant aspect of its nature or essence will thereby understand immediately that it must exist and why it must exist. Anyone who fully understands the relevant aspect of its essence will know the explanation of why the being exists, since that aspect transparently entails its existence.

---

[8]Cf. the selections in Burrill.
[9]Contrary to Munitz.

This idea of a necessary being is meant to put an end to the regress of why-questions.

There is only one loophole left, if you wish to insist that a mystery is expressed by 'Why does the universe exist?' You must insist that the existence of the universe has an "internal" explanation by reference either to the necessity of its own nature or to the necessity of a special being in terms of which (or whom) everything else is explained; and further, you must insist that even though this nature or essence necessitates or entails existence, still one who grasps the relevant aspect of the essence will *not* understand why the being exists. This loophole is very narrow, since the arguments designed to establish a necessary being typically entail also that one who understands the relevant aspect of its essence will thereby know the explanation of why the being exists. And our verdict on the very idea of a necessary being must be that the idea is rather dubious to begin with.

There is a strategy for reversing this verdict, or trying to, that deserves special attention. The strategy begins by assuming that every existing thing has an explanation. This is a version of the (in)famous Principle of Sufficient Reason (PSR). Next, it is admitted that some things can have no explanation in terms of anything else—God, for example, or the universe. But because they must have an explanation, according to PSR, it follows that they have one in terms of their own nature.

The trouble with this line of argument is that its major assumption is seriously in doubt. *Does* every existing thing have an explanation? There are excellent reasons for believing that not everything does, at least not in any sense of 'explanation' meant by defenders of PSR, as we see in §2.4. They mean that the factors sufficient for the existence of a thing are *logically* sufficient; the combined factors are supposed to necessitate the existence of the thing in the strong sense that it is logically impossible for the factors to obtain and the thing not to exist. Thus the existence of a thing is explained, in the intended sense, only if there are factors that logically necessitate its existence.

But consider a beta particle created at a particular instant by the spontaneous decay processes within the nucleus of a uranium atom. Quantum theory, under its usual interpretation, assures us that the existence of *that* beta particle created at *that* instant is *not* necessitated by the processes within the nucleus. Of course it *is* necessary that some beta particle or other would be created over a period of time but not that any would be created at the instant of the beta particle in question. It is not even highly probable that any would be created at that particular instant. Nor is this "uncertainty" simply a matter of our not knowing enough about the factors involved. According to quantum theory (again, under its usual interpretation), even if we knew all about them, the uncertainty would remain. The existence of that particular beta particle is not necessitated by the relevant factors, not because we do not know enough about nature but because nature is that way. The existence of that particle *has* no explanation, known or unknown, if explanation is taken in the sense intended by defenders of PSR.

Many other phenomena treated by quantum theory are like the beta particle. The theory is based on principles that both entail the falsity of PSR and are among the best established in contemporary physics. They were undreamed of when PSR was first articulated. Most physicists themselves were initially very reluctant to give up PSR, hence very reluctant to accept the quantum principles. Today the principles are nearly commonplace. PSR, itself largely a product of earlier science, has been rendered obsolete. It might conceivably stage a comeback in physics, but no one should bet on it.

Physics and its interpretation aside, there are other ways of casting doubt on the leading versions of PSR (as we see in §2.4). Some versions entail that *every* fact has an explanation, not just the fact that a thing exists. But if every fact has an explanation, and if (as PSRs require) the explanation must in turn mention facts, then these further facts have an explanation too, and so on, which raises the possibility of an infinitely long parade of explanations.

2.3. Infinite Parades of Explanation

> *In asking 'Why is there anything at all?' the questioner*
> *attempts to put an end to the indefinitely long series of*
> *questions and answers. . . . In seeking a* final *answer, he is*
> *seeking a statement which puts an end to the series of questions*
> *and answers.*
>
> —ALVIN PLANTINGA

Children ask 'Why?' almost endlessly, until we dull their gift of wonder. They marshal parades of why-questions in which each question seeks an explanation of the things mentioned in answer to the previous question. Occasionally they do it to get attention, or to irritate, or to tease. More often they are genuinely curious, and the questions, instead of coming all at once, file by over a period of days or months. If they have not already been discouraged from asking questions, eventually they may get around to asking why life and its earth are here, or the sun and planets, or the galaxies. By that time parents may long since have reached the limits of their knowledge if not their patience. Even if there is an encyclopedia in the house, often no one bothers to consult it.

There comes a point when even the encyclopedia is mute, or nearly so. Usually it comes when the question is why the cosmos exists or, if a creator is mentioned, why the creator exists. We all hope the parade of questions has an end, even if we have no real evidence that it does and no evidence that the parade must end just here, with mention of a creator. Why not end it earlier, with mention of the cosmos? Why not end it later, with mention of something "beyond" the creator? If we were taught that such questions are unfathomable by human beings or are matters of intuition and faith, we may shrug, parrot our teachers, and resume whatever preoccupied us when the child interrupted.

In the beginning is the question, childlike, but is there no end? Since we humans are all too finite, we could never actually construct an endless parade of explanations—one in which there is always a next. So the issue really is whether there would always be a next, even for an infinite intelligence. If it is logically impossible for there always to be a next in the parade, known or unknown, then the parade must end even for the most transcendent understanding. This section argues that in the case of very many explanation-seeking why-questions, there is necessarily an end.[10] It is logically impossible for there to be an infinite parade of explanations, when the explanations sought belong to a certain very broad category of explanations that include, among many others, those postulated by PSRs.

Whether the parade must end, or at least whether we can show that it must, depends on what category of explanations we are considering. Most explanations, if known, would provide materials out of which one could construct a justification of the belief that the thing to be explained exists or occurs, though normally that belief already is justified in some other way as well. For example, consider the discovery of PBB (polybrominated biphenyl, a toxic fire retardant once used in plastic consumer products) in the blood and tissues of Michigan's entire population. We explain this unsettling discovery by reference to an accident in which PBB was mixed with livestock feeds sold to farmers all over Michigan.[11] The explanation tells us that PBB entered the food chain and we would therefore be justified in believing that PBB occurs in the population dependent on that chain. (PBB is also found in other states

---

[10]The argument is a revision of one in Post (1980).
[11]Chen.

where Michigan farm products were sold.) Our knowledge of the explanatory factors leads us to expect or predict the occurrence of what was to be explained.

By way of contrast, consider a retired colonel who contracts leukemia. Suppose the explanation is that the colonel's unit was positioned two kilometers from an atomic blast during the early days of testing in Nevada.[12] The probability of his contracting leukemia is causally related to his distance from ground zero. But even though the probability is significantly greater than for someone in the population at large, still it is quite low—less than $1/100$. This is true even if it is highly probable that someone or other in his old unit would contract leukemia. Thus the explanation would not provide materials that afford a justification of the belief that this particular member of the unit contracted leukemia. The probability, though causally related to his distance from ground zero, is too small to warrant our predicting or expecting that he in particular would be affected.

We need a short way of referring to explanations that would provide materials out of which one could construct a justification of the belief that what is explained exists or occurs. Let us call them justification-affording explanations or, shorter still, J-A explanations. Note that a J-A explanation, even if known, is not in general itself a justificatory argument but merely provides materials out of which such an argument could be constructed by someone who knew the explanation.[13]

The category of J-A explanations is very broad. It includes explanations in which the explaining factors necessitate or entail the existence or occurrence of the thing explained, as in PSRs. And it includes those in which the explaining factors merely make it rather more probable that what is explained will occur than not. As to the nature of the explaining factors, they may range from lawlike regularities to statistical regularities, from physical events and processes to mental states, from atoms and the void to minds and intentions, from the observable to the unobservable, from the trivial to the profound. Clearly, J-A explanations range from scientific to nonscientific, and from the mundane to the otherworldly.

Could there be an infinite parade of J-A explanations in which each factor that does the explaining in one explanation is itself explained in the next? Suppose there were such a parade. Because each explanation in it would afford a justification, the parade would give rise to an infinite

[12]Cf. W. Salmon, 688–689.
[13]Cf. W. Salmon, 700.

parade of justifications in which each premise in one justification is itself justified by a further justification in the parade.

Could there be an infinite parade of justifications? The argument will be that if we allowed even one such parade, we could arbitrarily construct a justification of any contingent statement whatever, hence a justification of any contingent statement plus its negation (where 'contingent' means 'neither logically necessary nor logically impossible'). But being able arbitrarily to justify any contingent statement whatever, hence any plus its negation, is absurd. The relevant concepts of justification are inconsistent with such arbitrariness and inconsistency. So we must conclude that it is logically impossible for there to be an infinite parade of justifications. Therefore, it is logically impossible for there to be an infinite parade of J-A explanations.[14] A parade of explanation-seeking why-questions must end, at least when the explanations sought are J-A, as is typically the case.

It remains only to argue that if we allowed even one infinite parade of justifications, any contingent statement whatever could be justified. The point is not new, nor is the argument for it entirely new. But the argument will plug some old holes[15] and help us to see what *is* new: the implications for regresses of explanations.

We begin by asking what conditions inferential justification should satisfy. In particular, what is it for person P to be inferentially justified at time t in believing statement ψ on the basis of statement ϕ, or for ϕ to justify ψ for P at t? No answer appears as yet to have achieved consensus. Fortunately, none is required for our purpose. Most of the lists of conditions proposed in the literature include something like the following: at time t, (a) P believes ψ (dispositionally or occurrently); (b) P is justified in believing ϕ; (c) P believes that ϕ adequately supports ψ; (d) P is justified in believing that ϕ adequately supports ψ; (e) P believes ψ because P believes both ϕ and that ϕ adequately supports ψ; and (f) there is no defeater—that is, no statement χ such that P is justified in believing both χ and that $(\phi \ \& \ \chi)$ does not adequately support ψ.[16] For our purpose, conditions (a)–(f) may be refined or augmented in many ways, according to one's views about inferential justification. For example, let ϕ, ψ, and χ be *sets* of statements; or replace (d) by 'ϕ adequately supports ψ', or (f) by 'P is justified in believing there are no defeaters', and

---

[14]Contrary to Edwards (1967b), 119.

[15]Including one in Post (1980).

[16]Cf. Annis; and Fumerton, 564, plus Harman's (1976) counter to Annis with regard to what in effect are (a)–(e) above.

so on. Adopt any such plausible revision. Then construe 'ϕ justifies ψ' wherever it occurs below in terms of the revision. The argument below against infinite justificational parades would still work, with only minor modifications.

If anything counts as an inferential justification relation, logical implication does, in a sense to be specified, provided it satisfies appropriate relevance and noncircularity requirements. Let us say a statement ϕ *properly entails* a statement ψ iff ϕ semantically entails ψ, where the entailment is relevant and noncircular on any appropriate account. Thus if anything counts as an inferential justification relation, proper entailment does, in the sense that where ϕ and ψ are statements rather than sets of statements,

> (1) If ϕ properly entails ψ, then ψ is justified for P if ϕ is—provided P knows that the proper entailment holds and would believe ψ in light of it if P believed ϕ.[17]

(1) is a *weak* entailment principle. *Strong* entailment principles, to the effect that a *set* of rational beliefs is closed under entailment, are controversial at best, implicated as they are in the so-called lottery paradox.[18]

Now let ϕ_0 be a logically contingent statement, and adopt some (alphabetical) ordering of the infinitely many statements of P's language. Then construct the entailment-saturated parade

> (2) $\ldots, \phi_n, \ldots, \phi_1, \phi_0,$

where ϕ_i $(i>0)$ is the (alphabetically) first statement such that (i) ϕ_i properly entails ϕ_{i-1}; (ii) ϕ_i is not entailed by any set of $\phi_{j<i}$; and (iii) ϕ_i is not justified for P on the basis of any set of $\phi_{j<i}$. Also, assume that for each ϕ_i, P knows (or could come to know) that ϕ_i properly entails ϕ_{i-1}. And assume that P would believe ϕ_{i-1} in light of this entailment if P believed ϕ_i.

The construction of (2) presupposes that at every point in the parade *there is* some statement ϕ_i satisfying conditions (i)–(iii). This is one of those old holes to be plugged. But first note that *deductive* noncircularity in (2), which in the intended sense is guaranteed by (i) and (ii), does not entail *justificational* noncircularity, which is guaranteed by (iii). Even though no ϕ_i is *entailed* by any $\phi_{j<i}$, it does not follow that no ϕ_i is *justified* by any $\phi_{j<i}$, or by any *set* of $\phi_{j<i}$, either of which would induce

---

[17]We may wish to add that ϕ's entailing ψ is brought to P's attention. Cf. Schick, 25.
[18]Kyburg, 55–59.

justificational circularity. A person P might justify some ϕ_i in (2) on the basis *both* of ϕ_{i-1} (deductively) *and* of some set of $\phi_{j<i}$ (nondeductively). Hence we must require that ϕ_i is not justified for P on the basis of any set of $\phi_{j<i}$, not merely that ϕ_i is not entailed by any $\phi_{j<i}$. The need for this sort of requirement has been overlooked—another of those holes—in some attempts to show that a noncircular justificational parade could be constructed for any statement.[19]

Suppose we were to require the parade to contain no empirical statement ϕ_i that is logically equivalent to one of its own evidential ancestors $\phi_{j>i}$.[20] Even though this excludes one sort of justificational circularity, it allows others, in which ϕ_i is justified ("inductively," say) by some set of descendants $\phi_{j<i}$ in a parade where no statement is equivalent to one of its own ancestors $\phi_{j>i}$ (or indeed to any set of them). Thus constructing a parade that satisfies Cornman's requirement (a "Cornman parade") does not in general count as constructing a parade that is noncircular in the required full sense of (iii). Even though a Cornman parade could be constructed for any contingent statement, it would not follow that a justificational parade, noncircular in the required full sense of (iii), could be constructed for any contingent statement. Hence there is a hole in Cornman's attempt to show that a noncircular justificational parade could be constructed for any contingent statement ϕ_0.

To plug these holes, consider parade (2) and the presupposition that at every step there is a statement ϕ_i satisfying conditions (i)–(iii). It helps to consider an instance of (2). To construct one *modulo* some appropriate ordering of the statements of P's language, let χ be contingent and use *modus ponens* as follows:

$$(3) \quad \ldots, \; \phi \; \& \; \{\phi \rightarrow [\psi \; \& \; (\psi \rightarrow \chi)]\}, \; \psi \; \& \; (\psi \rightarrow \chi), \; \chi,$$

where χ does not entail ψ, $[\psi \; \& \; (\psi \rightarrow \chi)]$ does not entail ϕ, and so on. This sort of infinitely iterated application of *modus ponens* guarantees that for every statement ϕ_{i-1} in (3), there is a statement ϕ_i that satisfies (i) and (ii). Satisfaction of (ii) can easily be checked. As for (i), misgivings on the score of relevance can be met either by requiring that χ and ψ share some nonlogical vocabulary, that ψ and ϕ do, and so on; or more strongly by requiring that any such vocabulary in χ appear in ψ, that any in ψ appear in ϕ, and so on. *Modus ponens* is only one entailment form with which to construct instances of (2) that satisfy (i) and (ii);

---

[19]Oakley, 227, makes this mistake twice. Pollock, 27–28, avoids it but overlooks the need to guarantee that at every step there is some statement that satisfies (iii).

[20]As does Cornman, 289–290.

there are many others. Furthermore, there are complex or "mixed" instances of (2) in which the form by which ϕ_i entails ϕ_{i-1} is distinct from that by which ϕ_{i+1} entails ϕ_i. Whatever the entailment forms, we see that for any logically contingent ϕ_0 we can construct an instance of (2), such as (3), that satisfies (i) and (ii).

What about (iii)? Again, consider (3). In it, χ will justify for P a set J_0 of statements, possibly null and possibly infinite but definitely not universal. For either χ justifies every statement whatever for P or it does not. If it does, then since the negation of a statement is also a statement, every statement plus its negation is justified by χ, which is intolerable for rational justification (recall also that χ is contingent). Thus we can be sure there is some ψ that is not justified by χ, some ψ not in J_0. In particular, let ψ be the (alphabetically) first statement not in J_0 such that any nonlogical term in χ is in ψ, and χ does not entail ψ; thus ψ satisfies not only (iii) but (i) and (ii). Next, the set $\{\chi,[\psi \,\&\, (\psi \to \chi)]\}$ will justify for P a set J_1 of statements. As with J_0, we can be sure that there are statements not in J_1. Let ϕ be the first statement not in J_1 such that any nonlogical term in ψ is in ϕ, and $[\psi \,\&\, (\psi \to \chi)]$ does not entail ϕ; thus ϕ satisfies not only (iii) but also (i) and (ii). In this way we see that at every point in the parade there will be a next statement that satisfies (i)–(iii), hence that the parade is noncircular in the required full sense of (iii). It follows that for any contingent ϕ_0 one can construct an instance of (2) that satisfies (i)–(iii).

So much by way of preliminaries. Now assume, contrary to what is to be shown, that for some person P at a time t, and some statement ϕ_0,

(4) . . . , what justifies ϕ_{n-1} is ϕ_n, . . . , what justifies ϕ_1 is ϕ_2, what justifies ϕ_0 is ϕ_1.

(4) is a justification-saturated parade (for P at t), meaning that for every statement in the parade, what justifies it (for P at t) is an earlier statement. Thus the question of whether there can be an infinite justificational parade is to be construed as the question of whether there can be a justification-saturated one.

What is disturbing about a justification-saturated parade like (4) is that in it justification is supposed to accumulate for ϕ_0 merely as a result of P's being able endlessly to meet the demand for justification simply by appealing to the next inferential justification in the parade. Thus ϕ_0 is justified for P because P can appropriately infer ϕ_0 from ϕ_1, so that ϕ_0 is justified if ϕ_1 is, and ϕ_1 is justified. (We assume that the remaining conditions for inferential justification in (a)–(f) are also satisfied.) If we demand to know why ϕ_1 is justified, P replies that ϕ_1 can be inferred from ϕ_2, so that ϕ_1 is justified if ϕ_2 is, and ϕ_2 is justified. If challenged about ϕ_2, P replies as before, and so on.

Thus ϕ_0 satisfies the sound principle (accepted by all parties) that a statement is justified iff everything in its justificational ancestry is justified. Foundationalists insist only that not everything in the ancestry will be justified unless somewhere in it there are noninferentially (that is, immediately) justified statements. Coherentists deny this but require the inferential justifications at least to form a coherent circle of mutual support. Both therefore deny the "infinitist's" claim, as we may call it, that justification can accumulate merely as a result of endlessly meeting the demand for justification by appealing to the next inferential justification in a justification-saturated parade.

Clearly the infinitist is wrong, but why? Appealing here either to foundationalism or to coherentism would beg the question against infinitism. Instead, the non-question-begging answer is that once infinitists are allowed even one justification-saturated parade like (4), they are compelled to say that *every* instance of (2) that satisfies (i)–(iii) would *also* count as a justification-saturated parade. For there is no relevant difference between (4) and such an instance of (2). In each such instance, as in (4), every ϕ_i is appropriately inferrable from ϕ_{i-1} (via proper entailment), so that ϕ_i is justified if ϕ_{i-1} is. Moreover, in every instance of (2), no ϕ_i is justified by any set of $\phi_{j<i}$, thus assuring noncircularity, which goes beyond what (4) requires (and rightly so, if foundationalism is true). So if justification accumulates for ϕ_0 in (4), then surely it accumulates for ϕ_0 in each instance of (2) that satisfies (i)–(iii), such as (3). For in each such instance, P can not only endlessly meet the demand for justification by appealing to the next inferential justification but do so noncircularly.

But as seen, we can construct, for any contingent ϕ_0 whatever, an instance of (2) that satisfies (i)–(iii), hence for any such ϕ_0 plus its negation. It follows that every contingent statement plus its negation could be justified (for P at t). This reduces to absurdity the infinitist's assumption that there can be a justification-saturated parade. In any parade of justifications there must be a last, in the sense that there must be a largest number n for which 'what justifies ϕ_{n-1} is ϕ_n' is in the parade—unlike (4).[21] This leaves it open as to whether ϕ_n is immediately justified, as foundationalists would require, or justified by statements between it and ϕ_0, as coherentists would allow. In either case, as explained earlier, it follows that there cannot be an infinite parade of J-A

[21]The foregoing argument for this conclusion now meets an objection by Sosa (1980), 12–13.

explanations—not for practical reasons, such as the finiteness of our faculties, but for logical reasons. Even for an infinite intelligence such explanation must end.

Someone might object that this conclusion neglects important conditions that any adequate explanation must satisfy, such as (let us say) the condition that the statements in the explanation must be true.[22] But the objection overlooks the fact that a J-A explanation in which the statements are true is still a J-A explanation. Hence an infinite parade of them would still give rise to an infinite parade of justifications, with the same absurd result. In general, add any conditions whatever for what is to count as an explanation. So long as the explanations remain justification-affording, there cannot be an infinite parade of them. That is, for each parade there is a largest n for which 'ϕ_n' is in the parade.

A parade of explanations is one thing; a series of causes another. The latter is a series of causally related (nonlinguistic) events and regularities. Thus even though there can be no infinite parades of explanation (assuming we are speaking of J-A explanation), it does not follow that there cannot be, for example, an infinite series of physical events each caused by a temporal predecessor (where such a series need not be temporally infinite but might occupy a finite temporal interval).[23] For the type(s) of causation involved in the series might very well not be such that there is an explanation of each event by reference to its temporal predecessor; or if there is such an explanation, it fails to be J-A (as in the leukemia case above). Whether or not there could be an infinite series of causes in this sense would have to be settled by some other argument.

2.4. How to Refute Principles of Sufficient Reason

> *If we turn to the question of whether it is reasonable for me or anyone else to believe the Principle of Sufficient Reason, it is less than clear that our answer should be* negative.
>
> —William Rowe

> *The principle of sufficient reason . . . might properly be called a presupposition of reason itself.*
>
> —Richard Taylor

Toward the end of §2.2 we noted that under its usual interpretation quantum theory entails the falsity of Principles of Sufficient Reason.

---

[22]As Horgan has done, in correspondence.
[23]Cf. Misner, Thorne, and Wheeler, 813–814; Grünbaum (1967b), 83–86.

Thus no version of PSR seems to be "a presupposition of reason itself."[24] But some philosophers are totally unmoved by any implications that physics might have for metaphysics. No merely empirical argument will do. They want arguments a priori.[25] This section presents an argument a priori against the leading versions of PSR.[26] So far from being a presupposition of reason itself, PSR can be refuted by reason, arguing only from PSR's own concepts of explanation. Thus our answer to the question of whether it is reasonable to believe PSR will be a clear negative.[27]

As noted in §2.3, all versions of PSR postulate explanations that are justification-affording. The sufficient reasons they postulate are supposed to be logically sufficient for the explained states of affairs. Does every state of affairs (every "stoa") have a J-A explanation, or at least every stoa in some restricted class or kind? Since stoas get stated by statements, or perhaps are merely the shadows cast by statements, we may treat this question as though it asks whether every statement has a J-A explanation, or at least every statement in some restricted class of statements. Even if it is stoas (or events or things) that in the first instance are what get explained or what have explanatory significance, still the explanation, being J-A, would provide materials (statements) out of which a justificatory argument could be constructed, in which the explanandum is justified by the explanans (conjoined if need be with other material).

If not every statement has a J-A explanation, perhaps every true statement does, or else every contingently true statement, or else every true statement merely that a given thing or being exists, or whatever. But whether every statement in a given class has a J-A explanation depends crucially on what concept of J-A explanation is being used. In particular, it depends on whether the property that singles out the stoas in the class is "hereditary" with respect to that concept. A property P is hereditary with respect to a given concept of explanation iff whenever statement ψ is explained by ϕ, and ψ has P, then ϕ has P.[28] The idea is that in any parade of such explanations, P gets passed from each statement to the next.

The property of being true, for example, is hereditary with respect to any concept of explanation according to which the explanans statement ϕ must be true. And the property of being contingently true is

[24]Contrary to R. Taylor (1963), 86–87. Cf. Rowe (1975), 93.
[25]Cf. Warnock, and the counter to Warnock in Rowe (1975), 88–89.
[26]Based on Post (1980).
[27]Contrary to Rowe (1975), 268, 261–266.
[28]Cf. Quine (1972), 238, 247; Wengart, 409.

hereditary with respect to any concept of explanation according to which ϕ must both be true and logically entail the explanandum statement ψ. For if ψ is contingent and entailed by a true ϕ, then ϕ must be contingent as well as true. It follows that the property of being contingently true is hereditary with respect to the concepts of explanation presupposed by PSRs. For according to PSRs, the statement ϕ of the sufficient reason is supposed to be true, and the sufficient reasons are supposed to be logically sufficient, so that ϕ entails the statement ψ of what is to be explained.

Next we prove the Heredity Theorem for J-A explanation:

> HT. Given any concept of J-A explanation for which property P is hereditary, not every P-statement has such an explanation,

where a P-statement is one that has property P. For suppose ϕ_0 has such an explanation—say, by ϕ_1. Then if ϕ_0 has P, so does ϕ_1 (because by hypothesis P is hereditary for the concept of explanation being used). But if *every* P-statement has such an explanation, then ϕ_1, having P, would have such an explanation—say, by ϕ_2—and so on to infinity. This would give rise to an infinite parade of J-A explanations, which by §2.3 is impossible.

One immediate consequence of the Heredity Theorem is that not every true statement—not every truth—has a J-A explanation for which being true is hereditary. Thus any version of PSR is false which implies that every fact or stoa that obtains has an explanation in any such sense. For facts and stoas get stated by true statements; hence, if every fact or obtaining stoa had some J-A explanation for which truth is hereditary, then every true statement would have such an explanation, contrary to the Heredity Theorem.

As seen, all versions of PSR postulate explanations that are J-A. In addition, truth is hereditary for the kind of explanation postulated by PSR; the stoas stated in the postulated explanations are supposed to obtain, not merely to be probable in light of our evidence. Thus any version of PSR is false which claims that every fact or stoa that obtains has an explanation, since the postulated kind of explanation allows us to apply the Heredity Theorem.

Other versions of PSR claim less. Often they claim only that every logically contingent stoa has an explanation. But logically contingent stoas get stated by (are the shadows of) logically contingent statements. Hence if every contingent stoa had an explanation, then every contingently true statement would have one. As seen, being contingently true is hereditary with respect to the kind of explanation postulated by

PSRs. Since that kind of explanation is also J-A, the Heredity Theorem applies. It follows that any version of PSR is false which claims that every contingent fact or contingently obtaining stoa has an explanation.

Often some such version of PSR is appealed to in order to argue that the existence of the physical universe—the cosmos—must have an explanation in terms of something "beyond," presumably a divine creator.[29] For the existence of the cosmos constitutes a logically contingent state of affairs; it is logically possible for it not to have existed. So if every such stoa has an explanation, the existence of the cosmos would have one. But even then it would not necessarily have an explanation in terms of something "beyond." The explanation might conceivably have something to do with the nature of the cosmos itself, despite our misgivings in §2.2 about such "explanation." Even if there were an explanation in terms of something "beyond," this something would not necessarily be a divinity, let alone the one expected. But towering over all these difficulties is the demonstrated falsity of the presupposed version of PSR. Even if quantum theory should happen not to refute it after all, the Heredity Theorem would suffice.

Another version of PSR claims that every existing thing x has an explanation in the existence and causal power of something else y. That is, the existence of x is explained by the existence of y, where it is understood that $x \neq y$ and that y causes x to exist.[30] But if every existing thing x has an explanation, then every true statement of the form 'x exists' has an explanation. Further, if the existence of x is explained by the existence of y, then the statement that x exists is explained by the statement that y exists (where again it is understood that $x \neq y$ and that y causes x to exist). It follows that having the form 'x exists' is hereditary with respect to the sort of explanation presupposed by this version of PSR. For 'x exists' has that sort of explanation by 'y exists'; and, trivially, whenever the latter statement has the form 'x exists', so does the former. Since being true is also hereditary for PSR, as seen, it follows by the Heredity Theorem that not every true statement that a thing x exists has an explanation in the fact that y exists, where $x \neq y$ and y causes x to exist. Therefore this version of PSR is false, according to which every existing thing has an explanation in the existence and power of something else.

We turn now to a final version of PSR, which may also appear to be the least vulnerable. It claims merely that every existing thing has an explanation of its existence either in the existence and power of some-

[29]Cf. Ewing, 225.
[30]Cf. Post (1980), 48 and note 26.

thing else or in the necessity of its own nature. Let us call this version "Strong PSR," in view of its relative invulnerability. At least one philosopher believes Strong PSR has not been disproved and is all that is needed, by way of a PSR, for a valid Cosmological Argument for the existence of God.[31]

Yet even if Strong PSR should happen to escape refutation by the Heredity Theorem, it would remain dangerously vulnerable. Few things, if any, exist by the necessity of their own nature. Those that do we have been calling necessary beings. Those that do not we may call contingent beings. Clearly, then, Strong PSR entails that while every necessary being has an explanation in the necessity of its own nature, every contingent being has an explanation—a logically sufficient reason—in the existence and power of something else. But if under its usual interpretation quantum theory is true, then some contingent beings—like the beta particle—have no such sufficient reason in the existence and power of anything else (§2.2). So if quantum theory is true, as the best evidence has long indicated, then Strong PSR taken as a whole is false.

Physics aside, recall that a leading reason for wanting PSR was to show that there must be such a thing as a being explained solely by reference to its own nature. This was to reverse our verdict, toward the end of §2.2, that the very idea of a necessary being is highly problematic. The strategy for reversing the verdict was to assume that every existing thing has an explanation, then to grant that some things have no explanation in terms of anything else, and finally to conclude that they must have one in terms of the necessity of their own nature. But obviously, if the question is whether the very idea of a necessary being is legitimate, and with it the very idea of explanation of a thing by reference to the necessity of its nature, then to assume Strong PSR is to beg the question. Strong PSR makes use of that very idea.

But suppose we were to grant the legitimacy of the idea of a necessary being. Suppose further that now the question is whether there *is* a necessary being. And suppose someone assumes Strong PSR in order to show that there is one. Then once more the question would be begged. The reason is that Strong PSR presupposes the existence of a necessary being, the very point at issue. To see why Strong PSR presupposes this, assume that Strong PSR is true but that there is no necessary being. This is to assume that every being has an explanation, either in the existence of something else or in the necessity of its own nature, but that there is no being that has an explanation in the necessity of its own nature. It would follow that every being has an explanation in the existence and

[31]Rowe (1975), 73, 112–113.

power of something else. But this is a version of PSR we lately refuted with the Heredity Theorem. Thus one cannot consistently assume that Strong PSR is true but that there is no necessary being.

Hence Strong PSR implies by itself that there is a necessary being. That is, Strong PSR presupposes the very point at issue, whereas traditionally, of course, PSR was supposed to imply there is a necessary being only when conjoined with the further assumption that there exists a contingent being (namely, the world). Usually, Strong PSR is assumed in order to argue that the existence of a physical cosmos has an explanation by reference to something beyond it, and therefore that there is a being beyond the cosmos. The argument works only if one denies, correctly, that the cosmos or anything in it is a logically necessary being, and this is duly denied. But in the context of this denial, Strong PSR presupposes that there is a being beyond the cosmos, since it presupposes that there is a necessary being and the cosmos is not one. Hence theists are presupposing, unwittingly, that there is a being beyond the physical universe, when they assume Strong PSR in order to show that there must be one.

Aside from the vulnerabilities noted so far, how does Strong PSR fare with the Heredity Theorem? According to Strong PSR, every existing thing x has an explanation either in the existence of something else y, where y causes x to exist, or in its own existence when x is a necessary being. This implies that every truth of the form 'x exists' expresses a state of affairs that has an explanation either by what is expressed in the truth 'y exists' (where it is understood that $x \neq y$ and that y causes x to exist), or by what is expressed in the truth 'x exists' (where it is understood that x is a necessary being). This means, as seen a few paragraphs back, that being a truth of the form 'x exists' is hereditary with respect to explanation of the sort postulated by Strong PSR. It follows by the Heredity Theorem that not every truth of that form has an explanation of this sort, contrary to Strong PSR.

Thus Principles of Sufficient Reason are powerless to widen the only remaining loophole, if one wishes to insist that the existence of the universe is a mystery. There can be no such mystery, we saw, if there is no explanation, known or unknown, of why the universe exists. The reason is that the explanation-seeking question 'Why does the universe exist?' would be based on a false presupposition. For there can be no explanation of the universe in terms of anything outside, because there is nothing outside, given our all-inclusive use of the word 'universe' in this chapter. Hence if there is any explanation, known or unknown, it must be solely in terms of the nature either of the universe as a whole, or of some special being in terms of which (or whom) everything is explained, itself included. That is, it must be in terms of some necessarily existing being. By assuming a version of PSR, some have tried to argue that the existence of the universe, like the existence of everything else, has an explanation and hence an explanation in terms of some necessary being. But every suitable version of PSR is either refuted by the Heredity Theorem, or is inconsistent with quantum theory, or presupposes the problematic necessary being that was to be shown. Some versions fail on all three counts.

Even if someone could somehow show that the existence of the universe does have an explanation in some necessary being, there remains a further difficulty noted in §2.2: the arguments designed to establish a necessary being typically entail also that anyone who grasped the relevant aspect of this being's essence would understand why this being exists. Thus the explanation would be known, whereas only if it were unknown would there be a mystery.

Occasionally, I have spoken almost as though PSRs are used primarily to argue that there is a mystery of existence. Historically, they have been used more often to argue the opposite, by arguing that there is a necessary being (God) in terms of whom the sum total of what there is has an explanation, an explanation known at least to theists. But PSRs are as powerless for the purpose of arguing that there is no mystery as they are for the purpose of arguing that there is. Whatever their purpose, Principles of Sufficient Reason are a very poor bet. For to repeat, even if they somehow survived the challenge of quantum theory—a very big 'IF'—still they would either be refuted by the Heredity Theorem, or be question-begging in their intended application to show there is a necessary being, or both.

2.5. Ultimate Explanation

> *An ultimate explanation must be one that eliminates all mere happening.*
> —R. W. HEPBURN

> *I realized that I had discovered the key to Existence, the key to my fits of Nausea and the key to my own life. Indeed, anything that I managed to apprehend since leads back to the same basic absurdity. . . . No necessary being can explain existence: contingency isn't an illusion or a mere appearance that can be dissipated; it is the absolute . . . inconsequent: everything is inconsequential.*
> —JEAN-PAUL SARTRE

There cannot be an infinite parade of justification-affording explanations, known or unknown; any parade of such explanations must end, even for an infinite intelligence. A final explanation is one behind which there is no next, known or unknown. This much is clear from §2.3. But what should we say of the explanation that ends the parade? In what sense would it be "ultimate" or "fundamental"? Wouldn't its finality amount to some sort of inevitability or necessity? And mustn't a truly ultimate explanation represent a mystery, perhaps unfathomable?

We can make no headway with these questions so long as we continue to use only a loose idea of an ultimate explanation. We need a definition. As a first step we may define a final explanation as the last in a parade, even for an infinite intelligence. It is not a First Cause, if only because the type of explanation involved need not be causal. Also it need not be first in any temporal sense, if only because the type of explanation involved need make no reference to time. But the existence of final explanations is guaranteed by the argument in §2.3 that any parade of J-A explanations must end in an explanation beyond which there is no next, known or unknown, knowable or unknowable. If parades of other sorts of explanation must also end, as is likely, then there are final explanations that are not J-A. Otherwise the only final explanations are final J-A explanations.

In a final explanation the explaining factors explain something between them and the head of the parade. We might suppose that the final explaining factors, or final explainers, are themselves automatically unexplained, just by virtue of being final. We would be wrong, unless the concepts of explanation involved in the parade preclude any explaining factors from being themselves explained by some factors between them and the head of the parade. In other words, the concepts of explanation involved must be noncircular or, as we may also say, hierarchical. More precisely, let the following represent a parade of explanations:

(1) $\phi_n, \phi_{n-1}, \ldots, \phi_1, \phi_0.$

Here ϕ_0 heads the parade, ϕ_n ends it and therefore is final in (1), and each ϕ_i (other than ϕ_0) states facts or states of affairs that explain those expressed in ϕ_{i-1}. Explanation is noncircular or hierarchical, according to a given concept, iff in any parade of such explanations no ϕ_i states facts that are explained by the facts stated either in some $\phi_{j<i}$, or in some set of $\phi_{j<i}$. The idea is that the parade forms a hierarchy, in which each rank (except the final one) is completely subordinate to the next. That is, each rank depends on the next for its explanation but contributes nothing to the explanation of any rank behind it in the parade.

Explanation is hierarchical according to most concepts, perhaps according to all. For to begin with, if justification must be noncircular, as foundationalists believe, then obviously every justification-affording sort of explanation must also be noncircular, hence hierarchical. But even if justification can be circular, as coherentists believe, still much explanation is likely to be hierarchical, including J-A explanation. For we normally use the word 'explain' in such a way that if ϕ explains ψ, and ψ explains χ, then neither ψ nor χ, nor ψ and χ combined, can explain ϕ.[32]

Examples of this "sequential asymmetry" abound. Increased burning of coal in the Midwest for power explains increased acid rain and snow toward the northeast, which in turn explains the disappearance of all life from hundreds of lakes in the Adirondacks. But the reverse does not hold. The disappearance of the life does not explain the acid precipitation, nor does the latter, even combined with the former, explain the increased burning of coal. This example illustrates a further point: explanation has close ties with causation, since explanations usually refer to causes. But causation exhibits the sequential asymmetry, and is hierarchical. So we might expect explanation to be so as well.[33]

In any event, suppose the explanations involved in a parade are not only J-A but hierarchical. Then the final explainer in the parade—call it *F*—must itself be unexplained. Being first, there would be no next explanation in the parade that might explain *F*. And the hierarchical character of the kinds of explanation involved ensures that *F* is explained neither by itself nor by any factor or set of factors between *F* and the head of the parade. *F* would not only be unexplained; it would be ineligible for explanation, not even a candidate, neither admitting of nor requiring any explanation. (Indeed whether or not something is a final explainer, or any explainer, if there is no explanation of it, knowable or otherwise, then it too is ineligible for explanation. Nothing said so far precludes the possibility that there are some nonexplainers ineligible for explanation. But for the time being we are concentrating on final explainers.)

Final explainers that are ineligible for explanation are the unmoved movers of explanation, and we may well call them unexplained explainers, or ultimate explainers. Ultimate or unexplained explainers need not be what have traditionally been called first causes, even though they have much in common. The reason is that the variety of hierarchical J-A explanations is potentially very large, with causal explanations being only one kind, though a very important kind. A parade of hierarchical J-A explanations that made no reference to causes would

[32]But see Woodward.

[33]Cf. W. Salmon, 686–687: "Explanations demand an asymmetry not present in inferences. . . . The asymmetry is inherited from the asymmetry of causation." But see van Fraassen (1985).

also end with an ultimate explainer, which would be first but not a cause. Even if the explanations involved were all causal, the ultimate explainer would not necessarily be first in any temporal sense; some relations called "causal" make no reference to temporal order. And, again depending on the kinds of explanation involved, an ultimate explainer might or might not be physical or observable or knowable at all, or immutable or eternal or whatever. Of course an ultimate explainer might happen to have one or more of these properties. But we would have to show that it does by appealing to considerations beyond the mere fact that it is an ultimate explainer.

An ultimate explanation is one beyond which there can be no more. It is a terminus, a finality, a conversation stopper. The most garrulous must stand mute and accept. The reason is that to ask an explanation-seeking 'Why?' about an ultimate explainer is necessarily to ask a question based on a false presupposition. The question is equivalent to 'What is the explanation?' (§2.1). It therefore presupposes that there is one, known or unknown. But of course there is none, in the case of an ultimate explainer, and indeed in the case of anything else ineligible for explanation. Hence the question can express no mystery, unfathomable or otherwise. There is nothing to fathom, even for an infinite intelligence.

This does not mean that there can be no mystery about ultimate explainers. There can be plenty of mystery, and doubtless there is. For we may not know what the ultimate explainers are. We may not know which facts or states of affairs terminate those parades of explanation we initiate that do terminate. We know that at least some of them must terminate, even for an infinite intelligence; these are the parades of hierarchical J-A explanation. But do we know with what they must finally terminate? Do we know that the explainers we now happen to regard as final would be so for an infinite, all-knowing intelligence? Can we be certain that *our* stopping place is *the* stopping place?

The answer can only be, "Rarely, if ever." For recall all the ways in which we can fail to know the answer to a question (§2.0). No answer at all may occur to us, or only false ones; even if the answers that occur to us include the true one, we might happen to reject it in favor of another; or we might happen to accept the true one but have inadequate justification for believing it is true and hence again fail to know that it is true; indeed we may subsequently accept another. All these possibilities arise because of the distinction between truth and our criteria for truth. There are no relevant guaranteeing criteria and perhaps not even any warranting criteria (§1.3). The logical prerequisites for truth, while eliminating a relativism of anything goes, carry us only so far (§1.4–1.6). So the possibility of mystery, in the sense of truths we do not know and perhaps can never know, is assured.

It is sobering also to list the answers people have given, in effect, to the question of what the ultimate explainers are. The list coincides with a list of things taken to be the most fundamental or basic existents, according to various schools of metaphysics. It includes "the indefinite," atoms-and-the-void, Platonic forms, Aristotle's unmoved mover, Spinoza's one substance (God-or-Nature), spirit, pure consciousness, a life force, quanta, mass-energy, Being-as-such, process, History, God, Shiva, Tao (in its aspect as *tzu-jan,* the "self-so"), and so on and on. Each is supposed to represent the ultimate face of existence. Each is supposed to have no explanation in terms of anything else. And the enormous variety of answers suggests that there can be mystery aplenty, if not downright confusion, as to just what the ultimate explainers are.

Philosophers often have wanted a logically necessary being in order to put an end to indefinitely long parades of why-questions. For if there were a logically necessary being, it would have and need no explanation in terms of anything else.[34] Hence a why-question that seeks an explanation of it in terms of something else would be based on a false presupposition. Further, the relevant aspect of such a being's nature would logically entail the being's existence, rather as it is the nature of a plenum to be full. Asking why a necessary being exists would be like asking why a plenum is full. Just as the latter would betray failure to understand what it is to be a plenum, so would the former betray failure to understand what it is to be a logically necessary being. But we have been learning that no such being is needed. Philosophers who have wanted one for the purpose of ending parades of explanation could have been spared the trouble, the more so as the very idea of a logically necessary being is highly problematic in any case.

Since the idea is so problematic, and since there must be an end to the why-questions anyway, we may well wonder whether what ends the parade, though not a logically necessary being, nevertheless enjoys an unproblematic kind of necessity just by virtue of being ultimate. It does. Traditionally something is said to be contingent, in an important sense, if it is dependent for its explanation—explanatorily dependent— on something else. This explanatory contingency, as we may call it, is distinct from logical contingency. Something that is logically contingent may or may not have an explanation, hence an explanation in terms of something else, if only because any version of PSR is false

---

[34]Cf. Plantinga (1967a), 138–139. See further Franklin; Hick (1960); B. Miller.

according to which every logically contingent state of affairs has an explanation (§2.4). So a state of affairs that is logically contingent might or might not be explanatorily contingent.

Because an ultimate explainer has no explanation in terms of anything else, it is not explanatorily dependent on anything else. That is, it is not contingent; it is explanatorily necessary. If the existence of the universe—the whole of existence—is an ultimate explainer, then the existence of the universe is explanatorily necessary. It is not contingent or inconsequential unless these terms mean merely that it is logically contingent, that we can conceive that it might not have existed.

There are as many varieties of explanatory necessity as there are concepts of explanation according to which there are ultimate explainers. Given any such concept of explanation, there must be at least one explanatorily necessary state of affairs. States of affairs include those in which some being x exists. If the stoa in which x exists is explanatorily necessary, then we may say that x is an explanatorily necessary being.[35] In light of our argument that at least in the case of hierarchical J-A explanation there must be ultimate explainers, we are guaranteed that there are concepts of explanation—quite a few, in fact—according to which there must be an explanatorily necessary being. Note also that explanatory necessity is distinct from natural and physical necessity, and from what are usually called causal and factual necessity.[36]

We saw in §2.3 how very broad is the category of J-A explanations. Early in the present section we saw how such explanations are all likely to be hierarchical, whether from science or religion or whatever. Hence whatever the domain of discourse, so long as explanation-seeking is appropriate to it, and so long as the explanations sought are J-A, we can expect the domain to include mention of an explanatorily necessary being. But it is quite another question as to whether the different domains include the *same* necessary being. They might or might not, depending on whether the explanatory parades in different domains all happen to end in the same thing. At this point we have no reason at all to suppose they do.

In light of the finality and ultimacy of an explanatorily necessary being, and in light also of strong similarities between our argument for such a being and a certain strand of philosophical tradition, we may call the being metaphysically necessary.[37] Thus metaphysical necessity may be construed as explanatory necessity. Others have construed it as some

[35] Thus there is an alternative to construing Aquinas' 'necessary being' as 'logically necessary being', contrary to Plantinga (1967b), 22–23.

[36] Cf. Daher; B. Miller.

[37] Cf. Young.

sort of logical necessity.[38] Let them defend, if they can, the problematic notion of a logically necessary being. You and I have no need to do so, committed as we are only to explanatory necessity.

Evidently an ultimate explainer is metaphysically fundamental in some sense; it enjoys some sort of ontological priority. But so far, all we are entitled to say is that it is explanatorily fundamental or prior, meaning only that it is the explanatory ancestor of all the other things in the parade of explanations it terminates. And there are as many varieties of explanatory priority as there are varieties of explanation. Is some variety somehow more fundamental than the rest? Evidently not in any unconditional sense: different kinds of explanation are appropriate on different occasions, depending on our purposes and interests (§§2.6). Moreover, we remain free not to be interested in explaining things in the first place. Other ways of living and being occasionally prove more urgent. And there is the problem of whether the different domains all include the same ultimate explainer (or explainers). If not, we would have to show that one of the domains is more fundamental than the rest, in order to show that its ultimate explainer(s) would be more fundamental than those from other domains. But it seems most unlikely that one domain of discourse is unconditionally prior to the others (§§7.2–7.4).

Suppose E is an ultimate explainer, whether God or the cosmos or anything else, and suppose someone asks, "Why does E exist?" There is a strong temptation to reply, "That's just the way the world is." The reply is not exactly wrong, but it is not nearly strong enough, and it is potentially quite misleading. The stronger reply that must be made is, "Your question is improper, because it is based on the false presupposition that there *is* an explanation, known or unknown." And to say "That's just the way the world is" is potentially misleading insofar as it suggests—as often it is meant to suggest—that E is merely contingent and in no sense metaphysically necessary. But of course an ultimate explainer is metaphysically necessary, as lately noted. It is not contingent, brute, gratuitous, absurd, irrational, an accident or mere happening, in crucial senses of these terms. Let us see why.

To begin with, the status of an ultimate explainer E, compared to that of other things, is one of primacy: everything between E and the head of the parade is an explanatory descendant of E; E is the explanatory ancestor of them all. This elevates an ultimate explainer above the status of *mere* happening, even if in other respects it should prove to be a kind of happening. Furthermore, to call something brute, gratuitous,

[38]Cf. Geach's warning, 65, against construing Aquinas' notion of necessity à la Leibniz.

absurd, irrational, or an accident is to imply that it fails to satisfy some norm. In the present context, the implication is that it fails to satisfy some norm of rationality.[39] And the alleged norm is that there be some explanation of the thing. But this alleged norm is warranted only if some appropriate version of PSR is valid—usually some version according to which every logically contingent thing has an explanation. Since PSR is not valid, and since PSR could be a norm of rationality only if it were, it follows that the thing in question does not fail to satisfy a norm or expectation of rationality to the effect that the thing must have an explanation.

Thus in this respect an ultimate explainer E would not be brute, gratuitous, absurd, irrational, or an accident. At best, E would be those things only in light of an erroneous and obsolete conception of rationality and its norms—a conception according to which PSR is indelibly a part of rationality and leads us to expect that E has an explanation. To call E or anything else irrational or absurd on the ground that E has no explanation, known or unknown, is to betray an erroneous and obsolete conception of rationality. A correct conception, which rejects PSR, does not permit us to call something irrational, absurd, brute, or gratuitous merely because it is ineligible for explanation.

Of course if 'brute' and 'absurd' meant no more than "has no explanation," then E would be brute and absurd. But the words do mean more. They have strong pejorative meanings and are intended to have them. A contrast is intended between those things that do and those that do not satisfy some norm of rationality. Certainly this is meant by irrationalists, when they urge us to believe that existence is irrational or absurd because it does not conform to the requirements of presumptuous reason. But irrationalists are the ones who presume too much when they tacitly assume that some version of PSR must be part of rationality. They fail to see that other parts of rationality lead us to reject PSR, whether by way of quantum theory (§2.2) or by way of a priori arguments such as those based on the Heredity Theorem (§2.4).

Sometimes when people say that existence is absurd they mean that human values have no ground in existence, that the universe provides no meaning or purpose for our lives, no reason for our existence. Now existence may or may not be absurd in this sense. Whether it is we consider in §7.6. Here we need only note that even if existence were absurd in the sense of not conforming to a norm of rationality by virtue of having no explanation, still it would not follow that existence is

---

[39]There is more than a hint of this, e.g., in Rowe (1978), 10, and Rowe (1975), 17. Cf. also Young.

absurd in the sense of failing to satisfy the human demand that it ground our values and give meaning to our lives. Existence could do these things and yet have no explanation. Something within existence, though unexplained, could provide the values and the meaning—or the meanings.

2.6. The Secret of Chaco Canyon

> *Which factors are explanatory is decided not by features of the scientific theory but by concerns brought from outside. . . .*
> *Which property is counted as explanatory and which as explained seems to me clearly context-dependent. . . .*
> *Explanation is indeed a virtue; but still, less a virtue than an anthropocentric pleasure.*
>
> —B. C. van Fraassen

> *The world of explanations and reasons is not the world of existence.*
>
> —Jean-Paul Sartre

Philosophers have long wondered whether and how one could show definitively that there are ultimate explanations, knowable or not. They have been fascinated by the problem largely because they assumed that an ultimate explanation would necessarily have some deep metaphysical significance, something to do with *the* nature of existence, or *the* meaning. Some assumed that an ultimate explanation would surely refer to something beyond the physical universe. Some assumed that the referent would be an eternal, immutable First Cause or ground of everything else. Some assumed that it would be a logically necessary being, self-existent or self-caused. Others assumed that it would be identical with the physical universe as a whole. And still others assumed still other things. But all assumed that a proof that parades of explanation must end would be profoundly significant.

I am the last to wish otherwise, having constructed such a proof in §2.3, free of defects in the proofs to date. Alas, most philosophers simply took for granted, until recently, that explanation is an objective relation among the things explained, and that a parade of explanations corresponds with an order in reality, a hierarchy or chain of being. They forget that explaining is something *we* do in order to satisfy *our* wonder about the whys of things, and that what we wonder about and what satisfies our wonder are very variable affairs. So explanation may well not correspond with any objective or invariant relation among existents.[40] If not, this powerfully limits the metaphysical significance of an ultimate explanation.

Our discussion so far has left open whether explanation is an objective or invariant relation among things in the world. But we *have* been assuming (for the most part) that explanations are *veridical,* meaning that the entities or states of affairs mentioned in an explanation do exist, have the properties it assumes, and are related in the way it says. An explanation can easily be veridical even if the relation happens not to be an invariant. That is, '*x* explains *y*' can be true in about the same way as '*x* is simultaneous with *y*' can be true, yet not true *period* because not an eternal sentence, if only because '*x* explains *y*' is short for '*x* explains *y* for P at t*' (§1.5[vii]).

For example, there is a canyon in New Mexico, Chaco Canyon, which contains an isolated butte several hundred feet high. Near the summit three large rock slabs—each weighs about two tons—rest on a narrow, sloping ledge and lean against the cliff from which they came. The slabs are on the southeast side of the butte; they are slightly separated and cast various patterns of sunlight and shadow on the cliff behind them. Clearly, the positions and dimensions of the slabs—their total configuration—explain, in conjunction with the angle of the sun, the patterns of light and shade; the patterns do not explain the configuration. What could be more objective? The dimensions and shapes are properties the slabs possess in and of themselves, whereas their shadows are very accidental features. The direction of explanation here evidently must be from the configuration of the slabs to their shadows, not vice versa.

If one could show nevertheless that the patterns of shadow explain the configuration of the slabs, then we would be forced to make a choice. Either we must give up the asymmetry of explanation—according to which if *x* explains *y*, then *y* does not explain *x*—or else we must conclude that explanation is not objective, that *x* does not explain *y* *period* but explains *y* only relative to some person's interest or frame of reference, so that *x* could explain *y* relative to one while *y* explains *x* relative to another.

If we gave up asymmetry, we would also have to give up the hierarchical nature of explanation (§2.5); hierarchy entails asymmetry. But hierarchy and asymmetry are among the best established properties of explanation, even if a few varieties of explanation might prove not to have them. Giving up asymmetry for all varieties seems too high a price. We would have to conclude that explanation is not objective,

---

[40]Cf. van Fraassen (1977), 149.

though it can certainly be veridical. And indeed if we are interested only in the patterns of light and shadow, then the configuration explains the patterns. But suppose we are interested in how the slabs came to be there in the first place. The secret of Chaco Canyon is that they were deliberately placed there between 950 and 1150 A.D. by the Anasazi Indians, the builders of the great pueblos nearby, in order to determine accurately four positions of the sun that especially concern an agrarian culture: the solstices and the equinoxes. In fact, not only do the changing patterns of light and shadow mark these solar positions; certain patterns of moonlight and shadow mark the moon's phases, and some are associated with specific lunar eclipses.[41]

All this was achieved not only by the positioning of the slabs but by the careful carving of their edges into curves that translate the horizontal movement of the sun and moon into a vertical movement of light patterns on two spiral petroglyphs pecked into the cliff just behind the slabs, in such a way as to indicate solar and lunar position. Thus the patterns of light and shadow have certain desired characteristics for each position of the sun and moon, and these characteristics of the patterns explain why the slabs are positioned and shaped as they are. In short, *the patterns explain the configuration of the slabs,* since the slabs were made that way in order to cast precisely those shadows, just as the moving shadow of a sundial explains the shape and orientation of its gnomon.[42] From this point of view, the shadows are not at all an accidental feature of the slabs, any more than a sundial's shadow is inessential to its gnomon.

Of course, the configuration of the slabs is also explained by the aims of their creators, and this no doubt is a more informative and fundamental explanation than one which in the first instance mentions the shadows. But from the fact that there is another explanation, even in some sense a more fundamental one, it does not follow that the first is not after all an explanation. Likewise, from the fact that the question 'Why is the sundial's gnomon pointed that way?" may be answered by the explanation 'Because we want the shadow to do so-and-so', it does not follow that we could not as well answer, on occasion, with the explanation 'Because that way the shadow does so-and-so'.

Relativization to a context crops up elsewhere to somewhat different effect. An explanation-seeking why-question like 'Why are their headlights on?' may be answered by 'Because the switch is on' or by 'Because they're driving in a funeral procession'. Suppose both replies are

[41]Sofaer et al. Reyman questions whether the Anasazis were the builders, and others have even questioned whether the slabs are a solar marker in the first place, none of which affects the point of the example.
[42]Cf. van Fraassen (1977), 149, on Bromberger's flagpole example; and Glymour (1978).

veridical. Then the context determines which reply is the explanation sought. If our interest is in the reliability of the car's electrical system, the switch's being on is relevant. If our interest is in motives, driving in the procession is relevant. Neither reply is *the* explanation, though both are explanations. There appears to be no such thing as *the* explanation.

Even where no agent is involved—no one to make solar markers or to turn on lights—context has a powerful effect. The question 'Why does the sun have planets?' may be answered either by 'Because the disc that formed around the sun when it was formed separated into planets', or by 'Because the collapsing cloud of dust and gas that made the sun acquired a spin that made the disc that separated into planets'. Which of these explanations is to be preferred? That depends on how far back in the chain of efficient causes we are interested in going when we ask 'Why?' And that in turn depends on what would satisfy our wonder, what would give us the understanding we seek. There are circumstances, even, in which we would rightly be satisfied with an answer like 'The formation of most stars involves the formation of planets'. In like manner we sometimes answer 'Why is Richard so thoughtless?' with 'Many people are'.

Even if some variety of explanation should prove to correspond with an invariant order in reality, we have good reason to question its claim to priority. For we remain free not to be interested in that variety of explanation in the first place, or indeed in any variety. Other ways of mapping existence could be more important, at least on occasion. We might relate things to each other and to ourselves in terms of purely temporal (or spatiotemporal) order; or in terms of our feelings about them; or in terms of their potential contribution to realizing our deepest hopes; or in terms of degrees of complexity, with conscious organisms at or near the top; or, if a divinity exists, in terms of degree of participation in the divine; and so on.

Furthermore, can we be sure that the diverse parades of this alleged objective variety of explanation would all end in the same thing?[43] Consider a parade of such explanations that starts with the slabs' explaining their shadows. Would it end with whatever ends the parade that starts with an objective explanation of why someone's headlights are on by reference to driving in a funeral procession? For that matter, would it end with whatever ends the parade that starts with an objective explanation of the slabs by reference to their shadows?

It looks as though the proven existence of ultimate explanations, though obviously important for certain purposes, has little of the profound metaphysical significance most philosophers supposed it would

[43]Cf. Edwards (1967b), 106.

have. It does not follow from the existence of ultimate explainers that they represent *the* nature of existence, or *the* meaning, even assuming there is such a thing. This is true even though we can use the proven existence of ultimate explanations to legitimize the idea of a meta-physically necessary being, which then proves not to be contingent, absurd, irrational, gratuitous, or brute, and about which there can be no mystery as to why it exists.

2.7. Science and Ultimate Explanation

> *The one type of question [science] cannot deal with at all, is precisely that which is conveyed by our statement of the mystery of existence.*
>
> —MILTON MUNITZ

> *Someday . . . a point will be reached where the only unexplained features . . . will be the elements of the scientific framework. Beyond that point, the . . . theory of nature . . . will become a* vision *of nature transcending the realms of thought and language; leading out of science and into the world of* acintya, *the unthinkable.*
>
> —FRITJOF CAPRA

> *A question does not become intelligible merely because of the co-presence of a curiosity-feeling.*
>
> —TERENCE PENELHUM

The view is widespread and stubborn: science cannot possibly fath-om the mystery of existence. The mystery expressed by 'Why does anything at all exist, why not rather nothing?' represents an absolute limit on the pretensions of science and of reason generally. But those who made it through §2.2 can readily see what is wrong here. The question is equivalent to asking why the universe exists, which in turn is equivalent to asking what the explanation is of its existence. And the presupposition on which this is based, namely that there is some expla-nation, is false (unless, implausibly, someone can patch up the idea of a being whose very nature explains its existence, *and* show that one who grasped the relevant aspect of its nature *still* would not understand why it exists). So it is true that science cannot fathom why there is something rather than nothing, just as it is true that mathematics cannot fathom the way to trisect an angle using only compass and straightedge. What is pretentious is the question. It does not cease to have a false presupposi-tion "merely because of the co-presence of a curiosity-feeling" when we ask it.[44]

[44]Penelhum, 149.

Vision, mystical or otherwise, is as beside the point here as science and reason. There is nothing to be envisioned, nothing for insight to sight into, not even a void. The role of heightened states of vision and feeling need not be to provide explanations, even in response to why-questions that have no false presupposition. Such states of awareness may be authentic and invaluable without providing an ultimate explanation of anything. Just what might constitute their authenticity we consider in the final chapter.

An ultimate explanation, by definition, is one beyond which there can be no more, known or unknown, knowable or unknowable (§2.5). Since there is no further explanation to be known, there is none to be known not only by science and reason but by any means that allegedly transcend them. But can science, in contrast perhaps to something else, *identify* ultimate explainers? Can it provide explanations beyond which there can be no more, even for an infinite intelligence? Or must all ultimate explanations exceed the grasp of science?

Historically, one popular reason for supposing they must is that any explainer mentioned by science is contingent. We can imagine the world to have been otherwise, and we feel curious as to why it was not; there must be some further, nonscientific explanation. One trouble with this line of reasoning is that it presupposes PSR. Another is that even if there were a further explanation, it would have to be shown to be nonscientific. Frequently, we marshal a parade of nonscientific explanations that we believe ends with reference to a certain thing. But how do we know that the existence and properties of this thing do not have some scientific explanation as yet undreamed of? Hamlet's admonition, that "there are more things in heaven and earth . . . than are dreamt of in your philosophy," cuts both ways.

A different line of reasoning is that any explainer mentioned by science is subject to processes of change and decay, and there must be some unchanging and unchangeable being to explain them. This line of reasoning has all the troubles of the first plus some others (§§3.3, 3.4). In general, neither PSRs nor arguments for the existence of an ultimate explainer can be used to inflate our inventory of what there is, whether the list is drawn up by science or by anything else. They cannot be used to show that there must be something beyond the list to explain what is on the list. At best, the argument that there must be ultimate explainers can be used to show, on occasion, that something already on the list is an ultimate explainer of other things on the list. Independent reasons are required for determining what goes on the list in the first place, and whether anything on the list is somehow beyond the power of science to describe.

Physics continually revises what in effect are its proposals for ultimate explainers (not *the* ultimate explainers, if any, but the ultimate explainers in its domain). This occurs when the most basic theories in physics change and evolve in light of new experience. We might suppose that whatever is unexplained in one such theory gets explained, or ought to, in the next. We would be wrong, not just because some unexplained things continue to be unexplained, but because the very class of things eligible for explanation, according to the later theory, may change so radically as not to include what is eligible for explanation according to the earlier one.

Consider an arrow in flight. Why does it keep moving after it has left the bow? This question arises within Aristotle's physics, and much effort went into finding a good explanation. A subsequent favorite was that air displaced at the front rushed to the rear, where it pushed. The attempted explanation seems so quaint to us, so obviously inadequate, that we may say the arrow's continued flight was not really explained. But was it explained in Newton's theory? Not really. Within Newtonian physics, what is even eligible for explanation is not *continued* motion but *change* of motion—not why the arrow keeps moving but why it slows, why its path curves, why it stops. The *natural* motion of an object—the motion, according to Newton's theory, that neither admits of nor requires explanation—is a continued, uniform state of motion (or rest). The arrow's tendency to keep going is an instance of the principle of inertia, a principle so basic to the theory that neither it nor motions in accordance with it admit of or require any explanation. The principle expresses an ultimate explainer within the theory. Within the theory, the explanation-seeking 'Why do objects continue in a uniform state of motion unless affected by external forces?' is based on the false presupposition that there is an explanation. Thus does the evolution of scientific theories school us to revise our judgments of what is even eligible for explanation, and thereby our judgments of what is a legitimate object of wonder, as well as what satisfies that wonder.

Of course, from outside a theory, even a basic theory, we may ask 'Why?' about one of its ultimate explainers. But we must recognize that to do so is to contemplate the possibility of *another* theory, within which what was an ultimate explainer will have some explanation. We thereby assume some responsibility for at least sketching what this alternative theory might look like. Otherwise our 'Why?' might be idle, doing no work and based on none, but only on the co-presence of a curiosity-feeling and on unsubstantiated hope that there is some alternative. Furthermore, even if a later theory proves superior, we have no guarantee that what was an ultimate explainer in the earlier one will remain even eligible for explanation. Our 'Why?' may go the way of 'Why does the arrow keep moving?'

Clearly, one should not assume that progress in the evolution of scientific theories brings about a single parade of explanations in which later theories provide explanations for what was unexplained in an earlier one. Occasionally, a later theory may do so; more typically, a basic theory abandons the parade of explanations marshalled by earlier theories and marches to a different drummer. The later theory imposes new categories on existence, in terms of which different classes of things are deemed to be eligible for or to require explanation. Relative to the new classification, we marshal parades of explanation and tentatively designate the ultimate explainers in them.

At any given time, if asked what the ultimate explainers are, we have no choice but to answer in light of the best basic theory then available. That is, we have no choice but to use the theory that has so far best survived trial by prerequisites, that best satisfies any criteria for truth we may then be lucky enough to possess, and best exemplifies any other relevant virtues, including comprehensiveness and simplicity. The theory's ultimate explainers represent our current best guess as to what, even for an infinite intelligence, would terminate the parade of explanations marshalled by the theory. For, to repeat the rhetorical challenge from §1.4, what else could there be to go on?

Now suppose I were to ask an explanation-seeking 'Why?' about an ultimate explainer E within this currently best theory. Then either I do not know that E is an ultimate explainer; or I do not understand what an ultimate explainer is (in particular, that it has no explanation, known or unknown); or I understand all this and am proposing an alternative theory within which E does have an explanation. In this last case, as lately noted, I am obligated to tell you a bit about what this new theory would look like. Otherwise my 'Why?' risks being idle, and you have no indication that it is based on anything more than the co-presence of a curiosity-feeling.

Even if I can sketch the new theory, my 'Why?' may well fail to arise. The reason is that my new theory might not be as good as the present best theory. Only time will tell, of course, but the new theory might fail where the present one succeeds in satisfying the prerequisites and other virtues we require of good theories. Until the present best theory is successfully displaced, or at least called into serious question, we are forced to say that an explanation-seeking 'Why?' about E is based on a false presupposition so far as we can presently tell.

This does *not* mean that no one should work on the new theory. On the contrary, we are free to assume, for the sake of argument, that 'Why?' does arise and in this heuristic spirit to use the question, plus the curiosity-feeling it generates, to spur ourselves on. But this heuristic, creative use of 'Why?' should not be mistaken for a use according to which we are forced to say, and not for the sake of argument, that there *is* some explanation of *E*.

Let us apply some of these lessons to physical cosmology. According to a steady-state cosmology, hydrogen atoms constantly and spontaneously appear in empty space. The role of this hypothesis is so fundamental to the theory that it ought to be regarded as expressing an ultimate explainer within the theory (though even some of its proponents seem to have missed this point). To ask why or how the atoms appear is therefore improper, based as such a question would be on a false presupposition, unless someone is proposing an alternative theory within which the spontaneous appearance receives some explanation. This is rarely if ever done. Instead, those who persist in speaking of the "mystery" of the "creation" of the atoms in empty space give us nothing more to go on than their curiosity-feeling, plus perhaps some version of the dubious PSR. Unless and until these particular mystery-mongers do better, defenders of a steady-state theory (if there still are any) are entitled to dismiss the talk of "mystery" and "creation" as based on the false presupposition that there is some further explanation to be known (some "creator").

Big-bang cosmologies are now preferred by most physicists. Such theories do not explain the appearance of atoms in empty space; they deny that it occurs at all. Instead, they explain the observed expansion of the cosmos by reference to an explosion that occurred some tens of billions of years ago. Now suppose the "bang" was a genuine beginning (a first event), so that it was not preceded by an earlier contraction (a "big crunch") from which the present expansion is a rebound. Does this even point to a creator? Does it have an explanation? PSR is discredited—no help there. Our curiosity-feelings, no matter how intense, are powerless to ensure there is an explanation for what we are curious about—no help there, either.

The structure of big-bang theories themselves can shed some light here. Within such theories, certain global features of spacetime are ultimate explainers. In terms of these features (assuming they obtain) *every* stage of the expansion, *including the first,* would count as part of the *natural* behavior of the cosmos—the behavior to be expected, neither admitting of nor requiring explanation. If so, the big bang, strange as it seems, would be like the arrow's continued flight for Newton, or better, like the spontaneous appearance of hydrogen atoms for a steady-state cosmologist. Asking 'Why did the big bang occur?' would be like asking 'Why did this hydrogen atom come into existence?' It would also be like asking 'Why does the arrow keep moving?' Unless and until we construct not only a better physical cosmology but one in which what was unexplained has an explanation, asking 'Why?' about the big bang would be idle. Whatever our unschooled intuitions may suggest, this primordial event no more points to a creator or represents a mystery than the continued flight of an arrow points to a being who sustains it.

Nor can we say of the big bang that it is brute, gratuitous, absurd, irrational, or a mere happening. Toward the end of §2.5 we saw that none of these terms applies to an ultimate explainer. Instead we must say of the big bang that within our present best cosmological theory (or theories), it is metaphysically necessary. If the theory changes, as is highly likely, then some other event or events (such as vacuum fluctuation) and some other features of spacetime will be ultimate explainers, hence metaphysically necessary within the new theory. There remains mystery aplenty, perhaps more than we can fathom, as to just what the new theory might be and whether it is true.

3 Universe

*Before Euler's work it was customary to think that no concept
was to be used in physics or science unless it met certain
standards of metaphysics. . . . Euler's reverse consisted in
his . . . suggestion that the ideas and principles of
metaphysics ought to be regulated and determined by the
knowledge which physics has established.*

—ARNOLD KOSLOW

*The aim of cosmology is to determine the large-scale structure
of the physical universe.*

—G. F. R. ELLIS

*A true account of the actual is the rarest poetry, for common
sense always takes a hasty and superficial view.*

—THOREAU

3.0. Introduction

What if the physical universe were the whole of existence, the sum
total of what there is? That is the guiding assumption of this chapter,
made for the sake of argument, in order to grant physicalists one of their
most unsettling theses. The argument will be that if the physical universe were all, then it would be an eternal, immutable, uncreated, self-
existent, necessary being and the First Cause on which everything is
dependent. Furthermore, just as theologians sometimes talk of the God
beyond God, physicalists are committed to a universe beyond the universe. What this means, roughly, is that beyond what we presently call
the known universe, or beyond the universe as conceived through our
present scientific categories, is the true physical universe, or the Universe, as we may call it. The Universe is to be identified neither with *the*
way things are nor with some indescribable thing-in-itself.[1] Humans

[1]Nor with what Nozick, 150f., calls the beyond.

may or may not be able in principle some day to give a correct and complete characterization of the Universe. But the realist account of truth in Chapter 1 would force the physicalist, who is a realist anyway and thus scarcely needs urging, to assume that the Universe is there to be characterized.

Unless our present categories are completely adequate, which few believe, the Universe exists in addition to (or perhaps instead of) what we may call the "manifest" universe—the physical universe as it is presently known or categorized.[2] If our present categories are completely adequate, then it is the manifest universe that is eternal, immutable, uncreated, self-existent, necessary, and the First Cause. If they are not completely adequate, then strictly it is the Universe to which we should apply the terms 'eternal', 'immutable', 'uncreated', and so on.

All these terms are subject to construction. Much of the chapter consists in reconstructing them safely within the idiom of contemporary physics and physical cosmology. Despite the contemporary setting, what emerges is a cherished perennial in metaphysics—namely, an eternal, immutable, necessary being. Establishing the existence of such a being typically has been the first step in traditional theism. Indeed, when told of an eternal, immutable, self-existent, ultimate explainer of all else, anyone—not just theists—might be tempted to say, in the spirit perhaps of Aquinas, "and this all people call God." One should resist the temptation. The physical universe, whether manifest or true, seems most unlikely to have the personal attributes of divinity, however admirably it may exhibit such abstractions as eternity, immutability, self-existence, and so on. And even if the universe as a whole were called God, the result presumably would be pantheism, not theism. Pantheists might rejoice, but theists would find their suspicions confirmed about assuming, even for the sake of argument, that the physical universe is the whole of existence.

Still, being able to reconstruct even this much theism within the framework of an apparently hostile physicalism should make us wonder how much more might be accommodated. And if theism should prove not to be totally ruled out by an austere physicalism after all, we may wonder about other views and values commonly thought to be threatened by physicalist philosophy. Perhaps they can be joined with it, so that they and physicalism enrich each other while correcting each other's occasional extremes.

Obviously, we are getting ahead of our story, into some of the substance of later chapters. Even so, we need to anticipate a bit more. In

---

[2]With apologies to Sellars.

assuming, for the sake of argument, that the physical universe is all, we are *not* assuming that the only kind of truth is truth in physics, or even that truth in physics enjoys some sort of unconditional priority over other kinds. The existence and occasional priority of other domains of truth is quite compatible with the assumption that the physical universe is the sum total of what there is. For to say that everything is physical does not entail that everything is to be described or explained only in the language of physics, or even in the language of some other science, as we see in Chapters 4–8. As for priority, even if physical descriptions are prior in certain contexts for certain purposes, it hardly follows that they take priority in all contexts whatever the purpose. Physics supplies us with maps of the whole of existence—invaluable maps—but like all maps, they tell us only what is fundamental given certain interests. This is the inevitable consequence of maps' double abstraction: the selection of features of interest to their intended users or producers, and the further selection of only certain aspects of those features.

So there can be many domains of truth, hence many faces of existence, even if everything there is is included in the physical universe. Physicalism claims that there is but one set of bare bones behind and supporting all the faces, and that physics has no peer in telling us about the bones. The claim does not entail that the faces are not real, or that they are mere masks. I could as well argue that my own visage is not real or important but that only my skull is, on the grounds that it alone anchors the facial musculature, and that osteology has no peer in ascertaining the dimensions of skulls.

3.1. What Is the Physical Universe?

> *What is . . . essential . . . is something tantamount to treating the world as a great big object. (It is after all natural to us so to regard the world . . . as the upper limit of the series: Earth, solar system, galaxy, cluster of galaxies, . . .)*
>
> —P. T. GEACH

> *It is by no means clear . . . that the universe is an object. It is by no means clear that if a and b are just any objects, then there is an object c composed of a and b.*
>
> —ALVIN PLATINGA

> *First of all, is the World a Whole?*
>
> —JUSTUS BUCHLER

If the whole of existence is to be identified with the physical universe, then the physical universe plus everything in it forms a whole. In

§1.2 we warned against uncritical talk of wholes in the absence of a clearly understood part-whole relation. But when only physical entities are supposed to exist, the problem eases dramatically, for we can then use a spatiotemporal part-whole relation. Such relations are well understood—well enough, certainly, for our purposes.[3] Not that using a spatiotemporal part-whole relation ends all our troubles. There are many mathematical spacetimes, some of them extraordinarily at odds with common sense, including a few that may well represent the physical spacetime of our universe. Spacetimes differ widely as to the number of their dimensions, though most of those presently used in physics are 4-dimensional. They differ also in other crucial respects, such as whether they are (to use the technical terms) differentiable, connected, Hausdorff, paracompact, time-(space-)orientable, bounded, affine, with a Lorentzian metric, and so on.[4]

Can we define a part-whole relation that would apply to them all? It is essential that we do so if we want our definition of 'the universe as a whole' to apply no matter what the spacetime of the universe should happen to be. The spacetime generally presupposed in physics today certainly is not the last word; already there are serious proposals for change.[5] Fortunately, all spacetimes (including infinite-dimensional "superspace")[6] can be represented as sets of points, and every set is ordered by the subset relation.[7] The subset relation is a sound basis for a part-whole relation, defined as follows:

STPW. *x* is a spatiotemporal part (ST-part) of *y* iff the set of ST-points that constitute *x*'s ST-region is a subset of the set of ST-points that constitute *y*'s ST-region.

For example, consider a 3-dimensional Euclidean space. A room in a house is a spatial part of the house, since the set of spatial points that constitute the room's spatial region (the space the room occupies) is a subset of the set of spatial points that constitute the house's spatial region (the space the house occupies). Now introduce time, and think of the room and house as 4-dimensional solids extended temporally as well as spatially. Thus each occupies a region of spacetime. Provided that house and room are built at the same time and torn down together, then

[3]Cf. Eberle (1970a).

[4]Cf. Geroch; Hawking and Ellis, §§2.1, 2.6, 6.1; Friedman (1983), 350.

[5]Cf. Isham's survey of developments in quantum gravity, in Isham, Penrose, and Sciama.

[6]Thus I use 'spacetime' rather more broadly than Wheeler does when he discusses superspace in Misner, Thorne, and Wheeler, ch. 43.

[7]Not that sets need exist, strictly; cf. §4.1.

the set of ST-points that constitute the room's ST-region is a subset of the set of ST-points that constitute the house's ST-region. (Without the proviso, the two regions might diverge.) The 4-dimensional room is a spatiotemporal part of the 4-dimensional house.

In general, to use definition STPW, first choose a spacetime, however weird. Then let the interpretation of 'ST-point' and 'ST-region' in STPW vary accordingly. This presupposes, as do all treatments of applied geometry, that we know what it means for x to be *at* some ST-point, and more generally what it means for x to be at or occupy some ST-region (i.e., for a set of ST-points to constitute x's ST-region). This presupposition is minimal, harmless, and uncontroversial. Note in particular that it does not conflate ST-regions with their occupants, if any.

Controversy begins when one inquires what a spacetime point is. Roughly speaking, it is a location in spacetime at which some event occurs or could occur. But is the notion of a location definable in terms of something still more basic? Also, is a location something physical or merely an idealization? And what of the spacetime itself? Is it merely a convenient abstraction, just our way of representing the system of spatiotemporal relations among the concretely existing things and events? Or is it itself a physical thing, somewhat like an electromagnetic field? Definition STPW enables us to bypass such controversies, since it is neutral among the competing positions.[8] Whatever one's views on the status of ST-points and of spacetime, simply interpret the relevant terms in STPW accordingly. The result will still be a sound definition of 'part-whole' for the spacetime chosen.

Intuitively, we regard the physical universe as the unique spatiotemporal whole of which every physical existent is a part—approximately what Geach calls "the upper limit of the series: Earth, solar system, galaxy, cluster of galaxies . . ."[9] How shall we capture this intuition rigorously in a definition? To do so we must (i) define 'physical existent' and (ii) explain just how and in what sense the physical existents form a whole or a "series" with an "upper limit" or upper bound.

3.1.1. What Is a Physical Existent?

We cannot define a physical existent as anything that exists in spacetime. Being in spacetime is a necessary but not sufficient condition for something to be physical. Ghosts and spirits, if they exist, are in spacetime but presumably are not physical things. And if we view minds and consciousness, plus perhaps a life force, as nonphysical, we will not

---

[8]For an account of the competition, cf. Friedman (1983), chs. 6 and 7.
[9]In the epigraph for this section; Geach, 63.

want to say that being in spacetime is sufficient for something to be physical. For by virtue of being in time, if not necessarily spatially extended, minds and consciousness and the alleged life force are in spacetime, whence it would follow that they are physical after all. (They can be in time, hence in spacetime, without being spatially extended, by having zero-magnitude extensions along the spatial axes.)

Even physicalists themselves must refrain from defining 'physical existent' in such a way that merely having spacetime location is sufficient for something to be physical. They must not define their terms in such a way that merely stating what their position is would beg the question of whether it is true. Physicalism includes the claim that everything—hence everything in spacetime—is physical. If 'physical' were defined so that being in spacetime were sufficient for being physical, then simply by definition everything in spacetime would be physical. And this would beg the question against those who believe that some things in time, hence in spacetime, are nonphysical—such as spirits, minds, a life-force, or whatever.

Nor can the physicalist define a physical existent as what physics might someday divulge. This is far too vague. But it does remind us that our concept of the physical changes over time. Indeed it can change dramatically, so much so that what is called physical by a later generation would have been called supernatural by an earlier. Imagine, if we can, what someone two hundred years ago would have thought about radio, lasers, fusion, and black holes; about fields, quanta, and variably curved spacetime. Our own reaction to the physics of 3000 A.D. (let us hope there is some) would likewise probably be one of incomprehension if not disbelief.

Because our concept of what is physical changes over time, and because references to future physics are too vague, the physicalist, like everyone else, has no choice but to define 'physical existent' by reference to some explicit list of predicates drawn from the best of contemporary physics. The list must be from *physics* in order both to retain the connection between physicalism and physics and to acknowledge the impact of this most basic and comprehensive of the sciences on our changing concept of the physical. And the list must be from *contemporary* physics, not only because we cannot anticipate the evolution of physics for more than a few years at most, but also because we do not want to use an obsolete and erroneous concept of the physical (erroneous, so far as we can tell, in light of the best evidence available, which by the nature of the case must be largely from today's physics). We do not want to conceive of physical things as, say, all made of atoms like billiard balls, when some things are instead intangible, diaphanous fields, and when the atoms themselves are resonating sets of resonances that a crude billiard–ball materialism must reject as nonphysical (as indeed some diehard mechanists did in the early days of field theories).

The list would include some such predicates as 'is an electron', 'is a quark', 'is an electromagnetic field', 'is a 4-dimensional manifold', 'is a quantum field described by such-and-such equations', 'is a spacelike hypersurface', 'is a singularity', 'are pairwise related by a force obeying such-and-such equations', and so on and on. The list would be drawn up from the relevant papers, treatises, and textbooks in recent physics. Of course, there are different ways of formulating physics, taking different predicates as basic (that is, as undefined by others). Nothing in this or other chapters will turn on these differences (as we see further in §5.1). But in whatever formulation, the list should not include *negative* predicates, like 'is not an electron' or 'is not a quantum field'. For we want anything that satisfies a predicate in the list to be a physical existent. Something about which we know only that it is not an electron may or may not be physical; it could be a ghost, or a mysterious life force, or whatever (cf. §4.2). Thus we must restrict the list to *positive* physical predicates.

Even though everything that satisfies a predicate on the list is a physical existent, not every physical existent need satisfy a predicate on the list. Shoes are physical things, as are ships, sealing wax, cabbages, and if not kings, at least their bodies. Yet there is no mention of these or most other ordinary macroscopic things in the *Journal of Mathematical Physics* or like publications. Shoes and ships are made up of entities (electrons, protons, etc.) that satisfy predicates on the list. But it does not follow that shoes and ships themselves satisfy some predicate on the list, though they may happen to satisfy some complex predicates defined or constructed out of those that are on the list.

Of course, shoes and ships are related to each other and to the earth by a "force"—gravitation—that obeys certain equations. So it looks as though ordinary macroscopic objects would satisfy some predicate on the list after all (a "relational predicate"). Actually the matter is not so simple, but let us assume anyway that ordinary macroscopic objects would satisfy some such gravitational predicate. There remain some extraordinary ones that do not. Black holes, for example, ought to emit no particles at all, not even light, according to the gravitational equations. Yet according to quantum theory, they emit particles by a process called "tunneling" and will eventually evaporate out of existence. On the other hand, quantum theory suffers an incompleteness of its own, since it does not describe the gravitational processes by which black holes are formed (many of them, anyway) from collapsing stars. No quantum gravitational theory yet exists that is completely adequate to the job.[10]

In general, if we assume that every physical existent satisfies some predicate on the list, including relational predicates, we risk assuming that the equations that describe the relations are complete; that there are no relevant physical phenomena they are unable to describe, no matter how accurate our measurements. Obviously, this sometimes presumes too much. In addition, to assume that every physical existent either satisfies a predicate on the list or satisfies one defined by reference to those on the list is to make a dubious claim about the descriptive and defining power of the language of physics.

How, then, may the physicalist or anyone else define a physical existent? Roughly, as something made up or composed of entities that clearly do satisfy a predicate on the list. Shoes and ships are made up of electrons, protons, and so on. Black holes are made up of the mass-energy of, say, collapsed stars. And, to revert again to Geach's theme, the earth and the other planets are made up of particles and fields, as is the sun; the solar system therefore is made up of things that are made up of particles and fields; so too for galaxies, and so on.

But what does it mean to say "x is made up of y and z"? Roughly, it means that x is a spatiotemporal whole composed of y and z. That is, we start with y and z, then get x out of them, rather as we start with the sun and planets and then think of the solar system as composed of them, or with protons and electrons and then think of a cabbage as composed of them. Can we be more precise? Yes, via the notion of a spatiotemporal sum:

> STS. The ST-sum of y and z is the x whose ST-region is the union of y's ST-region with z's ST-region.

That is, the set A of ST-points that constitute x's ST-region consists of exactly the ST-points that are members *either* of the set B of ST-points that constitute y's region *or* of the set C of ST-points that constitute z's region (which again does not conflate regions with their occupants, if any). Since B and C are subsets of A, it follows by definition STPW, as desired, that y and z are ST-parts of their ST-sum x. In addition, it can be shown that the ST-sum x is what is technically known as the supremum (the least upper bound) of y and z with respect to the spatiotemporal part-whole relation defined in STPW.[11] The ST-sum is also

[10]Cf. Isham, Penrose, and Sciama.
[11]Cf. Eberle (1970a), 32–33.

sometimes called the ST-fusion. If y and z themselves are ST-sums of entities, STS allows us to speak in turn of the ST-sum of the latter, and so on.

Clearly, STS can be generalized so that we may speak of the ST-sum not just of two entities but of many:

> GSTS. The ST-sum of the entities in a given set is the x whose ST-region is the union of the ST-regions of all the entities in the set.

As before, the ST-sum is also called the ST-fusion or supremum of the entities, a special kind of upper bound. If some or all the entities themselves are ST-sums, GSTS allows us to speak in turn of the ST-sum of the latter, and so on, so that there can be ST-sums of sums . . . of sums of entities.

All physical entities are in spacetime, so that given any two whatever, each occupies a region of spacetime. By a law of set theory, the union of the two regions always exists and is unique. It follows that the ST-sum of any two physical entities exists and is unique, no matter how unrelated the two entities may be in other respects. For example, consider Alexander the Great's horse and the celebrated mole on Chairman Mao's chin. Horse and mole are separated in space and time and bear no significant relation to each other. Yet they form a spatiotemporal sum. So do one's little finger and the farthest galaxy, one's latest breath and the earliest dinosaur.

Of course, not every ST-sum is an *individual* or an *object* (at least not in any ordinary sense). Some are too scattered to deserve the title, too discontinuous in space and time, like Alexander's horse and Mao's mole.[12] But every ST-sum *is* a spatiotemporal *array*. In this minimal sense the sum is a thing, an entity, an existent. Thus we need not claim, as against Plantinga in this section's epigraph, that "if a and b are just any objects, then there is an *object c* composed of a and b," let alone an *individual c*.[13] We need claim only that there is an array composed of a and b, namely their ST-sum.

Indeed some ST-arrays are *random*. Label every electron in the universe by a number, then use a table of random numbers to select electrons at will, and consider the ST-sum of those selected. This sum is a random ST-array, so scattered and discontinuous spatially and tem-

---

[12]We can also agree with van Inwagen that the top half of the Eiffel Tower is not a "concrete material particular in the same sense as the Eiffel Tower itself." Cf. Cartwright.

[13]Plantinga (1967b), 19.

porally as not to be an object or individual in any ordinary sense. Even more radical gerrymandering is possible: from among the randomly selected electrons, choose only those at spacelike separation from each other; that is, no causal influence, not even light, can connect any two thus selected. The result is a random array whose parts cannot bear any causal relation to each other, gravity included (at least according to today's theories). It is exceedingly unlikely that so weird an array satisfies any predicate on the list of basic predicates drawn up from treatises in physics. This reinforces the idea that there must be physical existents that satisfy no such predicate.

Our rough idea of a physical existent was that it is an entity made up or composed of entities that clearly do satisfy a predicate on the list. Suppose we call the latter entities physical entities of a listed kind, or entities belonging to a listed category. Then a physical existent is either a physical entity of a listed kind or composed of such entities. More precisely,

> PE. x is a physical existent iff x is either a physical entity of a listed kind or the ST-sum of physical entities of listed kinds.

Actually PE can be shortened. Technically and trivially, each physical entity, whether it belongs to a listed category or not, has a spatiotemporal sum—namely, itself. Hence if x is a physical entity of a listed kind, then automatically x is the ST-sum of such an entity. So we can define a physical existent simply as the ST-sum of some entity or entities of the listed kinds.

Some physical entities will satisfy a predicate on the list, or at least a predicate defined by those on the list. Others may not. Some will be ordinary macroscopic objects. Others may not be objects in any familiar sense but random ST-arrays. All are in spacetime. But PE does not imply that all things in spacetime are physical. Note also that PE defines the notion of a physical existent in terms of a list of predicates drawn from the best of contemporary physics. As the list changes, so therefore does the notion of a physical existent.

3.1.2. The Sum of the Physical Existents

It remains to be explained just how and in what sense all the physical entities form a whole that we may call the physical universe. The key is GSTS, which allows us to speak of the ST-sum of many entities, indeed infinitely many if need be. Thus we have:

> PU. The physical universe is the ST-sum of all the physical existents.

By PU, the physical existents form a whole in the sense of their ST-sum, or fusion, or supremum. As such, it need not be an object or an individual or even a whole in any ordinary sense. But it *is* an array, of as many dimensions as the presupposed spacetime. In this minimal sense the universe is a thing, an entity, an existent. Even nonphysicalists must include it in their inventory of what there is if they have already included physical entities.

What PU defines, strictly, is the manifest physical universe. For the notion of a physical existent has to be defined, as seen, in terms of a list of predicates drawn from contemporary physics. When the term 'physical existent' in PU is spelled out according to PE, and the manifestness made explicit, we have:

> MU. The manifest physical universe is the ST-sum of all the entities that are either physical entities of a listed kind or ST-sums of physical entities of listed kinds.

Thus our very concept of the physical universe, like our concept of a physical entity, is a function of the kinds or categories used in physics at any given time. It is a function also of the spacetime we use, because of the unavoidable dependence on the notion of a spatiotemporal sum. So it is conceivable, though perhaps not likely, that some list of physical predicates could stay constant while we adopted a radically different spacetime. The result would be a change in both (a) our concept of a physical entity, because of PE's dependence on the notion of an ST-sum, hence on a previously chosen spacetime; and (b) our concept of the physical universe as a whole. In the history of physics, however, the choice of a spacetime has tended to be relatively stable, while the list of predicates changes more frequently.

Is the physical universe, as defined by MU, identical with the whole of spacetime? That depends on what one means by 'the whole of spacetime'. A spacetime from the point of view of mathematics is just a specially defined abstract set, even if it is the spacetime "of" the universe, as one says. Viewed this way, no spacetime could be identical with the physical universe, which is a whole or sum, not a set. If spacetime were defined not as the set but as the ST-sum of the locations or regions of all the physical existents (events, fields, objects), still the spacetime would not be identical with the whole physical universe, unless a physical existent were nothing more than its ST-region or location (which *would* be to conflate regions and their occupants, if any, or at least to identify them).

The view that a physical existent *is* nothing more than its ST-region is taken seriously in certain quarters.[14] The idea is that spacetime is a physical existent, perhaps a unique sort of field, and that the other things we call fields, plus the particles, events, and so on, are really only regions of spacetime endowed with special curvature. According to this space theory of matter, as it sometimes is called, there are not two sorts of physical existents—spacetime and mass-energy—but one. And this one existent, spacetime, is identical with the whole physical universe. The opposite view is that only the mass-energy exists. What we call spacetime is merely a convenient way of representing certain relations among the scattered bits and fields of mass-energy. This view is sometimes called the matter theory of spacetime, sometimes the relational theory.[15] Since spacetime does not exist, according to this view, the physical universe can scarcely be identical with it but only with the ST-sum of the bits and fields of mass-energy.

Neither view enjoys a consensus among physicists or philosophers. A third view does, at least for the present. It is a dualism, according to which both spacetime and the bits and fields contained within it are physical entities.[16] Defenders of this view can point to a predicate routinely used in gravitational physics, which they contend can only be satisfied by spacetime construed as an independent physical entity. The predicate is 'is a 4-dimensional manifold satisfying such-and-such equations'. Such talk of the manifold (or "the continuum") is to be construed, we are told, as talk of a physical entity somewhat like a field. Indeed we do often speak of the gravitational field equations. The other fields, plus the bits of mass-energy, occupy regions in the manifold or spacetime; they are its material contents. The ST-sum of the contents need not be identical with the spacetime, since there might be empty regions of spacetime, regions devoid of material contents. But the ST-sum of the contents *plus* the spacetime is identical with the spacetime. Thus in this dualistic view the whole physical universe would be identical with the whole of physical spacetime plus its contents, even though the whole formed only by the contents would not be.

MU is neutral among all three alternatives, as it should be. Whatever the physical status of spacetime, MU allows us to speak with clear conscience of the physical universe as a whole, meaning the ST-sum of all the physical entities. It is a further question whether spacetime is among the physical existents, or only the bits and fields of mass-energy, or both. MU has another considerable advantage. It does not construe

---

[14]Cf. Wheeler; Graves; and Grünbaum's (1973) critique of the view.
[15]For a critique, cf. Friedman (1983), ch. 6; Grünbaum (1977).
[16]Cf. Earman (1972).

the physical universe as a set or class of things. Many philosophers and others have severe doubts as to whether sets exist; talk of sets may be just a convenient manner of speaking about something else. But even if sets exist, they are extraordinarily abstract entities without any sort of spatiotemporal structure. The physical universe, on the other hand, has plenty of spatiotemporal structure. It is not a set, not even a maximal possible state of affairs, but a spatiotemporal whole.[17] It presents itself to us as an array or spread of things, as we grope our way through it from infancy on.

3.2. Mystery and the Universe

> *While physicists are probing and deciphering the secrets of the universe, a higher question yet remains: why does the universe exist?*
>
> —Letter to the Editor of *Newsweek*

> *If the world is an object, it again seems natural to ask about it the sort of causal questions which would be legitimate about its parts.*
>
> —P. T. Geach

> *After all it does remain incredible that the physical universe should just have happened. . . . It calls out for some further explanation of some kind.*
>
> —A. C. Ewing

Because we are assuming, for the sake of argument, that the physical universe exhausts what there is, many of the conclusions of Chapter 2 carry over virtually unchanged. Thus the existence of the physical universe has no explanation, even for an infinite intelligence, and the question 'Why does the physical universe exist at all?' is based on a false presupposition. Of course, most of us experience what Penelhum calls "the co-presence of a curiosity-feeling," a sense of mystery, when we ask 'Why does the universe exist?' But the feeling cannot make a false presupposition true, nor can we appeal to some Principle of Sufficient Reason to justify the curiosity-feeling. Even though we can treat the physical universe as "one great big object"—or at least as a great big array—and imagine it not to have existed, still we cannot infer that there must be some explanation of its existence. The required version of PSR is too thoroughly discredited. Nor can we infer that we may ask

---

[17]Cf. Nerlich (1979a), 439: "Physical space [is not] a *set* with points as members, but rather . . . a *whole* with points as parts."

about it *any* of the questions, causal or otherwise, that would be legitimate about its parts.[18] What is true of a part need not be true of the whole.

Clearly, the physical universe *could* "just have happened," with no further explanation, except insofar as this might imply that the universe is brute, gratuitous, absurd, or irrational. We saw in §2.5 how these terms typically presuppose a pejorative contrast between those things that do and those that do not satisfy some norm of rationality. The alleged norm is some version of PSR. But this betrays an erroneous and obsolete conception of rationality. Given an adequate, up-to-date conception, the universe is not absurd or irrational. Nor can PSR be used to inflate the physicalist's inventory of what there is on the ground that there must be something beyond the inventory to explain the existence of something in it, including the universe as a whole.

However, recall the distinction between the manifest universe and the Universe. Unless our present categories in physics are completely adequate, which is unlikely, the two are not the same. So the existence of the manifest universe may have an explanation by reference to the Universe. But even if it does, everything said so far about the universe will still be true, provided merely that we understand it as being about the Universe. Roughly speaking, the Universe is the unknown (or incompletely known) whole about whose parts physics attempts (or ought to attempt) to give us descriptions and explanations that are true and complete. Whether these potentially problematic terms can be made clearer we consider in §3.5.

Meanwhile, even if our notion of the Universe should prove too problematic we can assert the following. Each stage in the development of physics will have its own idea of the physical universe, defined in terms of the spacetime presupposed at that stage plus the list of physical predicates used at that stage. That is, each stage will have its idea of the manifest universe, defined by appropriate reinterpretation of the key terms in MU. But each stage consists of the best physics then available. Thus at each stage the idea of the manifest universe represents our best guess as to what the physical universe is (or what the Universe is, if we can make sufficient sense of the term). So far as the best evidence and arguments are concerned, the manifest universe of that stage *is* the whole of physical existence (or the Universe).

Now suppose I ask an explanation-seeking 'Why does it exist?' about the manifest universe within this currently best physics. Then we must say that my question is based on a false presupposition, so far as

[18]Contrary to Geach, 63.

the best evidence is concerned. For in light of that evidence, there exists nothing outside the manifest universe in terms of which it could have an explanation. And the notion of an 'internal' explanation would be as dubious as ever (§2.2).

Of course I might ask 'Why does the universe exist?' in the heuristic spirit noted toward the end of §2.7. But in this case, as we saw, I assume some responsibility at least to sketch what the new stage of physics might look like, within which the universe of the earlier stage receives some explanation. Otherwise, the 'Why does it exist?' is likely to be idle. Moreover, we have no assurance at all that, at some later stage of physics, what was called the universe at an earlier stage will remain even eligible for explanation (§2.7). The list of categories or the spacetime or both may change too radically. The question 'Why does it exist?' may go the way of 'Why does phlogiston exist?' Or better, it may go the way of 'Why does the universe exist that is composed solely of billiard-ball atoms in a 3-dimensional space enduring through a separate time?' The universe of a crude nineteenth-century materialism neither admits of nor requires any explanation within today's physics, or tomorrow's.

None of this implies that there can be no mystery at all about the universe, manifest or true. Certainly there is mystery aplenty in either case, even if we think only of the mysteries expressible in physics rather than in biology or psychology or some other domain. It is exceedingly unlikely that we yet know which spacetime is the spacetime of the universe, even assuming it to be one of the spacetimes that so far have occurred to us. It is unlikely also that our present list of physical predicates is the last word. And even if we happened to have an adequate list, plus also the correct spacetime, still it is unlikely that the laws so far formulated in terms of them are entirely correct or complete. "This huge world stands before us like a great eternal riddle," as Einstein said. Surrounded as we are by genuine mysteries, why squander the gift of wonder on the fakes?

If the physical universe is the whole of existence, so that there is nothing outside it, then there is nothing outside that could have created it. Since presumably a creator would be something not part of the physical universe, it follows that the physical universe is uncreated. Indeed it is not the *sort* of thing that could have such a creator, according to the physicalist, since by hypothesis every existent is a part of it. Of course, it is conceivable that some ST-part of the universe created the rest. But the word 'create' has strong, unavoidable associations with some sort of intelligent, purposeful agency. In the present context, it should be rejected in favor of the word 'cause', according to the physicalist, and even this word is not without its troubles. But even if a special part of the universe somehow is the cause of the rest, still we cannot conclude that the universe as a whole is caused or created, since in that case the special part would have to be its own cause. The notion of something's being its own cause, literally, is as troubled as the notion of something's existing by the necessity of its own nature. We do better to confess that the universe is uncreated, indeed not the sort of thing that could be created.

3.3. First Cause

> *The modern mind feels not the faintest axiomatic force in principles which trace contingent things back to some necessarily existent source.*
>
> —J. N. FINDLAY

> *There does not seem to be any good ground for supposing that the various causal series in the universe ultimately merge.*
>
> —PAUL EDWARDS

For the physicalist, then, the universe is not explanatorily dependent on anything. May we conclude further that it is explanatorily necessary? Not quite. An explanatorily necessary being was defined as an ultimate explainer, a final explainer ineligible for explanation. The universe is ineligible for explanation, clearly. But is it also an explainer, in particular a final one? That is, does some parade of explanations end with reference to the universe as a whole? If so, then the universe as a whole is an ultimate explainer and thereby explanatorily necessary.

It might seem obvious that there are parades of explanation that end with reference to the universe as a whole. After all, gravitation theory and cosmology are full of talk about the total mass-energy in the universe, and about such boundary conditions as that the universe be closed, and so on.[19] And such talk does play an essential explanatory role.[20] The trouble is that this sort of talk is not necessarily about the universe in the sense we have defined, as the spatio*temporal* sum of all physical entities. Instead, such talk is often about what is technically a spacelike hypersurface,[21] only a *part* of the ST-whole that is the universe. Roughly speaking, talk of the universe in physics frequently is talk about our 3-dimensional *spatial* universe at a given time, often the present. When it is said that the universe is expanding, what is meant is

[19]E.g., Weinberg (1972); Misner, Thorne, and Wheeler, 543, 549, 704, 705, 1181.
[20]Nerlich (1979b).
[21]Cf. Misner, Thorne, and Wheeler, 714f.

roughly that the "radius" of a certain volume increases with time. Clearly this is not to talk directly about the 4-dimensional entity that is the spatiotemporal sum of all the physical existents (assuming that the correct spacetime is 4-dimensional).

Furthermore, even if today's physics should prove to contain a parade of explanations that ends with reference to the universe as a spatiotemporal whole, tomorrow's might not—not only because its concept of the universe might be different from ours but because, even with respect to its own concept, the universe as a whole might play no explanatory role in the parades of explanation that tomorrow's physicists actually present or need.

Can we show nevertheless that there would always be some parade of explanation, even if it is not actually presented or needed by the physicists of the day, which ends with mention of the universe as a whole as it is conceived by the physics of that day? As a first step, recall the slabs in Chaco Canyon. We said that the slabs explain, via their configuration, the pattern of their shadows (relative to an interest only in the pattern). Even though the talk here is overtly of things rather than persons as explainers, the talk is elliptical, we saw, for some longer assertion like 'There is an explanation (for some P at t) of why the shadows have the pattern they do, by reference to the slabs' configuration'. Thus speaking in this way of entities or events as though they explain does not conflict with the context-sensitivity of explanation stressed in §2.6[22]—no more than granting that events and regularities may be what have explanatory significance conflicts with recognizing that explanations can nevertheless provide materials out of which arguments may be constructed (§2.3).

Now if the slabs thus explain the shadows, then so does the whole formed by the slabs plus the sun, as does the whole formed by the slabs plus the sun plus the cliff against which the slabs rest, plus the butte where the cliff is, plus the surrounding canyon rim, plus the rest of the earth, plus the solar system, and so on. Thus given that the slabs explain their shadows, it seems that various wholes of which the slabs are a part will also explain the shadows. That is, given that there is an explanation of why the shadows have the pattern they do by reference to the slabs' configuration, there are also explanations of this by reference to various wholes of which the slabs are a part. We may not be interested in or even aware of those explanations that make reference to ever larger wholes, at least beyond a certain point; nevertheless, the explanations are there should our scope of interest and awareness ever widen.

[22]Nor with Achinstein's arguments against the nonlinguistic view.

Now introduce time into the story. Regard the slabs as 4-dimensional spatiotemporal solids. Their spatial configuration will be an aspect of their spatiotemporal configuration. Thus the shadows continue to be explained by the slabs, now via their spatiotemporal configuration, in conjunction with the sun. Regard the sun too as a 4-D spatiotemporal solid. Just as the spatial whole formed by the slabs plus the sun explains the shadows, so too does the spatiotemporal whole formed by the 4-D slabs plus the 4-D sun, as indeed does the ST-whole formed by the 4-D slabs plus the 4-D sun plus the 4-D cliff plus the 4-D butte, and so on through the solar system and beyond.

Try another example. The disappearance of all life from many lakes in the Adirondacks is explained by increased acid rain, which in turn is explained by increased burning of fossil fuels in the Midwest and elsewhere. Since the acid rain is explained by the burning of fossil fuels, it is also explained by the fuel-burning plus the prevailing winds at the time. That is, it is explained by the whole that consists of the fuel-burning events plus the weather events. It is also explained by the whole formed by this whole plus the earth-sun whole that is responsible for weather, and so on through the solar system and beyond. Again, introducing time and going 4-dimensional would not affect the general idea: if one thing explains another, then so do various wholes of which the first thing is a part.

Notice that when one reaches the solar-system whole in these two examples, if not before, *there are parts of the whole that play no role in explaining the shadows or the acid rain,* if only because causal influences from those parts arrive too late, or are too little, to have any effect. Thus light from Pluto is too weak to influence the shadows, even that light which arrives in time. And since the speed of light is the absolute limit on the velocity of causal signals, no causal influence emitted by Pluto in the next hour can have any effect on the present state of the shadows, or on the acid rain. Thus there are ST-parts of the solar system—those outside certain past light cones—that can have no effect on certain events we explain, such as certain instances of acid rain, or of the shadows of the slabs in Chaco Canyon. Hence *when a thing is explained by reference to some whole, not every part of the whole need play a role in explaining the thing.* Typically, though not always, there will be parts that play no such role.

Such reflections suggest the following general principle of Explanation by Fusion:

> EF. If y explains z (i.e., if there is an explanation of z by reference to y), and if x is any ST-whole of which y is an ST-part, then

there is also an explanation of z—known or unknown, useful or useless given our interests at the time—by reference to x (i.e., x also explains z, though not necessarily in just the sense that y explains z).

It can easily be shown that if the explanation of z by reference to y is justification-affording and hierarchical (§§2.3, 2.5), so is the explanation of z by reference to x. EF can lead to some examples that sound odd but are not. Thus by EF, because the slabs explain the shadows, so does the ST-fusion or whole consisting of the slabs plus the mole on Chairman Mao's chin. The reason this sounds odd is that Chairman Mao's part of this whole contibutes nothing toward explaining the shadows. When we explain something by reference to some whole, ordinarily we do so by reference to some whole *all* of whose parts play an explanatory role. We are not then interested in the other wholes only *some* of whose parts play such a role. But we just saw that when a thing is explained by reference to some whole, not all the parts of that whole need play a role in explaining the thing. Chairman Mao's chin stands to the shadows in about the way Pluto does, despite their differences; influences from it are too little or too late to have any effect on the shadows.

Note also that by EF it can happen that z is itself part of a whole x by reference to which there is an explanation of z. This sounds odd but is not. It sounds odd because it suggests that z plays a role in its own explanation. The resolution of the seeming oddity is as before: when a thing is explained by reference to some whole, not all parts of that whole need play a role in explaining it. In particular, only parts other than z will play a role in explaining z.

In §2.6 we saw how arbitrary and anthropocentric are the ways of explanation. Even where the explanations are to be in terms of efficient causes, which explanation we should prefer depends on how far back in the chain of efficient causes we are interested in going in order to satisfy our wonder. In going back in the chain, we are carving up the world into various wholes, depending on the scope of our interest. EF formulates an important aspect of this connection between explanation and the various wholes we choose to notice or emphasize. Roughly speaking, the farther back we go in the chain of causes, and the more auxiliary explanatory factors we recognize, the wider is the whole that comes to our notice as having explanatory import. EF tells us to expect these further wholes. The widest ST-whole that can come to our notice in this way, or in any way, is the universe, the ST-supremum of all the physical existents.

Since every physical existent y is an ST-part of the universe, it follows by EF that

> EU. If there is an explanation of z by reference to a physical existent y, then there is also an explanation of z, known or unknown, useful or useless, by reference to the universe as a whole.

EU does *not* imply that the parades of explanation actually given or needed in physics are incomplete or otherwise inferior unless they are widened so far as to make reference to the universe. Nor does EU imply that each z has some explanation. Hence it does not imply that *everything* has an explanation (a version of PSR), whether by reference to the universe or by reference to anything else. EU implies only that everything that does have an explanation by reference to a physical existent also has one—known or unknown, useful or useless—by reference to the physical universe as a whole.

EU implies further that the various parades of explanation found in physics *do* merge. The point is not that the parades actually given or needed all end with some reference to the universe; rather, wherever they end, there is always some widening of them that ends by referring to the universe as a whole. Thus the universe is an explainer. Since the universe is ineligible for explanation, it follows that the universe is an ultimate explainer, though again this must not be construed to mean that everything has an explanation by reference to the universe or anything else. It follows also that the universe is an explanatorily or metaphysically necessary being, in the sense of §2.5, contrary to the conventional wisdom that "in a materialist theory there are no necessary beings."[23] Those of its properties that have no explanation by reference to properties of its parts also enjoy this sort of necessity. They are not contingent, nor are they brute, gratuitous, absurd, or irrational. They are metaphysically necessary. From physics to metaphysics is but a step. Can we develop this Aristotelian moral still further?

Traditionally, a first cause is something that is a cause of other things but itself has no cause. Yet the word 'cause' has many meanings. For each such meaning there may or may not be such things as first causes. The attempts to show that there must be first causes have fared so poorly that contemporary philosophers generally conclude that there are no first causes in any relevant sense of the word.[24] But there is one sense of the word for which we may now reverse this verdict. This is the

---

[23]Campbell, 184.
[24]E.g., Edwards (1967b); Munitz, ch. 6; Penelhum; Singh, 392.

sense according to which a cause is an explanatory factor, or an explainer, for short. (For example, instead of asking 'What explains acid rain?' we often ask, equivalently, 'What causes acid rain?' In both cases the answer would be 'increased burning of fossil fuels'.)

Whenever we thus use 'cause' and 'explanation' interchangeably, we are entitled to assert that there are first causes in the sense of ultimate explainers, which explain other things but themselves have no explanation. For we have a proof that there are such, in §§2.3 and 2.5 (also recall yet again that speaking of things as though they are explainers does not conflict with the context-sensitivity of explanation). We may usefully speculate that those philosophers who thought they could prove there must be first causes did so because they were thinking of parades of J-A explanations, in effect, and sensed that such parades must end. It is significant that these philosophers often denied they were using the word 'cause' to mean efficient cause, or to signify temporal priority.

It follows of course that the universe is a first cause. In saying that it is *a* first cause, we are not saying it is *the* First Cause. Traditionally, notions of the First Cause, or of the First Mover, have implied not only uniqueness but also that everything else is causally or explanatorily dependent on this First Cause. The latter claim is (or implies) a version of PSR. Is there some way to reconstruct a notion of the First Cause, safely within the limits of contemporary physicalism, without presupposing some version of PSR?

What is worrisome here are the events, entities, and processes within the universe that have no explanation, known or unknown, either because of quantum indeterminacy, or because they happen to be ultimate explainers, or both. How can we explicate a notion of the First Cause without implying that such events have an explanation after all? By relying once more on the concept of the ST-sum or fusion:

> FC. The First Cause is the ST-sum of all the ultimate explainers plus anything else that has no explanation (even for an infinite intelligence).

In §2.5, in passing, we called ultimate or unexplained explainers the "unmoved movers" of explanation. The metaphor is apt, not least because of its connections with traditional notions of a first cause. Provided we are not misled by the metaphor, we may happily call the First Cause the First or Unmoved Mover.

It just so happens that the First Cause, as defined by FC, is identical with the universe as a whole. The reason is that the universe is both an ultimate explainer and the ST-whole of which everything is a part. It follows that the ST-sum of all the ultimate explainers, which include the universe, is identical with the universe, as is the ST-sum of all the ultimate explainers plus anything else that has no explanation. The reason is that the ST-sum of any x plus the universe is their union (by STS, §3.1); and the union of any x with the universe, which contains everything, is identical with the universe (just as the union of any set A with the universal set V is V).

So the universe for the physicalist not only is uncreated, independent, and an explanatorily or metaphysically necessary being; it is also the First Cause or Unmoved Mover, the sum total of all the events, entities, and processes that explain but have no explanation, plus any that have no explanation and do not explain either. In this sense everything is metaphysically dependent on the universe. The point is not that everything has an explanation by reference to the universe, and is explanatorily or causally dependent on it; rather, everything that has an explanation is explanatorily dependent on the universe, and all other things are parts of the universe that share with it the ultimacy of having no explanation, known or unknown. They therefore share its metaphysical independence. Some of them will also share its necessity; these are the ultimate explainers. Others, if any, will not; these are the unexplained nonexplainers.

Because FC makes essential use of the notion of explanation, the notion of the First Cause inherits much of the anthropocentrism that afflicts explanation. In particular, we cannot attribute an unconditional priority to the First Cause, even if some variety of explanation should happen to correspond with an invariant order in reality. Other ways of mapping existence may well be more important, at least on occasion. To the extent that FC captures what was viable in traditional ideas about the First Cause, it follows that those ideas failed to have the sort of priority their authors often supposed.

The notion of the First Cause presupposes there are such things as ultimate explainers. The argument that there are depends in turn on showing that there cannot be an infinite parade of J-A explanations (§2.3). Thus our argument for the First Cause resembles so-called cosmological or first-cause arguments for the existence of God. One crucial difference is that we have rejected PSR. Another is that first-cause arguments typically try to establish the existence of a being outside the universe. But no such argument can inflate one's ontology, on pain of committing PSR (§3.2); there need be nothing beyond the ontology to explain the existence of things in the ontology. Nevertheless, cosmological arguments of a sort can sometimes be used, as here, to establish of something already in an ontology that it is the First Cause. When they can, cosmology recapitulates ontology, even though it cannot inflate it.

3.4. Eternal Universe

Only space-time entities are invariant and their laws covariant:
one cannot get invariance or covariance by taking space and
time separately. And it is sensible to take invariance and
covariance as a touchstone of reality.

—J. J. C. Smart

Henceforth space by itself and time by itself are doomed to fade
away into mere shadows, and only a kind of union of the two
will preserve an independent reality.

—Hermann Minkowski

The undeniable fact that passage in the sense of transiency of
the now is integral to the common-sense concept of time may
only show that, in this respect, this concept is anthropocentric.

—Adolf Grünbaum

In everyday usage 'eternal' signifies everlastingness. We say, "I'd be eternally grateful," meaning I'd be forever grateful. To say that something is eternal, in this sense, is to say that it is forever, or that there is no time at which it does not exist. *OED* lists a second meaning, which it both calls "metaphysical" and attempts to render as "not conditioned by time." What could this mean? It could mean (i) what is eternal is not subject to change, to becoming, to process, or to corruption and decay; or (ii) the eternal entity is not *in* time, so that its existence cannot be dated as past, present, or future or as before or after some event; or (iii) the entity consequently is not to be described by means of tensed verbs but by means of the tenseless present, as in sentences like 'Seven is a prime number'; or (iv) the entity itself has no aspects or parts distinguished by being transiently past, present, or future or still to come, relative to one another, but rather exists somehow "all at once"; or finally (v) the entity's "duration" is such that the entity neither ceases to exist nor comes into being. In addition, to say that something is "not conditioned by time," or is eternal, could mean *all* these things.

Traditionally, when metaphysicians and theologians have called something eternal, frequently they have indeed meant all of (i)–(v).[25] At any rate there is a family of traditional ideas about eternity, from Parmenides on, at the heart of which one finds (i)–(v). Different philoso-

---

[25]Cf. Kneale (1960), (1967); Stump and Kretzmann.

phers in this multistranded tradition tend to stress different aspects of eternity, sometimes to the point of denying that all of (i)–(v) are necessary for something to be eternal. Nevertheless, (i)–(v) trace the crucial lines of family resemblance. If we should uncover an entity with the properties mentioned in (i)–(v), we would be entitled to call it eternal in the second or metaphysical sense listed by *OED*.

Each of (i)–(v) contributes to the characterization of an eternal entity *negatively*, by denying that the entity has such-and-such temporal properties. The entity is said to be *not* subject to change, *not* in time, *not* describable in a language of tenses, and so on. This negative characterization of what it is to be eternal, which is the best anyone can do, has prompted many to wonder whether we really know what we mean when we call something eternal. For to define something by saying it is not this, not that, not the other, is not really to define it at all. But I do not offer (i)–(v) as a definition of 'eternal' (the term may or may not have a definition in sufficiently positive terms); instead, I offer them as tracing the essential lines of family resemblance among traditional ideas about eternity. When traditional philosophers called something eternal, (i)–(v) were fundamentally what they had in mind. We are merely following their usage of the term if we call an entity eternal that proves to have the negative properties mentioned in (i)–(v). We need not claim in addition that we have a sufficiently positive definition.

Obviously, one's concept of eternity depends heavily on one's ideas about time. This comes of characterizing an eternal entity as something not having such-and-such temporal properties. Traditional concepts of eternity therefore depend on traditional ideas about time; changes in the latter are likely to induce changes in the former. And on few subjects are we so separated from our predecessors as we are on the subject of time. A revolution divides us, begun by Einstein's strange new maps of time, space, and spacetime. We caught a glimpse of some of their radical implications in §1.5(vii), in connection with the concept of objectivity. There we noted what is called the relativity of simultaneity: ordinary simultaneity and ordinary before-and-after are not invariant properties or relations of events. Instead, they are in the eye of the beholder, contrary to common sense and traditional philosophy. This fact alone has profound implications for our ideas about time, as we shall see. All such ideas are affected, all our ideas about change and process, about past, present, and future, about beginnings and endings, and more.

An inevitable result of so fundamental a revolution is that ideas before cannot easily be compared with ideas after. For example, if the spacetime of our universe fails to have certain features—and it might well fail to have them—then the very idea of a beginning (or end) of time cannot even be *defined* for our universe; the traditional question of whether time has a beginning (or end) could not even arise (as we see in the final paragraphs of §3.4.5). On the other hand, if our spacetime does have the required features, then several nonequivalent definitions of a beginning of time are possible. All would be equally good as reconstructions, within spacetime physics, of the traditional concept of a beginning or end of time. There would be no one right way to represent the traditional concept of a first (or last) moment of time.[26] What we thought was one question ("Does time have a beginning or an end?") would be several, not necessarily with the same answer. The mathematics of spacetime as developed since Einstein forces us to draw distinctions that never occurred to our predecessors, indeed could not have occurred to them.

Since our ideas about time can be so fundamentally discontinuous with traditional ideas, how can we be sure our concept of eternity is not also fundamentally discontinuous or incommensurable? How can we be sure that in using the word 'eternal' we are talking about the same thing? We cannot. But traditional philosophers were not all talking about the same thing either, as lately seen. We are justified in saying they were all talking about eternity only because there are sufficiently strong family resemblances among the different things they did talk about. Likewise, if there are sufficiently strong family resemblances between our use of 'eternal' and theirs, we may use the word in good conscience.

In practice, this means that there must in turn be sufficiently strong family resemblances between our uses of the crucial temporal words in (i)–(v) and theirs; for example, when we say of something that it does or does not change or become, we mean, nearly enough, what traditional philosophers meant. So too must we mean what they meant, nearly enough, when we say of something that it is or is not in time; that it can or cannot be dated as past, present, or future or as occurring before or after some event; that it neither ceases to exist nor comes into being; and so on. In this way we remain entitled to use (i)–(v) to characterize an entity as eternal, despite revolutionary changes in the philosophy of time.

In what follows I do not often pause to argue that the required family resemblances are there; mostly, it is sufficiently obvious that they are. Nor do I pause to inquire whether the physicalist's characteristic views about time are entirely justified;[27] I mostly assume, though for

[26]Cf. Earman (1977), 109, 129.

[27]For example, Quine (1960), §§36, 52; D. C. Williams; Smart (1963), 132–142; Smart (1972); Grünbaum (1967a), (1967b); Baker.

the sake of argument, that they are. Given such views, plus some relatively uncontroversial views of others about time and change, it follows that the physical universe is eternal. Let us see why, by seeing why it satisfies each of (i)–(v).

3.4.1. Immutable

As an apple ripens, it changes. It reddens, softens, sweetens. What thus changes is the familiar 3-dimensional apple of common sense, or the 3-apple. To say that the 3-apple changes is to say that it acquires or loses various properties at various times; it is green and sour in the spring, red and sweet in the fall. Such an entity is said to be a continuant, something that persists through time, having various properties—the same or different—at different times. Its dimensions, like those of the 3-apple, are all spatial. It has no temporal dimension. Instead, time is entirely separate, simply a scale in the background by which to rank the continuant's changes and samenesses from earlier to later.

Now consider a 4-dimensional apple. The 4-apple is a solid, the 3-apple extended some months in the time direction as well as some inches spatially. Change in the 3-apple is a matter of different parts of the 4-apple having different properties, in particular those parts that are time-slices of the 4-apple (slices across its time-length at an instant; an instantaneous slice is not itself temporally extended, so it can be construed as 3-dimensional).[28] The earlier time-slices are green, the later time-slices red (or at any rate they have properties responsible for our attribution of these colors; §7.5). This is not something we *mean* when we say the object changes. It is something we *discovered* about objects, time, and change, largely as a result of a revolution in physics.

Why should we construe objects 4-dimensionally? Often we shouldn't (§§5.4, 7.1). When practical action impends, typically we do better to construe them commonsensically as spatial 3-objects that acquire or lose various properties at various moments of a separate time. Our reflexes are probably keyed to some such perception. Thus fussiness over the objectively correct account of change rightly takes a lower priority when we act and speak in our ordinary life-world. But when we are interested in finding the true account, the fussiness is entirely in order. Relative to this interest, the 4-dimensional view inspired by Einstein's theory is clearly superior. The reason, basically, is that the purely spatial properties essential for the 3-object to be a spatial thing in the first place—its length, breadth, depth, and shape—are not invariants (§1.5[vii]). Instead they are properties of projections of the correspond-

---

[28]Cf. Smart (1972), 4.

ing 4-object onto various systems of reference.[29] Thus the purely spatial properties go the way of ordinary simultaneity. By a fine irony the familiar 3-object, so long a paradigm of objectivity, turns out not to be objective enough. What has objective existence is the 4-object, because its essential spatiotemporal properties are invariants, the same for all frames of reference. If we are interested in truth *period,* rather than truth relative to some frame, then we must focus on the 4-object.

Does a 4-apple change? It does only if the whole 4-apple, like the 3-apple, has different properties at different times; for this is what we ordinarily mean by 'change'. But its having different properties at different times would entail that the whole 4-apple exists in a separate time with respect to which the whole 4-apple could be said to have one property at one time, another at another. This additional time would be a fifth dimension, not of the apple but of spacetime. It would be a hypertime.

Spacetime might someday prove (indeed may already have proved) to have five or more dimensions. But at the moment we are assuming for simplicity that it has four. If so, no sense can be made of the idea that the 4-apple changes. The picture of permanence-in-change simply does not apply to the 4-apple. The 4-apple is not a continuant. It is not even the sort of thing that *can* change, unlike the 3-apple. It cannot have various properties at various times, because there is no separate time in which it exists with respect to which it could be said to have one property at one time, another at another. The 4-apple simply has certain properties or does not have them, period.

Since the 4-apple is not a continuant, it is not even the sort of thing that can remain the same. To say that something remains the same, in ordinary parlance, is to say that it is unchanged—that the properties it has at one time are the same as those it has at a later time. Thus something that remains the same is a continuant, even if it is a continuant that happens not to acquire new properties or lose old ones at various times in its history. So the 4-apple is not the sort of thing that can either change or remain the same.

The picture of permanence-in-change is very hard to escape. The reason is that we are so accustomed to viewing everything concrete as a continuant. We acquire the habit in infancy—as we acquire our mother tongue—if we are not born already expecting a world mostly of permanence-in-change. Thus it is very hard to resist thinking of the 4-apple as just another continuant, just another instance of permanence-in-change. Suppose we do not resist. Suppose we insist on thinking of every spa-

---

[29]Cf. Born; Smart (1972), 6–8.

tiotemporal entity as something that can change. Then for every n-dimensional entity x_n, we must imagine that there is a further temporal dimension, $(n+1)$-time, with respect to which the whole entity x_n could be said to have various properties at various times. But if this $(n+1)$-time exists, then there is also an $(n+1)$-dimensional entity x_{n+1} that we must consider, a solid extended in the $(n+1)$-dimension as well as in the n-dimensions. If we now insist that x_{n+1} can change too, obviously we are forced eventually to accept an infinity of further temporal dimensions. We would have not only hypertime but hyper-hypertime, and so on, in a vicious regress. Hence our almost irresistible tendency to view objects as continuants cannot be a good reason for postulating a further time in which they could change. There is only one good reason for doing so, according not only to physicalists but to nearly everyone else. If physics requires a further temporal dimension in order to account for various phenomena, well and good. Otherwise the postulate is superfluous and falls to Occam's razor. In any case, not every spatiotemporal entity is something that can change.

The universe is the spatiotemporal sum of all the physical entities. Therefore, it has the same number of dimensions as the spacetime presupposed by the physics of the day. Again, for simplicity, let us think of the manifest universe as an enormous array that has four dimensions. It is a 4-universe, not a 3-universe enduring through a separate time. Like the 4-apple it is extended in time as well as space. Again like the 4-apple, and for exactly the same reasons, the physical universe is not a continuant, hence not the sort of thing that can either change or remain the same. In other words, it is not subject to change; it is immutable.

If tomorrow's physics were to adopt an n-dimensional spacetime, then its manifest universe would be n-dimensional. There would not be an $(n+1)$-dimension with respect to which the n-universe could be said to have various properties at various times. Thus at each stage of physics the foregoing arguments can be reiterated, so that at each stage the manifest universe as conceived at that stage would not be the sort of thing that could change or remain the same.

To say that the physical universe is not subject to change sounds odd, if only in light of cosmologists' talk of "the expanding universe." But as noted in §3.3, what expands is the 3-universe, roughly speaking, not the 4-universe. Expansion of the 3-universe is a matter of different time-slices of the 4-universe having different radii: the later the slice the larger the radius. If the 3-universe eventually contracts, still later time slices of the 4-universe have smaller radii, and so on. Nor does saying that the universe is not subject to change imply that change does not exist, or that our experiences of change and motion are illusory.

Though not itself subject to change, the universe contains a stupendous amount of change by virtue of containing an enormous number of ST-parts, like the 4-apple, whose different time-slices have different properties.

Since the universe is not the sort of thing that can change, it can hardly be said to be in process. It contains myriad processes, from the ripening of apples to the collapse of stars. It even contains a process we misleadingly call the expansion of the universe, meaning roughly the expansion of the 3-universe. But the 4-universe is not itself *in* process, nor can we say that it *is* a process. For according to the dictionaries, a process is either a phenomenon that shows a more or less continuous change in time or it is a series of such changes.

Change is also presupposed by our ordinary notion (or notions) of becoming. When a caterpillar becomes a butterfly, it changes; it comes to be a butterfly. The universe is no more subject to becoming than to change and process. Nor is it subject to corruption and decay. These too presuppose change. The 3-apple rots if eaten too late, meaning that it becomes brown and mushy. But the 4-apple does not rot. Decay of the 3-apple is a matter of the 4-apple's final time-slices being brown and mushy. And if our 3-universe decays or runs down, then certain time-slices of the 4-universe have corresponding properties. But the 4-universe does not decay or decline. To say so, as we have seen, would bring time into the account twice over.

"If moons decay and suns decline, how else should end this life of mine?" The 3-life that is my 3-body while I live can end in no other way. But what of my 4-life, the 4-object that is my body extended not only spatially but some threescore and ten years in the time direction? Like the 4-apple, it neither declines nor decays. Yet it too is "cut off," both in the biblical sense and in the sense that it has a last time-slice, corresponding with my death, the end of my 3-life. In §3.4.5 we inquire whether the universe has a last time-slice, and whether this would mean that it ceases to exist. We inquire also whether it has a first-time slice, and whether this would mean that it comes into being.

3.4.2. Not in Time

Is the universe in time? Not if saying so entails, as typically it would, that the universe is something that endures through a separate time, acquiring and losing various properties, or even remaining the same. For the universe is not a continuant. Is the universe in time in the sense that its existence can be dated by reference to some event? 4-apples are in time in this sense. Those that correspond with the 3-apples in supermarkets are all located A.D. Some others are located B.C. In temporally locating the existence or occurrence of a 4-object, we choose some event *outside* it and inquire whether the object is located before, after, or simultaneous with that event. If we tried to locate the occurrence of a 4-apple by reference to some event contained within it—an event that is thus a part of it—the best we could do would be to locate the occurrences of its *parts* relative to the event. We could not locate the occurrence of the *whole* 4-apple relative to the internal event. One of its parts would be the event, by hypothesis, and hence trivially simultaneous with it. But its other parts would occur before, after, or simultaneous with the event. The special case in which the event is the whole 4-apple would give us a totally uninformative date: the 4-apple would be simultaneous with itself. So the whole 4-apple would be located neither before nor after the event, nor simultaneous with it (except in the totally uninformative case in which the event is the 4-apple itself).

Is there some event outside the universe with respect to which we could temporally locate it? Obviously not. The universe, by definition, is the ST-sum or supremum of all events. So it cannot be in time in this sense. The question 'When is the universe?' is every bit as defective as 'Where is the universe?'

In what other sense could the universe be said to be in time? Occasionally, to say of something that it is in time is to imply it has an end (or beginning) such that there are other things that go on after its end (or before its beginning), as when we contrast our fleeting lives with "the everlasting hills." Whether the universe has an end or a beginning, and in what sense, is not at all clear (as we see in §3.4.5). But even if it does, there can be no other things that go on after its end or before its beginning. For there are no other things. The universe, by definition, includes them all.

Finally, to say of something that it is in time could mean that it has parts distinguished by being transiently past, present, or future relative to one another; or that it comes into being and/or ceases to exist. These meanings are treated in §§3.4.4 and 3.4.5. The universe will prove not to be in time in these senses either.

3.4.3. Tenseless

If we say that the solution to '$x + 5 = 12$' exists, we do not mean anything that could be countered by the reply, "That was yesterday." Our use of the verb 'exists' is tenseless. Tenseless verbs allow us to construct eternal sentences. The sentence 'Seven exists', like the sentence 'Seven is a prime number', is an eternal sentence. The truth-value of its tokens does not vary with the time of utterance. By contrast, if numbers had datable existence, the truth-value presumably would vary for sentences like 'Seven existed', 'Seven will exist', and 'Seven now exists'. These sentences sound odd precisely because they contain tensed verbs, whereas numbers are not the sorts of things whose existence is datable. Seven either exists or it does not. If it exists, it does not exist in the past, present, or future or before or after the event that is our utterance of 'Seven exists'.

So too for the universe. If we utter 'The universe exists', meaning that it now exists, we are presupposing that the universe exists as a whole simultaneously with the event of our utterance. That event, like all events, is a part of the universe. But we lately noted that in dating the existence or occurrence of something, we must do so with respect to an event that is not part of it. Therefore, tensed uses of 'exist' about the universe are out of order. The universe neither *was* nor *will be* nor *is now*. It *is*.

Nor can we use tensed verbs to ascribe properties to the universe. Either it has the property or it does not. For to say that the universe had, will have, or now has the property entails that it has the property at some time, and that it might not have it at some other time. But this entails that the universe is the sort of thing that could change, contrary to our reflections in §3.4.1. The universe is to be described not by means of tensed verbs but by means of the tenseless present we use in sentences like 'Seven is a prime number' and in eternal sentences generally. Clearly, this is not to say that the universe is like a number in other respects. Nor does any of this imply that tensed discourse is always eliminable or reducible, or that it never enjoys priority over the tenseless. Indeed the opposite often happens, as we see toward the end of §5.4.

3.4.4. Existing "All at Once"

Does the universe have parts distinguished by being transiently past, present, future, or still to come, relative to one another? Much depends on what these terms mean. When traditional philosophers, plus some others, deny that an eternal entity has parts still to come, they are mainly concerned to distinguish the sort of changeless "duration" it enjoys from the duration of changing things in our normal experience, which at one time are in the future but become present and fade into the past. ("Real duration gnaws on things, and leaves on them the mark of its tooth.")[30] In this sort of view, ordinary things are victims of a temporal becoming that is not merely a matter of their occurring (tenselessly) before or after some event (or at various clock times). In addition, they are subject to temporal becoming, being transiently future,

---

[30]Bergson, 48.

present, past. They are supposed to have successively the temporal properties of futurity, nowness, and pastness.

If we are interested in truth *period,* rather than truth relative to some point of view or frame of reference, then the relevant things or parts of the universe for us to consider here are the 4-objects (as in §3.4.1). The 4-objects, we saw, cannot change. Rather, change is a matter of their different time-slices having (tenselessly) different properties. *If* a whole 4-object could successively acquire the temporal properties of futurity, nowness, and pastness, then (assuming these are indeed properties) it could change. At one time, relative to some ongoing now, it would be future; at a later time, past. Since the 4-object does not change, it cannot be subject to such temporal becoming. *In this sense,* the universe, if it is to be split objectively into parts, has no such parts still to come, or past, present, or future relative to one another.

Even if the temporal properties are not really properties of the object after all, still the object cannot be said objectively to be past, present, or future in the ordinary sense. The reason is that the occurrence of an object or event at present, or now, is not an objective or invariant matter.[31] Suppose I say, "The space shuttle is landing now." If what I say is true, the shuttle is landing at that very moment—the moment at which I utter 'The space shuttle is landing now'.[32] That is, the landing occurs simultaneously with my utterance. But because of the relativity of simultaneity, the landing is simultaneous with my utterance with respect to some frames of reference (including my own) but not with respect to all. Thus suppose I am in New York, whereas the landing is in California. To some observers moving very fast relative to my frame, the landing would occur before my utterance; to some others, after.

Clearly, 'future' and 'past', in normal usage, are no more objective than 'now'. With respect to them all, we have to ask *who?* That is, we have to ask *whose* future? *whose* past? *whose* now? Depending on whose it is, one and the same event or other ST-part of the universe might or might not be still to come relative to another, and might or might not occur now. There is no such thing, objectively speaking, as the state of the universe *now,* and no such thing as an objective, ongoing now with respect to which events could be past, present, or future.[33]

There is a technical sense in which one event can be said to occur before or after another. Thus x occurs absolutely before y, or is in y's absolute past, iff x lies either within or on y's backward light cone (the

[31]Cf. Baker.

[32]Not that this is an *analysis* of 'now'. Cf. Sosa (1979), 30–36.

[33]Contrary to McCall, who gives insufficient reason for rejecting frame-invariance as a criterion of objective existence.

set of ST-points from which a light ray could reach y). And x occurs absolutely after y, or is in y's absolute future, iff x lies either within or on y's forward light cone (the set of ST-points that a light ray could reach from y).[34] If x lies outside both light cones, it cannot be compared with y as absolutely before or after. It is absolutely elsewhere. It can be made to look either earlier or later than y, depending on what reference frame is chosen. It is certainly not objectively present or simultaneous with y in any ordinary sense.

This last fact alone shows that the objective, technical notions of before/after and past/future are distinct from the commonsense notions that traditional philosophers have in mind when they speak of parts that are past, present, or future relative to one another. According to common sense, an event that is neither past nor future must be present; and an event that occurs neither before nor after another must be simultaneous with it. Thus even though some events and objects in the universe occur absolutely before (after) some others and are in the absolute past (future) of some others, it hardly follows that they are past, present, or future relative to one another in the sense or senses meant by common sense and traditional philosophy. Moreover, being successively future, present, and past in this ordinary sense entails, as we saw, that the objects change or could change and/or that they are subject to temporal becoming, a sort of passage or succession of moments that spells transience for the objects. But the absolute temporal relations just defined entail no such thing.

The duration of the universe and its 4-objects, if 'duration' is the right word, is such that their parts are not still to come relative to some ongoing now, or transiently past, present, or future relative to one another. The universe and its 4-parts neither were nor will be nor are now. They are, they exist, in the tenseless sense that is so foreign to our ordinary life-world. It is foreign also to the belief that only those things exist that are present, a belief held by Augustine, for example, according to whom "the past no longer exists, and the future is not yet in being."

3.4.5. Without Beginning or End

Will the universe cease to exist? Did it come into being? Does it have a beginning or end, in the sense of a first or last time-slice? The crucial insight here is that even if the universe should prove to have a first or last time-slice—a very big IF, as we shall see—nothing follows as to whether it comes into being or ceases to exist.

Of course, the phrases 'comes into being' and 'ceases to exist' might

[34]Cf. Taylor and Wheeler, 36–40.

have meant nothing more than "has a first (last) time-slice." But ordinarily they mean something very different. Traditionally and commonsensically, they mean "once did not exist and later did" and "once existed then did not." Besides using tenses, these phrases inject the notion of *dated* existence—existence before or after some event—into the ideas of coming into being and of ceasing to exist. But the universe, as we saw in §3.4.2, is not the sort of thing whose existence has a date. Its first time-slice, if it has one, might be located n billion years B.C. Certain other time-slices are located A.D. The familiar difficulty now recurs: some parts are located before, others after the dating event, but when does the *whole* exist?

Someone might object that the appropriate question here is *not* 'When does the whole exist?' but 'When does the whole *begin* to exist?' The latter question presupposes that before a certain time the whole universe does not exist, then later it begins to exist. Presumably, the time before which the whole does not exist would be the date of its first time-slice (assuming there is a first), some n billion years B.C. This would also be the date at which the whole "begins to exist," if we can make sense of this phrase as applied to the universe.

What could it mean to say that the ST-whole which is the universe begins to exist? Suppose it means that before n billion B.C. the whole does not exist, whereas at that date and for some time after, the whole does exist. Unfortunately, of course, this would again require us to date the existence of the universe as a whole. We could say that one part of the universe—its first time-slice—is located n billion B.C., and the remaining parts are later. But what about the whole? Is it located n billion B.C., or later? Neither answer makes sense. As so often happens, we encounter here a question about parts that makes no sense for the whole. Moreover, it is problematic as to whether the question makes sense even for the parts, as we soon see.

What else could it mean to say that the universe begins to exist at a certain date? If it meant only that its first time-slice is located at that date, we would not be forced into the absurdity of trying to date the whole of which the first time-slice is but a part. But normally it means much more. For *we are accustomed to speaking of temporal beginnings and endings in connection with entities we conceive of as existing in a 3-space which itself persists through a separate time.* Thus the anthropocentrism of the space-plus-separate-time view infects nearly all our talk of beginnings and endings.

In particular, we ordinarily infer that an entity begins (ceases) to exist from the mere fact that, like the 3-apple, it is bounded in the past (future) time direction, meaning roughly that it is finitely old (young).

But we do not infer that it begins (ceases) to exist from the fact that it is bounded spatially. Otherwise, we would have to say that the 3-apple, which is bounded in all three spatial directions, ceases to exist just as soon as it begins.

If we take the 4-dimensional view of spacetime seriously, and refrain from invidious, anthropocentric distinctions among the four directions in which 4-objects are extended, we can no more infer that the 4-object begins (ceases) to exist from the fact that it is bounded in the temporal direction than we can from the fact that it is bounded in the three space directions.[35] Its having a first and a last time-slice is no more significant in this respect than its having outermost space-slices (for example, the skin of the 3-apple at its largest). The 3-objects in a 3-space are not said to begin or cease just because they are spatially bounded in one or more of the three directions. This is true even if the spatial extent of the object happens to coincide with that of the space itself. Likewise, the 4-objects in the 4-space that is spacetime cannot be said to begin or cease just because they are spatiotemporally bounded in one or more of the four directions. This is true even if the spatiotemporal extent of the 4-object should happen to coincide with that of the spacetime itself.

The reason we *can* say of the 3-objects that *they* begin to exist, or cease, is that we think of the 3-space which contains them as *itself* a continuant, persisting through a separate time. At one time the 3-space contains certain 3-objects; at a later time it contains others (not excluding objects whose spatial extent coincides with that of the space itself). Thus at various times various 3-objects come into existence in the enduring 3-space and subsequently disappear, like bubbles in beer. That is, they begin to exist, then cease. Our ordinary talk of beginning and ending implies that space is a continuant.

The 4-space that is spacetime is not a continuant. There is no separate time, hence none through which it could endure. It follows that we cannot sensibly say that at one time the 4-space contains certain 4-objects and at a later time others, including objects (if any) whose spatiotemporal extent coincides with that of spacetime. We are therefore prevented from saying that at various times various 4-objects bubble into existence in the enduring 4-space and subsequently cease to exist. They neither begin to exist nor cease. They are, they exist, tenselessly, at various ST-locations or regions in the spacetime. Clearly, then, even if the universe—meaning the 4-universe—happens to have a first or a last time-slice, we cannot infer that it begins to exist or ceases, or that it

[35]Cf. Smart (1972).

comes into being or passes away. On the contrary, we are prevented from saying that the 4-universe begins to exist or ceases (unless this means only that it has a first or a last time-slice).

We have been assuming for simplicity that spacetime has four dimensions. Nothing crucial depends on this assumption. The foregoing argument works for n dimensions as well as for four. An n-universe, whose spacetime is n-dimensional, would neither begin to exist nor cease, even if it had a first or a last time-slice. At each stage of physics, the manifest universe as conceived at that stage would not be the sort of thing that comes into being or ceases to exist.

Does the universe have a first or a last time-slice ? No one knows. The evidence and the theories presently available to physical cosmologists are inconclusive. Even if big-bang theories should happen to remain the best accounts of the evolution of the 3-universe, they cannot tell us by themselves whether the big bang was a true beginning—the first time-slice of the 4-universe—or whether it was preceded by an earlier contraction. Part of the problem is that quantum theory evidently is required to tell us more about the superdense state at or immediately preceding the explosion. Gravitation theory tells us only so much. No synthesis of the two theories yet exists that is adequate to the job, though there has been some progress.

Nor is it likely that our present concepts of spacetime would remain unaffected by a synthesis of theories at so fundamental a level. Spacetime might fail to have certain properties we presently take for granted, among them some properties that are presupposed by the very idea of a first or a last time-slice. That is, in defining the idea, one must assume that spacetime has certain properties. If it does not, the question whether the universe has a first or a last time-slice cannot even arise.[36] Still other properties presupposed by the very idea of a beginning or end might someday be rejected because of developments in physics outside quantum theory.

What are some of the properties a spacetime must have in order for the very notion of a first or a last time-slice to be meaningful? Brevity requires some technical terminology not fully explained here, though the general ideas will be clear enough.[37] To begin with, the spacetime S must be time-orientable (roughly speaking, at no ST-point of S can we transform a forward into a backward light cone by means of a continu-

[36]Cf. Earman (1977).
[37]With regard to this and the next three paragraphs, cf. Earman (1977), and Hawking and Ellis.

ous transformation that always keeps timelike intervals timelike). If S is not time-orientable, then the very notion of forward-direction-of-time-at-a-point cannot be defined for S. (There is a spacetime involved in one kind of solution to Einstein's gravitational equations that is not time-orientable—namely, the elliptic interpretation of de Sitter spacetime.) The definition of 'time-orientable' presupposes in turn that S is a manifold, and that S is differentiable, compact, and of a certain topology.

Not only must S be time-orientable; it must have a global time order, meaning that it contains no closed future-directed timelike curves. If S does not have a global time order, then neither does it have a global time function t such that the real number $t(x)$ assigned by t to the ST-point x is less than $t(y)$ whenever there is a nonzero timelike or lightlike curve from x to y. And if S does not have a global time function, then S has no time-slices either. For a time-slice of S is defined as a set of ST-points x in S such that $t(x)$ is a constant: a particular real number. (Gödel spacetime, which is involved in another kind of solution to Einstein's equation, contains no time-slices.)

If for any of the above reasons S has no time-slices, then of course they cannot be dated. Talk of their occurring n billion B.C. or A.D. would make no sense. So the question 'When is it located?', which we saw makes no sense for the universe, would not in general make sense for its parts either, should the spacetime of the universe fail to have one or more of the presupposed properties listed above. And of course, if S has no time-slices, then we cannot ask whether there is a first one or a last. Because of certain global features of S, concepts definable on the local scale may not be definable on the cosmological.

Is there a beginning or an end of time? It is natural to suppose that the existence of a first or a last time-slice would correspond with the beginning or end of time. Curiously, it need not. The reason, basically, is that even if a spacetime S has a first or last time-slice, S might still contain timelike curves that are unbounded in the future or past direction (i.e., timelike curves such that proper length as measured along them from a certain point assumes arbitrarily large values). If so, time would be without end (beginning), even though S has a last (first) time-slice. Even if the existence of a first (last) time-slice should happen after all to correspond with the beginning (end) of time, still the concept of a beginning (end) of time can be defined only if S has at least the global features listed above. If it does not happen to correspond, the problems involved in defining 'beginning (end) of time' are even more complex than those involved in defining 'first (last) time-slice'. For there are several equally good but nonequivalent ways of defining or representing, within the general theory of relativity, the traditional notion (or notions) of a first or a last moment of time. But even if there were just one right way of doing so, and even if there were a first or a last moment of time, still the ST-whole that is the universe would neither come into being nor cease to exist, for the reasons lately given.

Thus all of (i)–(v) apply to the universe: (i) it is immutable, since it is not subject to change, to becoming, to process, or to corruption and decay; (ii) it is not in time in relevant senses, so that its existence cannot be dated as past, present, or future or as before or after some event; (iii) it is not to be described by means of tensed verbs; (iv) it exists "all at once," having no parts distinguished by being transiently past, present, or future or still to come, relative to one another; and (v) its "duration" is such that it neither ceases to exist nor comes into being. It follows that the universe is eternal. It follows also that those philosophers and theologians are wrong who believe that according to contemporary naturalism generally, and to physicalism in particular, "all is becoming, all is changing, all is in passage out of the past and into the future, and so all causes and effects come and go—and all is mortal—and nothing else is real."[38]

In light of characteristically physicalist assumptions, we have learned so far that at each stage of physics the manifest universe according to that stage must be construed as uncreated (§3.2), as explanatorily independent (§3.2), as metaphysically necessary (§3.3), and as the First Cause or Unmoved Mover on which everything is metaphysically dependent (§3.3). In addition, the manifest universe is eternal in that metaphysical sense which is contrasted with everlastingness. It exists all at once, in the classical phrase, except insofar as this implies that the universe might be the sort of thing the whole of which could exist at a moment.

Given these properties, we may now add that the universe is self-existent, in the traditional sense of a being at once eternal and not dependent for its existence on anything else. A surprising amount of traditional theism can therefore be reconstructed within an apparently hostile physicalism. As remarked at the outset, no one should now say, with respect to the eternal, immutable, necessary being, "and this all people call God." But we should at least begin to wonder whether theism is totally excised after all by the physicalist's razor, and whether the remaining features of at least some theisms may be reconciled with an austere physicalism, contrary perhaps to all expectation.

[38]Gilkey (1969), 54, who expresses the idea in order to reject it.

3.5. The Universe beyond the Universe

> *The game of science is, in principle, without end. He who*
> *decides some day that scientific statements do not call for any*
> *further test, and that they can be regarded as finally verified,*
> *retires from the game.*
>
>   —K. R. POPPER

> *In giving up dependence on the concept of an uninterpreted*
> *reality, something outside all [conceptual] schemes and science,*
> *we do not relinquish the notion of objective truth—quite the*
> *contrary.*
>
>   —DONALD DAVIDSON

'Beyond' expresses a spatial metaphor, or perhaps spatiotemporal. There is nothing literally beyond the universe, since by definition it is the ST-sum or supremum of everything. More precisely, it is the ST-sum or supremum of everything that is either a physical entity of a listed kind or an ST-sum of such entities (§3.1.2). This is the manifest physical universe. We can define no other. Any such definition, we saw, must be based on a list of predicates from contemporary physics, and on a contemporary theory of spacetime. Otherwise, the definition is either obsolete or too vague.

We can easily imagine changes in the list, or in the theory of spacetime, or in both. Indeed changes are inevitable, certainly at today's stage of the unending game of science. Thus "beyond" the manifest universe of today's physics there lies tomorrow's. Just how tomorrow's physics will differ from today's, with respect to its list of predicates and its spacetime, we cannot predict. Probably we can have a good approximate idea of what the list and the spacetime will look like for the next five years; beyond that point we are reduced largely to guessing.

For similar reasons we can only guess at the relations between the manifest universe, as conceived at the present stage of physics, and the manifest universe as conceived at a later stage. We do not know how many of the predicates on today's list will still be presumed true of any entities: whether, for example, many or all of them will go the way of the predicate 'is a luminiferous ether'. We do not know whether the spacetime presupposed at the earlier stage will be thought entirely wrong or approximately correct, nor do we even know just what 'approximation' would mean here.

Hence we do not know whether we can now give any positive description of the manifest universe as it may be conceived at a later stage—say, a millennium hence. For we do not know which of our positive predicates—if any—are true of the manifest universe as conceived a millennium hence. Is it 4- or 5- or 11-dimensional? Is its space-time a manifold? differentiable? temporally orientable? Does it have a Lorentzian metric? a global time order? time-slices? causal signals faster than light? Does it satisfy Einstein's equations? quantum theory? Does it contain what *we* mean by 'mass-energy'? Does it contain what we mean by 'fields'?

We should not go so far as to assert that the manifest universe according to physics a millennium hence would *not* satisfy any of our present positive predicates; we should not assert that we may at least describe it negatively, as not 4-dimensional, not temporally orientable, not general-relativistic, and so on. For we do not know that it would be none of these things. Nevertheless, in a fundamental sense we are reduced to a *via negativa*: we are not entitled to ascribe any positive predicate, drawn from our present list, to the manifest universe as it would be conceived a millennium hence. Nothing positive is known about it, even if nothing negative is known about it either. To this extent it is wrapped in mystery.

Are physicalists committed to the existence of such a universe beyond the universe, with respect to which we must refrain from positive predication? To begin with, physicalists are not instrumentalists. Physical theories are not merely convenient tools for predicting and calculating; they also describe and are true or false. If true, the entities they mention exist and are not merely convenient fictions. The physicalist, by definition, is someone who believes that such entities exist (and no others, save their ST-sums). More precisely, physicalists believe that at any given time we are entitled only to whatever inventory of entities the current best evidence in physics requires. They recognize that the evidence continually changes, that it always has and therefore is likely to do so at least for some time to come, and that consequently our best estimates as to which theories are true must change too—plus, inevitably, the list of predicates—as we successively replace theories with others deemed simpler, more comprehensive, and less at odds with the evidence.

Physicalists, then, by virtue of their realist commitment to the truth-or-falsity of physical theories, as well as to the pursuit of such truth in physics as humans can find, are committed to the ongoing trial by prerequisites at the heart of truth-seeking in every domain, and at the heart therefore of the unending game of science. Granted, some physicalists occasionally speak as though the latest stage of physics were the last word. Usually such talk is just rhetorical excess. In any case, it is incompatible with their own prior commitment to physics as a means of seeking truth, and with their own recognition that many of our present theories and predicates are no more likely to survive trial by prerequisites than our predecessors'.

The physicalist therefore is committed to a universe beyond the universe, meaning that today's definition of the phrase 'the manifest universe' is likely to be distinct from the definition that would be given a millennium hence. For despite the fact that the two definitions would fit the same form MU (§3.1.2), still the list of predicates plus the presupposed theory of spacetime would likely be different. And since we cannot predict the ways in which they would differ, so that we do not know which of our positive predicates, if any, are true of the universe as defined a millennium hence, it follows that the physicalist must refrain from ascribing to it any positive predicates on the list of predicates drawn from today's physics.

So far, nothing has been said in this section about the true physical universe, or the Universe. Intuitively, the Universe is the unknown (or incompletely known) whole about whose parts physics attempts (or ought to attempt) to give us descriptions and explanations that are true and complete. There is not much one can do to make this intuitive idea more specific. Even though the whole it speaks of is a spatiotemporal whole, no one yet knows which spacetime is involved, or even whether it is any of the spacetimes that so far have occurred to us. Hence we do not know specifically what we mean when we speak of the whole that is the Universe, or of its parts, which physics attempts to describe and explain, since the definition of a whole requires that a spacetime be specified (§3.1).

Even if we knew which spacetime to use, still we would not know which of the many possible ST-wholes or sums we mean when we talk of the Universe. Granted, the Universe would be the ST-sum of all the "physical existents." But what, in this context, could that mean? A physical existent, by PE in §3.1.1, is the ST-sum of certain listed physical entities. Which list should be used, when we are talking about the true universe? We do not know, unless we know that it is today's list. Surely we do not.

Suppose we took the following line. The list to use is the one used by the physics that would give the true and complete account. But then we must ask, "The true and complete account of *what?*" The Universe? The physical existents or phenomena? Either answer lands us in circularity, if we are looking for a definition of the Universe, or for some characterization more specific than the intuitive one above. Circularity aside, there are severe problems about what completeness means here— the completeness of physical descriptions and explanations. For we need to ask, "Complete with respect to what aim?" Relative to one sort of aim or interest, physics might someday be complete; relative to another, it might not.

Worse still, the spacetime S of the Universe might be such that it is observationally indistinguishable (OI) from a distinct spacetime $S*$.[39] Roughly speaking, to say that S and $S*$ are OI is to say that for every ST-point x in S there is an ST-point x' in $S*$ such that the region of S which can possibly be observed from x is ("spacetime-wise") identical with the region of $S*$ which can possibly be observed from x'. It can be shown that if S and $S*$ are OI, and if S has a global time function (§3.4.5), then $S*$ need not have one. Other global features $S*$ need not have, even when S does have them, include temporal orientability, compactness, inextendibility, possession of no closed timelike curves, and certain (other) causal and/or deterministic features.

Why worry about observational indistinguishability? Because physics might never be able to ascertain the spacetime of the Universe, even in light of all the possible observations (meaning all the observations from each point in spacetime). And there are other, more familiar ways in which theories in physics might well be underdetermined by all possible observational evidence (as Quine has long emphasized).[40] So we can ill afford to characterize the Universe by reference to what physics might someday achieve, even should physics be practiced ideally and forever. In like manner we can ill afford to define truth as what science would achieve if practiced ideally and forever, even aside from objections on the score of violating neutrality among the domains of discourse.

For all these reasons, then, we must make do with the intuitive idea of the true physical universe, or the Universe, as the unknown (or incompletely known) whole about whose parts physics attempts (or ought to attempt) to give us descriptions and explanations that are true and complete (relative to some generally accepted aim or aims).

Suppose that physicists a millennium hence are lucky, and the manifest physical universe, as they conceive it, indeed happens to be the Universe. The very possibility shows that the Universe is not to be thought of as some completely uninterpreted reality, a thing-in-itself outside all conceptual schemes, physics included. Rather it stands to us roughly as the elephant stands to the blind men of the story (§1.5[vii]). Our groping and probing give us a revisable stock of predicates and hypotheses, either true so far as we can presently tell or at least not yet eliminated in the ongoing trial by prerequisites. From these predicates

---

[39]Cf. Glymour (1977); Malament.
[40]But see M. Wilson.

and hypotheses we then project a whole elephantine universe—a manifest universe that represents our current best guess as to the specific character of the Universe. Like the blind men, we believe that our predicates and hypotheses, though revisable, are somehow prompted in part by a reality that our instruments touch here and there. We believe that the Universe is a causal factor in our adopting certain predicates and hypotheses, and in our rejecting them eventually in favor of still others. The Universe has a say in the ongoing trial by prerequisites. It is not completely uninterpreted, or "ineffable."

Physicalists, then, by virtue of their prior commitment to objective truth, are committed to a true physical universe beyond the manifest universe as conceived by today's physics. Physics may or may not someday reach a stage at which the manifest physical universe, as conceived at that stage, is the Universe. Even if it reaches it, there may then and forever be no way of knowing for certain that it has done so. Hence there is mystery aplenty about this universe beyond, with respect to which we must refrain from positive predication. We *can* say of the universe beyond that it is eternal, but only because 'eternal' is characterized negatively, by denying certain temporal properties (§3.4). By the same token, we can say that it is immutable, uncreated, independent, necessary, and the self-existent First Cause. If for some reason we must reject all talk of some such true universe beyond the universe, then at each stage of physics, nevertheless, the manifest universe as conceived at that stage is eternal, immutable, independent, necessary, and the self-existent First Cause.

If these properties seem fusty, it is largely because modern science and philosophy are widely supposed to have buried them. We now see how a proper use of scientific philosophy would exhume them. There may be no other way, or at least no better way, to resurrect these ideas, which perennially display their power over us to fascinate and console.

4 Nonreductive Physicalism

How do you go about reducing Constable's or James Joyce's world-view to physics?

—Nelson Goodman

Anti-reductionist arguments are irrelevant to the truth of physicalism.

—G.P. Hellman and F. W. Thompson

4.0. Introduction

The time has come to replace the rough idea of physicalism we have so far relied on with something more precise. The rough idea is that only the basic entities and processes of mathematical physics exist, plus their complex combinations—often wholly novel—into stars, planets, life, consciousness, and more. Nothing at these higher levels can occur without some corresponding occurrence at the level of physics—not the flicker of an emotion, not a stir in the womb. And the truths at the higher levels are in some sense determined by or manifestations of truths at the level of physics. All that we are and all that we can hope to be we owe to the dispositions of the basic physical existents.[1]

This rough idea sufficed so long as we concentrated on the status of the physical universe as a whole. We could ignore problems about what sort of relation is supposed to obtain between the physical entities, as defined by PE in §3.1.1, and organisms, sentience, intentions, values, and the rest. But physicalism claims to be a kind of unified theory or synthesis of all the diverse sciences, and indeed of all the domains of truth in or out of the sciences. Physicalism thus claims to provide the

---

[1]Cf. Quine (1976), 228.

new, unified picture of existence that should replace the largely medieval one shattered piecemeal by successive discoveries in the sciences. So we must inquire into the techniques of this alleged unification.

Until recently, physicalists and others generally assumed that the key relation, if physicalism were to succeed, must be one of reduction. Physical reduction, in the sense relevant here, occurs when terms from another domain are defined solely by terms from physics. Different views as to the variety of definition admissible for this purpose give rise to different varieties of reduction. The strongest variety requires that the two terms—one nonphysical, the other from physics—be fully synonymous, or at least "translatable" one into the other without significant loss of meaning. The weakest requires only that they be coextensive. Somewhere between is a coextensiveness that is not accidental but entailed by the laws of science, hence a lawlike coextensiveness. And there are still other varieties of reduction weaker than synonymy but stronger than accidental coextensiveness.

In some cases a variety of reduction does succeed. Thus the absolute temperature of a gas is identical with the mean kinetic energy of its molecules; the two terms are lawlike coextensive, thanks to the kinetic theory of gases. And thanks to ongoing discoveries about DNA and RNA, a few terms from Mendelian genetics (some structural terms, like 'heterozygous') are coextensive with certain terms from molecular biology, though perhaps not (yet) lawlike coextensive.[2] A few more terms from Mendelian genetics might be reduced to those of molecular biology if Mendelian genetics were to be suitably modified.[3] Indeed it often happens that a theory must be modified if reduction of its terms is to succeed; what is loosely called reduction of that theory's terms to those of another is really reduction of the modified theory's terms.

In many cases, notoriously, reduction either has been shown to fail or has not been shown to succeed to the satisfaction even of many physicalists. Talk about persons, intentions, consciousness, and the functional states of organisms, for example, seems especially resistant to reduction even of the weakest kind, whereby the terms need only be accidentally coextensive with certain terms from neurophysiology and eventually from physics.

There is no need to review here the obstacles encountered by the reductionist enterprise. They are numerous, severe, and vigorously expressed by many authors, including a growing number of physicalists.[4]

[2]Cf. Kimbrough.
[3]Cf. Hull, ch. 1.
[4]For analytical surveys of the major problems with reductionism, see Margolis (1984), chs. 2 and 4; Boyd (1980); Block.

Perhaps the most insurmountable obstacle is that certain functional states and intentional states seem not to be identifiable with any particular physical states, and not even with finite sets of alternative physical states. One and the same functional or intentional state can be realized or embodied in an indefinite variety of distinct physical systems, perhaps even in an indefinite variety of physically specifiable states of the same physical system. Functional and intentional states are defined without regard to their physical or other realizations.[5]

The idea that physicalism does not after all entail reductionism is not especially new and by now may even be widely accepted. Yet a number of recent sketches of nonreductive physicalism are mute on the following urgent questions. If no variety of reduction need obtain, what then *is* the relation between the physical phenomena and the nonphysical? How *are* the terms and truths in other domains related to the terms and truths in physics, if not by at least accidental coextensiveness? How can physicalists bring off their attempt to unify all the domains, in or out of the sciences? In what sense are the truths in the higher domains—biology, psychology, history, and so on—determined by or manifestations of truths at the level of physics, if not via some sort of reduction? How can it be that nothing occurs at these higher levels without some occurrence at the level of physics, so that there is "no difference without a physical difference"?[6]

Answers to these challenges appear below in the sections on the physicalist's minimal theses, the weakest that one could accept and remain a physicalist. In slogan form, the minimal principles are: (i) "Everything is physical" (§4.1); (ii) "No difference without a physical difference" (§4.2); (iii) "All truth is determined by physical truth" (§4.3), and, if not already implicit in these three, a realism of the sort explained in §1.1. The realism would be implied if, for example, the kind of systematic unity that (i)–(iii) presuppose requires our physical theories to be true, not merely empirically adequate, as seems likely.[7] The challenges are met in the sense of explaining what the minimal principles are by which physicalists believe they can relate the other domains to mathematical physics and thereby achieve their kind of unification.

Of course, merely explaining what the minimal principles are is not directly to argue for their truth. It is simply to give some clear idea of what they are and how they function, and thereby to answer the com-

---

[5]An argument for combining functionalism with a variety of reductionism (namely, type-type identities) appears in Jackson, Pargetter, and Prior. See also Richardson, but esp. Lycan (1981).

[6]Quine (1978b), 162–163, 166.

[7]Cf. Friedman (1979), 280.

plaint that "in the literature it is possible to find at least a half dozen accounts of what [physicalism] is, no pair of which is equivalent and all of which are desperately obscure."[8] The principles to be explained are modifications of those due originally to Hellman and Thompson,[9] but they prove equivalent, nearly enough, to some of the notions of "supervenience" subsequently developed by others.[10] Eventually, someone might develop minimal physicalist principles that are preferable. If so, suitable revisions in this chapter and some to follow would be required. But the improved principles would so closely resemble those discussed in §§4.1–4.3 that no very fundamental changes would be necessary.

The minimal version of physicalism is distinguished from other versions by a number of things it is *not*. The following list of *nots* will serve also to preclude stereotyping this version as just more of the same dreary old materialist dogma.

To begin with, the minimal version does not exclude emergent entities and properties (such as—presumably—organisms, persons, works of art, languages, and so on, plus certain of their properties). An entity or property is emergent or "novel" with respect to a domain (such as physics), roughly, if our term for it cannot be defined by any terms from the domain (hence not "predicted" by any truths from the domain). The kinds of definition relevant here are those mentioned above, which range from full synonymy to accidental coextensiveness. Thus an entity or property is emergent with respect to a domain if the term (or terms) for that entity or property cannot be reduced to any term from that domain in any of the above senses of reduction. Since nonreductive physicalism requires none of these varieties of reduction, it is clearly compatible with the existence of emergent entities and properties.

Nor is the minimal version eliminative, as we see in §§4.5–4.6. It does not entail, for example, that there are no persons, minds, feelings, sensations, thoughts, freedoms, or whatever. Nor does it entail that all talk about such things is either false or meaningless or otherwise defective, or that it ought to be replaced or even someday *might* be replaced by talk about purely physical things.[11]

Further, it is not an identity theory, typically so-called (according to which all properties and states of things are really physical properties

---

[8]G. Wilson, 67.

[9]Hellman and Thompson (1975), (1977).

[10]Kim (1978), (1979), (1982), (1984a), (1984b); Horgan (1982), (1984); Haugeland; Lewis (1983a). See Teller (1984) for a valuable critical survey and unification of work on supervenience and determination.

[11]In contrast with the eliminativisms of Rorty (1965), (1970); Feyerabend; Churchland (1979), (1981), (1985). Cf. Shope.

and states). True, like all versions of physicalism, the theory must require that any entity mentioned outside physics—a person, say—is
identical with *something* in the physicalist's inventory of what there is. In
this trivial, limiting sense the minimal theory is an identity theory,
meaning, in the jargon of the trade, a token–token identity theory
(meaning in turn that each particular entity or event of some general
type N is identical—token-identical—with a particular mathematical-
physical entity or event, even if the type N is not itself identical—type-
identical—with any physical type). But of course *any* metaphysics is an
identity theory (that is, a token–token identity theory) insofar as it must
claim that everything at bottom is somehow token-identical with or
constituted from certain basic entities or processes, whether physical,
mental, spiritual, or whatever. When a theory does not entail that everything is at least token-identical with something or other in some
ontology O, then either the theory is not a metaphysics in the first place,
or it is one whose inventory exceeds O.

Note also that an entity or state x could be token-identical with
something in the physicalist's inventory *without* being token-identical
with something in the inventory that satisfies a term (or a complex of
terms) from physics or even the neurosciences (where a [complex of]
P-term[s] is understood to be a first-order open sentence whose only
nonlogical words are the P-terms). The vocabulary of physics and neuroscience, in this sort of case, would be incapable, by itself, of picking
out or individuating x; for x would not be denoted by any term from
(or definable by) such a vocabulary (where a term is said to be definable
by a given P-vocabulary only if the term is [necessarily] coextensive
with some first-order open sentence whose only nonlogical words are
from the P-vocabulary). We could not say that x is *nothing but* a physical
entity, meaning that *all* of x's (characteristic) traits are physical traits.
Moreover, certain states and (other) abstract entities (if abstracta exist)
can be token-identical with something or other in the physicalist's inventory, as we see in §4.1, without being token-identical with some
spatiotemporal whole composed of parts that are basic physical entities.
We could not say of such an x that it is nothing but some whole
composed of such parts.

Thus nonreductive physicalism, unlike identity theories typically so-
called, does not require x to be individuatable by any clearly physical or
other scientific term, does not require x to be some ST-whole composed
of basic physical entities, and perhaps above all does not require nonphysical states and properties to be type-identical with physical states or
properties.[12] Nor does the minimal version entail any particular theory

[12]Contrary to Armstrong, among others. Cf. Place, Smart (1963).

of mind, whether an identity theory (again typically so-called), eliminativism, functionalism, or whatever—though of course these theories are all motivated by some sort of materialism (and functionalism by a nonreductive sort).

Nor is the minimal version an "embodiment" theory, according to which a person, say, is a particular embodied in a certain physical entity, where the embodiment relation is *sui generis*—a relation neither of instantiation, nor set membership, nor composition of parts into a whole. Instead, embodiment is said to be a relation such that if x and y are both particulars, then x is embodied in y iff (a) x is not identical with y; (b) the existence of x presupposes the existence of y; (c) x instantiates some properties that y does and some properties that y does not; (d) the individuation of x presupposes the existence of some embodying particular; and (e) y is not a part of x.[13]

The problem with embodiment versions of physicalism is not that the embodiment relation is unclear (though some philosophers might argue that it is fatally unclear). Rather, the relation is all too clear in precluding x—which is not a universal but an embodied particular—from being identical with (cf. clause [a]) or composed of (clause [e]) *any* embodying entity y, whether or not y is denoted by some physical term. But if x is not identical with *something or other* in the physicalist's inventory, then x exceeds the physicalist's ontology. Embodiment versions, evidently, are not really versions of physicalism; they posit an extra sort of entity. By contrast, the minimal version avoids the embodiment relation, relying instead on relations of instantiation or realization (§4.5) to characterize the relations between bodies and properties or states of persons in such a way that persons do not exceed the physicalist's inventory of what there is, and yet are not nothing but physical things.

Nor does the minimal version violate the methodological autonomy of the various domains. Each domain continues to enjoy its own methods of investigation and understanding, its own vocabulary for describing and explaining matters within its scope. Each can proceed without waiting to see how its terms, its descriptions, or its explanations would connect with those of some domain closer to physics. None need fear that physical terms or methods are necessarily superior to its own with respect to matters within its scope. Indeed physical terms and methods will often be inferior with respect to such matters (§§4.5, 4.6, 5.1). This is so despite the unity of method we saw in §1.5, which is simply the trial by prerequisites. Such unity is quite compatible with diversity of

[13]Margolis (1978), 25.

vocabulary and of modes of description and understanding. The trial by prerequisites is realized in each domain by means appropriate to that domain.

Nor does the minimal version of physicalism preclude the existence of abstract entities like sets or numbers. Whether such things exist is left entirely open. When we speak of sets and numbers, or of (other) universals, what we say may be regarded either Platonistically, as referring to such entities, or nominalistically, as a mere manner of speaking (§4.1).

Nor is this version dogmatic about what the basic physical entities are, or vague about them. It is not dogmatic, as we saw in §3.1, because it realizes that our concept of the physical changes as physics itself changes in the ongoing trial by prerequisites. It is not vague, because it provides a specific definition PE (§3.1.1) of a physical existent in terms of a definite list of positive predicates from physics at any given stage.

Nor is it committed to some mirror theory of truth—though of course it is committed to a realism of the sort elaborated in §1.1—or even to some causal relation between words and the world in virtue of which there is an objective fact of the matter as regards the reference of our terms (§1.1). It does not even require the terms to have any *precise* reference, determinate or otherwise (§4.4). The physicalist can heartily agree that vagueness and tortured but novel usage often are indispensable, in everything from poetry to physics, for creating momentous new ways of seeing ourselves and our worlds. Metaphors especially are essential in this regard, though exploration of a physicalist accommodation of metaphor must await §§5.2–5.3.

Perhaps above all, this version is, in at least three fundamental senses, not monopolistic. First, it is not monopolistic in the sense that all domains of discourse beyond physics either are reducible to physics or else are somehow defective. Reducibility, once again, is irrelevant; so too is extensional isomorphism, a relation we encounter in §4.6, which is even weaker than merely accidental coextensiveness.

Second, it is not monopolistic in the sense that physics enjoys unconditional preeminence or priority over all other domains of truth. Naturally, only if physics enjoys *some* kind of priority will it seem significant that all other truths are somehow determined by physical truths. But the priority physics enjoys is highly conditional. *If* we are interested in the kind of objectivity, comprehensiveness, and explanatory power that physics pursues, then the truths of physics take on a corresponding priority, in light of which it seems significant that all other truths are determined by them. In many other contexts we remain free, and often even obligated, to be interested in other sorts of truth and to value them more highly. Indeed there are senses in which physical truth is dependent on certain other truths—evidentially dependent, for example, and semantically dependent. The point will be elaborated in §§5.0 and 5.3, and throughout Chapters 7–8. Here we need only emphasize that the principles to be explained in §§4.1–4.3 do not entail unconditional priority or preeminence for physical truth. Indeed no principles should, since there is no unconditional priority to be enjoyed by any domain, if we may believe §§7.2–7.3.

Third, the minimal physicalist principles are not monopolistic in the sense of entailing that physics in particular or science in general describes the ultimate nature of existence, or the way the world is. There is no such thing, no such thing as *the* face of existence (§§7.2–7.4). There are as many faces as there are aspects or attributes of the whole of existence (§§1.2, 4.6, 5.3), some of which are expressed by today's vocabularies and some of which are not (§5.4). Even though they are all attributes of one and the same thing, it does not follow that this one thing of which they are all attributes is or represents the way the world is, as we see in §4.6, or that "the physical world [is] the world."[14]

Finally, the minimal version is not dogmatic about the principles that constitute it. They operate both as higher-order empirical theories and as regulative ideals in the pursuit of a physicalist unification of the domains. In either case they are as subject to trial by prerequisites as any other theories and ideals. In order to subject them to the trial, we must be clear as to exactly what they are. To this we now turn. Having seen so many things the minimal version is not, the time has come to see what it is.

4.1. "Everything Is Physical"

> *Henceforth, we shall use 'physics' to mean 'physics plus mathematics'. . . . Physicalism asserts, roughly, that everything is exhausted . . . by mathematical-physical entities.*
> —G. P. HELLMAN AND F. W. THOMPSON

> *It would be satisfying to contrive a systematic account of the world while staying strictly within an ontology of physical objects.*
> —W. V. QUINE

Physics is impossible without mathematics. Yet mathematics is full of terms for abstract entities like numbers, sets, relations, functions, and the rest. Some physicalists—the Platonistic ones—believe abstract en-

---

[14]Quine (1978a), 25.

tities do exist. Some believe further that we are forced to posit the abstract entities for much the same reason that we are forced to posit physical entities like electrons or quarks: without them, physics could not develop theories of very great scope and simplicity. The argument, roughly, is that in order to develop such theories, physics requires a certain amount of mathematics, which in turn is up to its neck in numbers, sets, functions, and all that can be defined in terms of them. So in order to do physics we must assume that such abstracta exist.[15]

Nominalistic physicalists will have none of this. According to them, the mathematical talk that appears to commit us to sets and the like is a mere manner of speaking.[16] When mathematicians say, "There is a function such that for a given argument x there is a unique value y satisfying a certain predicate," what they say can be thought of as merely an abbreviated way of saying something like, "There are rules of calculation such that if we were to follow them, then given the numeral N_x for X, eventually we would write or utter a unique numeral N_y whose concatenation with a certain predicate results in a true sentence."[17]

In general, to eliminate Platonic talk of numbers and functions, and indeed of sentence types, the nominalist thus resorts to judicious use of certain counterfactuals about what tokens we would write or utter were we to follow some rule. What of the rules themselves? The nominalist must suppose that they too are things that have been or could be written or uttered. To talk of an unwritten rule is to talk of inscriptions we would write if we were to write replicas of various morpheme tokens in some appropriate order. Thus we encounter more counterfactuals, more talk of possible but nonactual inscriptions or utterances, and recourse to modal notions generally.[18] This is the price nominalists must pay, if price it is, for their puritanical abstinence from Platonism. Conversely, the price for abstinence from counterfactuals and talk of possible but nonactual entities seems to be the Platonist's inflated inventory of what there is.

We need take no stand on these hoary and tangled debates. But we do need to make provision for talk of certain abstracta, in any characterization of physicalism, just in case the nominalist is wrong. If the mathematics required by physics forces us to say that the abstract entities exist, then physicalism cannot be the view simply that everything

[15]As for example Quine (1976) argues, 244, 259–264.
[16]Cf. Chihara, and Field (1980), among others.
[17]Cf. Chihara, 179, 180, 220, and esp. 191.
[18]As when Bonevac, 67, bases his nominalism finally on the notion of "combinatorial possibility," or Field (1980) resorts to modal operators.

is physical. Instead, it must be the view that everything is *mathematical*-physical; everything is either an abstract entity of mathematics or a concrete entity of physics.

Disjunctive formulations of physicalism such as these are acceptable to the nominalist. For they do not imply there are any abstract entities. Henceforth, let us present the principles of physicalism thus disjunctively, where necessary, lest we violate our neutrality between nominalists and Platonists. But let us also enjoy the enormous convenience of talk about numbers, sets, relations, and the rest. Nominalists are free to regard our talk as a mere manner of speaking and to eliminate, if they can, all our terms for abstract entities in favor of terms more to their liking.

Of course, the disjunctive formulations themselves require further specification. They are hopelessly vague, failing precise characterization of what it is to be a physical entity and what it is to be a mathematical entity. What it is to be a physical entity was explained in §3.1.1: a physical entity, by PE, is an ST-sum of entities that satisfy a positive predicate on the list drawn from contemporary physics. Can we be equally specific about mathematical entities? Yes, and we can be brief, too, if we may assume that the mathematical entities required for physics can all be constructed out of sets. Numbers, functions, spaces, manifolds, tensors, and the rest can all be thought of as special sets from various ranks in the hierarchy of sets familiar from set theory. If, on the other hand, numbers are not sets,[19] then we may construe them as properties of sets[20] and construe properties in turn as outlined below. The first rank $R(1)$ consists of the sets of physical entities, including the null set. $R(2)$ consists of the sets of sets in $R(1)$; $R(3)$ consists of the sets of sets in $R(2)$; and so on. In general, where α is a successor ordinal, $R(\alpha+1)$ is the power set of $R(\alpha)$; where α is a limit ordinal, $R(\alpha)$ is the union of all the ranks at a lower level than $R(\alpha)$. When physicalists say that x is an abstract mathematical entity, they can be construed as saying, in effect, that x is a set in some rank $R(\alpha)$ of this hierarchy built on a ground level of concrete physical entities.[21]

We can now spell out just what the physicalist slogan 'Everything is physical' stands for. The slogan abbreviates the physicalist's Inventory Principle:

[19]As argued by Benacerraf.

[20]Following Maddy.

[21]Following Hellman and Thompson (1975). The notion of rank is John von Neumann's, not to be confused with that of type-level. Cf. Mendelson, 214.

> INV. Everything whatever is either an ST-sum of entities that satisfy a positive predicate on the list from physics, or else is a set that belongs to some rank $R(\alpha)$ in the hierarchy defined above.

INV requires only that every existent be identical with *something or other* among the mathematical-physical entities. It does not imply that every existent, or even many, must be identical with a mathematical-physical entity individuated by some term or complex of terms from mathematics or physics, or indeed from any other science. In §3.1.1 we noted that there are random ST-arrays, as well as other weird physical entities, that need satisfy no individuating term on today's list or tomorrow's. We noted also that ordinary macroscopic things like shoes and ships need satisfy no such term or complex of terms. Already, then, we should have a lively sense for the limits of mathematical-physical vocabulary as a means of picking out various entities, well before we consider such phenomena as sentience, consciousness, and so on. For the limits may already be illustrated among the inanimate phenomena themselves. Whatever they may once have thought, physicalists can cheerfully concede that there may be more things in heaven and earth than the mathematical-physical vocabulary can say, although there are no more things than are dreamt of in their Inventory Principle. One of the things it dreams of, notably, is the universe as a whole, the eternal, immutable, metaphysically necessary First Cause on which everything is dependent (§§3.2–3.5). Clearly, INV allows for the existence of some surprising things.

In §4.0 we remarked that even for the physicalist there could exist certain entities that are not token-identical with any ST-whole of basic physical entities. What this means, we now see, is that there could be such things as sets, numbers, relations, functions, and the rest, though the nominalistic physicalist rejects them. We also remarked that states of entities can be in the physicalist's inventory without being token-identical with some ST-whole. It follows that the states must be construed somehow as special sets or relations. To say that an entity x is in a certain state may be construed as saying that x is a member of some appropriate set, as we see in §4.5, or that x bears some appropriate relation to its surroundings, its parts, and/or itself. How this set or relation is to be specified or expressed is another matter, depending mainly on what state x is supposed to be in. Here the point is that there is no need to speak of embodiment (§4.0)—of x's embodying the state—but only ultimately of set membership.

What of properties, or attributes? Their distinctive feature, for our purpose, is that coextensiveness of two predicates is only necessary, not sufficient, for the predicates to express the same property. In addition, the two predicates must at least have the same intension (roughly, the same "meaning"). It is supposed to be in virtue of their common intension that they are coextensive. The strongest variety of sameness of intension is logical equivalence, in virtue of which, for example, the two predicates 'tender and juicy' and 'juicy and tender' presumably express the same property. Somewhat weaker is synonymy, in virtue of which 'bachelor' and 'unmarried male' would express the same property. Weaker still is lawlike cointensionality: two predicates are lawlike cointensional iff they are coextensive as a matter of scientific necessity. Whether lawlike cointensionality of a couple of predicates—such as 'absolute temperature' and 'mean kinetic energy of the molecules', in the case of an ideal gas—is (always) sufficient for expression of the same property is a question we may leave open.

How can physicalists make room for properties in their inventory? By identifying a property (whether or not it is expressed or expressible) with a function from possible worlds to sets of things—the property's extensions—in the worlds. Thus a property, ontologically speaking, is a special set, a function, rather high in the hierarchy of sets, and hence safely within the physicalist's inventory. This is true even though many properties presumably can be expressed (when they can be) only by predicates from domains well beyond mathematics and physics.

But what in the world is a possible world? In §1.1 we construed a possible world provisionally as a triple $<D, P, R>$, where D is a set of entities, and P and R are sets of genuine traits- and relations-in-extension. A better policy would be to construe worlds not as a matter of (extra) entities at all but merely as a heuristic device to help analyze various modal assertions. And it does seem likely that we could have a naturalistic account of modality that (i) does not reduce modal idioms to, or translate or paraphrase them into, purely extensional or other nonmodal terms; (ii) does not assert the existence of possible worlds or any other possibilia; and (iii) affirms that (some) modal discourse is objectively true or false by virtue of being based on actual physical facts. That is, "One can be a realist about modal truth, and hold it to be objective, without being a *modal* realist."[22]

No doubt this is largely true, but we need to allow for the existence of (some) possible worlds just in case it is wrong. For in the course of modeling modal discourse, we do often seem compelled to speak of there being such-and-such possible worlds. Nor would that be the

[22]Mondadori and Morton, 20.

worst of it, from the point of view of physicalists who would like to reject possibilia altogether. For in the very formulation of their own minimal theses, they seem committed to the existence of nonactual worlds, or at least to nonactual circumstances or states of affairs that count as ways this world might have been.

Consider the slogan that physical truth determines all truth whatever. To say that one thing determines another is to say that given the way the first is, there is one and only one way the second *can* be. For example, given the state of a deterministic system at one time, there is one and only one state it can be in at a later time. That is, given the system and given any hypothetical other in the same state, the state the two are in at a later time will also be the same (§1.1.1). We get rid of the modal word 'can' here by quantifying over systems and their states.

This seems harmless, until we reflect that often there is only one actual system in the precise state in question; the hypothetical other we imagine to be in that same state is not actual but only possible. Furthermore, physicalists themselves want likewise to say that, given the physical state of the world, for each nonphysical vocabulary N, there is one and only one N-state the world can be in. That is, given the world, and given any other world in the same physical state—or given a physical duplicate[23]—the two are also in the same N-state for each N. The price for eliminating 'can' seems to be quantification over worlds or other possibilia. The same difficulty arises for the physicalist's slogan 'No difference without a physical difference', as we see in the next section.

Physicalists are among the most adamant actualists. How might they accommodate the talk of possibilia that the very formulation of their minimal theses seems to require? There have been attempts to construct or represent possibilia within a physicalist inventory. Even Quine, in order to model the propositional attitudes of some nonverbal creatures, works hard to construe worlds as what in effect are alternative combinations or distributions of mass-energy in spacetime, where the different combinations are in turn merely sets of ST-points occupied by some form of mass-energy.[24] In a related development, Cresswell takes a world to be a set of "basic particular situations," which for a physicalist can be a set of occupied ST-points.[25] A complete state of the world would therefore just be or be determined by a set of ST-points—namely, those that are occupied. The points in turn can be represented by quadruples of real numbers, thence eventually as sets.

---

[23]As Lewis (1983a) puts it.
[24]Quine (1969), ch. 6.
[25]Cresswell.

Worlds, then, would be actually existing things in the physicalist's inventory; they would be sets. And the main primitive or undefined notion here—that of a bit of mass-energy occupying or being at a certain ST-region, including a point-region—seems relatively unproblematic. As we saw at STPW in §3.1, it is presupposed by all treatments of applied geometry. Nor need we think of occupation of a point as by particles only. We can easily also speak nonatomistically of the degree of intensity of a field at a point, and nondeterministically of merely the probability that something occurs there.

Objections to combinatorial representations of or proxies for worlds have mostly been on another score: namely, that there are notions of possibility they cannot represent.[26] For example, it surely seems possible that there should have been more particles or more bits and fields of mass-energy than there actually are. Yet we cannot say so, if we are limited to speaking of rearrangements only of the actual ones. Fortunately, there is a strategy for meeting this "inflated-universe" objection. One merely lets further sets represent or go proxy for the extra entities.[27] Of course, this strategy abandons a purely *combinatorial* approach.[28] But physicalists are wedded to no such approach; they need only stay within their inventory. If letting further sets go proxy for the extra entities violates pure combinatorialism, so much the worse for pure combinatorialism.

There are some technical problems in letting sets stand in for the extra entities. Consider the truth that there might have been more stars. To preserve this truth, suppose that to the actual extension of 'is a star' we add in some world W the null set, let us say, to represent an extra star (or stars), thus rendering 'There are more stars' true in W. The trouble is that we also want to assert the truth that necessarily no star is a set, that there is no world in which some set is in the extension of 'is a star'. Yet in W the null set is in this extension, and we have a contradiction.

How do we avoid this sort of fiasco? By not assigning all the actual sets to the predicate 'is a set'.[29] Instead we assign to 'is a set' a structure of sets isomorphic to the actual-world sets but beginning at some rank higher than the null set. Indeed there is no limit to how high we may go. Thus for any ordinal α, all sets of rank lower than α may be used as stand-ins for possibilia, and any set of rank α may be designated as the

[26]Cf. Lycan (1979).
[27]As do Hellman and Thompson (1977).
[28]As Lycan (1979), 305, points out.
[29]Again following Hellman and Thompson (1977).

(new) null set. Then we may systematically reinterpret all mathematical terms accordingly (so that each such term is assigned the image of its actual extension under a 1-1 ∈-isomorphism from the actual universe of sets to the new universe that begins at rank α). Clearly, there will always be enough sets to go around—enough to serve as stand-ins for possibilia and enough others to do mathematics—and yet necessarily no set is a star (since nothing in the extension of 'is a set' as now reinterpreted is in the extension of 'is a star'; of the actual-world sets, only at some rank lower than α would there be any in the extension of 'is a star').

Even though the technical problems may thus be met, they probably do not constitute the major sort of misgiving about representing possibilia within the physicalist's inventory. The major misgiving, as before, is that there are notions of possibility not representable in this way.[30] But whether there are is not here to the point. Here we are concerned only to accommodate talk of possibilia just so far as it is needed in the formulation of the physicalist's minimal theses. It will turn out that *physically* possible worlds are adequate to this narrower task (§§4.2, 4.3). Roughly, they are the worlds in which the laws of physics are true (and in which the only entities are those allowed by INV). It is relatively easy to represent such worlds in the manner envisaged above, inadequate though such representations might be for worlds that operate according to a radically different physics (and geometry) or that contain no physically law-governed things at all but only irreducibly spiritual things, or whatever.

A possible world, then, is still a triple $<D,P,R>$, where (a) D is now a set both of ST-points (represented in turn as quadruples of reals) and of things (or their set theoretic proxies) that can be said to occupy them, and (b) P and R tell us (among other things) which such points are occupied and by what (or to what degree of field intensity or of probability). A *physically* possible world (a P-world) is one in which this distribution of occupied/nonoccupied over the ST-points is in accord with the laws of physics. If this does not entail that the things in D (except for sets) are all physical entities of the actual-world kind, and if the purposes for which we need P-worlds require that the things in D (sets aside) all be of this kind, then we can easily stipulate additionally that (c) the concrete things in D be of this kind (or be decomposable into entities of this kind). This would be simply to stipulate that each world's contents satisfy INV.

---

[30]Again, cf. Lycan (1979), 305–312.

4.2. "No Difference without a Physical Difference"

> *Nothing happens in the world . . . without some redistribution*
> *of microphysical states. . . . If the physicist suspected there was*
> *any event that did not consist in a redistribution . . . allowed*
> *for by his physical theory, he would seek a way of*
> *supplementing his theory. Full coverage in this sense is the*
> *very business of physics, and only of physics.*
>
> —W. V. QUINE

> *There clearly are missing premises between 'nothing happens*
> *without some redistribution of microphysical states' and 'full*
> *coverage'.*
>
> —HILARY PUTNAM

We encounter another slogan, potentially misleading: "No difference without a physical difference." What does it stand for? Roughly
this: suppose there is a difference between x and y expressible in the
vocabulary of some domain or other; then there is also some difference
between x and y expressible solely in the vocabulary of physics. Thus
imagine two emotions, however subtly distinguished by novelist or
poet. There should also be some distinction between them expressible in
physical terms, if the slogan is right.

Why is the slogan potentially misleading? Because it may suggest a
form of reduction. This can happen if the slogan is construed as standing
for the erroneous Reductive Discernibility Principle:

> RD. If there is a distinction between x and y expressible by terms
> from some domain, then there are terms solely from physics
> which express that same distinction.

Why is this reductive? Suppose there is a distinction between x and y
expressible in some domain beyond physics, meaning there is a predicate N from that domain such that N is true of x and false of y or vice
versa. Then by RD, not only is there some physical predicate P that
likewise distinguishes x from y, but this P expresses the same distinction
as N. But if P is to "express the same distinction" as N, in the usual
sense of this phrase, then minimally, P must be true of the same things
as N and false of the same things, which is to say that P must be
coextensive with N, which is just a weak form of reduction.

How might we construe 'No difference without a physical difference' nonreductively? The temptation is to let it stand for what may
be called Quine's Full Coverage Principle:[31]

---

[31]Quine (1978a), 25. Cf. Quine (1978b), 162–163.

QFC. Given a nonphysical N that distinguishes x from y, there is some physical P that also distinguishes x from y.

QFC is equivalent to 'If x and y are N-discernible, they are also P-discernible', or 'P-indiscernibles are N-indiscernibles'. QFC does not imply that P makes the same distinction as N. It implies only that for any pair of things distinguished by N, there is some P that also distinguishes them. Given some *other* pair of things distinguished by N, there may well need to be some *other* physical predicate that distinguishes *them*. Thus P might be true of only one of the things N is true of, and hence not coextensive with N.

Is there a gap, as Putnam suggests in the epigraph above, between 'No difference without a physical difference' and 'full coverage'?[32] Not at all: 'No difference without a physical difference' is simply what 'full coverage' *means* for Quine. That is, full coverage in the sense in which it is "the very business of physics" is just what QFC spells out; this is the force of Quine's phrase "in this sense," also quoted above.[33]

There *is* a gap, and a dangerous one, but not where Putnam locates it. Instead, the gap is between full coverage and monopoly (§4.0, 4.6), should a physicalist assert not only QFC but also that the physical world is "the only real world," as has Quine, or further that it is *the* way the world is, or *the* face of existence. But QFC can be true even though these other, monopolistic claims are false. QFC can be true even though it is false that physics enjoys some sort of unconditional preeminence over any other domain of truth, in virtue of which the physical world is supposedly the only real world. Full coverage in the sense of QFC just means that any distinguishable things are physically distinguishable. It does not mean that there are no domains of truth outside physics or that they are any less important. Indeed for many purposes they are more important, if only because their vocabulary often enables us to individuate things that physics cannot, and these things—emotions, thoughts, intentions, values, and more—form the worlds we most often live in.

The real problem with QFC is that it is too easily satisfied. It is equivalent to 'Any two N-discernibles are P-discernible'. This is automatically true if either there are no two N-discernibles, or every two things are P-discernible. Thus if the N-vocabulary happens to be so impoverished as to be incapable of discerning anything at all, then Quine's principle holds for N, trivially, by virtue of a false antecedent. Worse, if the physical vocabulary is only barely so rich as to discern any

[32]Putnam (1979), 614.
[33]Quine (1978a), 25.

two nonidenticals, then again QFC holds trivially, for every N. That is, if the Identity of Physical Indiscernibles is true (as Quine believes when, e.g., he insists of translation that there is no difference in meaning without some physical difference), then QFC is trivially true, by virtue of a true consequent.

Clearly, QFC is too weak to express much of what physicalists have in mind when they say that there being a nonphysical difference depends on there being a physical difference. What they mean is not just that there *is* no difference without a physical difference but that there *can be* none. This is the Modal Nonreductive Discernibility Principle:

> MND. For any P-world W, if x and y are N-discernible in W, then they are P-discernible in W,

where x and y are P- (N-)discernible in W iff there is some P- (N-)property, relations included, that x but not y has in W. Quine is notoriously suspicious of modal principles, but in view of the basically Quinean account of physically possible worlds at the end of §4.1, MND need not offend.

MND expresses a regulative ideal. It tells us to keep looking for a physically distinguishing property even if there is no immediate prospect of finding one. Of course, if we were to fail in too many cases to find some such property, or for too long, that would cast doubt on MND. But the physicalist believes that we have been successful often enough to warrant MND. If we should ever have good reason to suspect that the list of physical properties from today's physics is insufficient to discern certain discernibles, we should improve the list. The ideal we pursue, as expressed by MND, is to create a physics whose list of physical properties suffices to discern all discernibles whatever. Of course, physicalists might some day be proved wrong in their belief that the ideal is realizable at some future stage of physics if not now. But the mere possibility that the ideal is mistaken is no reason for abandoning it. Remember its past successes; but even more, notice that by proceeding as if the ideal were sound, we are far more likely to find physical properties that do discern certain recalcitrant discernibles than if we had doubts about the ideal. Why court loss of nerve?

Note also that MND applies when the difference between x and y is in terms of some functional and/or intentional role x plays in a wider environment, rather than in terms of some state of x in isolation. We discuss this sort of case toward the end of §4.5, when better equipped to do so. The key insight is that the P-property that distinguishes x from y need not be realized by x in isolation but can be a relation between x and

a much wider context. MND is entirely congenial with holistic or ecological thinking.

Over the years philosophers have used the word 'supervenience' for
many relations. Its first contemporary use, and still in many ways its
core use, seems to have been by Hare for a relation expressed also by
MND (with *P*-worlds replaced by logically possible worlds).[34] Hare's
idea, like Davidson's later,[35] was that a set of properties supervenes on
another whenever two things exactly alike as regards the latter sort of
property must be exactly alike as regards the former. In Hare's example,
St. Francis' moral properties supervene on his descriptive properties if
anyone exactly like St. Francis as regards descriptive properties must be
exactly like him as regards moral properties. In particular, if St. Francis
is a morally good person, so must anyone be who is exactly (or even
only relevantly) like him in descriptive respects. Thus MND is equivalent to an important kind of supervenience.

One might suppose that if the *N*-properties supervene on the
P-properties in this sense, then all the *N*-truths are fixed or determined
by the *P*-truths. In fact, this does not follow, mainly for two reasons.
First, determination requires us to look at worlds pairwise, as lately seen
in §4.1 and earlier in §1.1.1, whereas MND takes worlds one at a time.
Second, even if we take worlds pairwise and even if any two individuals
distinguishable in and between them are physically distinguishable, still
it does not follow that *all* the *N*-truths in the two worlds are the same.
So even though MND expresses a kind of supervenient dependence of
the nonphysical on the physical, it does not express the kind of dependence we call determination, let alone determination of all nonphysical
truth by physical truth.

Of course we might interpret the slogan 'No difference without a
physical difference' not as MND but as 'No difference *between worlds*
without a physical difference between them', or as 'Worlds that are
physical duplicates are nonphysical duplicates' (for an appropriate class
of worlds).[36] And this does express a kind of supervenience, even if it is
not what Hare called supervenience (or what G.E. Moore earlier had in
mind by another name).[37] But more important, it also expresses determination, to which we turn in the next section.

Meanwhile, let us consider whether supervenience, in any interest-
ing sense, must after all be reductive. Start with the core sense of MND
shared by Moore, Hare, and Davidson (though the last may have had

[34]Hare (1952), 145. Cf. Post (1984a), 321, 326; and Kim (1984b), 161–162.
[35]Davidson (1970), 88.
[36]Following Lewis (1983a).
[37]G.E. Moore, 261.

something stronger in mind as well).[38] That is, the N-properties super-vene on the P-properties iff

(1) P-indiscernibility entails N-indiscernibility.

Obviously (1) will be of interest only if what the N-properties are said to supervene on are clearly or uncontroversially P-properties—in the pre-sent instance, clearly *physical* properties. We should not allow 'P' to range over properties that may or may not be physical.

In particular, we should not let the range of 'P' include (all) the complements or negations of physical properties, since the complement of a physical property is not in general itself a physical property (there may be an occasional exception). The property of being an electron, for example, is clearly physical, whereas its complement is not (when com-plementation or negation is taken to be exclusion negation);[39] if it were, we would have to say of anything that has it—of anything not an electron—that it has a physical trait: namely, the trait of not being an electron. We would have to say that numbers, sets, pains, thoughts, and more are partly physical simply because they are not electrons. Nor would there be any reason why we should not allow the same for any other kind of property. The complement of a moral property, then, would itself be moral, and we would have to say that electrons have moral traits simply because they are not morally good (and not morally bad). Worse, perhaps, we would have to say that everything whatever has properties of every kind, since each thing would have the comple-ment of many a property of each kind.

Indeed some philosophers (Armstrong, for example) go so far as to deny that the complement is a property at all, or at least a genuine property or universal (perhaps on the ground that allowing it to be one is to desert naturalism). Nor is the issue merely terminological. Suppose we were to define a physical property as whatever is expressed by a complex of admittedly physical terms. Since 'x is not an electron' is such a complex, this policy would rule that the property of not being an electron is physical. We would have to say of abstract sets and the like that they have some physical properties, of electrons that they have moral properties, and eventually of everything that it has properties of every kind. Yet there is a considerable difference between, on the one hand, the "physical" properties that are projected merely by the sen-tence-forming operations of first-order logic and, on the other, the *genuine* physical properties, or (in another idiom) those that correspond

[38]On Davidson, cf. Kim (1984b), 157, 162, 164.
[39]Cf. Post (1984c).

with (genuine) universals. Precisely what the nature of the difference is, and its source, we need not pause to inquire. It is enough to note that whereas we would unhesitatingly say of an electron that it has a genuine physical trait, we would hesitate to say the same of something known only not to be an electron.

It follows that a relation of supervenience will be of interest, or will clearly have the intended sort of application, only if its formulation does not presuppose that the complement of a *P*-property is always itself a *P*-property (as the formulations of Moore, Hare, and Davidson do not). It follows further that even if its formulation presupposes no such thing, arguments to the effect that the relation after all is reductive will fail to persuade if they presuppose that the complement is always a *P*-property. Yet this presupposition enters the leading argument for the reductiveness of supervenience. The argument begins by letting *P* and *N* be "two nonempty families of properties . . . closed under the usual Boolean . . . operations, complementation, conjunction, and disjunction."[40] This is done in connection not only with (1) but with supervenience in the following three senses:

(2) Necessarily, for any *N*, if *x* has *N* then: there is a *P* such that *x* has *P*, and if any *y* has *P* it has *N*.

(3) Necessarily, for any *N*, if *x* has *N* then: there is a *P* such that *x* has *P*, and necessarily if any *y* has *P* it has *N*.

(4) Worlds that are *P*-indiscernible are *N*-indiscernible.[41]

Kim calls these weak, strong, and global supervenience, respectively. (4) is equivalent to 'No difference between worlds without a physical difference' and also to 'Worlds that are physical duplicates are nonphysical duplicates'. Hence (4) expresses determination.

Kim argues that (1) and (2) are equivalent. The argument presupposes that a *P*-maximal property is itself a *P*-property, where a *P*-maximal property is a maximally consistent conjunction (mcc) of *P*-properties *and their complements*.[42] For example, consider the purely physical properties of being an electron (E) and having mass (M). There are four mcc's of E, M, and their complements: EM, $\overline{E}M$, $E\overline{M}$, $\overline{EM}$. Of these, only the first is clearly a physical property. By contrast, the property of not being an electron and having no mass ($\overline{EM}$) is possessed by numbers, abstract sets and much else we would decline to call even partly

[40]Kim (1984b), 157–158.
[41]Kim (1984b), 163–165. (2) is essentially (S), and (3) essentially (?), in Blackburn (1985b).
[42]Kim (1984b), 163, at "Let G be the B-maximal property of *x*."

physical; and doubts easily arise about $\overline{\text{EM}}$ and probably $\overline{\text{EM}}$. Hence neither the mcc's of P-properties and their complements nor therefore the P-maximal properties are by any means all P-properties themselves, and the argument for the equivalence of (1) and (2) rests on a problematic presupposition. Note that this would hold even if 'P' (and 'N') in (1) and (2) ranged over no complements.

Kim further argues that given the supervenience of N on P in sense (1), then within each world, and for each N, there is a P^* such that all and only the x's that have P^* have N. This is to claim accidental coextensiveness of the relevant P^* and N, a weak form of reduction. The trouble is that P^* turns out to be a P-maximal property,[43] hence not in general itself a physical property. The same problem affects his argument that supervenience in the strong sense of (3) implies that for each N there is a P^* *necessarily* coextensive with N.[44] Again this would hold even if 'P' and 'N' ranged over no complements.

Finally, Kim argues that (3) is equivalent to (4), hence that determination (or "global supervenience") is the same as supervenience in his preferred, strong sense. Given his argument that (3) is reductive, it would follow that determination itself is reductive after all. But even if (3) implies (4), the argument for the converse rests on the assumption that a P-maximal property is itself a P-property.[45] It also rests on the non sequitur from 'x has P^* in world W, and P^* does not entail N' to supposing that x does not have N in W.[46] So even if supervenience in the strong sense of (3) implies determination, the converse does not hold. Determination of N by P can obtain in the absence even of accidental coextensiveness of any N and P.

4.3. "All Truth Is Determined by Physical Truth"

> *It is not the purpose of this view to leave any aspect of life out of account.*
>
> —W. V. QUINE

Physicalists believe that their theory is superior to all others in accounting for the faces of existence. What is the most charitable in-

---

[43]Kim (1984b), 159.

[44]Kim (1984b), 170. Blackburn (1985b), 52, follows Kim here, as does McFetridge, 250.

[45]Kim (1984b), 168, at the move from "if any G is in B and x has G, G fails to entail F" to "the B-maximal property of x does not entail F," and also later.

[46]Kim (1984b), 168, at "Since B* does not entail F, we can consistently suppose that $-F(x)$ in w#." Hellman (1985), n. 3, likewise finds this step problematic.

terpretation of this claim? The claim is not that anything that can be accounted for or explained in nonphysical terms also has some purely physical explanation; rather, the explanation may now and forever belong to some nonphysical domain of discourse. Our explanation of various emotions, say, or of our experience of temporal becoming and the twilight fleetingness of life, may always belong primarily to psychology and literature, both of which have their own modes of insight and understanding, plus their own vocabularies for describing and explaining matters within their scope. The physicalist's claim is no threat to the explanatory autonomy of the higher domains, or to the insight and understanding they can provide when physics cannot.

Instead, the claim is that for all their diversity, the domains enjoy a kind of unity in which their truths are determined by truths at the level of physics, so that any explanatory power the nonphysical truths have will be, in some derivative sense, part of the explanatory power of physics, or at least a manifestation of its comprehensiveness. If no aspect of life is left out of account,[47] the reason is that the nonphysical truths which describe or explain some such aspect are themselves determined by truths at the level of physics, even when there is no explanation proper at that level.

Understandably, then, determination might appear to be an exclusively physicalistic relation, or to presuppose physicalism. Nothing could be further from the truth. Even though the relation is of great use to the physicalist, it is potentially just as useful to other metaphysicians. If pressed about what the relation is between *their* basic or unifying truths and all other truth, if not some sort of reducibility, they too might argue that the former determine the latter. The concept of determination is metaphysically neutral, even though claims about what determines what are not. The core idea is merely that given the way things are in a certain respect, there is one and only one way they can be in some other respect. That a couple of physicalists[48] were the first to explore and apply the relation is accidental.

Some physicalists and others later explored what proved to be essentially the same relation under another name: 'supervenience'.[49] But 'determination' is less a term of art and is perhaps preferable on that score alone. More important, 'determination' in ordinary usage comes closer to conveying the core idea. For to say one thing determines another, in

---

[47]The epigraph is from Quine (1976), 227.

[48]Hellman and Thompson (1975).

[49]See n. 10, above. Kim's relation may well not be one of supervenience, ironically, since according to Post (1984c), it does not fit the schema in Teller (1984). But see Teller (1985).

ordinary parlance, is to say the first delimits or fixes how the second can be; or that given the first, there is one and only one way the second can be. By contrast, 'supervenience', according to the dictionaries, principally means "to occur as extraneous (upon)," which hardly conveys the dependence intended.[50] So let us continue to talk mostly of determination, even though the relation is equivalent (nearly enough) to a number of relations later called supervenience.

Ordinary usage yields a clue further as to what the sense is in which the physicalist (or other metaphysician) now claims to account for or explain various matters. For ordinarily, if we wonder why a certain thing is as it is, our question is answered when (but not only when) we learn that it had to be that way, given the way some other thing is. That is, our question is answered when we learn that this is the one and only way the thing could be, given the way the other is. In short, the matter is accounted for or explained, in an important sense, when we learn that it is determined by something else (which is not to say that we may not subsequently wonder why this further thing is as it is, or why and how it is determinative). And as we shall see, such determination is compatible with our being unable to predict or deduce or even express the way the thing will be, given a knowledge only of the way the further thing is.

Hellman and Thompson express the determination relation model-theoretically, in terms of structures (where a structure is a domain D of entities plus an assignment of elements in D and sets of their n-tuples).[51] Their idea is that P-truth determines N-truth in a class α of structures iff given any two α-structures s and s^*, if the same P-sentences are true in s and s^*, then the same N-sentences are true in s and s^* (where the same P- or N-sentences are true in both iff for every such sentence ϕ, ϕ is true in s iff ϕ is true in s^*). That is, P-truth determines N-truth in α-structures iff given any two such s and s^*, if s/P (the restriction of s to the P-terms) is elementarily equivalent to s^*/P, then s/N is likewise elementarily equivalent to s^*/N. The class of structures they choose is the class of those that model scientific possibility, or according to them those in which the laws of science are true and the vocabulary of pure set theory and mathematics has its standard interpretation.

Thus they formulate the determination principles in terms of the models of a fairly rich background theory that includes today's physics. Since today's physics is incomplete and probably wrong, it follows that there are no precise, general determination principles that we know how

---

[50]As Hellman (1985), n. 3, points out.
[51]Hellman and Thompson (1975).

to formulate. The principles must be regarded as schematic in this respect (as they are in others), to be filled in or revised as advancing physics dictates.[52] This surely is right, as is the companion idea that precisely which class of structures should be chosen depends on the specific purpose for which a given determination principle is wanted. The same is true of possible worlds explications of determination, despite the impression possible-worlds talk may occasionally give of some completely theory-independent access to worlds, as when we talk unqualifiedly of physically possible worlds. Our idea of precisely which worlds are the physically possible ones must be filled in or revised in light of ongoing developments in physics.

Two objections to model-theoretic explications are of interest. The first[53] is that physicalists presumably want the laws of nonphysical science to be determined, nontrivially, by physical truth; yet if a is a class of structures in which (among others) the laws of science are true, then automatically and trivially, physical truth determines the laws of science (since automatically the same scientific law-sentences are true in any two s and s^* in a). The same problem confronts possible-worlds explications, according to which, roughly, P-truth determines N-truth in a class W of possible worlds iff given any two worlds W_1 and W_2 in W, if W_1 and W_2 are the same in all P-respects (or else are the same as regards which P-sentences are true in them), then they are the same in all N-respects (or else in their N-truths). But if W_1 and W_2 are scientifically possible worlds, meaning at least that they are the same in that the laws of science are all true in them, then again physical truth trivially determines the laws of science, for the same reason. In both cases, the solution is simply to let the class of relevant possibilia—structures or worlds—be the physically possible ones in which certain bridge principles that connect the relevant vocabularies are true.

The second objection is that model-theoretic formulations of determination seem vulnerable to trivial counterexamples.[54] The counterexamples take the form of structures that seem to satisfy the stated constraints on what is to model the relevant sort of possibility and in which the same P-sentences are true, but in one of which a simple N-sentence is true that is not true in the other. Thus let s and s^* be two structures in which the same P-sentences are true and the vocabulary of pure set theory and mathematics receives its standard interpretation. Suppose

[52]Hellman (1985).

[53]Raised by Horgan (1982), n. 12, and in correspondence.

[54]As pointed out by Thomas Conner via Teller (1984), 142, and independently by Horgan (in correspondence).

further that the domains of s and s^* contain the same actual individuals, including Nixon, but whereas the assignment function in s assigns an extension that includes Nixon to the N-predicate 'resigned in disgrace', the function in s^* assigns to the same predicate an extension that does not include Nixon. Then s and s^* satisfy the stated constraints, but 'Nixon resigned in disgrace' is true in one but not the other.

Obviously, further constraints must be imposed that hold certain meanings constant throughout the relevant class of structures, so that 'resigned in disgrace', for example, is assigned the same extension in each. This is easily accomplished by choosing as the background theory that the structures are to model one that includes the appropriate state-ment of meaning-connections.[55] Of course, if the predicate is assigned a set of actuals, as it must be (§4.1), then we seem limited to saying of each actual president that he did or did not resign in disgrace, whereas presumably it is true that there might have been more presidents who did so. This is the inflated-universe objection all over again (§4.1). A plausible way out, as before, is to let certain abstracta among the actuals go proxy for the extra individuals. Then meanings could be held con-stant, not only in the sense of actual extensions but in the sense of potentiality for reference to new cases.

Thus the second objection is not necessarily fatal to model-theoretic explications of determination. But it does show that such explications must be more complex than possible-worlds accounts, which have meaning-constancy already built in and therefore avoid the counterex-amples simply and directly. For this reason and others it is easier, if metaphysically less neutral, to explicate determination in terms of possi-ble worlds, or ways the world might have been. And as seen, the possibilia needed for *this* purpose, if not necessarily for all purposes, can safely be represented within the physicalist's actualist inventory of what there is.

Variations there are in possible-worlds accounts of determination, but they all share a common pattern or schema: P determines N, in a class of worlds, iff any two worlds in the class that are the same with respect to P are the same with respect to N.[56] The variations mainly are in what class of worlds to use, and in what respects they are to be the same. The variation I shall refer to as the physicalist's Principle of the Determination of all Truth by Physical Truth is

[55]As does Hellman (1985).

[56]Teller (1984) identifies a still more general schema of which nearly all significant varieties of determination and supervenience appear to be instances. Again, Kim's may be an exception, and therefore Blackburn's. Cf. nn. 41 and 49, above.

TT. Given any two *P*-worlds, if the same *P*-sentences are true in both, then the same *N*-sentences are true in both,

where to say that the same *P*- (*N*-)sentences are true in both is to say that for every such sentence ϕ, ϕ is true in one iff ϕ is true in the other. The notion of truth-in-a-world was defined in §1.1.1, and that of a *P*-world at the end of §4.1.

TT is a way of saying that given a distribution of truth-values over the *P*-sentences, there can be one and only one distribution over the *N*-sentences. If sentences somehow offend as truth-bearers, then propositions and/or facts may be pressed into service, as we see in §5.4. Since not every fact need be expressible, TT thus amended is compatible with there being inexpressible and hence irreducible facts, including perhaps facts about what it is like to be a bat or some other subject, which nevertheless are determined by purely objective, physical facts.

While TT is overtly about sentences and their truth-values, still determination is a matter of how things are in the world. For according to §1.1, the world determines truth (even if it does not determine reference). A fortiori, the world determines not only physical truth but also whether it is true that physical truth determines all truth, hence whether TT is true. Furthermore, the physicalist can easily formulate his principle of truth-determination in the first place not as TT but as directly about how things are in the world, along the following lines:

TT*. Any two *P*-worlds indiscernible as regards the physical properties and relations of the things in them are also indiscernible as regards their things' nonphysical properties and relations.

That is, given the way things are physically, there is one and only one way they can be nonphysically. TT merely engages in a bit of semantic ascent that proves useful later on.

Other variations in possible-worlds accounts of determination are plausible and for certain purposes perhaps preferable. Lewis begins with the notion of a natural property, then characterizes a property as alien to a world iff it is not instantiated in that world and is not constructible out of natural properties all of which are instantiated in that world. He then formulates "Minimal Materialism" as the contingent supervenience thesis that "among worlds where no natural properties alien to our world are instantiated, no two differ without differing physically; any two such worlds that are exactly alike physically are duplicates."[57] This is

---

[57]Lewis (1983a), 364.

designed to imply that each such world is a materialistic world, one in which the medium in which all properties are realized is physical—not spiritual, say, or mental, or whatever.

Thus Lewis's principle is designed to imply not only TT* (nearly enough) but INV, as it should if it is to express a minimal materialism. But principles of supervenience or determination are claims only about the existence of certain correlations or dependent variations. The claim is that the physical and the nonphysical are so correlated that given the way something is in physical respects, there is one and only one way it can be in nonphysical respects; there can be no variation in the latter without some variation in the former. Yet of course the assertion merely of a correlation notoriously entails nothing as to the nature of the medium in which the correlation is realized, and therefore nothing as to what we may include in our inventory of what there is. Thus it seems wise to separate inventory principles from claims of determination and supervenience, though of course there is nothing wrong with asserting their conjunction, provided the evidence supports our choice of inventory.

Still other variations occur among possible-worlds accounts of determination. Thus Lewis's resembles an earlier one by Horgan,[58] which differs in what is to count as an alien property. Since Lewis introduces the notion of an alien property mainly in order to ensure that the relevant worlds are all materialistic ones, and since requiring them all to satisfy the Inventory Principle would ensure the same result, we can bypass this difference between Horgan and Lewis simply by so requiring, as we envisaged at the end of §4.1. Likewise we may hope to bypass further differences between these formulations and others. Whatever the final, ultrarefined variation proves to be, the result is a physicalism "unencumbered by dubious denials of existence, claims of ontological priority, or claims of translatability."[59]

TT is an ontological or metaphysical principle, not epistemological. Even if we knew all the P-truths, still we could not say what the N-truths are if we knew only that P-truth determines N-truth. Further principles would be needed, and much stronger ones, if we wanted to ascertain what the N-truths are on the basis of a knowledge only of the P-truths. The project of trying to find such principles, or at least what kind of principle they would be, is a challenging one.[60] But physicalists are committed to no such project, nor should they be concerned if it fails. Their claim is not that the N-truths can be *ascertained* from the

[58]Horgan (1982). Cf. Horgan (1984), n. 3.
[59]Lewis (1983b), 358.
[60]On which Horgan (1984) has made a start, under the rubric 'cosmic hermeneutics'.

physical but only that they are *determined* by the physical. Given the physical, the rest have to be as they are, but how they are does not have to be ascertainable or predictable. Nor need the evidence for principles of determination be evidence to the effect that the nonphysical is thus ascertainable. Mostly the evidence is very different and far easier to obtain, as we see in §5.1.

But why does physical determination hold in our world, if not because of some deeper relation that would enable a Laplacean demon, let us say, to calculate all truth from physical truth?[61] The trouble with this question is that it presupposes that there is some explanation for why the determination holds in our world. Unless the discredited Principle of Sufficient Reason is true, there need be none. Physical determination might well be one of those ultimate facts about the world that neither have nor require explanation but are simply ineligible for explanation (§2.3). Whether, in addition, physical determination is an ultimate explainer depends on whether there is something it explains (§2.5). A good case can be made that there is (§5.1), but a minimal physicalism is not committed to saying so.

In this connection it is worth noting that TT need not be a logically necessary truth but can be contingent (and probably is). That is, TT need not be true in every possible world, as it might have to be if it quantified over logically rather than merely physically possible worlds. Of course, if TT were a necessary truth, that would reduce or eliminate the temptation to seek an explanation of why it is true. But even if (or even though) it is contingent, the request for an explanation is improper if and to the extent that it presupposes the erroneous PSR. Note also that even if TT were a necessary truth, empirical investigation might well still be the only way to discover that it is true and to justify our belief that it is true; that a truth is necessary does not entail that it is knowable only a priori. And even if TT were necessary, hence true in every world, still we could not refute it merely by conjuring a pair of wild worlds in which the same *P*-sentences are true but not the same *N*-sentences. To counterexample TT, it is necessary instead to describe a pair of uncontroversially *physically* possible worlds in which the same *P*-sentences are true but not the same *N*-sentences (where again a *P*-world may well need to be one that satisfies INV, as well as the other requirements). This is not so easy, as we see in effect in §5.1.

TT is a minimal determination thesis, at least with respect to some stronger ones discussed in the literature. For example, Horgan and Hellman separately mention versions that would apply to ST-regions

---

[61]Cf. Horgan (1984).

within *P*-worlds, rather than to entire *P*-worlds.[62] Such versions would be stronger than TT because they would require that each *N*-phenomenon x be determined by *P*-phenomena within some relatively small ST-region around x, whereas by TT the relevant *P*-phenomena need not be thus local but can be global. But the weaker TT seems preferable, if only to provide for the possibility (shall we say the likelihood) that there are nonphysical truths about the world that are true only in virtue of the totality of the *P*-phenomena. In the same spirit we noted in §1.1.2 that correspondence notions of truth should allow for truths that are true only in virtue of (because they are about) the whole of what there is. Also, there are problems in specifying how large the "relatively small region" must be, within which the *P*-phenomena determine x. Furthermore, if determination holds for every relatively small ST-region, it need not also hold either for the whole world or for all the truths about the whole world.[63]

In any case, once in possession of TT or an equivalent, we can easily explicate the notion of the specific *P*-phenomena that are the ones to determine some given *N*-phenomenon x. In the manner of §1.1.2, we merely define them as the *P*-phenomena that form the least set that suffices to determine x (or if there is more than one such set, their union). Likewise, we can explicate the notion of the local ST-region within which the *P*-phenomena determine x, as the ST-region in which the *P*-phenomena of no subregion determine x (or if there is more than one such ST-region, their ST-sum). Local determination principles probably are too strong, but TT enables us anyway to speak of the specific *P*-phenomena that determine some given *N*-phenomenon, and of the relevant local ST-region (if any) within which the *P*-phenomena determine the *N*-phenomenon. Thus TT combines specificity with the same allowance for holistic or ecological thinking that we saw in the physical discernibility principle MND.

There are principles of determination/supervenience that imply both TT and MND. Thus someone might express physicalism, or a component of it, as the thesis that given any two *P*-worlds, there is no difference either between them or between any two things within them without some physical difference. This is equivalent, nearly enough, to the conjunction of MND and TT (and possibly INV, depending on what a *P*-world is). But even though there is nothing wrong with conjoining the principles, we do better to state them separately, if only

[62]But they do not adopt them: Hellman (1985), 611, and earlier in correspondence; Horgan (1982). Cf. Lewis (1983a), 359.

[63]As Horgan and Hellman separately point out: Hellman in correspondence; Horgan (1982).

to be clear as to how different their claims are about the expressive power of the language of physics, or about the relations between physical and nonphysical properties and events. The language of physics might be capable of discerning all discernibles within each world, yet its truths incapable of determining all or many N-truths, and vice versa. The physicalist, of course, believes that the language of physics is capable of doing both, at least at some later stage of physics if not now. TT is as much a regulative ideal as MND, and in the same senses, with the same sort of justification (§4.2). To paraphrase Quine, if as physicists we suspected there was any event whose traits were not determined ultimately by phenomena allowed for by our physical theory, we would seek a way of supplementing our theory. And if challenged to define the comprehensiveness that physics seeks, we have a ready reply: physics is truly comprehensive or complete when MND and TT are both true; they are what 'full coverage' means.

The minimal physicalist principles, then, are (i) everything whatever is a mathematical-physical entity; (ii) every discernible must be physically discernible; (iii) all truth is determined by physical truth, and, if not already implied by (i)–(iii), a realism of the sort described in §1.1. Variations on all three are possible, as seen, and some such variation may be preferable for certain purposes. But the variations closely resemble INV, MND, and TT, as also seen, so that no very fundamental changes would be needed in what lies ahead that is based on them. Family quarrels among physicalists over the final, ultrarefined formulation of their principles should not be allowed to blind others, let alone themselves, to the profound implications the minimal theses have in whatever variation.

4.4. Determination by Reference

Thus far we have spoken of the determination of one kind of fact or one kind of truth by another. Can we come closer to the world?
—G. P. HELLMAN AND F. W. THOMPSON

Reference is supposed to obtain or not obtain, between a word and the world, regardless of our intent in using the word. This contrasts with the more ordinary intentional sense of 'refer', according to which I can refer to whatever I like when I use a word, even a word like 'unicorn', whether or not there are any unicorns. According to some physicalists, what the terms from a given domain refer to, in the nonintentional sense, is no mere accident. For they believe that

TR. All reference is determined ultimately by physical truth.

According to TR, the references even of the physical terms are physically determined. Physics is so comprehensive as to apply to itself, in
the sense that physical reference is determined by physical truth. Some
other physicalists, following Quine, deny not only TR but that reference is determined by *any* kind of truth.[64] Still other philosophers reply
that at best the Quinean arguments for indeterminacy show only that
reference is not determined by truths about the behavior of speakers,
including verbal behavior and dispositions to respond in certain ways to
the linguist's queries. Truths about behavior, they point out, hardly
exhaust the totality of physical (or other) truths that could well be
relevant to determining reference.[65]

Both sorts of physicalist agree that the physical facts determine all
the facts, including the facts of semantics. They merely disagree as to
whether there is a fact of the matter about reference. If there is, then in
accord with TT it must be determined ultimately by physical truth. If
there is not, then there is no truth of the matter to be determined, and
TT remains satisfied. If there is no truth of the matter, then a term refers
to this thing or that only relative to some way of translating the language the term belongs to. And which translation to use would itself be
undetermined by the physical truths (since otherwise, reference would
be determinate after all).

To the extent that disputes over the determinacy of translation and
reference represent a family quarrel within physicalism, we can ignore
them. But there is a related issue we cannot ignore. Many concepts of
truth seem to presuppose some notion of objective reference. We may
wonder, then, whether a sentence could be true—objectively true, true
in the realist's sense—if there were no fact of the matter as to its terms'
reference. If not, and if reference is indeed inscrutable, then the physicalist's commitment to realism is undercut, ironically by a physicalist's
own arguments—Quine's—for the inscrutability of reference. But in
§1.1 we saw that a realist concept of truth does not presuppose an
objective or determinate relation of reference between terms and pieces
of the world. Thus even if reference is inscrutable, and even if no sense
can be made of the notion of the intended interpretation of our words,
the truth-values of our whole sentences are nevertheless determined by
the world. We saw further how to define an unproblematic correspondence between true sentences and the pieces of the world in virtue of

[64]Cf. Quine (1960), ch. 2; Quine (1969), ch. 2; Quine (1970b).
[65]Cf. Friedman (1975); Hellman and Thompson (1977), Appendix; Tuana.

which they are true. So even if there is no fact of the matter as regards reference, still our words do not stray so far from the world as to frustrate realism or a correspondence theory of truth.

Whether or not reference is determined ultimately by physical truth, we may wonder[66] whether

RR. All reference is determined ultimately by physical reference,

and (if not) whether

RT. All truth is determined ultimately by physical reference.

Neither RR nor RT implies that reference is determinate. Only if physical reference itself were determined by some sort of truth would it follow via RR that there is a fact of the matter as regards reference.

What are some of the logical relations among TT, TR, RT, and RR? TR, as lately noted, does not follow from any of the other three. For simplicity, suppose further that the truth-value of a sentence is determined by the reference of its terms (a supposition that some theorists of truth would reject; fix reference, they say, and still the truth-value can depend also on something else, such as on whether the sentence is warrantedly assertible). Granted the supposition, TR still does not follow from any of the others, but they all follow from it. Also, RT follows from each of the other three, while none follows from it. Thus TR (the determination of all reference by *P*-truth) is the strongest of the four, logically speaking, and RT (the determination of all truth by *P*-reference) the weakest.

Even though RT is the logically weakest, and even though it therefore is a candidate for being the minimal physicalist determination principle, we probably would hesitate to call a position physicalist if it asserted RT rather than TT (the determination of all truth by *P*-truth), even if it also asserted INV and MND (the Inventory and the modal *P*-discernibility of all discernibles). A reason is that by tradition and perhaps by definition, a physicalist is one who holds that the way the world is physically is a matter of what the physical facts about it are, not of the reference of our terms (or not necessarily; under some rather strong assumptions, the two are equivalent). Another reason is that reference—even *P*-reference—may strike us as a less secure notion than truth, since as seen, truth is determined by the world even if reference is not.

---

[66]As have Hellman and Thompson (1975).

It is conceivable, perhaps even likely, that some of these four determination principles apply to certain domains but not to others. For example, RR might apply to chemistry but not to psychology: the reference of chemical terms, but not psychological, would be determined by *P*-reference. Or RT might apply to molecular biology but not to psychology. But TT, the principle of the determination of all truth by *P*-truth, would apply to all the domains, according to the physicalist. Otherwise, the aspects of life expressed within some domain would be left out of account; INV and MND, by themselves, do not imply that or reveal how the insight and understanding unique to a given domain are also, in some derivative sense, part of the explanatory power of physics, or at least a manifestation of its comprehensiveness (§4.3).

Clearly, the possible varieties of physicalism are greatly multipled. Physicalists could differ widely as to what determination principles apply within what domains. Indeed, with respect to one and the same domain, physicalists could differ as regards which of its terms have their reference determined by physical truth and which do not; or which have their reference determined by physical reference and which do not. Nor is that the end of the variety. Determination of or by reference might fail. Yet determination of or by *partial* reference might succeed.[67] Such "partial" principles might apply to some domains but not to others, while the straight principles remain in effect elsewhere. The conceivable combinations seem endless. The unity in all this variety would be provided by the minimal INV, MND, and TT.

Even though RT is the logically weakest of the lot, RT makes a substantial claim: nonphysical truth is determined by *P*-reference, hence by how our uses of terms at the level of physics select (or "disclose"; §5.3) various pieces of the world, or "carve up the noumenal dough."[68] To appreciate the significance of this claim, we need to see how it contrasts both with TT and with RR.

TT can be false even when RT is true. That is, determination of all truth by *P*-truth might fail, while determination of all truth by *P*-reference succeeds. This suggests that physicalists might fall back on RT if the logically stronger TT were to be eliminated. They could argue correctly that any evidence for TT is also evidence for RT (since TT implies RT), and they could try to show that evidence alleged against TT does not count against the weaker RT. Then they could try to reconstruct physicalism by using RT, rather than TT, as their minimal determination principle. This would involve explaining how, despite

---

[67]Cf. Field (1973), (1974).
[68]Field (1982), 561.

the remarks above, a physicalist properly so-called is not committed to TT. This might be done by explaining how and in what sense the faces of existence are accounted for, in virtue of RT rather than TT—how the unique insight and understanding of various domains are also, in some derivative sense, part of the explanatory power or scope of physics in virtue of the determination of all truth by *P*-reference. To this end, an embattled physicalist might argue that the explanatory power of physics, or at least its empirical adequacy and comprehensiveness, depends in large measure on how its terms select or individuate various pieces of the world. Conceivably, therefore, if improbably, determination of truth by *P*-reference could be all a physicalist really needs.

The contrast between RT and RR is just as instructive, though in a different vein. RR can be false even when RT is true; that is, determination of all reference by *P*-reference might fail, while determination of all truth by *P*-reference succeeds. Now suppose RR is false, *perhaps* because some nonphysical terms, unlike the physical terms, *do not have any precise reference* (as is the case with 'bald', 'yellowish', possibly 'angry', and so on). Either they fail to refer to anything, or they are so vague that there is no clear boundary between what in the world they do or might refer to and what they do not (which does not entail they do not refer to anything at all). They may be so ill-defined, their usage so nebulous, obscure, and tortured, that even in an objectively correct translation scheme they have no precise reference (as would be the case with 'bald' and 'yellowish'). Notorious examples are familiar from religion, politics, and some philosophy, though I will name no names, and examples abound in other domains as well.

Despite this flaw in the vocabulary in question—indeed sometimes because of it—such terms can often be used to express truths. That is, certain sentences that contain the defective terms can often be true (or false), as is 'Some bald men sport wigs'. When they are true, then like all truths, their truth would be determined by physical truth, granted TT, and by physical reference, since TT implies RT. Thus construed, RT allows physicalists to express their confidence that vocabulary at the level of physics does have precise reference, and that such physical reference determines all truth, without their having to concede a similar respect for the nonphysical vocabulary in question. It follows that the determination of all truth by *P*-truth and/or *P*-reference does not presuppose that a nonphysical term must have a precise reference among the mathematical-physical entities, or among any entities. Like reducibility, precision is a red herring.

As a corollary, physicalists, whatever they may sometimes think, need heap no scorn on a domain of discourse just because some or all of its terms fail to have precise reference by their standards. They can well afford to admit—indeed to insist—that vagueness and novel or even tortured usage often are indispensable for certain purposes, including the creation of momentous new ways of seeing ourselves and our worlds. Metaphors are especially powerful in this regard, and we explore a physicalist accommodation of metaphor in §5.3. Physicalists can revel in the myriad ways language works, including the occasional lack of precise reference. And all the while they can reflect that the diverse domains also enjoy a unity in which truths at the level of physics determine the truth-values of sentences elsewhere, even when they contain terms whose reference, if any, is utterly obscure.

4.5. Emergence: From the Physical to the Nonphysical

> *Emergent entities . . . though linked to entities that are*
> *materially composed . . . cannot themselves be characterized*
> *solely in terms of composition or material attributes. . . . There*
> *is a profound sense in which human persons cannot be*
> *physicalistically reduced.*
>
> —JOSEPH MARGOLIS

When all is said and done, what sorts of relations, according to the physicalist, are supposed to obtain between the basic physical entities and such seemingly nonphysical things as sentience, consciousness, persons, intentions, and culture generally? Not all is said and done, of course, not in this volume or in a hundred. Physicalists doubtless will continue to elaborate their principles in ways undreamed of. More to the point, many of the details about how persons, say, are related to the physical entities must surely be provided by special disciplines, not all in the sciences. Neither the physicalist nor anyone else can anticipate just how the relevant disciplines will evolve.

Philosophers there are who exploit this necessary incompleteness of detail to excuse any and all shortcomings of physicalism. They promise that advances in the relevant special disciplines will answer our questions and bear out the physicalist principles. But why should we believe in advance that advances in biochemistry, neurophysiology, psychology, linguistics, and so on will conform to the physicalist's vision? One reason, according to physicalists, is that the principles operate as regulative ideals. If we suspected that some truths about thoughts, emotions, intentions, and the rest were not determined by truths at the level of neuroscience, and beyond neuroscience at the level of physics, then we should improve our physics, or try to, perhaps by revising the list of physical predicates or even the physical inventory itself. To take an extreme sort of example, it is conceivable that so-called ESP phenomena are evidence of a "force field" not now recognized in physics. That is, the new field would not be identical with any vector sum of the basic forces presently thought to be sufficient (let us say the gravitational, electromagnetic, and the weak and strong nuclear forces). If so, the proper course, endorsed by physicalism, would be to enrich our basic list of predicates so as to develop a theory of the new force within physics.

This regulative character of the principles, with their consequent flexibility, can be reassuring. But it is hardly sufficient—indeed it is beside the point—for answering our questions about the relations between persons, say, and the purely physical entities listed at the *present* stage of physics. That, after all, is what we really want to know. For if the kinds of relations envisaged by the physicalist between today's physical and the nonphysical could not obtain *even in principle,* then no advances in any disciplines could possibly bear them out. There must be a plausible and coherent framework of envisaged relations which the advances could illustrate. Otherwise they could just as easily testify to some antiphysicalist moral.

Whatever the framework, it must begin with the fact that any physicalism worthy of the name is committed to INV, according to which everything is identical with some mathematical-physical entity, though not necessarily with one that is individuated by a mathematical-physical term. INV entails that even where we distinguish the physical from the nonphysical, still a nonphysical entity is identical after all with some mathematical-physical entity. To give the point an air of paradox, we may say that nothing but mathematical-physical entities exist, yet not everything is nothing but a mathematical-physical thing. What does this mean?

Start with properties. Let us say that a property is nonphysical as regards its domain status, or is domain-nonphysical, iff every predicate that either expresses it (in case it is actually expressed) or would express it (in case it is only expressible) belongs to some domain other than physics. This characterization requires further clarification, below, but let us go along with it for now.[69] The urgent point is that even though a property can be nonphysical as regards its domain status, still the property will be a mathematical-physical entity, assuming it satisfies INV. That is, its *inventory* status is unaffected by its *domain* status; its status as a mathematical-physical *entity* is unaffected by what sorts of predicates *express* it. And properties do satisfy INV, in virtue of being functions

---

[69]See also §5.4 on inexpressible properties.

from possible worlds to extensions (§4.1). Thus a property is a set somewhere in the hierarchy defined in §4.1, and therefore a mathematical entity, hence mathematical-physical, even though it can be domain-nonphysical, depending on which predicates would express it. This is the sense in which a property can be nonphysical and not nothing but a mathematical-physical thing, yet identical after all with some mathematical-physical entity.

What about entities not in the hierarchy of sets? According to INV, any such concrete x is identical with some ST-sum of entities that satisfy a positive predicate on the preferred list of physical predicates. Let us also say, equivalently, that x is composed of physical entities of a listed kind. As repeatedly emphasized, even when x is thus physically or materially composed, it does not follow that x is individuated by any physical term. To that extent, then, and in that special sense, x is a nonphysical entity if and when it is not individuated by any physical term. To that extent also, x is not nothing but a physical entity. Let us say of any such x that x is wholly nonphysical as regards individuation. This is one sense in which a concrete or spatiotemporal entity x can be nonphysical, yet identical after all with some physical entity.

Are there any concrete entities not individuated by some purely physical term? If not, no concretum is wholly nonphysical as regards individuation. Fortunately, this question can be left open by minimal physicalism, as ultimately I do here. Even so, I suspect there are (perhaps must be) concreta not physically individuated (even when they are to be individuated merely as this concretum or that, rather than as a person, say, or an inscription, or whatever). The reason is that the only initially attractive argument that they are all physically individuatable seems in trouble. The argument assumes that each concretum occupies its own unique spatiotemporal region, that it could thus be individuated as this concretum or that by its ST-region, and that such ST-locations can always be specified by mathematical-physical descriptions. We are then to infer universal physical individuatability. One problem with this argument is in its opening assumption, to which there are counterexamples in the form of, say, two chemical reactions in the same flask, two radiations in the same cavity, and so on. Another problem is in the third assumption; there may well be more occupied ST-regions than there are descriptions. For even though there is a countable infinity of the latter, there could well be an uncountable infinity of the former, as would be the case if some sort of continuous field or perhaps background radiation is distributed through all spacetime, so that each of the uncountably many ST-regions is occupied by some distinct subfield of the field (distinct perhaps also because the field intensity varies infinitesimally from point to point).

Even if no concrete entity x can be wholly nonphysical as regards individuation, it does not follow that x can be characterized solely in terms of composition or in terms of physical properties. This would follow only if *all* x's properties were physical or compositional (or reducible to physical or compositional properties). If, at the other extreme, all x's properties are irreducibly nonphysical, then let us say that x is wholly or purely nonphysical as regards properties (not that there need be any such x). If some of x's properties are physical and some are irreducibly nonphysical, then x is partly physical and partly nonphysical as regards properties.

Thus x could be partly or perhaps wholly nonphysical as regards its properties, and also composed of whatever counts as matter according to today's physics. This is another sense in which a concrete or spatiotemporal entity x can be nonphysical yet identical after all with some physical entity. If we put both senses together, we may say that such an x can be nonphysical, wholly or partly, as regards individuation and/or properties, yet identical with some physical entity or other (though this should be interpreted so as to exclude the case in which x is partly physical as regards individuation but wholly nonphysical as regards properties).

Part of what nonreductive physicalism envisages, then, is a monism of entities (the mathematical-physical) combined with a dualism of their properties (the nonphysical and the physical). And this dualism of properties allows the physical entities to be subdivided, as regards their properties, into the purely physical entities and the wholly or partly nonphysical entities. Thereby we are again prevented from saying that everything is *nothing but* a physical entity—meaning that all its properties are or are reducible to physical properties—even though nothing but physical entities exist. Actually a *pluralism* of kinds of properties is required, unless all the nonphysical properties are identical with or in some sense reducible to a special class of nonphysical properties, which is exceedingly unlikely.

Some properties presumably have multiple domain status. That is, such a property would be expressed by predicates from different domains. For example, if 'water' and 'H_2O' express the same property, and if these two predicates belong to distinct domains (roughly the vernacular and the physical-chemical, respectively), then the property they express has dual domain status. Clearly, if a concrete thing x has a property with multiple domain status, and if one of the domains is physics, then x can be neither wholly nonphysical as regards properties nor wholly physical (assuming irreducibility).

In § 4.0 we characterized emergent entities or properties roughly as those which cannot be reduced to any from the domain with respect to which they are said to be emergent.[70] This rough characterization works well enough for properties: a property is emergent with respect to a domain P iff it is reducible to no P-property. But the rough characterization works less well for entities, meaning the concrete, spatiotemporal ones. The idea would be that x is emergent with respect to P just if x is wholly non-P as regards individuation. The trouble is this. Even when x—a person, say—is not wholly nonphysical as regards individuation, often we wish to say that x is emergent, on the ground that x's key properties are nonphysical. So we ought not limit the emergent concreta to those not suitably individuatable. We should also include those whose key properties are irreducible to the properties of the domain in question. Hence distinctions are in order. Let us say that x is emergent with respect to P as regards individuation iff x is not individuated by any P-term. Let us say further that x is wholly emergent with respect to P as regards properties iff none of x's properties is reducible to any P-property. Clearly, x might be nonemergent as regards individuation, yet mostly emergent as regards properties.

We need one last batch of terminology. This concerns states of entities (or of systems of entities). Let us construe states of entities (or of systems) as certain (complex) properties of those entities (or systems). For example, if to be in a functional state is to bear certain causal or other relations to various things and states, then the functional state is the property of bearing just those relations to those things and states. A functional state then is a functional property, an intentional state is an intentional property, and so on. Construing states as kinds of properties allows us to construe realization of a state simply as instantiation of the appropriate property. There is no need to invoke an additional, *sui generis* relation of embodiment. Of course, we remain free to speak of embodiment if we mean just realization and if realization in turn comes to instantiation.

States typically are not defined by reference to the stuff of which the entities are made that can realize them. Entities composed of very different stuff could all realize one and the same state, whether the stuff is biological, electronic, bionic, or mental. Even Tinkertoys will do. And even for an entity composed of a given stuff, a functional state, for example, typically is not defined by reference to any physically specifiable states of the entity (sometimes called structural states). Thus one and the same functional state could be realized in the same entity (or system) x when x is in any one of a perhaps indefinite variety of distinct physical (or structural) states.

[70]On emergence, see further Klee.

These possibilities have given rise to powerful arguments against the reducibility of various states—functional, intentional, logical—to physical states, or even to natural states.[71] Thus if a certain intentional state, say, is not type-identical with any natural state, then it would not be type-identical with any brain state or process, though of course one's brain certainly can be in or realize some such intentional state. An intentional state would be a state of a physical entity but not a physical or natural state of that entity.

Suppose some concrete entity (or system) x realizes a state emergent with respect to the natural sciences in general and the neurosciences in particular. Then presumably there is also some physical state x realizes. Yet the presumption may be a shade too strong. To say that x realizes a physical state normally suggests that x realizes a state expressed by a predicate from today's physics (though we may not know which one). Yet it is possible, in many cases, that the expressive power of present-day physical language falls short of expressing the structural state x happens to be in when x realizes the emergent state in question. Indeed the language even of the whole of natural science may on occasion fall short in this respect. What we must say instead is that when x realizes some state that is emergent with respect not only to physics but to natural science, then there is also some state or other at the level of physics that x realizes, though not necessarily one expressed by any predicate from today's physics or even from today's natural science, and perhaps not from tomorrow's either.

Expressible or not, what is the relation between this physical state P and the emergent state N that x also realizes? They cannot be identical, or the same state, since by hypothesis N is emergent. Nor can we say in general that necessarily if x realizes N, then x realizes P. For N might be defined in such a way that x can realize N when x is in the physical state P and also when x is in a different physical state. We cannot even say, in general, that whenever x realizes P, then x realizes N. For N might be defined in such a way that no structural-physical state of x is sufficient for x to realize N. Instead, it may be that x realizes N only when x realizes a certain (sort of) structural-physical state in some wider context. If so, the relations x bears to certain other things—via its cultural role, say, or its linguistic role, or (other) intentions about it—must be taken into account, in addition to x's structural-physical state. The relations between x's physical states and x's emergent states often obtain only or largely in virtue of x's place in a wider environment.

Can the physicalist say something more positive here? MND (the

---

[71]See Margolis (1984), chs. 3–4, for a critical survey.

P-discernibility of all discernibles) implies that for any difference in the emergent states *x* realizes, there is some physical difference between *x* in one of its emergent states and *x* in another. The difference need not have to do with *x* in isolation from its surroundings; it can also be a matter of a relation between *x* and a wider context. Thus MND applies even when the emergent states in question are so defined that no structural-physical state of *x* is sufficient for *x* to realize one of the emergent states, but, instead, is sufficient only in a wider context.

Can the physicalist say still more? TT implies that truths at the level of physics determine which emergent states *x* realizes. But this does not mean that physical truths about *x* in isolation will always suffice to determine which states *x* realizes. On the contrary, TT is designed with an eye to the necessity, on occasion, of taking into account *x*'s relations to its surroundings, if all the truths about *x* are to be determined by truths at the level of physics. The latter truths can range over anything, including what in various nonphysical domains would be called *x*'s cultural role, or its linguistic or ecological role, or whatever.

Descend now from the thin air of these abstractions to the ground of an example. The slabs in Chaco Canyon, we may suppose, are a solar marker (lunar, too) in an ancient pueblo observatory (§2.6). Even in calling them a solar marker we presuppose that they played a certain cultural role (a role, as it turns out, in the agrarian society of the Anasazi Indians). They are a solar marker mainly in virtue of certain relations they bear to that culture, just as a hammer is a hammer largely in virtue of its role as a certain tool. The structural-physical states of the slabs—their composition, size, weight, shape, and even their orientation to the sun and the butte—do not by themselves make the slabs a solar marker, as we see further below. It is only because these physical states are realized by the slabs in the wider, cultural context that they are a solar marker.

Presumably, the property of being a solar marker is emergent with respect to physics and indeed natural science. For a solar marker is such only in virtue of certain intentions, and intentions are widely supposed to be irreducible to natural properties or relations. Assuming that the property of being a solar marker is emergent, Chaco Canyon yields a clear case in which the physical truths about *x* in isolation (the system of the slabs) hardly suffice to determine that *x* does (or does not) instantiate a certain emergent property. A much wider set of truths at the level of physics must be brought in. Such truths will determine whatever it is about the Anasazis and the slabs that determines that the slabs are a solar marker.

By no means does this imply that physicists could tell us the slabs are a solar marker if only they were to bring in the relevant physical truths about the culture. One reason is that such truths would be enormously complex and unwieldy; better by far to let anthropologists tell the story in their own terms. But there is a deeper reason why physicists are out of their depth here, so long as they use only their special vocabulary. Anthropologists tell their story largely in terms of the intentions of the Anasazis. Intentional states, we have supposed, are irreducible. Therefore, the physicist's story could not express the Anasazis' intentions, even though it could express the physical truths that determine what the intentions were. Since the physicist's story could not express the intentions, it could not tell us that the slabs are a solar marker. For they are a solar marker only in virtue of those intentions. Even if physicists could have predicted the existence and the structural-physical state of the slabs, unlikely though that is, still they could not have told us that the slabs are a solar marker.

The same is true of any other entities that realize certain properties in virtue of some functional-intentional role (still assuming the irreducibility of the latter). Inscriptions, for example, and utterances are much more than mere physical marks or sounds;[72] hammers are much more than shaped stone, steel, or wood. As with the slabs in Chaco Canyon, no physical-structural truths about hammers and inscriptions even in their wider context could tell us that they are cultural entities. Nor could such truths tell us that the inscriptions belong to a language, let alone what language they belong to and what they mean within it. If only because language is so intimately involved in what it is to be a person, persons too would slip through the physicist's conceptual net, though not the physicalist's. For the physicalist can allow—indeed insist on—the use of an irreducible nonphysical vocabulary to express the properties essential for something to be a person, whatever those properties prove to be.

In view of all this, what finally can be said about the relations between an emergent state N that x realizes and the structural-physical state P that x happens at the same time also to realize? In the case of the slabs, what anthropologists discover is that the emergent state or property of being a solar marker is realized in stone, and not, as it might have been, in wood. They discover also that it is realized in stone in an ingenious way: the sun's horizontal motion is translated into a vertical one. This contrasts with the possibly less sophisticated way in which a

[72]Cf. Margolis (1978), 20–21, and chs. 5, 10, 12.

solar marker is realized at Stonehenge. And we learn also that there were no solar markers much before constructions like those at Stonehenge and Chaco Canyon. Here is something new under the sun.

In short, the relation between P and N in this case is accidental, historical, particular, and novel. There is no general sort of connection—hence no lawlike connection or even constant conjunction—between the slabs' structural-physical state and their being a solar marker (though there are some one-way generalizations from N to the complements of some P-states, such as 'Necessarily, any solar marker is not a dome that blots out the whole sky').[73] A totally different configuration of stone (and wood), such as that at Stonehenge, can also be a solar marker. And slabs in the same configuration, but formed by chance as the butte weathered, would not be a solar marker (unless subsequently used as such). The slabs are a solar marker only because the Anasazis made them so. It never happened quite that way before, and it will never happen exactly that way again. This is part of the fascination in learning just how the Anasazis did it, and part also of the fascination of all art.

Natural sciences higher than physics often are no better off in expressing, or reducing, or predicting, or explaining. They too must confess that the relation between the natural states they can express and certain emergent properties they cannot is historical, accidental, unique. From this point of view, persons—who are partly if not wholly emergent as regards properties and individuation—are to some extent works of art. They are made the persons they are in large part by their own prior decisions, plus also the intentions of others. Even if a person's body were duplicated down to the last microstate of its tiniest particle, still the duplicate need not be identical with the original person, or realize that person's every property. The reason is that particular persons are the persons they are partly in virtue of certain functional relations they bear to their culture, relations that involve the intentions of others and of themselves earlier in life. There is no guarantee that the duplicate would bear the same requisite relations to the culture, no guarantee that others in the culture would or could accord it the same roles (as parent, as daughter or son, as possessor of rights, and so on). Indeed if the roles required the duplicate and the original to be in the same place at the same time, the roles could not be the same.

Even if the roles did not require this, duplicate and original still might have different roles, if only because one has a birth certificate

---

[73]Here I am indebted to Hellman. Complements of P-states, however, are not in general themselves P-states, by §4.2.

while the other has a cloning certificate (not that origins are essential to the identity of every kind of thing). In like manner the Anasazis, if presented with a duplicate of their solar marker, would not have accorded the religious role to the duplicate that they doubtless accorded the original, if only because *they* made the original, their toil endowing it with much of its aura. Similarly, a perfect forgery of a Rembrandt—even an exact replica down to the last microparticle—would not have the same status as the original, however stunning it might be as a technological achievement. We would not say that there were two Rembrandt paintings, any more than we would say that there were two Anasazi solar markers. There is only one, the original, utterly unique in the way it emerged.

Persons are no more likely to be identifiable as such by reference solely to their structural-physical properties than are hammers, artifacts, artworks, or the meanings of our inscriptions and utterances. In the emergence from the physical to the nonphysical, by the time we have reached the human level—if not long before—we have entered a profoundly different realm.

4.6. Comprehensiveness versus Monopoly

> *The pluralist['s] . . . typical adversary is the monopolistic materialist or physicalist who maintains that one system, physics, is preeminent and all-inclusive, such that every other version must eventually be reduced to it or rejected as false or meaningless.*
>
> —NELSON GOODMAN

We can tighten our belts without narrowing our minds. Such is the message of nonreductive physicalism. That is, we can tighten our inventory of what there is so as to include just the physical, without presuming reducibility of everything, or even of very much, to physics, and therefore without presuming that everything is nothing but a physical thing. A monism of entities is entirely compatible with a pluralism of properties and with everything the pluralism implies for the autonomy of domains beyond physics and beyond all the sciences, as we lately noted in connection with works of art. The phrase 'monopolistic physicalist' contains no redundancy, whatever Goodman may think,[74] since some physicalisms are monopolistic and some are not.

Minimal physicalism is not monopolistic, in several senses. Being nonreductive, the minimal principles are truth-preserving without re-

---

[74]The epigraph is from N. Goodman (1978a), 4.

quiring even accidental coextensiveness of the relevant terms. Nor do they require the still weaker relation that Goodman elsewhere calls extensional isomorphism between terms from disparate domains (by which certain structural relations among the terms from one domain, rather than their extensions, are preserved by terms from another).[75] Nor is minimal physicalism monopolistic in the sense that physics enjoys unconditional preeminence over all other domains. To be sure, only if physics enjoys some kind of priority will there be much significance in such principles as that all truth is determined by physical truth, that there can be no difference without a physical difference, and that everything is some mathematical-physical entity or other. But the priority involved is highly conditional: *if* we are interested not only in the kind of objectivity physics pursues but also in its all-inclusive or comprehensive coverage and its characteristic types of explanation, then the minimal principles will seem correspondingly significant. If we are interested instead in, say, what the evidence is for a physical theory, or in what and how its terms mean, then certain evidential or semantic truths acquire a corresponding priority. And if we are interested in explaining the slabs in Chaco Canyon as a solar marker, then we must speak with anthropologists, and think with them too.

The relevant difference here between physics and anthropology is not that the former cares about objective truth while the latter does not; they both care. Instead, the difference has something to do with the comprehensiveness of physics, in contrast with the narrower scope of anthropology. In some sense, physics applies to every region of space and time,[76] whereas anthropology applies to human beings and their works, including their language and culture, all of which are limited to our planet and to a certain time. Discoveries in anthropology, like the one about the solar marker in Chaco Canyon, typically are to the effect that this or that emergent cultural state or property is realized in some particular way at some place and time. The relation between the realized emergent property and what realizes it typically is accidental, historical, and wholly novel (§4.5). This is true even when what is realized is some cultural or linguistic universal, assuming there are such.

Yet physics encounters its share of the accidental (as in quantum indeterminacy), the historical (as in the expansion from the big bang), and the novel (perhaps in the big bang itself). The contrast with other domains as regards comprehensiveness has more to do with emergence

---

[75] N. Goodman (1966). Cf. Hellman (1978); N. Goodman's reply (1978b) seems based on a captious reading.

[76] Cf. Earman (1978).

and with abstraction. Notoriously, physics abstracts away from all those properties of a thing—including its emergent properties, if any—that are irrelevant to framing hypotheses that apply everywhere in spacetime. Physics therefore concentrates on such properties as mass, motion, energy, spatiotemporal relation and configuration, and so on.

The same emphasis on complete generality often leads physics to concentrate not so much on ordinary things as on some of their extraordinary parts—the particles and fields of which they are composed. Certain physical properties of the ordinary things are then explained by reference to certain properties and relations of the parts. Nearly as often, certain physical properties of a thing are explained by reference to a larger environment of which it is a part, as when the earth's orbit is explained (via general relativity) in terms of the curvature of spacetime induced by the sun and all the planets. Holistic thinking is essential not only to ecology and some religions but also to much contemporary physics.

Whatever the means in physics, the end is the same: to frame theories so general as to apply everywhere everywhen. *All* objects, regardless of place or date, remain at rest or in uniform motion unless subjected to an external force, according to Newton. *All* objects, everywhere everywhen, have a velocity not exceeding that of light, according to Einstein. *All* objects have no determinate momentum and position simultaneously, according to quantum theory. In *all* interactions, mass-energy is conserved. And so it goes.

This sort of comprehensiveness in physics—its characteristic all-inclusiveness—must not be confused with monopoly. To be about everything is not to say everything about it, or even to try. Monopoly sets in when someone supposes that discourse outside physics is false or meaningless unless it can be reduced to the vocabulary required for framing these ultrageneral physical theories. It sets in also when someone supposes that such generality, or its pursuit, is more important—according to some absolute scale—than anything else, thus downgrading the value of everything from art to zoology.

The claims of nonreductive physicalism also are completely comprehensive. *Everything,* everywhere everywhen, is some mathematical-physical entity or other, even though few things (if any) are nothing but physical things (§§4.5, 7.5, 7.6, 8.1). Given *any* nonphysical difference, there must be some physical difference or other. And *all* nonphysical truth is determined by physical truth. Monopoly sets in only when someone insists that this sort of comprehensiveness must be conjoined with universal reducibility, or else with some doctrine of the unconditional priority of physical truth.

Occasionally, physicalists assert—or seem to assert—that physics describes "the only real world," or perhaps *the* world, *the* way things really are. When they do so, they again commit monopoly, though not quite in the senses discussed so far. Minimal physicalism is not monopolistic in this sense either. Neither its own comprehensiveness nor its emphasis on the pursuit by physics of combined comprehensiveness and objective truth implies that physics describes the only real world. Of course, if this means merely that everything is composed of mathematical-physical entities, then what is asserted is merely INV (§4.1). But usually much more is meant when someone asserts (or denies) that physics describes the only real world. Often the idea is that only those things denoted or expressed by a clearly physical term are real. This would rule out any property emergent with respect to physics, such as the property of being a solar marker, plus other functional-intentional properties. But if such properties were "unreal," then strictly speaking there would be no solar markers or other cultural artifacts, which is absurd; there *are* solar markers. The only relevant way to deny their reality is to fall back on the discredited view that what is irreducible is nonexistent.

Perhaps what is meant, when one says that physics describes the only real world, is that its predicates are true of physical entities. But the same can be said of other domains of truth. The predicate 'is a solar marker', for example, is true of a physical entity: namely, the array of stone in Chaco Canyon (plus the one at Stonehenge). Perhaps what is meant is that physical predicates are true of physical entities, and such entities are the only real ones. But this merely conjoins what can be said of other domains of truth with an assertion of INV. As repeatedly seen, this is quite compatible with the existence of an enormous variety of things that can hardly be said to be nothing but physical things. Thus the world or, better, the worlds of emergent entities (including artifacts, art works, language, persons, and more) stand proof against the view that physics describes the only real world. Again, a monism of entities is entirely compatible with a pluralism of properties.

It is compatible also, for closely related reasons, with a pluralism of worlds, where a world is roughly any collection or realm of things describable *as* such-and-such—say, *as* a solar marker—only in the vocabulary of a certain domain. Thus there are as many distinctive worlds in this sense as there are domains of properties irreducible one to another, even though there is only one world in the sense of the sum total of what there is (§3.1). Is a monism of entities and the universe they compose compatible as well with a pluralism of faces of existence? That it is would be clear *if* we could equate a face of existence with a world.

But we cannot equate them. A domain of truth in a vocabulary from our language at present expresses a face of existence, according to §1.2, though not every face need be so expressible. This means there are at least as many distinctive faces of existence as there are present domains of truth, regardless of whether the properties expressed by terms from the domains are reducible. So the faces would outrun the worlds, since irreducibility of the relevant properties is essential to the latter but irrelevant to the former.

Faces of existence ought not to be distinguished on the basis solely of irreducibility. Our choice of vocabulary to describe ourselves and our relations to other things can make an enormous difference in what we feel and think, even where the vocabulary is reducible to some other we might have chosen instead. The two sorts of description typically have effects on us, and on what we may become, which are largely independent of the reference of their terms. Sense, association, imagery, and so on, have the main effect (§5.3). Sameness of reference is largely beside the point here.

Better by far to equate a face of existence with a "global-sentential property" of the whole of existence—namely, the property of there being a certain vocabulary such that if it belonged to our language today, it would form a domain of truth about the universe or some of its parts (though this characterization will be revised in §5.3, to take account of the role of metaphor). The whole domain of truth may then be said to express the property. As regards inventory status, a global-sentential property is like any other. Unlike most properties, it is instantiated by the universe as a whole. The distinctive vocabulary of the sentences that would compose a domain of truth gives rise to a distinctive global-sentential property, and thereby to a distinctive face of existence, regardless of any reducibility that might hold from one vocabulary to another. A particular vocabulary "indexes" the corresponding global-sentential property, which we may therefore call a "vocabulary-indexed global-sentential property," though that is a jawbreaker.

According to the physicalist, all we are and all we can hope to be we owe to the dispositions of entities at the level of physics. This can sound depressing. Then we reflect that we are emergent beings. What we are and what we can hope to be is hardly exhausted by what can be expressed in physics or indeed in any of the sciences. We are not nothing but physical objects sailing in a physical sea, not even nothing but natural objects. In the emergence from the physical to the nonphysical, by the time we have reached human beings (if not long before), we have entered an irreducibly different realm. If the minimal principles of physicalism are true, then that realm owes everything to the dispositions of the physical entities, yes. But among those entities are some individuated by no term from physics, persons included, whose dispositions are what make their realm so different. For it is persons who make solar markers, artworks, languages, and so much else.

Thus it is that all we are and all we can hope to be we can express only with the help of the arts, literature, morality, religion, philosophy, and more. Many aspects of life are therefore physically or even scientifically inexpressible. At the same time it can also be true, as we have granted for the sake of argument, that nonreductive physicalism leaves no aspect of life out of account.

5   Relating the Domains

People had become tired of the manyness of things. It was when Thales began talking about the oneness of things that they began to hear the kind of thing they wanted to hear.

—R. G. Collingwood

To see the aim of philosophy as . . . the truth about the terms which provide ultimate commensuration for all human inquiries and activities—is to see human beings as objects rather than subjects.

—Richard Rorty

5.0. Introduction

There are many ways of relating the domains. Vocabulary from one might denote mere myths relative to the truths from another.[1] Or the first vocabulary might be derived or abstracted from the other by deleting various words.[2] Or it might be enriched by adding words from the other, or by adding tenses and other indexicals. Truths from one might constitute the main evidence for or against certain assertions in the other. The truths might instead imply something about the interest or significance, in a certain context, of truths from the other. Or they might describe in a different order, or with different emphasis, certain entities described by the other.[3] The possible ways of relating the domains seem endless.

So also are there many ways of unifying them. One way is to note that they share some feature, say a concept of truth that applies to them all (§§1.1–1.6). They therefore share the logical prerequisites for truth, however much they differ in how best to conduct the trial by prerequi-

[1]Christian.
[2]Goodman (1978a), 14.
[3]Goodman (1978a), 7–14.

sites. This unity of method is compatible with enormous diversity from domain to domain as regards ways of trying to reach agreement on whether the prerequisites have been satisfied, and additionally on whether various claims are true. The domains, or many of them, may well be incommensurable with respect to ways of resolving disagreement,[4] yet entirely commensurable in the sense of having the same truth-concept.

Not that such commensuration is "ultimate," if indeed any feature is. The domains have in common still other features, which on occasion are more significant. For instance, every domain is such that in many contexts we may freely choose to use its vocabulary rather than some other. We may choose to use the language of the marketplace or the bedroom rather than the language of science. Our choice can have enormous effects on us and others, especially if we persist in using one vocabulary to the exclusion of others. We are "a self-defining animal,"[5] not least because of the effects on ourselves of our chosen vocabulary. Accepting responsibility for such choices often is far more urgent than pursuit of truth.

Not even conversation is "the ultimate context" within which the domains may be arranged.[6] For there are other legitimate interests and purposes we sometimes pursue, including some that can result in unification. From the time of Thales one such interest has been in finding some one kind of thing of which everything else is somehow a manifestation such that the way the former is determines how the latter will be.[7] Thales thought the one thing was water. How quaint. Yet for his day it was a brilliant guess. Water was the only substance known to exist in three key forms, liquid, gaseous, and solid. Positing water as the stuff of which everything is composed therefore had a certain explanatory power and a certain power to unify the sciences of the time, which seem to have been rather compartmentalized. What intrigued Thales' contemporaries was his idea that there is one underlying stuff, rather than his belief that it was water.[8] Later philosophers denied that the one stuff was water but retained the presupposition that despite all differences everything is somehow a manifestation, not necessarily via composition, of some one kind or some limited variety of kinds of existent, not necessarily kinds of "underlying stuff" or "substance."

This presupposition, in various forms, has inspired efforts to unify

[4]As Rorty (1979) suggests, 315–316.
[5]C. Taylor, 49. Cf. Rorty (1979), 349–352.
[6]Contrary to Rorty (1979), 389; see also 317, 372, 378–380.
[7]Cf. Feinberg.
[8]Cf. Collingwood, 201–205.

the sciences ever since. Many a metaphysician has sought unity in some limited variety of existents or processes, a unity according to which the properties of these unifiers determine the properties of all the diverse things in which they are manifested. Candidates for the basic unifiers have included Anaximander's indefinite, Parmenides' unchangeable plenum, Democritus' atoms and the void, the Pythagoreans' numbers, Plato's Forms, Aristotle's matter and substance plus its movers, Descartes's two substances, Spinoza's one substance, Hegel's Spirit, Whitehead's actual occasions of becoming, and so on and on. No wonder Collingwood concluded that Greek monotheism and much Christian theology were meant to express and perpetuate Thales' presupposition, which had to struggle against the polytheism of the day.[9]

What, according to the physicalist, is supposed to make physicalism superior to all these other varieties of metaphysics? First we must ask, "Superior in what respect?" The physicalist's answer must be that it is superior not only as regards unifying the domains in terms of a limited variety of entities manifested in all the diverse things the different domains are specifically about, but as regards unifying them in such a way that how these diverse things are is determined by how the unifying entities are. Thus physicalism is alleged to be superior with respect to achieving an aim shared by most metaphysicians from Thales on. Whatever the priority some such metaphysics may enjoy, physicalism included, it is conditional on the interest or value of that aim.

What such metaphysicians share is neither some view of mind as the mirror of nature, contrary to Rorty, nor some related foundationalist view of knowledge, nor even some theory of truth. Systematic philosophers engaged in unifying the domains in terms of a limited variety of entities are interested primarily in what there is. They can differ enormously on how we are supposed to know it, and on how truth and our knowing (if any) are related to what there is. They can even agree with Rorty and others (as I do) that all we can ever know is what-there-is-under-a-description.[10]

At the same time they can differ on the status of the vocabulary used to describe the basic or unifying existents. Doubtless most such metaphysicians have supposed that the vocabulary must enjoy some unconditional priority, since they often suppose that it describes *the* nature of things, some underlying essence, which provides the ultimate commensuration for all the domains. Some have gone further and supposed that the vocabulary should be used in all inquiry. And some have even

[9]Collingwood, ch. 21.
[10]Rorty (1979), 377–378.

supposed that all culture should be remade along the lines of a model or paradigm implied, according to them, by the privileged vocabulary in its intended use. When they suppose any of these things, obviously, they commit monopoly (§4.6).

Whatever these philosophers and their opponents may sometimes have thought, positing unifying entities of which everything else is a manifestation need not entail that there is any such final vocabulary. Physicalism, of all things, affords an illustration. Minimal physicalism does not require that physics describe *the* nature of things, *the* only real world, or an underlying essence, even assuming there are essences. A monism of entities is compatible with a pluralism of properties, of worlds, of faces of existence, and of equally privileged vocabularies. It is compatible also with a pluralism of modes of insight and explanation expressible only in other domains. All this is true of other varieties of metaphysics when they do no more than posit certain unifiers. To echo the deliberately paradoxical saying in §4.5, it is quite possible both that nothing but the unifiers exist, and that not everything is nothing but one of the unifiers. A metaphysician must make further assumptions, beyond an inventory of unifiers, to be forced into committing monopoly. Unfortunately, many metaphysicians do make the further assumptions.

Minimal physicalism is superior to the views of many of these metaphysicians, then, at least as regards avoiding monopolistic pretensions. But there are still other metaphysicians in this multistranded tradition who may also avoid committing monopoly. What is supposed to make physicalism superior to *their* views? To begin with, it must at least be true that the posited unifying entities do exist. Yet many of those posited by other metaphysicians in the tradition can be seen *not* to exist, according to the physicalist. For the claim that they do cannot survive the trial by prerequisites.

The objectivity prerequisite is especially telling in this regard. In §1.5(vii), and later in §3.4, we saw how the claim that a certain thing exists can be true *period* only if its identifying properties are invariants, rather than properties of a projection of something else onto a system of reference. We saw further how the noninvariance of ordinary simultaneity would thereby force us to deny objective existence to such things as "the ongoing present" and the "now" with which the present contents of consciousness are simultaneous.[11] Yet nearly all traditional metaphysicians—including traditional atoms-and-the-void materialists—posit some kind of unifying entity or event or being or process whose identifying properties are not invariants (as may well be the case

---

[11]But see §5.4 for some qualifications.

with Whitehead's "actual occasions of becoming," at least as they are interpreted by some of the later Whiteheadians). Such unifying entities do not enjoy objective existence. At best they are projections or appearances on our screens of reference. Nor is it at all clear that the spirit of these traditional views could be retained in any revision that takes adequate account of the implications of contemporary physical theories of spacetime.

Nevertheless, some nonphysicalist inventories of unifiers might prove to satisfy the truth-prerequisites, including objectivity. If so, what would be the physicalist's response? Not only must the unifiers exist; it must also be possible to unify all the domains of discourse in terms of them, and to do so in such a way that truths about the unifiers determine the truths in all the domains. But to unify them all, one must at least unify the sciences, whereas in fact the truths in the various sciences are *not* determined by truths about nonphysical entities (or by alleged truths about alleged nonphysical entities). Instead, they are determined by truths about physical entities. Or so the physicalist is prepared to argue.

I shall say something about the premises of this argument in a moment. Notice first that with the help of an additional premise, the argument justifies far more than its immediate conclusion. Its immediate conclusion is merely that even if the alleged nonphysical unifiers existed, the domains still would not all be unified in terms of them. Now assume as an additional premise that the domains are all unified in terms of physical entities in such a way that all truth is determined by physical truth. Then there is a definite sense in which everything is accounted for on this physical basis, as we noted in §4.3. But in that case no further entities would be necessary, and Occam's razor comes into play. We would have no need of the hypothesis of nonphysical unifiers. Hence we would be justified in denying that there are any in the first place. This goes far beyond the conclusion merely that the domains would not be unified in terms of them.

Those who would champion nonphysical unifiers must therefore challenge the physicalist's belief that it is not necessary to multiply entities beyond the physical. In connection with the foregoing argument, this entails challenging the physicalist's premises. The key premises are two. The first is that the truths in the sciences are not, as a matter of fact, all determined by truths about nonphysical entities. The second is that all truth, not just truth in the sciences, is determined by physical truth.

Because it takes a theory to kill a theory, the first premise can be challenged successfully only by presenting a whole metaphysics—a competitor to physicalism—according to which the truths in the sciences *are* all determined by truths about something nonphysical. This competing view would have to be fully clarified and defended. Its candidates for the unifiers must exist. Its notion of determination would have to be explicated and defended against charges of reduction and monopoly. Finally, we would want to see at least some of the details about how particular truths in a particular science are supposed to be determined by truths about the alleged unifiers, as we do see in the next section in the case of physicalism. Sweeping generalizations would be no more persuasive here than in the service of physicalism. At every step along the way, antiphysicalists would be haunted by the realization that minimal physicalism might already have succeeded admirably in unifying the sciences. Thus they would have to argue extra hard for their extra entities. One such argument might be that such entities are required for determining truths in domains beyond the sciences.

This brings us to the physicalist's second premise, according to which all truth, not just truth in the sciences, is determined by truth at the level of physics. This second premise is fatally easy to challenge so long as determination entails reduction. It is easy to challenge also if determination entails that the modes of explanation in all the domains must be those employed in physics, or at least those employed in natural science. But, as seen, determination entails neither reducibility nor explainability nor the other kinds of monopoly.

Only one challenge remains. How could we ever tell in practice whether particular truths in one domain are determined by truths in another, if not by way of some sort of reducibility or explainability? This question is familiar from §4.3. We address it, at long last, in the next section. But many truths contain metaphors and other figures often thought to defy any physicalist approach. In §5.3 we consider how the physicalist might argue that such truths also are determined ultimately by physical truths. In Chapter 6 we do the same for truths that contain value terms, especially principles of morality. Truths about subjective experience are considered in §§5.4 and 7.1. Still other truths outside the sciences come in for treatment in Chapters 7 and 8.

Along the way we see why the minimal physicalist principles imply no devaluation of the truths whose determination they describe. On the contrary, some of those very truths entail that certain values or interests frequently ought to take precedence over the aim relative to which physicalism enjoys whatever priority it has. Physicalism, like most other brands of metaphysics since Thales, aims at finding some limited variety of entities of which everything else is somehow a manifestation such that truths about the former determine the truths about the latter.

Yet it can and does happen that among the latter truths are some that entail that this very aim frequently ought to give way to others. In this sense, therefore, the unifying entities manifest themselves in many truths, including truths to the effect that those selfsame entities are much less significant, on occasion, than other things. It follows that one of the ways the physical manifests itself is in its own occasional insignificance.

5.1. Connective Theories

> *The philosopher . . . is confronted by two conceptions, equally*
> *public, equally non-arbitrary, of man-in-the-world, and he*
> *cannot shirk the attempt to see how they fall together in one*
> *stereoscopic view.*
> —WILFRID SELLARS

Talk of determination, perhaps no less than of reduction or of translation, invites the rejoinder, "Put up or shut up." The physicalist owes us an account of how we could ever tell whether various truths are determined by truths from physics, if not by way of reduction, translation, or even extensional ismorphism. Not that establishing reducibility is without its problems, even where it obtains. Indeed showing that determination obtains is normally easier than showing reducibility, even though this section may occasionally give the contrary impression, concentrating as it does on determination rather than on the greater difficulties involved in knowing how to tell when we have successful reduction.

To begin with, determination is transitive, meaning that if (in the same class of worlds) Φ-truth determines Ψ-truth, and Ψ-truth determines X-truth, then Φ-truth also determines X-truth; likewise for determination of and by reference. Such transitivity induces no hierarchy among the domains. For even though determination is transitive, it is not antisymmetric. That is, if Φ-truth determines Ψ-truth (where $\Phi \neq \Psi$), then Ψ-truth may or may not determine Φ-truth; if Ψ-truth does also determine Φ-truth, we have an instance of codetermination. Hence determination is not a strict partial ordering and cannot by itself induce any hierarchy among the domains of truth, even in the slightly weaker sense of 'hierarchy' from §2.5. Probably there is no linear hierarchy among the domains anyway, stretching from physics on up. The most popular criteria for ranking them, such as degree of complexity or of comprehensiveness, are too vague; we can agree that physics is the most comprehensive, in some sense (§4.6), but how can we rank geology, say, as compared to meteorology, or anthropology as compared to history?

The significance of transitivity is not that it induces hierarchy but that it conduces to division of labor. Physicalists need not shoulder the heroic, hopeless burden of describing some direct relation between the truths of anthropology, say, and those of physics, in virtue of which we may infer that the latter determine the former. Instead, they can point to a lot of intervening disciplines—such as archeology, psychology, biology, geology, astronomy, chemistry, and so on—no one of which suffices to determine anthropological truth, but only a cluster of several or all of them in conjunction (§4.5). Then they can remind us that the truths of physics can more readily be seen to determine those of its near neighbors, such as astronomy and chemistry. The latter can more readily be seen to determine the truths of disciplines a bit further removed from physics, and so on, until finally we reach the truths of anthropology. Provided that determination holds at each step of the way, we may infer by transitivity that physical truth determines anthropological truth.

Thus the problem of establishing determination divides into a lot of local problems that concern relations between clusters of domains, clusters that in some sense are near neighbors—near enough, anyway, for there to be direct relations between the clusters in virtue of which we may infer that the truths in one determine those in the other. (What are to count as near neighbors we discuss toward the end of the section.) Inquirers in particular domains or clusters that thus adjoin will often already have explored various relations between them, including relations in light of which, perhaps unbeknown to those inquirers, we may infer determination. This means that as physicalists we can let particular disciplines do most of our work for us, as they explore the relations between themselves and their neighbors.

How in practice is local determination supposed to be inferable? Of course, it may be inferred, in some cases, from reducibility of the terms and sentences of one domain (or cluster of domains) to those of another. But this hardly exhausts the direct ways in which terms and sentences can be related across adjacent domains so as to justify an inference to determination. Defenders of "unified science" need not claim that "there are procedures for translating any significant utterance into . . . the language of unified science,"[12] whatever that language is supposed to be, *if any*. Nor need they attempt some impossible feat of

[12]Contrary to Rorty (1979), 348–349.

stereoscopic vision.[13] The typical result of staring at apples and oranges through a stereoscope is not a hybrid but a headache.

The simplest way to discover local determination is to observe it. This requires no Sellarsian stereoscope. Two masses of gas exactly alike in relevant mechanical respects may be observed repeatedly to be alike also in some given thermodynamic respect. Or two cells exactly alike in relevant molecular-biological respects may be observed always to be alike in some given aspect of their overt behavior. Or two organisms alike in relevant neurological respects may be observed always to be alike as regards their learning ability. In these and scores of other cases we observe determination of a class of Ψ-truths by a class of Φ-truths (assuming that 'repeatedly' and 'always' point to a lawlike regularity). Clearly, assertions of determination are capable of empirical support (and rejection).

Unfortunately, in all examples like these, determination is all too local. Determination in the case of a couple of entities, even when the entities are entirely representative of their kind, falls short of determination of *all* Ψ-truth by Φ-truth. In practice this gap is filled in one of two related ways. The first is to observe lots of determinations of lots of classes of Ψ-phenomena by Φ-phenomena. Suppose all sorts of thermodynamic properties of a wide variety of entities are observed to be determined by mechanical properties of those entities, by observing that whenever the entities are alike in relevant mechanical respects, they are alike also in given thermodynamic respects. Then we may justifiably infer that all thermodynamic properties are determined by mechanical properties and hence that all thermodynamic truth is determined by mechanical truth (provided, of course, no canons of sound inductive inference are violated).

Such a lot of miscellaneous determinations would be unwieldy. Also there are severe limitations on what can be directly observed of determination, just as there are limitations on direct observational evidence for most other generalizations. Typically, therefore, we resort to theories that systematize the otherwise miscellaneous determinations across two adjacent domains. Such theories are the means by which we carry on when observation falls short. They enable us, when successful, to claim determination for classes of phenomena whose determination we cannot observe. When especially successful, they lead us to discover determination for classes of phenomena when we would not otherwise have expected it.

[13]Contrary to Sellars, 5.

Thus it is that in practice the strongest evidence for determination of Ψ-truth by Φ-truth most often comes in the form of theories that successfully connect Ψ-phenomena with Φ-phenomena. Therefore, the physicalist must explain what a *connective* theory is, what counts as its *success,* and what sort of *inference* is involved in inferring, from the success of a number of such theories, to the determination of Ψ-truth by Φ-truth. A connective theory $T_{\Phi,\Psi}$, for two domains D_Φ and D_Ψ, consists of (i) an interpreted internal theory T_Φ, whose nonlogical vocabulary consists solely of terms from D_Φ; (ii) a set A of auxiliary assumptions required for application of T_Φ to particular cases; and (iii) a set $B_{\Phi,\Psi}$ of bridge principles whose nonlogical vocabulary consists solely of terms from both D_Φ and D_Ψ. The bridge principles constitute one kind of auxiliary assumption and form a subset of A. But because of their special significance we designate them separately. Roughly speaking, a bridge principle $P_{\Phi,\Psi}$ connects Φ-phenomena with Ψ-phenomena.[14] Bridge principles are what make a theory that contains them a connective theory.

Illustrations are in order. That old workhorse of an example, the kinetic theory of gases, will serve as a start, though some of its features could mislead. In one of its formulations,[15] its internal theory T_Φ contains only such nonlogical terms as 'mass', 'velocity', and 'position', as they are applied to randomly moving particles. That is, T_Φ is expressed in the language roughly of classical particle mechanics in its Newtonian formulation; if certain statistical concepts or theses are added, T_Φ would instead be in the language of classical statistical mechanics. Thus T_Φ is a theory about the behavior of classical particles. Under the auxiliary assumption that molecules can be treated as particles, T_Φ applies to the molecules and affords a theory of the behavior of randomly moving molecules.

The bridge principles of the kinetic theory include not only the vocabulary of T_Φ but also terms for such thermodynamic and other macroproperties of gases as their temperature, diffusion rate, viscosity, heat conduction, volume, pressure, and so on. One such principle $P_{\Phi,\Psi}$ is the hypothesis that the diffusion rate of a gas is proportional to the average velocity of its molecules. Another is the hypothesis that its absolute temperature is (or at least has the same quantitative magnitude as) the mean kinetic energy of its molecules. Still another is the hypothesis that the pressure exerted by a gas in a vessel results from the molecules' impact upon its walls. Clearly, the bridge principles are designed

---

[14]Cf. Spector, 32.
[15]Cf. Sneed, ch. 6.

to express some of the specifics involved in regarding various thermodynamic (and other) properties of gases as manifestations of certain mechanical properties of randomly moving particles. They are designed also to enable the kinetic theory to entail such things as that whenever two masses of gas are alike in relevant mechanical respects, they are alike also in given thermodynamic respects.

We remarked that some features of this illustration could mislead. For example, in the kinetic theory, T_Φ consists of laws. But connective theories, as defined above, can have internal theories that contain no laws, nor even any lawlike truths. Another potentially misleading feature is that the kinetic theory often is presumed to effect a reduction, to the theory T_Φ, of certain laws about gases framed in the Ψ-vocabulary. But a connective theory need not result in any such reduction.

Reduction here is a special case of *theory* reduction. The reduction of a theory T_Ψ to a theory T_Φ, it is widely agreed, requires at least that (a) T_Ψ be logically entailed by T_Φ plus a set of bridge principles that are laws; (b) every primitive predicate of T_Ψ be lawlike-coextensive with some predicate (or complex of predicates) of T_Φ; and (c) each kind of entity mentioned by T_Ψ be identical with some entity (or sum of entities) mentioned by T_Φ, where the identity is expressed by one of the bridge principles (which again is to be a law). So construed, theory reduction entails, via (b), the reduction of at least some Ψ-terms to Φ-terms, in the sense of lawlike coextensiveness. Some philosophers of science argue further that it entails the identity of the Ψ-properties with certain Φ-properties,[16] though we need not pause to inquire whether this is so.

For in any event a successful connective theory often results neither in theory reduction nor in term reduction. And as noted, its bridge principles need not be laws or even lawlike. It follows that successful connective theories need not be true in all physically possible worlds or even in all scientifically possible worlds. The kinetic theory of gases, though it is a familiar example of a successful connective theory (successful in its day, that is, or to an approximation), can mislead in these respects and perhaps in others.

The theory of evolution, in one or another of its versions, might be an example of a connective theory $T_{\Phi,\Psi}$ in which T_Φ contains no laws (depending on what one's notion of a law is and, above all, what counts as the theory of evolution), and perhaps no lawlike truths either.[17] In

[16]For example, Causey (1972a), (1972b).
[17]Cf. Smart (1963), ch. 3. But see Rosenberg; M. B. Williams; Rosenberg and Williams.

any case, certain bridge principles seem not to be lawlike. Thus consider 'Phylogenetic change in the characteristics of a species results from mutations in the species' genetic DNA, together with selective pressures from the environment'. The reason this is unlikely to be lawlike is that there may well be scientifically possible worlds (such as a world of self-reproducing automata) in which the genetic stuff in which mutation occurs is not DNA and not even protoplasmic. Moreover, the mechanisms of mutation in the genetic stuff might be very different from whatever they are in this world.

Connective theories are not limited to the empirical sciences. Logicism—the theory that mathematics is a branch of logic—contains as its internal theory T_Φ the truths of what it counts as logic (usually a higher-order predicate calculus). Among its bridge principles are certain contextual definitions that connect terms and sentences of mathematics with those of T_Φ. Another example appeared briefly in §4.1, when we mentioned a theory according to which numbers are sets. To construe numbers as sets is to invoke a theory that connects numbers and the truths about them with sets and truths about them. Its internal theory T_Φ is (a version of) set theory. Its bridge principles (in one formulation) include things like 'Let the number 0 be the null set ∅, let 1 (the successor of 0) be {∅}, and in general let the successor of each natural number n be {n}'.

Nor are connective theories limited to the sciences, empirical or formal. In the next chapter a couple of bridge principles that connect facts with values figure as premises in an argument to show that the facts determine the values. And some theologies contain an internal theory T_Φ about God, couched solely in a religious vocabulary, plus bridge principles that connect the religious vocabulary with a secular one. A main purpose of such a connective theory is to show that certain secular phenomena actually are manifestations of whatever is described by T_Φ, so that various truths about the former are determined by truths about the latter. Truths about God's benevolence, for instance, are supposed to determine that human suffering, even when described in secular terms, is not pointless. And since the world is supposed to have been created by God, everything in it is potentially a manifestation of God. A sentence like 'God created the world' may be the most fundamental bridge principle of all, in such a theory. Whether this sort of theory is successful is another story (§8.0). Typically, there are severe problems as to whether its internal theory is true or even coherent; problems as to whether its auxiliary assumptions are ad hoc; problems about the intelligibility of its bridge principles; and other problems about whether the theory adequately explains the variety of facts it claims to explain (which is not to imply that all or even very many theologies aim to be explanatory in this same sense).

The domain status of a connective theory $T_{\Phi,\Psi}$, obviously, is at least dual. Often it is multiple. This can occur when the Ψ-vocabulary actually contains terms from many domains, as is the case when $T_{\Phi,\Psi}$ is especially comprehensive. $T_{\Phi,\Psi}$ will have multiple domain status also when its internal theory contains terms from a cluster of several domains. The "solar-marker theory" of Stonehenge and the slabs in Chaco Canyon has an internal theory composed of truths from, among others, astronomy, geology, meteorology, and physiology (to help explain how mere flesh could have quarried the huge stones and levered them into place). The theory connects these truths with the anthropological term 'solar marker', as well as with related terms and the sentences in which they occur.

Notice also that a connective theory need not be construed as a collection of sentences, even interpreted sentences (though for convenience we have done so and will continue mostly to do so). Instead, $T_{\Phi,\Psi}$ may be construed as, say, a conceptual structure that generates a variety of Ψ-claims and may be represented by a complex predicate from set theory that has a wide variety of possible models.[18] This can be done in such a way that $T_{\Phi,\Psi}$ has close affinities with Thomas Kuhn's paradigms and Imre Lakatos' research programs.

Furthermore, the distinction between the two connected vocabularies Ψ and Φ obviously does not coincide with a distinction between the observational and the theoretical. Often the Ψ-vocabulary will not be observational at all. In any case, by connecting Ψ-vocabulary to the internal theory T_{Φ}, a connective theory will ensure that the Ψ-terms thus connected are to that extent theory-laden. This is because T_{Φ}, in conjunction with $B_{\Phi,\Psi}$, will place some constraints on the use of the connected Ψ-terms, thereby effecting a degree of conceptual change. By the same token, the bridge principles in $B_{\Phi,\Psi}$ provide partial criteria for the interpretation and application of the Φ-terms, thereby enriching our comprehension of Φ-phenomena, and again effecting a degree of conceptual change.

So much, then, for our sketch of what a connective theory is. What counts as its success? Since we want it to be true, it must satisfy the logical prerequisites for truth. In practice this means that its internal theory, auxiliary assumptions, and bridge principles must survive the trial by prerequisites. Or at least they must survive better than those of its competitors. And of course the theory should satisfy any criteria of truth we might be lucky enough to possess (§1.3).

Not only do we want a connective theory to be true; we want it to enjoy the other virtues relevant to such theories (§1.6). The main virtues

---

[18]In the manner of Sneed, 288–296, or Stegmuller, 177–202.

are comparative simplicity and a particular kind of comprehensiveness. The comparative simplicity of two connective theories is rarely if ever a purely quantitative matter. It involves a qualitative comparison, application by application, of their respective internal theories, auxiliary assumptions, and bridge principles. These judgments are among those usually best left to specialized inquirers working in one or more of the adjacent domains the theory connects. It is they who can usually best judge whether, say, one theory's greater economy as regards ontology (its positing fewer Φ-entities) outweighs the other's greater economy and naturalness as regards auxiliary assumptions.

What of comprehensiveness? The kind relevant here, namely consilience, has to do less with the number of Ψ-truths that $T_{\Phi,\Psi}$ explains than with their variety.[19] One theory is more consilient than another, with respect to explaining Ψ-phenomena, if it explains more classes or kinds of Ψ-truths than the other. The tricky notion here, of course, is that of a class or kind of Ψ-truth. No analysis seems adequate. But none is required. The specialists in the adjacent domains usually have no trouble agreeing on the division of Ψ-facts into classes.

Thus there was general agreement, in the case of the kinetic theory of gases, that facts about diffusion rates fall into a different class from those about relations among pressure, volume, and temperature (even though there are some connections between the two classes). Therefore, there was general agreement that diffusion and pressure-volume-temperature phenomena constitute two different applications of the internal theory (a theory in particle mechanics). The two therefore testify to the consilience of the kinetic theory (and of mechanics). On the other hand, the many instances of the law that the pressure of a fixed mass of gas at constant temperature is inversely proportional to its volume are all facts in the same class. There could be infinitely many of them, yet they would not testify to the theory's consilience.

A theory may explain kinds of facts different from those it was designed to account for. Such a theory is valued over one that accounts merely for the classes of facts familiar at the time it was proposed. The latter enjoys only static consilience; the former, dynamic. A theory is dynamically consilient at time t just in case it is more consilient at t than when it was first proposed. And one theory is more dynamically consilient than another, roughly, when the former has succeeded in adding more classes of facts explained than the latter.[20]

---

[19]Cf. Thagard (1978), who elaborates William Whewell's account.

[20]Thagard (1978), 84, who also points out that dynamic consilience has affinities with Lakatos' notion of "progressive problemshifts."

Best of all is a connective theory that achieves dynamic consilience by conservative means: it requires no modification of its internal T_Φ or its auxiliary hypotheses A (beyond augmenting its bridge principles $B_{\Phi,\Psi}$, if need be). This conservative dynamic consilience contrasts with the radical sort, which involves changes in T_Φ and in A (as well as in $B_{\Phi,\Psi}$). Even when such changes are not ad hoc, we are no longer speaking strictly of the same connective theory. The reason is that connective theories, as defined above, are individuated by their internal theories, auxiliary assumptions, and a core of bridge principles—the ones included in the theory when it was first proposed.

The successful connective theory, then, is one that is superior to its alternatives as regards simplicity, consilience (preferably dynamic), and satisfaction of the logical prerequisites for truth, plus any criteria for truth we might have. Now in what circumstances may we infer from the success of a number of connective theories to the conclusion that Φ-truth determines Ψ-truth? And what sort of inference would this be?

The ideal circumstance occurs when there is a happy family of connective theories for the two domains D_Φ and D_Ψ. That is, each theory in the family consists of some T_Φ, A, and $B_{\Phi,\Psi}$; the theories are consistent with each other; and they cover the Ψ-phenomena in the sense that even if no one theory in the family explains all the Ψ-phenomena, each theory explains some, and taken together the theories do explain all the Ψ-phenomena.

Now suppose that all the theories in this happy family are successful in the sense lately sketched. What would best explain the success of this happy family of theories that connect Φ-phenomena with Ψ-phenomena? According to the physicalist, the best explanation would be that the Φ-phenomena determine the Ψ-phenomena. For if they do, then any two things alike in the relevant Φ-respects are of necessity alike in given Ψ-respects. That is, any two things alike in their Φ-properties are alike in their Ψ-properties. But then any *one* thing that has the relevant Φ-properties also is of necessity the way it is as regards the given Ψ-properties; given the way it is as regards its Φ-properties, there is one and only one way it can be as regards its Ψ-properties. The knowledge of this connection, together with the knowledge that some particular thing x has those Φ-properties, would enable us to understand why x is as it is as regards those Ψ-properties: it has them because that is the only way it could be, given its Φ-properties. So determination of the Ψ-phenomena by the Φ-phenomena would explain why all the theories in the happy family are successful. Given determination, it is understandable why all these familial connective theories have so far survived the trial by prerequisites. And given determination, we would expect that these theories, which are designed to be consilient, would enable us to explain Ψ-phenomena by reference to their connections with Φ-phenomena, when the latter are in conditions specified by the theory's auxiliary assumptions A.

This inference to determination from the success of the theories in the happy family would be reinforced if all or even some of the theories were designed to systematize otherwise miscellaneous cases of determination already known to exist across the two domains; that is, cases in which it is known that two things alike in certain Φ-properties would be alike also in certain Ψ-properties. The inference would be further reinforced if some of the theories, though they contain different internal theories couched in different subclasses of the Φ-vocabulary, nevertheless turn out to be equivalent in some appropriate sense.[21] This would make it more likely that determination within the phenomena is responsible for the equivalent theories' success, rather than some lucky coincidence in our formulation of one or more of the theories.

Suppose, then, that determination would explain the success of the happy family. Why should we suppose further that this is the *best* explanation? To begin with, the physicalist is entitled to rule out coincidence. It is very unlikely that *all* these compatible connective theories satisfy the truth-prerequisites, collectively explain every variety of Ψ-phenomena (by virtue of covering all the Ψ-phenomena), and do so more simply than their alternatives just by chance. There must be *some* sort of connection between the Φ- and the Ψ-properties which, in combination with our activities of constructing the theories and subjecting them to the trial by prerequisites, influenced the evolution of those theories. This intimation of a noncoincidental relation is enormously amplified if some of the theories in the family, though independently discovered, prove equivalent in some appropriate sense.

Of course, ruling out coincidence does not leave determination as the only possible explanation. Perhaps the Ψ-properties are *identical* with the Φ-properties (where the identity holds, say, in every P-world). Certainly this would explain the success of the theories that connect Ψ-phenomena with Φ-phenomena. But such lawlike identity, the physicalist can reply, is a plausible hypothesis only when the bridge principles in the theories take the form of or imply the relevant identity statements. This is rarely the case (see further §5.2). Moreover, there is a sense in which property identity is just a special case of determination. For if all Ψ-properties are identical with Φ-properties, then automatical-

[21]On some of the difficulties in defining and establishing such equivalence, see Sneed, ch. 7, esp. 187.

ly a thing's Φ-properties determine its Ψ-properties. It follows that the hypothesis of determination, being logically weaker, will always be at least as well confirmed as the hypothesis of property identity.

What about *causation?* If the Φ-phenomena cause the Ψ-phenomena, again the success of the connective theories would be explained. But to the extent that causation is a clear notion at all, according to the physicalist, it too may well conflict with the form of the relevant bridge principles. And here it too is just a special case of determination. For if x's having certain Φ-properties is in the intended sense the cause of x's having certain Ψ-properties, then x's Φ-properties determine x's Ψ-properties. Hence the hypothesis of determination will always be at least as well confirmed as that of causation.

The physicalist will continue in this manner to deal with every alternative explanation, or try. Each alternative either will not explain as well as the hypothesis of determination, or will be at odds with the form the bridge principles take, or will turn out to be a special case of determination. Furthermore, determination explains the success of connective theories even when neither the phenomena they connect nor their properties are identical and when none is the cause of the other. Thus the determination hypothesis explains a much greater variety of kinds of cases of success and enjoys correspondingly greater consilience than its competitors. Or so the physicalist will contend.

In any event, we see clearly what sort of inference is involved in inferring determination from the success of the diverse connective theories in a happy family. For the most part, it is just old-fashioned inference to the best explanation, roughly what Peirce called abduction. By whatever name, it is used constantly in the sciences, in other disciplines, and in daily life. Darwin explicitly used it for his theory of evolution, as did Lavoisier for his oxygen theory of combustion and Fresnel for the wave theory of light.[22] Other historical examples abound. And for every self-conscious use, there are scores of other uses throughout the sciences and indeed all the domains. Some philosophers even venture to argue that all inductive inference is inference to the best explanation,[23] though we need not concur.

Early in this section we saw how the problem of establishing physical determination divides into a lot of local problems, thanks to transitivity. The local problems are those of finding direct relations between a couple of adjacent (clusters of) domains D_Φ and D_Ψ, in light of which one could infer that Φ-truth determines Ψ-truth, even when reducibility

[22]Cf. Thagard (1978), 77–78.
[23]Harman (1965), e.g.

and translatability fail. And now we see what a couple of those direct relations are, according to the nonreductive physicalist. First, D_Φ and D_Ψ are so related when there is a happy family of successful connective theories for D_Φ and D_Ψ—a family in which the theories are compatible and cover the Ψ-phenomena. Second, they are so related, as seen, when we have observed lots of determinations of lots of classes of Ψ-phenomena by Φ-phenomena.

We see further how physicalists can let someone else do most of their work for them. The local inquirers in D_Φ and D_Ψ often will already have observed lots of limited determinations. In addition, they often will already have constructed successful connective theories that form a happy family. Such theory construction goes on all the time, as part of the activity of neighboring disciplines. In the ideal circumstance envisaged above, it results in a direct relation between D_Φ and D_Ψ in light of which, perhaps unbeknown to the local inquirers, determination of Ψ-truth by Φ-truth may be inferred. The Hegelian might well see here an analogue of "the cunning of reason."

When are two domains near neighbors? All of us already know a lot about what domains are neighbors, thanks to our background knowledge of certain relations among the various sciences, other disciplines, and culture generally. But two domains hitherto supposed quite distant can be *made* neighbors by the creation of a theory that successfully connects them. Newton made neighbors of the heavens and such earthly phenomena as the mass and acceleration of a projectile. Darwin did so for genetics and the geographical distribution of species. Often even the mere promise of a successful connective theory suffices to induce neighborliness. We still do not have a very comprehensive theory to connect genetics with molecular biology, yet before the structure even of DNA began to be traced, there were tentative declarations of direct relations between the two domains. Clearly, our judgments about which domains adjoin reflect, among other things, our knowledge about successful connective theories and about the promising possibility of such a theory.

Frequently, we are justified not only in expecting such a theory but also in believing that eventually there will be a whole family of successful connective theories that are compatible and cover the phenomena. This can occur, for example, when the local inquirers have already observed a number of determinations of strategic classes of Ψ-phenomena by Φ-phenomena, so that the situation is ripe for some brilliant theorist to systematize the rest. Thus the ideal circumstance in which we already possess a happy family of connective theories is not the only one in which truth–determination may be inferred. In this the physicalist is lucky. Life rarely is so ideal.

Earlier, we said that a successful connective theory for D_Φ and D_Ψ offers explanations of Ψ-phenomena; otherwise, it would have no consilience. Does this conflict with what was said earlier still, in §§4.0 and 4.3, about the explanatory autonomy of the domains? No. The existence of a successful connective theory for D_Φ and D_Ψ, even where D_Φ is closer to physics, is compatible with the continued use of explanations of Ψ-phenomena that contain only the Ψ-vocabulary. For example, we may continue on occasion to explain the overt behavior of a cell by reference to its functional relations with its surroundings, rather than by reference to its molecular constituents, even if the latter sort of explanation is available in virtue of some appropriate connective theory.

Indeed the connective theory must take account of the relations among the Ψ-phenomena reflected in the explanations that use only the Ψ-vocabulary. If it too flagrantly violated too many of them, it would hardly be successful; rather than explaining the Ψ-phenomena, it would explain them away. Thus the achievements of inquirers within D_Ψ place constraints on any attempt to impose theories that would connect D_Ψ with some D_Φ closer to physics. This point is related to the fact, noted earlier, that the bridge principles provide partial criteria for the interpretation and application of the Φ-vocabulary, thereby effecting a change in our conception of the Φ-phenomena.

Repeatedly in Chapter 4, and again in §5.0, we asked, "How could we ever tell in practice whether truths in one domain are determined by those in another, if not by way of some sort of explainability?" What we had in mind was the explainability of Ψ-phenomena *purely in Φ-terms*. But the explanations of Ψ-phenomena offered by a connective theory need *not* be purely in Φ-terms. The bridge principles, which contain both sorts of terms, play an ineliminable role. Only if the Ψ-terms were reducible to Φ-terms would there be an explanation purely in Φ-terms, and perhaps not always even then, depending partly on one's idea of what an explanation is.

In any event, connective theories, whose domain-status is at least dual, offer only explanations that mix Φ-terms with Ψ-terms in the bridge principles. So the explainability of Ψ-phenomena by successful connective theories, which is a component of one way of telling whether determination obtains, is compatible with the claim that determination need not be detected via some sort of explainability purely in Φ-terms. This is one reason why "to explain a phenomenon is not to explain it away. It is neither the aim nor the effect of theoretical explanations to show that the familiar things and events of our everyday experience are not 'really there'."[24]

Even if one could somehow argue that there is an explanation purely in Φ-terms, still it would not follow that there is an explanation purely in terms from *physics*. While determination is transitive, explanation probably is not (except for deductive explanations, which are useless here because they require the Ψ-terms in their conclusions to be included among the terms in their premises—that is, among what would be the Φ-terms). If transitivity fails for explanation, then there can be an explanation of X-phenomena in Ψ-terms, and of Ψ-phenomena in Φ-terms, yet no explanation of X-phenomena in Φ-terms. We could not infer from a lot of local explanations among intervening domains that the phenomena in, say, anthropology have an explanation purely in terms from physics.

That there must be some such physical explanation of the anthropological is highly unlikely anyway, in view of the physical irreducibility of functional and intentional properties. So even if explanation were transitive, we would be forced to conclude that somewhere in the chain of intervening domains, explanation of Ψ-phenomena purely in Φ-terms breaks down. Determination and explanation are very different, even though determination of one sort of phenomena by another underlies many an explanation.

5.2. Bridge Principles and Metaphors

> *The multiplication of . . . disciplines is a familiar feature of the intellectual scene. Scarcely less familiar is the unification of this manifold which is taking place by the building of scientific bridges between them.*
>
> —WILFRID SELLARS

> *I stood in Venice on the Bridge of Sighs, a palace and a prison on each hand.*
>
> —BYRON

> *Metaphor is probably the most fertile power possessed by man.*
>
> —JOSÉ ORTEGA Y GASSET

Bridge principles are what make a theory that contains them a connective theory. They therefore tend to do most of the work of relating terms and sentences from one domain to those of another, when the truths of the former determine those of the latter, since connective

[24]Hempel, 78.

theories (or happy families of them) are the principal means by which determination is established. It follows that whether the terms from one domain are reducible to those of the other depends heavily on what forms the bridge principles happen to take. If they all have the form, say, of identity statements, then normally we must infer reducibility. If instead some of them have the form of a universalized biconditional, then the predicates are at least accidentally coextensive, hence weakly reducible.

The nonreductive physicalist must therefore explain how the bridge principles often assume forms that do not entail reducibility. The best way to do so is by presenting lots of examples of nonreductive bridge principles from a variety of theories across a variety of domains. Some of the theories would be from the sciences, but many would not. Not all the bridges between domains are scientific, even when they justify an inference to determination of truth in one domain by truth in another.

Here are a few examples of nonreductive bridge principles from the sciences, by no means exhaustive:

(1) The diffusion rate of a gas is proportional to the average velocity of its molecules.

(2) Light of exactly one wave length λ is produced by the energy ΔE released by an electron "jump" (where $\lambda = (h.c)/\Delta E$).

(3) Oxygen is necessary for combustion.

(4) The nerve gas tabum (characterized by its molecular structure) blocks nervous activity in humans.

(5) Phylogenetic change in a species' characteristics results from mutations in the species' DNA, in conjunction with selective pressures from the environment.

(6) Patients report memories so vivid that the remembered events seem to be occurring then and there, when certain areas of the temporal cortex are stimulated by microelectrodes.

(7) To say that mass points behave thus-and-so is to say that particles of given mass behave the more nearly thus-and-so the smaller their volumes.

None of (1)–(7) entails an identity, whether of properties or of concrete entities. In (1), for instance, that two magnitudes are proportional entails not their identity but only a correlation; hence (1) does not entail that the property of having a certain diffusion rate is identical with the property of having a certain average molecular velocity (though in conjunction with *other* parts of the kinetic theory it might entail this).

Example (2) merely states that one thing is produced by another, as do (4) and (5); (3) states a necessary condition and (6) a correlation. And the whole point of (7) is to enable us to talk about mass points without identifying them with anything; there are no points with mass. So too for frictionless surfaces, perfectly isolated systems, and other ideal objects.[25] Likewise, none of (1)–(7) entails coextensiveness, even accidental, of their principal terms.

Example (7) also shows how principles can connect whole sentences with whole sentences. The bridges need not be directly between terms—as in (1)–(6), in effect—but indirectly, via their containing sentences. According to (7), the truth-value of 'Mass points behave thus-and-so' is the same as that of 'Particles of given mass behave the more nearly thus-and-so the smaller their volumes'. This sameness of truth-value presumably holds in every physically possible world, since many a law of physics is formulated (or formulatable) in terms of the behavior of mass points or other ideal objects. It follows that the truth-value of each sentence in (7) is determined by that of the other.

Note also that (7) connects whole sentences in such a way that not every term has a referent, let alone the same referent as some term has in the determining domain. The point of (7) is to give 'Mass points behave thus-and-so' a truth-value even though 'mass point' has no referent when construed literally. In this respect, (7) is representative of a whole class of principles. This will become especially significant in Chapter 6, when we discuss sentences that contain value terms, and in Chapter 8, when we discuss some that contain 'God'.

Members of this class often have the air of definitions or stipulations, or even of explications, analyses, paraphrases, or translations. But we have already seen, in effect, that such things can be regarded as bridge principles in a connective theory (recall the examples from logicism and from the theory that numbers are sets, in §5.1). When they serve as such principles, they are to be judged in light of their contribution to the theory's success, including its survival in the trial by prerequisites, plus its simplicity, comprehensiveness, and dynamic consilience. Definitions, paraphrases, and the like are just as subject to revision as so-called factual claims, even if in practice the definitions occasionally are among the last to be revised.

Should we say that (7) *translates* one sentence into another? Not if translation is supposed to preserve anything more than truth-value. For that is all (7) does, consonant with the rest of its role in legitimizing our

[25]Cf. Quine (1960), 248–249.

continued use of the phrase 'mass point'. Since translation is widely supposed to preserve various other dimensions of meaning—reference, sense, emotiveness, etc.—it seems wise not to call (7) a translation, strictly speaking.[26] The same is true of most other bridge principles. And even if they were translations, they would hardly be translations "into the language of unified science," whatever that is, but into the vocabulary of the relevant internal theory, which can be almost anything.

The next example of a bridge principle is from outside the sciences:

(8) Humans are wolves.

It may seem odd to construe (8) as a bridge principle. For what is the connective theory to which it belongs? The theory need be nothing explicitly stated. It need only be implicit, its outlines to be guessed from the context in which the metaphor occurs. Thus we may guess that its internal theory T_ϕ consists of certain sentences about wolves, not necessarily true, couched in a vocabulary that normally can apply literally to wolves (such as 'run in packs', 'prey on the weak', 'aggressive', 'scavengers', and so on). *Which* vocabulary for wolves T_ϕ contains, and which sentences, can only be guessed from the context and the intent of the author of (8), in conjunction with our understanding not only of wolves but of humans. Our understanding of humans reciprocally affects our judgment about what is supposed to be in T_ϕ.

In the case of many metaphors, including (8), T_ϕ tends to be drawn from what has been called "the system of commonplaces associated" with the metaphorical word ('wolves' in this case).[27] But often T_ϕ does not coincide with the associated commonplaces.[28] Often T_ϕ includes only some of them: it might include 'Wolves prey on the weak' but not 'Wolves are bushy-tailed'. And T_ϕ might also include things that are not at all commonplace. The context in which the metaphor occurs might well be such that the metaphorical word has been provided novel or deviant associations by its author or speaker.[29]

Assuming that we have a rough idea of what is in T_ϕ, then T_ϕ and the bridge principle 'Humans are wolves' jointly have certain implications, such as 'Humans prey on the weak', 'Humans run in packs', and so on. One effect of these implications, and thereby of the metaphor, is

[26]Cf. Quine (1960), 248–251.
[27]Black (1962), 40.
[28]As Black (1979), 29, now notes as well. Cf. Scheffler, 117–118.
[29]Brooke-Rose contains numerous examples.

to emphasize certain (alleged) characteristics of humans while pushing others into the background. Thus the connective theory, like the metaphor, organizes our view of humans to some extent by selecting certain characteristics to emphasize at the expense of others.[30] In this respect it is just like a map (a kind of "seeing as") that abstracts away from everything except what is of interest to its intended users or producers. Metaphors have been compared to filters.[31] They could equally well be compared to maps.

Every metaphor can be regarded as a bridge principle in some implicit connective theory, though of course metaphors do much else as well, and not only in poetry. The spirit of this claim is less to explain metaphor than to shed light on theories, and in any case to point to a kind of direct connection between theories and metaphors so far unremarked in the literature.[32] Even if not every metaphor can be regarded as a bridge principle in some connective theory, nevertheless (8) represents an enormous class of metaphors that in effect are bridge principles. Here are a few more:

(9)   A balloon is a frustrated explosion.

(10) Argument is war.

(11) Time is a river.

(12) Life is a game of chance.

(13) Love is a work of art.

None of these entails reducibility of one domain to another. None expresses an identity (between humans and wolves, arguments and wars, and so on) or even coextensiveness (of the predicates 'is a human', 'is a wolf', and so on).

Furthermore, a metaphor's implications need not entail coextensiveness of *their* terms. For example, 'Humans are scavengers'—perhaps one of the implications of 'Humans are wolves', depending on the context—hardly entails coextensiveness of 'is a human' and 'is a scavenger'. Nor do metaphors generally entail isomorphism, extensional or

---

[30]Cf. Rothbart, 11; Black (1962), 41.

[31]Black (1962), 39–40.

[32]Rothbart, 610–613, now makes a closely related point but does not notice the likely explanation of why metaphors can do so much to promote theoretical unification: they are already bridge principles in connective theories that subsequently can be enlarged so as to achieve the unification. Cf. Eberle (1970b), 222. Boyd (1979) discusses scientific metaphors that are constitutive of certain theories, but he stops well short of the present claim.

otherwise (§4.6), between the domains they connect. No thoroughgoing sameness of structure is implied between discourse about wolves and discourse about humans, or between arguments and wars, time and money, and so on.[33] Finally, like 'Love is a work of art', many metaphors do not presuppose that their terms have a precise reference (though often they do have precise reference).

Because metaphors can be construed as bridge principles, they afford examples in which such principles do not entail reducibility, isomorphism, or precise reference of the relevant vocabulary. On the other hand, their significance in this respect is limited. The reason is that very few metaphors if any are bridge principles in a connective theory $T_{\Phi, \Psi}$ that is supposed to facilitate an inference to determination of Ψ-truth by Φ-truth. Even if 'Humans are wolves' were a completely successful metaphor, we would refrain from inferring that truths about wolves determine the truths about humans. Yet it is in connection with determination that physicalists need to produce examples of nonreductive bridge principles. For physicalists must explain how determination could be established, if not by way of some sort of reducibility. An essential part of their explanation is that determination may be inferred where there is a happy family of connective theories, or at least the reasonable promise of one. And they must show further, by means of examples, how the bridge principles in such theories need not entail reducibility, isomorphism, precise reference, and so on. Bridge principles that are metaphors, though they ordinarily entail none of these things, are therefore of limited use for this purpose.

Metaphors are far more significant in suggesting models that guide the construction of theories[34] that do facilitate an inference to determination. Indeed models—such as a billiard-ball model of gas molecules—have often been construed as extended or systematically developed metaphors. And so they frequently are, offering programs or paradigms that guide the construction of theories to connect various domains. The billiard-ball model influenced the evolution of the kinetic theory of gases at every turn. The root metaphor ('Gas molecules are billiard balls') operated less as a bridge principle itself than as a source of possible analogies, some of which were subsequently reflected in the bridge principles of the kinetic theory. The bridge principle 'An increase in the pressure of a gas results from an increase in the average velocity of the molecules' reflected an analogy with a property of the billiard balls: the net force they exert on the sides of the table increases with their average

---

[33]Cf. Eberle (1970b), 222–224, 229.
[34]Cf. Leatherdale; Boyd (1979); Kuhn.

velocity. In this extended sense, many of the theory's bridge principles are among the implications of the root metaphor.

Suppose we have a connective theory that is thus constructed in light of a metaphor. It does not follow that the nonreductiveness of metaphor will be inherited by the theory. There are, after all, reductive versions of the kinetic theory of gases and of some other connective theories inspired by metaphor. Nevertheless, one may plausibly speculate that relatively few connective theories constructed in light of a metaphor are reductive. The reason is that most of their bridge principles will reflect certain analogies, roughly of the form "A stands to B as C stands to D." (For example, the pressure of a gas stands to the average velocity of its molecules as the net force of the billiard balls stands to their average velocity.) Most of the time, C stands to D in no reductive relation (this is the speculative part). Hence, most of the time, A will stand to B in no reductive relation, so far as the analogy is concerned. And it is A's standing to B that the bridge principle expresses. So the bridge principles would not be reductive. If most of them reflect this sort of analogy, then their containing theory is less likely to be reductive too.

5.3. Metaphor

> *In all aspects of life . . . we define our reality in terms of metaphor. . . . We draw inferences, set goals, make commitments, and execute plans, all on the basis of how we structure our experience, consciously and unconsciously, by means of metaphor.*
>
> —GEORGE LAKOFF AND MARK JOHNSON
>
> *Everyday language is a forgotten and therefore used up poem.*
>
> —MARTIN HEIDEGGER

Of all the ways of relating a couple of domains, metaphor is probably the most frequent. Surely it is one of the most fertile. Many a metaphor blithely juxtaposes vocabulary from domains hitherto deemed utterly disparate, as in Newton's implicit 'The moon is a falling projectile'. Equally often, metaphors juxtapose vocabulary from within one and the same domain, vocabulary that nevertheless belongs in some sense to different categories or kinds, as in 'Humans are wolves'. Call the former sort of metaphor *inter*domain, the latter *intra*domain.

Whether inter- or intradomain, metaphors extensively structure how we perceive, feel, think, and act and how we relate to each other and ourselves. As an illustration of how powerful and pervasive the influence of a metaphor can be, consider 'Time is money'.[35] Because money is a limited resource, and a limited resource is valuable, the metaphor 'Time is money' implies the metaphor 'Time is a limited resource', which in turn implies the metaphor 'Time is valuable'. We are so accustomed to conceptualizing time this way that we seldom realize that these are indeed metaphors—metaphors in which a number of terms whose home ground is the marketplace are applied to time. They sustain and are sustained by such more or less literal expressions as

> How do you *spend* your time?
>
> We're living on *borrowed* time.
>
> This gadget will *save* you hours.
>
> That flat tire *cost* me an hour.
>
> She's *invested* a lot of time in him.
>
> You need to *budget* your time.
>
> *Put aside* some time for relaxation.
>
> Is that *worth your while?*
>
> You don't *use* your time profitably.
>
> *Pay me* for my time with your time.

Clearly, in our culture we understand and experience time largely as the kind of thing that can be spent, borrowed, saved, budgeted, and so on. And we act accordingly, so that for better or worse our basic everyday activities and much of our consciousness are structured extensively and profoundly by the metaphor. Doubtless this helps explain why we have so little true leisure. Fortunately there is nothing necessary about this way of conceptualizing time. Cultures there are, perhaps all nonindustrialized, in which no such metaphors are used of time, with corresponding differences in the way time is experienced. Few things affect the ways of human being so deeply as metaphors for time.

In §§1.2 and 4.6 we provisionally characterized a domain of discourse as some relatively distinctive kind of talk that both expresses and creates or sustains an image (or set of images) of ourselves and our worlds. Metaphor may well be the principal means by which we create and sustain such images and therefore the principal means by which a domain of discourse influences perception—including self-perception—

---

[35]From Lakoff and Johnson (1980a), as is much of the rest of this paragraph. Cf. Lakoff and Johnson (1980b).

plus feeling, thought, action, and our relations with each other. In a sense to be explained, the domain contains a variety of metaphors, often implicit or even explicit in its lexicon, which change over time. Some are relatively permanent (like 'Time is money', in our culture), and some are fleeting (like Mark Twain's 'A palm tree is a feather-duster struck by lightning'). We remarked in §5.0 that we are self-defining animals not least because of the effects on ourselves of our chosen vocabulary. Here we may add that the effects may well be primarily by way of the metaphors we create with the vocabulary; these become, permanently or fleetingly, part of the discourse of a domain. In all of us there is something of the poet, a vehicle for transforming domains of discourse and for creating new ones, if only by way of slang.

The idea that a metaphor becomes part of the discourse of a domain D_Φ can be made clear enough in the case of intradomain metaphors. Such metaphors juxtapose vocabulary already in D_Φ (as in Shakespeare's 'Old fools are babes again', or perhaps even de Gaulle's 'Old age is shipwreck'). There is no problem, then, in classifying them as among the sentences of D_Φ. If in addition the metaphor becomes deeply entrenched as, say, one of the commonplaces of D_Φ (something to which its speakers would automatically assent), or more deeply still as part of the lexicon (as is 'high' used of status), then we may say that the metaphor has become part of D_Φ and that D_Φ contains the metaphor. Normally, such metaphors either are instances (or reflections) of some more general metaphor (such as 'Time is money') or are themselves rather general in their implications, with extensive effects on the structure of the concepts expressed by vocabulary from D_Φ.

In what sense could an *inter*domain metaphor become part of the discourse of a given domain? Such a metaphor juxtaposes vocabulary from at least two distinct domains. Which one would it belong to? This question is analogous to a question about bridge principles in a connective theory $T_{\Phi, \psi}$. The bridge principles of $T_{\Phi, \psi}$ belong neither to D_Φ nor to D_ψ. Instead, their status is multiple, relative to D_Φ and D_ψ (indeed irreducibly so, if the ψ-terms are not reducible to the Φ-terms). We saw in §5.2 how a metaphor can be construed as a bridge principle in an implicit theory $T_{\Phi, \psi}$. So the domain status of a metaphor, relative to D_Φ and D_ψ, is multiple (and generally irreducibly so). But there is no reason why the metaphor could not be regarded as belonging to a *third* domain D_X, which consists in part of vocabulary from both D_Φ and D_ψ plus interpretations of the vocabulary consonant with the metaphor. (More on such interpretation below.)

Just as (a family of) successful connective theories can make near neighbors of domains D_Φ and D_ψ hitherto supposed quite distant

(§5.1), (a family of) cognitively successful metaphors can create a third domain D_X out of D_ϕ and D_ψ. (Cognitive success in a metaphor is much like success in a theory, as we shall see.) A metaphor thus present at the creation clearly is part of the discourse D_X. Indeed *all* our domains of discourse today may well have arisen out of prior distinct domains largely by such metaphor-driven metamorphosis ("language is a forgotten . . . poem").[36] Many a word contains evidence to that effect in its etymology ("trailing clouds of etymology," as J. L. Austin says). And we noted early in this section just one of many possible illustrations of how pervasive metaphor is. If language should indeed prove metaphorical through and through, then that fact would support and provide further content for the widespread idea that language is theory through and through. Everyday language would have its source in forgotten theory, largely because it would have its source in forgotten metaphor, or a "used-up poem."

Occasionally, it may be impossible to tell exactly where one domain ends and another begins. One reason why the boundaries often are so blurred and shifting is that interdomain metaphors typically work by slow degrees; we cannot readily tell just when a new domain has emerged out of older ones. Another reason is that one and the same vocabulary or set of terms may be used to express different metaphors. For example, greater knowledge and understanding of humans and wolves might conceivably if improbably lead us to endorse 'Wolves are humans'. Or, using the vocabulary of time and the marketplace, we might find ourselves thinking of time not as a limited resource but as a blank check written on an infinitely large account. Thus *vocabulary by itself is insufficient to individuate one domain from another,* convenient though it has been to pretend on occasion that vocabulary is all.

Let us henceforth think of a domain of discourse roughly as some relatively distinctive kind of vocabulary together with a particular set of entrenched metaphors that juxtapose the vocabulary in their special way. Thus a domain includes at least a vocabulary plus a set of sentences that are or express the entrenched metaphors. Two domains are distinct, then, not only if they have different vocabulary, but if they have the same vocabulary but different sets of entrenched metaphors. By requiring the metaphors to be entrenched, we allow a domain to remain the same despite its containing very different fleeting metaphors at different times. Naturally, whether a metaphor is entrenched or just when it becomes entrenched cannot always be determined precisely. There is some vagueness also in just what is to count as a metaphor. Nev-

[36]Heidegger (1971), 208. Cf. Lakoff and Johnson (1980b).

ertheless, this rough characterization of a domain of discourse is adequate for our purposes.

A domain of truth was defined in §1.2 as the set of true sentences couched in the vocabulary of a given domain. Entrenched metaphors are among the sentences ordinarily taken to be true by those who discourse within the domain. Thus we must face the issue of what it might mean to call a metaphor true (or false, for that matter). We can do no better than the Tarski schema. But is that good enough? Applied to Shakespeare's 'Life's but a walking shadow', the schema yields the seemingly innocuous 'Life's but a walking shadow' is true iff life's but a walking shadow. Yet it can sound odd to ask "True or false?" of 'Life's but a walking shadow'. The issue of literal truth or falsity, it would appear, cannot arise, at least not in this case. The role of metaphors, perhaps all of them, appears not to include being true or false.[37]

However, metaphors have presuppositions. In this they are no different from other sentences. Among the presuppositions of 'Life's but a walking shadow' are such things as that there is a shadow, all insubstantial; that it moves ("struts and frets his hour upon the stage"); that there is something more substantial which casts the shadow; that there is something upon which it is cast, plus a light source (perhaps some "brief candle"); and so on. If one of these presuppositions is false, then the metaphor is neither true nor false, though of course it would remain exceedingly powerful in other respects.

All this is quite compatible with the Tarski schema. Indeed it is a consequence of it, via the successful-presupposition prerequisite (§1.5[iii]). According to this prerequisite, when we apply the schema to a metaphor, as to any sentence, we are not claiming that it *is* true or false. We are only claiming something highly conditional: *if* it is true, then such-and-such, and vice versa. Because a presupposition is a necessary condition for a sentence ϕ to be true or false, the schema has the further consequence that if all ϕ's presuppositions are true, then ϕ is true or false (since the conjunction of all the necessary conditions is a sufficient condition). In the case of an entrenched metaphor, which we are inclined to call true, evidently we believe that all its presuppositions are true. If we are justified in believing that they are all true, then we are justified in believing that the metaphor is true or false. Thus suppose we are justified in believing that all the presuppositions of 'Time is money' are true (such as that there is a limited resource, hence a valuable one, which can be spent, saved, borrowed, and so on). Then we are justified in ascribing truth or falsity to the metaphor and its implications. And

---

[37]But see Davidson (1978); Boyd (1979); M. Bergmann; Stern (1983), (1985); Novitz.

we would be free to argue that it is *false* that time is money, and that it is true instead that time is, say, a perpetual loom (assuming that the latter has no false presuppositions either).

Identifying a metaphor's presuppositions is as difficult as identifying its implications, to which of course they are closely related. The reason is that even in context, we may be unable to identify the implicit connective theory $T_{\phi,\psi}$ (including above all the internal theory T_ϕ) of which the metaphor is a bridge principle; and even if we succeed in identifying $T_{\phi,\psi}$, we may be unable to see all its implications. Despite such difficulties, we know what it means to call a metaphor true or false, thanks to the Tarski schema and §1.1,[38] just as we know what it means to call a nonmetaphorical sentence true, despite not knowing on occasion *whether* it is true or even whether it is true or false.

Because our language and experience are metaphorically structured to such an enormous extent, one may be tempted to conclude that understanding is prior to truth, or that "a theory of truth . . . is dependent on understanding,"[39] or perhaps that "truth as disclosure" is prior to propositional truth. There is a sense in which such conclusions are exactly right. Before we are entitled to ascribe either truth or falsity to a sentence, we must interpret its terms. Normally, our interpretation must accord with at least the entrenched metaphors in the domain, and often with some novel ones as well. So we must allow the interpretation to be guided by the lexicon and the context. For example, instead of mindlessly assigning the set of wolves to the predicate 'is a wolf' as the latter occurs in 'Humans are wolves', we do better to assign it the set of wolves (possible or actual; §4.1) about which the implicit internal theory T_ϕ would be true. And our assignment to the term 'humans' will also be guided by the context and our best guess as to its role in 'Humans are wolves', as well as in the implicit connective theory $T_{\phi,\psi}$.[40]

Once an interpretation of the terms is thus assigned in light of $T_{\phi,\psi}$, it can still happen that the metaphorical sentence has no truth-value because of presupposition-failure. To see what the presuppositions *are,* we must understand the sentence under its assigned interpretation. To see whether they are *satisfied,* we normally look toward some extralinguistic circumstance or aspect of experience in order to ascertain, as best we can, whether the presuppositions fit the circumstance as we understand it. "What is relevant at this point is not what is *presupposed*

[38]See also Novitz.

[39]Lakoff and Johnson (1980a), 486.

[40]The needed details of this account of interpretation, it happens, are now provided by Stern (1985).

but what *actually* is the case."[41] If the way we understand or concep-
tualize the circumstance—the way it is "disclosed"—is structured by a
metaphor in (or reflected by) the very sentence at issue, then of course
we normally judge that the presuppositions fit. But if our understanding
of the situation—the way it is disclosed or "becomes present"—is not
thus structured, we are more likely to judge differently. Because of the
extent to which our understanding is determined by our discourse,
frequently only a powerful poet or theorist can disenthrall us from the
discourse so that we may judge that the presuppositions do not fit,
despite entrenched metaphors to the contrary.[42]

There is another sense in which, on occasion, understanding is prior
to truth, a sense familiar from §1.6, on virtues of beliefs besides truth.
Among these are such virtues of successful connective theories as simplicity, comprehensiveness, and consilience, valued because they con-
duce to understanding. On many occasions we are more in need of a
coherent rendering of various phenomena or experiences than we are in
need of strict truth. Of two theories tied on the score of satisfying the
truth-prerequisites, we prefer the one that is ahead on simplicity and
consilience. If it is far enough ahead, we may accept it even though it
seems not to satisfy the truth-prerequisites quite so well as the other.
Such priority is not unconditional, obviously, and depends on whether
at the time we are more in need of truth or of simplicity, consilience,
and related virtues.

In like manner many metaphors, perhaps all of them, are valued
more highly for their power to inject coherence into a bit of experience
than for their strict truth, if any. Indeed of two metaphors the more
successful, cognitively speaking, is the one that enjoys greater simplicity
and consilience, preferably dynamic. Thus cognitive success in a metaphor, unlike that in a connective theory, does not depend on satisfaction
of the prerequisites for truth. It is only when we begin to ascribe strict
truth to the metaphor that the truth-prerequisites become relevant. The
comparative simplicity and consilience we ascribe to a metaphor mean
merely the simplicity and consilience of the implicit connective theory
of which the metaphor is a bridge principle.

These cognitive virtues are not by any means the only virtues metaphors enjoy.[43] Metaphors in poetry are not usually aimed at cognitive
success even in the above somewhat relaxed sense. And often we value a

[41]Stern (1985), 708, though our uses of 'presupposition' differ somewhat.
[42]On this process of getting "unstuck" in science, cf. Rothbart, 610–612.
[43]Scheffler's analysis, 79–130, of the leading theories of metaphor is also an analysis,
in effect, of the leading virtues of metaphor.

metaphor as a guide to action and feeling, matters usually more related to the metaphor's simplicity and consilience than to its truth, if any. Thus in construing a metaphor as a bridge principle in a connective theory, we are not saying that its use is primarily for theorizing versus action, or for orientation and contemplation versus realization and feeling. Often the choice of a metaphor is not just the choice of a map or a way of seeing (§5.2) but of a way of life. And those who get to impose their metaphors on us, by virtue of being in power, can impose a way of life. Once again, 'Time is money' is instructive.

A face of existence was defined in §4.6 as a global-sentential property of the whole of existence. The property is expressed by a whole domain of truth, and we spoke of the property as being indexed by the vocabulary of the domain. But we have just been learning that vocabulary alone is insufficient to individuate domains of discourse. Entrenched metaphors must be taken into account. What effect does this have on our notion of a domain of truth, and thereby on our notion of a face of existence? None. A domain of truth remains the set of true sentences from a domain, *including* its true entrenched metaphors (if any). If two domains of discourse have the same vocabulary but different sets of entrenched metaphors, *and* if none of the metaphors is true (or false), then the two domains will turn out to have the same domain of truth. Ordinarily, this is no problem. Nevertheless, should it become necessary to distinguish two domains of truth even in this sort of case, we may do so by means of the distinct vocabularies-cum-metaphors from which they are descended.

There is no need, either, to revise our view that a whole domain of truth expresses a face of existence. Since the domain of truth includes any metaphors from a discourse that are true, this accords such metaphors the role they deserve as among the crucial means we have of disclosing faces of existence. But we probably ought not continue to speak of the global-sentential property expressed by a domain of truth as indexed solely by a vocabulary. It seems preferable to regard such a property as indexed by a vocabulary together with the relevant metaphors. Thus a face of existence is a vocabulary-cum-metaphor-indexed global-sentential property of the whole of existence—only that is a mouthful.

A domain of truth, metaphors and all, will automatically be consistent (since any set of truths is consistent). But a domain of discourse can happen to be inconsistent, if only because it can contain entrenched metaphors that are inconsistent with each other. Everyday language, or our ordinary conceptual scheme, probably offends in this regard, despite the fact that establishing the inconsistency of a couple of its metaphors is never easy. At first glance 'Time is money' seems inconsistent with 'Time is a river'. Actually they are consistent, in all likelihood, since they can be construed as being about time in different respects. Only if they were both about time in the same respect would they be inconsistent and the metaphors truly mixed. By way of contrast, 'Time is a river' and 'Time marches on' seem to be about time in the same respect. If so, they are inconsistent; rivers don't march. Truly mixed metaphors, it would appear, are to be shunned not merely for inelegance but also for inconsistency.

Does metaphor present special problems for physicalism? One problem might be that physicalists are unable to account for the creative process, much of it subconscious, by which new metaphors occur to us, plus new implications of old ones. 'Language arrives' is Heidegger's phrase for this mysterious and often unbidden welling-up in us of what in effect are new ways of disclosing faces of existence. But it is not the physicalist's job to account for such matters. The division of labor allowed by transitivity of determination entitles physicalists to refer us to the relevant disciplines for whatever explanation this creative process may prove to have. Nor are physicalists burdened with the claim that the process is nothing but some physical or natural process. They are free to regard our power of metaphor, and indeed all culture, as a manifestation of the awesome fertility of the physical, despite the fact that the physical and the human are irreducibly different.

Another problem arises in connection with the principle TT of the determination of all truth by physical truth (§4.3). TT may seem to require a literal-mindedness that renders it inapplicable to metaphorical truths. But we noted as early as §4.4 that TT is compatible with a thoroughgoing vagueness and indeterminacy of reference of the terms in the sentence whose truth is said to be determined. To the extent that vagueness or indeterminacy should happen to be involved in a metaphor, they are no obstacle to applying TT.

Furthermore, much depends on how the phrase 'metaphorical truth' is being used. If it refers to a metaphor that is strictly true, hence one with no false presuppositions, then talk of the determination of such truths presents no problems beyond those involved in the determination of any other sort of truth. Indeed a metaphor's having (so far as we can tell) no false presuppositions, hence its being strictly true or false (so far as we can tell), would be an excellent criterion of literalness, or at least of its conventionality or degree of entrenchment. By this criterion, entrenched metaphors are among those that people normally judge to be literal, rightly or wrongly, and that poets, philosophers, and others sometimes seek to deliteralize by calling attention, in effect, to a false presupposition.

The phrase 'metaphorical truth' might instead refer to a metaphor that is not strictly true or false but is in some relevant sense powerful, startling, open-ended, moving, or whatever. 'Life's but a walking shadow' could be an example. If so, it is nonliteral, or strictly neither true nor false, and TT does not apply to it. Instead, we explicate the so-called "truth" of the nonliteral metaphor in whatever way seems appropriate. We might say that the "truth" in the metaphor is a matter of seeing life as insubstantial, brief, flickering, dependent, and dark. Usually, such truth will be closely related to the metaphor's simplicity and consilience, the simple yet novel and striking way in which it implies and unifies in one figure a variety of features brought to the foreground by the metaphor itself.

Even in the case of nonliteral metaphor, however, there is room for some use of the principle of truth-determination. For there are many ways in which a metaphor can misfire or be inapt, ranging from poor taste to failures of fact. 'A palm tree is a feather-duster struck by lightning' would misfire in the absence of certain facts about the shape of palm trees and of feather-dusters, about the appearance of fronds and feathers, and about the effects of a lightning strike. Not that the content of the metaphor, whatever that might be, is necessarily exhausted by these or any other facts. Rather, the point is that if certain things were not true of palm trees, of feather-dusters, and of lightning, the metaphor would be inapt in approximately the same way as is 'A palm tree is a brick wall struck by gossamer'—a complete dud.

It is at the level of truths necessary for a metaphor to be apt that determination still has room to work, even when the metaphor itself is strictly neither true nor false. According to the physicalist, such truths, like all truths, are determined by truths at the level of physics. This does not imply that we always or even very often know exactly which truths are necessary for the metaphor to be apt—that is, which ones constitute what we may call its factual ground. Frequently, the metaphor is so rich and suggestive that there is little or no prospect of our finding everything in its factual ground, even in a given context of its use. Such a metaphor is open-ended, or endlessly suggestive of similarities that would not have been disclosed without the aid of the metaphor itself. By contrast, the factual ground of 'A palm tree is a feather-duster struck by lightning' is nearly exhausted by the fact that palms and struck feather-dusters are similar as regards a certain splayed, drooping shape.

Suppose, then, that the principle of determination of all truth by physical truth applies to "metaphorical truth," either by way of applying to a metaphor that is strictly true or to the factual ground of a metaphor that is neither true nor false. Most theories in physics, including those we presently deem true, are constructed in light of extended metaphors. And much physical vocabulary has its source in forgotten metaphor, or a used-up poem. But even when some such metaphor is not strictly true, as is perhaps always the case, its factual ground is nevertheless determined—and to that extent its aptness or fruitfulness accounted for—by truths at the level of physics. Thus there is a sense in which the poetry that precedes physics is also grounded in physics.

5.4. Discussing Sundials with a Bat

> *What is it like to be a bat?*
> —Thomas Nagel

> *Sebastian never alluded to his work in her presence: it would have been like discussing sundials with a bat.*
> —Vladimir Nabokov

The next chapter lays to rest the traditional objection that physicalism entails subjectivism in morals. The opposite sort of objection, emphasized by Nagel, is that physicalism fails to be subjective enough. It cannot capture what, in our role as moral agents, is our idea of ourselves as the source of our own actions. And it cannot capture what it is like to *be* the persons we are, experiencing our own moral dilemmas. Indeed "every subjective phenomenon is essentially connected with a single point of view, and it seems inevitable that an objective, physical theory will abandon that point of view."[44] So the problem arises not only in morals, according to Nagel, but wherever some phenomenon is essentially connected with a single point of view, such as that of a bat, or a human, or the here-now, or whatever.

Suppose Nagel is right that there is something it is like to be a bat, even though we are unable to understand or to express what it is like. Indeed for every sentient species, presumably, there is something it is like to be a member of it. And for a particular member—say, for a particular human—there is something it is like to be that individual. Suppose further that even if we could express what it is like, there is no way to reduce what it is like to purely physical or other objective terms, as Nagel argues, because in the process of translation the subjective character of the phenomenon will be left out. Objectification omits perspective, or the subjective point of view, precisely because viewing things objectively is to view them, so far as possible, from no particular point of view.

As Nagel himself emphasizes, the heart of his argument is an "objec-

[44]Nagel, 167, 199.

tion to the reducibility of experience. . . . The reduction can succeed
only if the species-specific viewpoint is omitted from what is to be
reduced."[45] And if the specific viewpoint is omitted, then it is hardly
accounted for by physicalism or by any other objective approach; so too
for the subjective character of experience generally.

As an objection to universal reducibility and the "wave of reductivist
euphoria" he is reacting against, Nagel's insight may well be decisive.
We need not inquire. For in any case, nonreductive physicalism would
not be implicated. The nonreductive varieties can cheerfully admit that
indeed there is (or may well be) something it is like to be a bat; that what
it is like is inexpressible and unknowable; and that even if what it is like
could be expressed, still it could not be expressed by, or otherwise
reduced to, scientific or any other objective discourse. It need only be
determined, in the sense that the facts about what it is like to be a bat are
determined by facts at the level of physics. That is, the physical phenomena determine the subjective phenomena that constitute what it is
like to be a bat, in the fourfold sense of determining (a) that there are
such phenomena, (b) which ones there are, (c) what it would be like to
experience them, and (d) what their (other) properties are. Once more,
expressibility is beside the point. Contrary to Nagel, physicalists need
not "insist that everything real must be brought under an objective
description."[46] Comprehensiveness can be achieved without monopoly.

Still, how could purely objective phenomena determine subjective
phenomena? Isn't subjectivity beyond the reach not merely of reducibility but even of determination? Not if there is a fact of the matter
as to what it is like to be the subject, as we see in (i)–(iii) below. And
Nagel holds that there is a fact of the matter. There are "facts about
what mental states are like for the creature having them," even though
"facts about what it is like to be an X are very peculiar." Some of them
may be so peculiar as not to consist in the truth of any propositions
expressible in human language, being "beyond the reach of human
concepts." As Nagel also says, "we can be compelled to recognize the
existence of such facts without being able to state or comprehend
them."[47]

Here the challenge to physicalists is threefold. Assuming for the sake
of argument that Nagel is right, they must (i) find room for facts in their
inventory of what there is, including facts not consisting in the truth of

[45]Nagel, 175.
[46]Nagel, 165, 210.
[47]Nagel, 201, 168, 171.

any humanly expressible propositions; (ii) define the relation of determination between two realms of such fact; and (iii) indicate how we could ever tell in practice whether some given subjective phenomenon (humanly expressible or not) is determined by certain objective phenomena. In effect this involves solving what Nagel calls the mystery of how the subjective character of experience "could be revealed in the physical operation" of the experiencing organism.[48]

(i) A fact for Nagel consists in the truth of a proposition, humanly expressible or not. To find room for facts in this sense, therefore, one must find room for propositions. To do so, recall how properties were accommodated, expressible or not, as functions from possible worlds to extensions (§4.1). Similarly, let propositions be functions from possible worlds to truth-values. As such, they are mathematical entities, hence mathematical-physical as regards their inventory-status. Just as physicalists can include even inexpressible properties in their inventory, so can they include facts about what various experiences are like for the subject having them, even if such facts are inexpressible in any language. They need not argue that knowing what an experience is like is the possession not of some sort of information but of certain abilities.[49]

(ii) Defining the determination relation for facts, as opposed to true sentences, is a straightforward extension of the definition in §4.3. Thus in P-worlds the Φ-facts determine the Ψ-facts iff given any two such worlds, if the same Φ-facts obtain in both, then the same Ψ-facts obtain in both. Clearly, this does not require that the facts be humanly expressible. So too for the phenomena they are about.

(iii) Provided the subjective phenomena are humanly expressible, we can tell what determines them in the same way we saw in connection with the physical determination of other phenomena (§5.1). Since determination is transitive, no direct relation between physics and the subjective need be claimed. Instead, we are to take advantage of the work of the relevant intervening disciplines. Their work, to the extent it is complete, justifies an inference to determination either from the success of a happy family of connective theories (say in psychobiology), or from observing the determination of classes of subjective phenomena by phenomena expressed in a cluster of neighboring objective domains, or typically from both.

The relevant idea of observing a subjective experience presents no problem here, any more than for Nagel, for to observe it is not to have it or even to be able to understand what it is like to have it. Instead, to

---

[48]Nagel, 172.
[49]As does Lewis (1983b), 122–132. Cf. Peacocke.

observe the experience is to observe that it occurs, perhaps by listening to a person tell us he or she is having that sort of experience, or by hearing the cries of an animal in pain, or by seeing a face and reading body language, or whatever. And we can observe certain correlations between the occurrence of the experience and various organic states, including the determination correlation.

Thus the subjective character of an experience could be "revealed" in the physical operation of the experiencing organism, if we must use Nagel's word, in the sense of our seeing that it is determined by that operation (or by that operation in relation to a wider environment). The subjective character need not be revealed in the physical operation in the sense of being identical with or otherwise reducible to it, hence in that sense read off from it. No term that expresses what the experience is like for the experiencing organism (even if there is such a term) need be even accidentally coextensive with any term (or complex of terms) from the sciences or indeed from any objective discourse. Hence the subjective experiential state need not be type-identical with any structural-physical state of the organism, though of course it will be realized or embodied in the organism.

The same subjective state might even be realized at different times in the same organism via different structural-physical states. For as seen in §4,5, physicalism does not require the same state to be realized the same way, whether in each individual, in all individuals, or in all species. And the state might be realized in very different substances, from protoplasm to microchips to Tinkertoys. The connection between subjective states and their physical realization could therefore be accidental, historical, particular, and novel. If so, many discoveries in the psychobiology of bats would in this respect be like typical discoveries in anthropology, to the effect that this or that emergent state or property is realized in some particular way at some place and time.

What about humanly *in*expressible subjective phenomena? How can the physicalist argue that they too are determined by the physical phenomena? Basically, on grounds of continuity and simplicity. As regards expressibility, experiences come in degrees, from the expressible through the partly expressible to the wholly inexpressible. "The distance between oneself and other persons and other species can fall anywhere on a continuum."[50] Human experiences are mostly toward the expressible end, other species' mostly toward the inexpressible. The progressive inexpressibility corresponds with our progressive inability to take up the other's point of view.

[50]Nagel, 172 n.8.

Now suppose the physicalist is right in claiming that the expressible experiences are physically determined. There appears to be no relevant difference, between the expressible and the partly or wholly inexpressible experiences, in virtue of which the former but not the latter could be granted determination. If reducibility or translatability were being claimed, then degree of expressibility would matter. But determination is a relation among the phenomena, expressible or not. And if all the many observed phenomena (say, the expressible ones) in a given class (say, the class of *all* subjective phenomena) are determined, then all the phenomena whatever in that class are determined, unless there is some relevant difference between them that would obstruct this routine inductive inference.

Discussing subjective experience with a reductivist might be like discussing sundials with a bat. But the physicalist need leave no such aspect of life out of account, even if it cannot be expressed by purely physical or other objective vocabulary.

Our subjective experience of time seems especially resistant to such reduction. Our experience of passage and becoming, of the now and the present, seems utterly inexpressible in the objective temporal idiom of physics. For physics deals with spatiotemporal invariants, deliberately abstracting from point of view, frame of reference, or what things are like for us here now. But the irreducibility or ineliminability of our subjective temporal experience and our use of tenses is irrelevant as regards whether the corresponding subjective phenomena are determined by the objective phenomena with which physics deals. They are determined in the fourfold sense of its being physically determined that there are such subjective temporal phenomena, which such phenomena there are, what it is like to experience or have them, and what their (other) properties are.

Nor does it follow from the physical determination of our subjective temporal experience that the experience is any the less fundamental. The comprehensiveness of physicalism does not entail monopoly, either in the sense that tenseless discourse enjoys some sort of unconditional priority or in the sense that it describes the way things are in themselves (whatever that might be), let alone in the sense that it translates or reduces tensed discourse.

Nagel is rightly disturbed by the monopolistic pretensions of certain forms of physicalism in particular and objectivism generally. Many of them do claim absolute priority or dominance for the objective view, on the ground that the view somehow includes or accounts for the individual and his personal views. But such inclusiveness or completeness implies no such dominance, nor does it imply that the objective view is "the *right* way for the individual to look at the world and his place in it."[51] Inclusiveness like completeness is always relative to some aim or purpose (§§3.5, 4.6, 5.0, 7.3). Only when we are pursuing the relevant purpose or purposes need we employ an objective idiom. We remain free to be interested in other things, and sometimes we are obligated to be.

For example, communication and other conversation could well require me to orient myself and my listener in time, by treating my utterance in effect as the origin on the time axis, relative to which things are spoken of as past, present, or future.[52] If so, then on such occasions, as on some others, tensed discourse takes priority over tenseless. Furthermore, there are many ways of unifying the phenomena, and subjective ways are surely among them. A map of everything in polar coordinates centered on us is no less a map, and no less inclusive, than a map that is coordinate-free.[53] The important thing is to know which map to use on what occasion for what purpose. Such knowledge is less a matter of metaphysics, traditionally conceived, than of wisdom.

If one's purpose is to express a face of existence, then it is unwise to use tensed or other subjective idioms. For we defined a face of existence in such a way that only a domain of truth can express one, where truth meant truth *period*. Hence the objectivity prerequisite applies (§1.5[vii]), and only eternal sentences satisfy it. Tensed and other sentences whose truth-values vary with the time, person, and context of utterance cannot express a face of existence, even though such sentences often are indispensable for other equally valuable purposes, including unifying things in the world in terms of how they look to us from here now, or even how they feel (§7.5).

How things look or feel from here now is itself determined by purely objective phenomena, according to the physicalist. Thus the objective phenomena also determine why the subjective point of view often is nearly true, or true with certain qualifications, or true relative to some time and place. In this extended sense, determination of all truth by physical truth applies not only to strict truths from a given domain, but also to "truths" couched in a subjective idiom, such as 'You promised me a rematch here today'. Even if this sentence could not be turned into an eternal one by supplying names, locations, and dates, nonetheless on those occasions when its utterance is true, its truth would be physically determined. Or, to put the point propositionally, on those

---

[51]Nagel, 197; cf. 209–210. See further §7.1 below.

[52]As Polakow argues in ch. 5, esp. 102–104.

[53]On coordinate-free physical geometry, see Misner, Thorne, and Wheeler, 5–8.

occasions when uttering the sentence expresses a proposition, the truth-value of the proposition is physically determined.

Still, the real test of wisdom is less a matter of knowing which idiom to use for a given purpose than of knowing which purpose to pursue. When ought we to engage in conversation or gesture or art, and when ought we to seek objective truth and such expression of the faces of existence as we can achieve? When ought we to map everything in polar coordinates centered on us, and when ought we to try unifying the phenomena physicalistically? And what kind of "ought" is this, or what kinds? Are these oughts, like moral oughts (§6.1), determined by purely physical phenomena? If so, then the values these oughts represent would be manifestations of the physical phenomena. But some of these values entail that certain moods or purposes or interests frequently ought to take precedence over the aim relative to which physicalism enjoys whatever priority it has (§7.1). So again we would see that one of the ways the physical phenomena manifest themselves is in their own occasional insignificance and in the occasionally far greater significance of other things, including the subjective.

6 Fact and Value

Philosophy's central problem is the relation that exists
between the beliefs about the nature of things due to natural
science and beliefs about values.

—JOHN DEWEY

From the viewpoints of Gadamer, Heidegger, and Sartre, the
trouble with the fact-value distinction is that it is contrived
precisely to blur the fact that . . . to use [a given] set of true
sentences to describe ourselves is already to choose an attitude
toward ourselves.

—RICHARD RORTY

6.0. Introduction

"Materialistic . . . philosophers deny that the objective world of
matter in motion has any place for moral goods. . . . Good and
evil . . . are rather men's internal and variable reactions to the ways in
which they are stimulated by the world."[1] So we are told in a major
encyclopedia article, and indeed the verdict is widely accepted. It was
Democritus himself, after all, who held that because there are only
atoms and the void, our values are mere conventions. Yet this inference
is unsound, as we shall see; physicalism is entirely compatible with
objective values. Or as one contemporary physicalist puts it, "Materialism is consistent with . . . our special status as moral beings. The
right kind of material object can posses intrinsic worth."[2]

On the other hand, the thesis merely that physicalism is compatible
with objective values is not very exciting or even very new. More
revealing would be a physicalistically acceptable argument that there are
objective values in the first place. §§6.1–6.3 provide such an argument,

[1]Gewirth, 979.
[2]Levin, 227.

by explaining how moral truth is determined by purely descriptive truth, whatever the moral truths happen to be and whatever the best way of discovering and justifying them.[3] The existence of objective values is a matter not of extra entities but of there being a truth of the matter as regards the correctness or incorrectness of our value judgments, a truth of the matter determined by objective, natural fact. If the physicalist is right that natural fact in turn is determined by physical fact, it follows that the correctness of our value judgments is determined ultimately by truths at the level of physics. Those physicalists are wrong who insist that "no . . . scientific facts about the world can by themselves determine what we should do,"[4] or who believe that objective values are incompatible with persons as emergent beings.[5]

But is there such a thing as purely descriptive truth in the first place? If not, it could hardly determine value; the fact-value distinction would be doomed. Yet we presuppose some such distinction merely in asking whether purely descriptive truth determines moral or other normative truth. Of course, the fact-value distinction is doomed in any case if it means there is a domain of discourse such that our choice or continued use of it involves no value presuppositions whatever.[6] In *that* sense there *is* no purely descriptive or factual discourse. Not only our decision to use but our acquiescence in continuing to use a discourse, however objective the discourse is, reflects or presupposes as well as reinforces values we may scarcely perceive. Often the values are revealed only in the domain's entrenched metaphors. The discourse comes trailing clouds not just of etymology but of value, purpose, emphasis, and mood.

And yet in another sense we can distinguish between descriptive and valuative discourse just as surely as we can distinguish between what the House of Representatives does and what it ought to do. Without some such distinction we would be defenseless against cynical remarks like "An impeachable offense is whatever the House says it is" (as then Representative Gerald Ford said with regard to Earl Warren). What the House *ought* to do cannot be reduced to or expressed as what it *does*. And *this* distinction, between what descriptively is the case and what would be better (or worse), gives every indication of being vital to civilized life. So in this sense there is such a thing as purely descriptive truth, even though there is another sense in which no discourse, including the pur-

---

[3]The argument appears in Post (1984a), a revision of which forms the core of §§6.1–6.3.

[4]Smart (1963), 154.

[5]As does Margolis (1978), 254–258.

[6]As I take Rorty (1979), 363–365, to be saying.

est description, is value-free. For our decision to use one discourse rather than another reflects and reinforces certain values, even if—strictly speaking—the discourse, via its distinctive vocabulary, expresses none.

Modern science chose to use descriptive, objective discourse (not overnight, but the essential commitments seem to have been made by the end of the seventeenth century), which made it look as though the world could contain no entelechy, no *telos,* no element of value whatever.[7] Values were banished from nature, along with much else that matters to us. All efforts to get the values back in have seemed unconvincing. Indeed no such effort can possibly succeed, assuming the irreducibility of values to facts, so long as (i) the world is identified with the totality of fact, and (ii) the only sense in which the world could contain or exhibit an element of value is via derivability from or reducibility to the factual.

The flaws in this history are increasingly easy to see. One consists in construing the chosen factual discourse as expressing *the* way the world is, via identifying *the* world with what the discourse can describe or express. This is just a form of monopoly, rejected in §4.6. Another flaw consists in supposing that there are no alternatives to reduction and derivation as ways of showing that the world contains an element of value after all, or that *ought* is entirely a function of *is.* That there is a plausible alternative is one of the lessons of the next three sections.

Of course, if ought could be reduced to is, then ought would be determined by is. For in general, reduction is sufficient for determination. Again, reduction means a term-term relation whereby ought would be coextensive (of necessity or at least accidentally) with some construction on is, and in that sense definable by is. But determination means that a distribution of truth and falsity over whole sentences about what is the case would allow one and only one such distribution over whole sentences about what ought to be the case. In particular, given the purely descriptive or natural facts about the world (including us), one and only one account of our obligations would be correct. If in turn the descriptive facts are determined by facts at the level of natural science, as the physicalist believes, then ought would itself be determined by facts at that level. Nature and morals would be ontologically reunified, the natural phenomena determining the moral, despite their bifurcation since the seventeenth century, roughly when teleological concepts had begun to be eliminated from natural science.

Notoriously, no reduction of ought to is has achieved consensus, to

[7]Cf. Nozick, 399.

put it mildly, and none is likely to. Antireductivist arguments in ethics evidently are too powerful, if not conclusive. But even though reduction is sufficient for determination, it is not necessary, as we have seen. Further, moral oughts, at least, are indeed determined by is. The argument for this determinacy, outlined in the next section, is nonreductive and surprisingly simple, granted just two premises—one of them unproblematic, the other less so. In any case the argument applies no matter what the best way of justifying or defending moral claims might be, and no matter which such claims are correct. And it applies to moral first principles, not just to particular judgments made in light of them.

Nor does the argument presuppose that ought is either derivable from or entailed or implied by is. The correctness of moral claims can be grounded in nonvaluational, noninstitutional brute fact, in the sense of being determined by it, even if no ought or imperative or prescriptive can be deduced from or defined by any is or indicative. The same then proves true of the correctness of all value judgments (subject to a minor proviso). To the determinacy of moral valuation we may therefore provisionally add the determinacy of valuation generally.

The argument for the determinacy of valuation is outlined in §6.1. Some caveats about the argument, especially about one of its premises, appear in §6.2. The main caveat is that *the argument as it stands in §6.1 is meant neither as a non-question-begging proof of objectivism nor as a non-question-begging refutation of subjectivism or antirealism in morals.* Instead, the argument there is meant only to undermine what has always been the final, indispensable argument for subjectivism. This is what Mackie calls "the argument from queerness": objective values would have to be very queer sorts of things, because their relation with facts is so mysterious, being a matter neither of entailment or implication, nor of derivation, nor of reduction or definability, nor even of supervenience or "resultance" (the latter two relations being either unclear or, when clear, not strong enough to capture the relation required by objectivists).[8] Better by far to replace the alleged objective values with some sort of subjective response that can be causally related to stimulation by the natural features on which the alleged values are said to be resultant or consequential. Or so the argument goes. As against this, what §6.1 shows is (only) that there is an intelligible, unqueer alternative to the listed relations.[9] The assumption that these are the only alternatives is false.

Mackie himself explains why the argument from queerness is indis-

---

[8]Mackie, 41; on resultance, see Dancy.
[9]And to those listed in Nozick, 538–539, 568.

pensable. Without some such argument the mere fact of widespread moral disagreement does not by itself imply that there are no objective values about which to disagree, any more than disagreement in science implies that there really is no truth of the matter there.[10] Or as Nozick remarks, "It is because we do not see how an objective ethics is *possible* that we worry about irresolvable moral disagreements."[11] And as Sturgeon argues, anyone who finds it plausible that objective values play no explanatory role in our account of the world must already have been persuaded by some other consideration that there are in the first place no objective values to play the role.[12] Indeed if anything, the presumption should be that there *are* objective values. For this is what ordinary usage of moral terms overwhelming presupposes, as does most of our actual moral reasoning, including those of our explanations that appeal to moral properties (as in 'Mother Theresa's goodness won her a Nobel Prize', 'Hitler's depravity won him universal condemnation', and so on).[13] Hence, as Mackie sees, subjectivists like himself are compelled to advance an error thesis: our ordinary usage and reasoning, entrenched for millennia, are massively in error, for there really are no objective values. And Mackie is far more candid than most subjectivists in acknowledging that the burden of proof is on those who advance any such thesis. The argument from queerness is meant to discharge this burden.[14]

It follows that if we can undermine the argument from queerness by showing the falsity of one of its assumptions, then not only is the presumption that there are objective values undefeated and in full force, but we are free to treat ordinary usage and normal moral reasoning and explanation as powerful independent evidence against subjectivism, and in particular against its thesis that a couple of genuinely conflicting moral judgments can be equally correct, there being no real truth of the matter in the first place. If we can undermine the argument from queerness by showing how an objective ethics is possible, we need not worry so deeply about irresolvable moral disagreements and the occasional seeming irrelevance or impotence of moral explanations of various admitted facts. Without the argument from queerness, or something very like it, subjectivism has little to be said for it.[15]

[10]Cf. Peterson.

[11]Nozick, 17.

[12]Sturgeon (1985), 57, 73. McDowell, 117–122, independently argues to much the same effect. See also Sayre-McCord, §§5–6. The contrary view, that objective values are explanatorily impotent, is argued, ultimately unsuccessfully as I see it, in Harman (1977), (1985), (1986); Blackburn (1985a); Zimmerman.

[13]Cf. Sayre-McCord, §6.

[14]Cf. Brink (1984), 112.

[15]Cf. Brink (1984). See also Lichtenberg.

How the argument for determinacy undermines the argument from queerness is explored further in §6.3. This occurs partly in the course of contrasting the determinacy of valuation with Quine's thesis of the indeterminacy of translation. The determinacy of valuation enables us to define 'correspondence with the facts' for value judgments, first principles included, and to explicate the notion of the class of facts with which such a judgment would correspond. Not for us is Quine's lament: "Science, thanks to its links with observation, retains some title to a correspondence theory of truth. . . . It is a bitter irony that so vital a matter as the difference between good and evil should have no comparable claim to objectivity."[16] So too may we reject the view that problems about what sort of reality, if any, a given moral judgment corresponds with are a reason for abandoning a correspondence theory of truth.[17] What a true moral judgment corresponds with, what makes it true, is a definite class of objective, natural facts, not some shadowy Platonic realm "out there," perhaps beyond space and time. Moral realism, meaning simply a realist theory of truth applied to moral judgments, does not require us to posit any sort of entity or reality beyond what we already recognize.[18]

6.1. The Determinacy of Valuation

> *What is the connection between the natural fact that an action is a piece of deliberate cruelty . . . and the moral fact that it is wrong? . . . . The wrongness must be somehow 'consequential' or 'supervenient': it is wrong because it is a deliberate piece of cruelty. But just what* in the world *is signified by this 'because'?*
>
> —J. L. MACKIE

> *The evident failure of theorists to provide acceptable definitions of moral terms in natural terms has provided non-naturalism and non-cognitivism their strongest argument. That truth in ethics is determined by nonmoral facts is a plausible alternative worth pursuing.*
>
> —G. P. HELLMAN AND F. W. THOMPSON

A number of philosophers have suspected that there is some sort of nonreductive relation of resultance from facts to values. Hence merely asserting that there is one is hardly news. What is needed is an argu-

---

[16]Quine (1978c), 43.

[17]Rorty (1982), xvi, holds this view. Cf. McDowell, 121–122.

[18]Contrary to Blackburn (1985a), 11, where moral realism is likened to realism about mathematical entities.

ment. Here is H–N. Castañeda's: "The unity of the world demands the unity of an effective reason, and this demands the unity of the contents of thinking, all thinking, in one master Representational Image. There *must,* therefore, be bridging implications connecting propositions and practical noemata." The idea that the facts have no value implications is "wholly out of order, by running against the 'grain' of reason."[19]

Unfortunately, the argument is question-begging. It assumes that the world has a certain sort of unity, when the question at issue is whether it does.[20] That is, we were wondering whether the world is a unity that contains an element of value, whether values are "part of the fabric of the world."[21] To be told simply that the world's unity demands this, by way of demanding an effective reason, hardly advances the discussion. Nor does it help to be told that the contrary idea runs against the grain of reason, since again what Hume and others were wondering about in the first place was in large part whether reason might be mistaken here (the massive-error thesis in another form). Another trouble with the argument is in its assumption that reason and the world's unity demand bridging implications from facts to values. Why implication? Why not a relation of resultance or determination that requires neither implication nor reduction, above all in light of the severe difficulties in establishing the required kinds of implication from facts to values?

We do better to look elsewhere for an argument, and to begin by recalling what we ordinarily mean by determination. When we say one thing determines another, we mean that given the way the first is, there is one and only one way the second can be (§§1.1.1, 4.3). In particular, to say that the world determines which distribution of truth-values over our value judgments is the correct one is to say that given the way the world is, there can be one and only one correct distribution. That is, given the natural or descriptive properties (relations included) of the world's entities, there can be one and only one correct distribution. This in turn is to say that given the natural properties, and given any other world whose entities have the same natural properties, the same distribution is correct in both worlds. Equivalently, given worlds W_1 and W_2 in which the entities have the same natural properties (that is, for every such property P, x has P in W_1 iff either x or x's counterpart x' has P in W_2), then the same value judgments are true in W_1 and W_2. For simplicity, let us continue to think of possible worlds as physically

[19]Castañeda (1975), 333. Cf. Castañeda (1973).
[20]A similar difficulty may afflict the appeal to "organic unity" in Nozick, ch. 5.
[21]Hare (1957), 47, who uses the phrase only to deny that it expresses a genuine issue. Cf. Hare (1985), 42; Mackie, 21.

possible worlds. Then the relevant notion of determination, in the case of moral judgments, can be captured by

> DD. The world determines moral truth in P-worlds iff given any P-worlds W_1 and W_2 in which the entities have the same natural properties, then the same moral judgments are true in W_1 and W_2.

Parallel but modally distinct notions of determination result from DD depending on which class of possible worlds replaces the P-worlds.

In ethics, talk of determining or grounding morals typically refers to ways of formulating and defending various principles and actions. This preoccupation with problems of discovery and justification is understandable, in light of our frequent doubts and disputes about what to do when, on the basis of what principles. But because of this preoccupation, 'determine' typically has an epistemic meaning in ethics, whereas its meaning according to DD is purely semantic or ontological. In particular, determination in the sense of DD does not by itself enable anyone to identify *what* the moral truths *are* from a knowledge only of the natural facts. Given a pair of worlds in which the same natural facts obtain, and even given a list of those facts, still we could not tell which moral judgments are true in the pair, if all we knew was that moral truth is determined by natural fact. In addition, and for closely related reasons, determination by itself does not enable anyone to reduce, or define, or derive, or justify any of the moral truths from descriptive truths. The autonomy of morals therefore is secure, even if moral truth is determined by purely descriptive truth.

Contrary to what one might expect, talk of such determination does not itself presuppose that our moral judgments have a truth-value. Rather, the idea is that given the world, then whether or not they are strictly true or false, nevertheless if we pretend they are and distribute those values over them, there is one and only one correct such distribution. Thus despite understandable impressions to the contrary, saying in this sense that the world determines moral truth, or that the natural phenomena determine the moral phenomena, does not presuppose cognitivism as regards the moral judgments, though in the end the determination provides powerful support for cognitivism.

DD does presuppose the notion of a moral judgment's being true-in-W. This was defined in §1.1.1, à la Tarski. But a Tarski-style account is of little (further) use in explaining what it means for a moral judgment to be true. Granted, the definition of truth-in-W becomes a definition of truth when W is the actual world. But the result, in the case of the atomic sentences, is the uninformative schema 'ϕ is true (in the actual world) iff the elements assigned to ϕ's individual terms exist and are related by what is assigned to ϕ's predicate'. Correspondingly uninformative clauses mount as we pursue the recursion upward to ever more complex sentences. The result is on par with saying that 'Torturing cats is morally wrong' is true iff torturing cats is morally wrong. It remains unclear what is the nature of the reference or satisfaction relation, *if any*, between the moral terms and the world, and in particular whether the relation can support a robust correspondence notion of truth for moral judgments. Likewise, it remains unclear how to go about giving truth-conditions for moral judgments, and above all what the purely natural conditions are that supposedly determine a moral judgment's truth-value.[22] It is of no help at all to be told that the necessary and sufficient conditions under which 'Torturing cats is wrong' is true are those in which torturing cats is wrong.

If Tarski's theory is of no help here, what is? Begin with a further clarification of DD. It is a commonplace, accepted by all parties, that moral properties (or at least our ascriptions of them) supervene on natural properties in the sense that nothing can differ in its moral properties without differing also in its natural properties. And it may seem that the righthand limb of DD asserts no more than this, since it is equivalent to saying that if W_1 and W_2 differ as regards what moral judgments are true in them, then they differ also in the natural properties their entities possess. Now this does reveal a connection between determination and supervenience: namely, that determination is one among the many relations variously called supervenience. But 'supervenience' here has a weak and a strong sense. In the weak sense, supervenience of the moral on the natural means there can be no moral difference without some relevant natural difference, *as relevance is judged from the point of view of one's own moral principles.* This is the sense in which Hare, no moral realist, asserts supervenience.[23] In the strong sense, alien to Hare, there can be no moral difference without some relevant natural difference, where a natural difference is morally relevant or not, independent of the moral principles one happens to hold.

There is a parallel distinction in the case of determination. In the weak sense, acceptable to Hare, the natural properties *in conjunction with the principles one happens to hold* determine one and only one distribution of truth-values over the totality of our moral judgments. In the strong sense, the natural properties alone determine the correct distribution

---

[22]As Wong, 17–22, points out.
[23]Hare (1952), 145.

over our moral judgments, first principles included. And of course it is
the strong sense that realists have in mind when they claim determination of moral truth by the world. So yes, supervenience is accepted by
all parties, but only in the weak sense, from which one cannot infer
determination in the intended, strong sense.

This weak supervenience of the moral on the natural is the first
premise in the argument for the determination of moral truth by the
world. Hence we need a more precise characterization. The basic idea is
that there can be no moral difference without some relevant natural
difference; a couple of worlds relevantly alike as regards natural properties must be alike as regards the moral status (permissible, impermissible, obligatory, right, wrong, good, bad) of persons and actions. Furthermore, since we are to treat like cases alike, such "equity" requires
that the rules or principles to be followed in treating one case are to be
followed in treating any relevantly similar other. Thus a couple of
worlds relevantly alike as regards natural properties must also be alike as
regards the rules or principles to be followed in them. Supervenience,
then, or the Equity Principle, as I shall call it, may be characterized by

> EP. For any W_1 and W_2 relevantly similar as regards natural prop-
> erties, an act A has a certain moral status for person P in W_1 iff
> A has that same status for any relevantly similar P^* in W_2; and
> a substantive moral rule, principle or first principle R is true (or
> at least correct or to be followed) in W_1 iff R is true (or correct
> or to be followed) in W_2.

Though we need not assume so in what follows, EP is equivalent to
certain weak versions of universalizability, such as the principle that "if
it is wrong for someone else to do something, it would be wrong for me
to do that in a similar situation; in other words, if it is okay for me to do
something, it can't be wrong for anyone else in my situation."[24] Likewise, EP may be equivalent to certain versions of the Golden Rule, the
rule of law, formal justice, and the generalization principle, provided the
versions are sufficiently formal or nonsubstantive. Note also that equity
principles, notoriously, provide no criteria for what are to count as the
relevant descriptive similarities. Such criteria are supposed to be supplied by the substantive principles of one's moral theory (which principles may actually entail EP, so that EP is not strictly additional).[25]
Hence the term 'relevantly similar' acts as a kind of place-holder, or
blank, to be filled differently in different contexts according to guidelines expressed by substantive principles.

[24]Harman (1978), 159. Cf. Hare (1963); Lycan (1969).
[25]Cf. Carr.

Often supervenience and universalizability principles are stated in terms of circumstances rather than worlds. The idea is that an act performed by P in a given circumstance has a certain moral status iff it has that same status when performed by any relevantly similar $P*$ in any relevantly similar circumstance. Circumstances, however, can be construed as possible worlds. For even if a circumstance is technically only a piece of a world, rather than itself a maximally complete possibility, the remainder of the world is presupposed background. What we imagine, when we imagine a circumstance, is in effect the circumstance or piece surrounded by the rest of the actual world unchanged (except for whatever further change is entailed by the change of that piece). But this is just to imagine a possible world differing from ours in that piece (plus in whatever is entailed by the change).

Since we are treating different circumstances as (slightly) different possible worlds, one cannot object to EP that an act A could have a certain status for P and a different status for $P*$ because $P*$'s circumstances differ from P's. As soon as the circumstances relevantly differ, the worlds relevantly differ; morally relevant circumstances cannot vary within a given world when different circumstances are themselves being construed as different worlds.

So much, then, for our first premise. As for the second, imagine that someone judges a certain act morally permissible, while someone else judges it impermissible. The two judgments are genuinely conflicting. No one should assent to them both, nor presumably would the persons who make them. Even though they disagree about *which* judgment we should assent to, they agree that two genuinely conflicting moral judgments should not both be assented to by the same person, and in that sense cannot both be correct. Our second premise is not this but the significantly stronger principle that given a moral judgment and its denial, one or the other should be given assent by both parties (whether they know it or not) and in that sense is correct. This is a kind of bivalence for moral judgments, though it stops short of attributing truth or falsity to them—an attribution that realists normally will go on to make. More generally, given any exhaustive set of two or more mutually conflicting alternative moral judgments, just one member of the set is correct. That is, just one should be given assent; or, if we are in a mood to pretend they have truth-values, just one should be assigned truth. In turn this implies Meta-Ethical Antirelativism:

MEA. If we pretend our moral judgments are true or false, and distribute those values over the totality of the moral judgments, then among all the possible mutually conflicting such distributions, only one is correct.

MEA is to be taken in a strong sense, not weak.[26] In the weak sense we could "universalize" our principles in line with EP, distributing truth-values over the moral judgments accordingly, thus arriving at the one and only one "correct" distribution induced by our principles in conjunction with the facts; and all the while others could do the same with *their* principles, arriving at their very different one and only one "correct" distribution. In the strong sense of MEA, there is only one distribution allowed, and one of these distributions—ours included—may or may not be it; among all the possible mutually conflicting principles persons might use in making their own distributions, only one is correct (or to be given assent).[27]

Doesn't invoking MEA at this stage beg the question against the antirealist? We see in the next section why it does not. Doesn't invoking MEA amount to assuming what is to be shown—namely, that the facts determine which of our moral judgments are to be given assent? No. Even if just one member of an exhaustive set of genuinely conflicting moral judgments should be given assent, and likewise just one distribution of truth-values over our moral judgments, it does not follow that *which* distribution is to be given assent is determined by the facts or by anything else. Thus the determinacy amounts to much more than MEA, just as it amounts to much more than EP. But the determinacy does follow from the conjunction of EP and MEA, as we see in a moment.

Note first that many philosophers who are not moral realists could accept MEA. This is because the concept of truth involved need not at this stage be a realist concept. Instead of amounting to some sort of correspondence, it could be a matter of coherence or reflective equilibrium among our considered judgments, or a matter of warranted assertibility by ideal inquirers in light of all their long-run evidence, or whatever. What moral realists eventually must add to MEA, in order to express their characteristic position, is that the concept of truth here should be a realist one, according to which truth is independent of coherence and other evidence, even the evidence of ideal inquirers over the long run, and of course independent also of our beliefs about what is morally right. That is, among all the possible distributions of truth and falsity over the moral judgments, not only is just one of them correct; what determines which one is correct is not belief about what is morally

---

[26]Here I am indebted to correspondence with Norman Dahl.

[27]The "quasi-realist" in Blackburn (1985a), 5–6, 11, seems committed to MEA (in the strong sense), not as a "second-order metaphysic of morals" but as "a first-order attitude."

right, not even coherence or the long-run evidence of ideal inquirers, but in some sense the world.

What then is the argument for this determinacy? Consider a P-world W_1 together with its entities' natural properties. Suppose that in W_1 the moral judgments are to be assented to or not, hence that in W_1 they are correct or not, to be followed or not, or whatever. Thus we may pretend they are true or false in W_1. In line with MEA, this is to suppose that in any set of mutually conflicting moral judgments, one at most is true in W_1, first principles included; truth-in-world-W is nonrelative in the sense that given an exhaustive set of conflicting alternatives, exactly one member is true in W, and one's favorite candidate may or may not be it. Likewise, exactly one distribution of truth-values over the moral judgments is correct in W.

Now suppose, contrary to what is to be shown, that there is another P-world W_2 in which the entities have the same natural properties as in W_1, yet there is a moral judgment true in one of W_1 or W_2 but not the other. This is to suppose that a change in distribution of truth-values over the moral judgments, such as the change between W_1 and W_2, does not require a change in the natural properties. But because W_1 and W_2 are the same as regards natural properties, the persons, acts, and circumstances in either world are indiscernible from those in the other in all natural respects. It follows that the persons, acts, and circumstances in the two are similar (because indiscernible) in all natural respects, hence in all *relevant* natural respects. Thus they are relevantly similar, as are the worlds W_1 and W_2 that contain them. And this is true even if we haven't the faintest idea which natural respects are morally relevant.

But if W_1 and W_2 are relevantly similar, then according to EP, (i) an act has a certain moral status (of being obligatory, permitted, wrong, etc.) in W_1 iff it has that same status in W_2 (because both the persons who perform the act and the circumstances in which it is performed are relevantly similar, however relevance is defined). Hence (ii) the persons in W_1 have the same obligations as those in W_2 to act and to be treated in various ways. And also according to EP, (iii) a moral principle or rule is true in W_1 iff it is true in W_2, first principles included. Furthermore, every moral judgment asserts either (i) the moral status of some particular act or compound of acts, either act-tokens or act-types; (ii) an obligation (or compound of obligations) of or to some particular person or persons; or (iii) some general principle or rule, first principles included. It follows that there is no moral judgment true in one of W_1 or W_2 but not in the other after all, first principles included; a change in truth-value of a moral judgment does require a change in the natural properties. That is, given any P-worlds in which the entities have the same natural properties, the same moral judgments are true in them as well. By DD this is just to say that the world determines moral truth in *P*-worlds.

We cannot yet draw the stronger, cognitivist conclusion that the moral judgments are true or false. From the fact that there is no moral judgment true in one of W_1 or W_2 but not the other, it does not follow that there is some moral judgment true in one of them or in any other world. Nevertheless, what we may conclude is nearly as strong. Given the purely natural properties of people and things, whether or not the moral judgments are true or false, if we pretend they are and distribute those values over them, then there is one and only one such distribution allowed (in the strong sense, explained above).

Nor may we conclude that this one correct distribution would be "intrinsically motivating" in the sense that anyone aware of it must necessarily be motivated to act morally, in accordance with it.[28] Such a conclusion is in any case no part of the moral realism I advocate, which again is simply a realist theory of truth applied to moral judgments. There can be objective values, in the sense of a truth of the matter as regards the correctness of moral judgments, without such values being intrinsically motivating. Of course, there cannot be such values for one who holds that (a) if there is one true morality, then everyone has sufficient reason to conform to it, and (b) if one has sufficient reason to conform to a morality, then necessarily one will be motivated to act in accordance with it.[29] But both (a) and (b) are highly problematic. And even if (b) were to prove true, so that where morals are concerned there can be no gap between justification and motivation, still there could be a gap between truth and justification, contrary to (a). That there often is a gap between truth and justification is of course one of the realist's characteristic claims, so that to assume (a) without argument would be question-begging.

If Mackie (or anyone else) denies that there can be objective values that are not intrinsically motivating, then "this . . . raises very sharply the question of what the objectivity is that Mackie is denying."[30] If his argument from queerness is meant to show only that there are no objective values construed as intrinsically motivating or action-guiding, then moral realists need not be so concerned to undermine the argument (though its major premise will still fail to have listed all the relevant alternative relations that might obtain between facts and values). On the other hand, if the argument from queerness is meant to show that there

[28]Cf. Harman (1985), 30.
[29]As does Harman (1985), 34–35.
[30]B. Williams, 205. See also Brink (1986); Mackenzie.

are no objective values whether or not they are intrinsically motivating (as Mackie often seems to intend), then realists do need to undermine the argument. But in this case no one can object to the present strategy for doing so that it overlooks the fact that Mackie usually construes objective values as intrinsically motivating.

It is a commonplace that if two people agree on moral first principles, then moral disputes between them can be resolved by appeal to the purely descriptive facts of the case. But the determinacy of moral valuation goes well beyond this, in two respects. First, the purely descriptive facts about the actual world determine which is the correct distribution of truth and falsity over moral judgments about particular cases, by (i) and (ii), regardless of anyone's agreement either on these cases or on principles by which such agreement might be reached. Second, the facts determine which is the correct distribution not only over judgments about particular cases, but also over general principles and rules, by (iii). Thus even if we cannot agree on which moral first principles are true in the one correct distribution, which ones they are is still determined by purely descriptive truth just as much as is the truth of any particular judgments they subsume. Nor need we presuppose that the moral first principles are strictly true or false in order either to say this or to show it, as seen.

Even if we were entitled to the cognitivist conclusion that the moral judgments are true or false, we would not yet be entitled to conclude that they are true or false in the realist's sense. This is because the concept of truth involved in the presupposed MEA, as pointed out, need not be a realist concept but could amount instead to coherence or to warranted assertibility or whatever. Granted, MEA and EP jointly entail that the world alone determines moral truth, but this implies mainly that moral truth is not determined only by the-world-in-conjunction-with-the-moral-principles-one-happens-to-hold, as perusal of the argument shows. Left open is the question of whether what determines moral truth is, say, the part or piece of the world that consists of the (long-run) evidence that warrants assertion of the moral judgments in question. Thus verificationists, pragmatists, and coherentists can agree with the moral realist that the world determines moral truth, but disagree as to what it is in the world that at bottom does the determining.[31] Just as cognitivism does not follow from the determination jointly entailed by EP and MEA, realism does not follow from the cognitivism.

[31]Cf. Brink (1984), 117n: "A coherentist theory of moral truth would be incompatible with moral realism." Cf. Sturgeon (1986a).

To assert a realist version of cognitivism, therefore, the realist must assert not only that moral judgments are true or false but that the truth and falsity involved are realist truth and falsity, so that (among other things) the truth of a moral judgment is independent of warranted assertibility, of coherence, and so on. This is just an instance of the realist's characteristic "declaration of independence," unpacked in §1.1.1. But this is not enough. We want also to know what positive account realists can give of what in the world *does* determine the truth of a given moral judgment, if not evidence, coherence, or antecedent moral belief. That is, what in the world does a true moral judgment correspond with, and what precisely is this relation of correspondence? We return to this challenge in §6.3.

Meanwhile, what about values generally, in addition to moral values? They too prove determinate, subject to the proviso that they obey a suitable analogue of EP and MEA:

> EA. For any relevantly similar W_1 and W_2 and any value term V: V (or its negation) applies to x in W_1 iff V (or its negation) applies to any relevantly similar y in W_2; and a general principle R about the V-values is true (or at least correct) in W_1 iff R is true (or at least correct) in W_2; further, for each W, only one member of an exhaustive set of conflicting V-judgments is correct in W.

Here x and y can be anything—paintings, sunsets, persons, purposes, moods, emotions, whatever. How many of our value terms obey EA? I suspect they all do, at least on those occasions when it is appropriate to give reasons for or against the claim that V applies in a given instance, or that a principle or rule involving V applies. If I claim that a certain painting is great art while another is not, I must be prepared to point eventually to some relevant descriptive difference between the two (something to do with color, texture, design, subject, technique, etc.). This includes the case in which the second painting is a perfect forgery—even an exact replica down to the last microparticle. In that case the descriptive difference in virtue of which one is great art and the other only great technology would presumably have something to do with who made the painting—Rembrandt, say—and how he did it.

But even though all our value terms may well obey EA, we need not assume they do. For what is being claimed is not that all nonmoral values are determined by the world but only that they are determined to the extent that they obey EA. The argument for this determinacy of valuation is of exactly the same form as the one lately given to show the determinacy of moral valuation. Merely replace every reference to moral judgments with a reference to *V*-judgments. Thus all values are determined by the world, whatever the values and whatever the best way of analyzing and justifying them, provided only that they obey EA. It is not far to argue that normative epistemological matters of justification and knowledge are determined by the world and that truth-values are determined by the world even if reference is not, as seen in §1.1. As also seen, this does not entail treating 'true' as a full-fledged value term; we need only treat 'true' as satisfying an analogue of EP and MEA.

6.2. Objections and Replies

> *The chief and most lasting illusion of the mind is the illusion*
> *of its own importance. What madness to assert that one*
> *collection of atoms . . . is right or is better, and another is*
> *wrong or worse!*
> —DEMOCRITUS, IN GEORGE SANTAYANA'S
> *Dialogues in Limbo*

We turn now to the caveats. It is a consequence of DD that judgments true in every world, or even only in every *P*-world, have their truth-value determined, trivially, by natural fact. For if they are true in every *P*-world, then automatically, for any *P*-worlds W_1 and W_2, the same such judgments are true in W_1 and W_2, and the consequent of the operative conditional in DD is satisfied. Necessary falsehoods likewise have their truth-value thus trivially determined, as would judgments (if any) that are necessarily neither-true-nor-false. Thus if moral first principles were true in every *P*-world, their truth would automatically be determined by natural fact. The argument lately given for their determinacy would be unneeded and uninformative.

However, few philosophers today, and none of those at whom this chapter is aimed, believe that moral principles are true in every *P*-world, nor do I. Mackie, for example, clearly holds that the principles apply (even if they are not true or false) only in those worlds in which not only are there persons, but persons in conditions of relative scarcity who are either selfish or capable only of limited sympathy, and who agree that it is important to eliminate or at least to reduce certain evils.[32] Such worlds obviously form a proper subset of the *P*-worlds. According to Rawls, "First principles are not . . . true in all possible worlds. In particular, they depend on the rather specific features and limitations of human life that give rise to the circumstances of justice."[33] Again it is

[32]Mackie, 165.
[33]Rawls, 565. Cf. Nozick, 545.

obvious that we are talking about a restricted subset of the *P*-worlds. And in different ways, Hume, Hobbes, the Sophists, Stevenson, Hare, Quine, Smart, Harman, and many others all deny, in effect, that moral principles are true in every *P*-world, let alone in every world. For they hold that such force as the principles have, whether or not it is the force of strict truth, depends on specifics of human wants and needs in the specific conditions of our world.

Even intuitionists are not committed to regarding moral principles as true in every *P*-world, provided intuitionism is defined as (i) the rejection of descriptive definability or reducibility of moral terms, which express nonnatural properties, conjoined with (ii) an insistence on a priori intuition and self-evidence as the only ways of knowing the principles about these nonnatural properties. For from the assumption that such a principle is known a priori and its terms are irreducible, it does not follow that it is true in all worlds, or even in all *P*-worlds. (Think of a world in which we were given innate a priori knowledge of the engineering principles of the strength of materials that exist in no other world.) In this regard the tendency of some intuitionists to compare moral principles to mathematical axioms can mislead, though of course some intuitionists may in fact hold, in addition to (i) and (ii), that the principles are true in all worlds.

It might be objected that moral principles, as normally stated, are only elliptical expressions of underlying principles that are indeed necessary.[34] Just as 'Thou shalt not kill' is elliptical for something like 'In circumstances other than self-defense, capital punishment, or a just war, thou shalt not kill', so also is the latter itself elliptical for 'Given the specific human wants and needs in the specific conditions of our world, then in circumstances other than self-defense, capital punishment, or a just war, thou shalt not kill'. In general, each principle or rule *R* is similarly only elliptical for a conditional of the form 'Given the overarching conditions *C* that obtain in our world, then *R*'. And clearly, such a conditional will be true in every world, unlike *R,* which normally is true only in worlds in which the conditions *C* obtain.

The trouble with this move is that it is too general. Once we allow it here, there is no way of blocking it in domains where it clearly goes wrong. Thus consider the statement O that the period of the earth's orbit is 365.25 days. O's truth is entailed by particular fact or initial conditions C in conjunction with physical laws. Thus O is not true in every *P*-world but only in those *P*-worlds in which C; O is not *P*-

[34]As has Sosa, in correspondence.

necessary, hence in that sense not lawlike. But now why couldn't some-one argue, as above, that O is elliptical for an underlying statement that *is* P-necessary? After all, the conditional 'Given C, then O' is true in every P-world. In this way one can always boost a contingency into a necessity, whence it follows (still arguing as above) that empirical truths at bottom really are true in every P-world. Indeed why stop with P-necessity? Why not ascend all the way and insist that underlying every moral or empirical or other kind of statement ϕ, there is a truly funda-mental statement of that kind that is true in every *logically* possible world? This fundamental statement is a conditional whose consequent is ϕ and whose antecedent expresses conditions which are such that ϕ is true in any logically possible world in which they obtain.

Clearly, something has gone wrong. No such argument would per-suade us that all empirical truths really are (or are elliptical for) empirical truths that are true in every world. But if the argument goes wrong here, it goes wrong when applied to principles of morality, unless of course someone can point to a relevant difference between the two cases. Even though there are important differences, I can think of none relevant here. The mere fact that one can always boost a contingency into a necessity, by inserting appropriate conditions into some condi-tional's antecedent, does not show that the underlying principles of morality are necessary.

For all these reasons it seems wise to assume, if only for the sake of argument, that moral principles are true (or at least are correct, or to be followed, or apply) in some P-worlds but not all. We thereby deprive ourselves of the dubious opportunity of arguing, in light of DD, that their truth-value is trivially determined by natural fact in P-worlds. On the contrary, the determinacy of such nonnecessary principles has long seemed anything but trivial. Thus the argument in §6.1 is neither un-needed nor uninformative, since it works even for nonnecessary first principles—assuming, of course, that we are entitled to its premises.

The first premise—EP—may seem inconsistent with certain theories of morality. Consider views according to which right and wrong de-pend on the arbitrary command of a willful divinity. Couldn't such a being command one person to do X in given circumstances and also command another, similar person to do the opposite in precisely the same circumstances? Indeed so. But even though what might be called the "natural" circumstances would be the same—the two persons' powers, inner states, relations to surrounding people and things—there would nevertheless be a crucial, purely descriptive respect in which the total morally relevant circumstances differ. For according to arbitrary-command views, the fact that the command is given is morally relevant (indeed it is the only relevant fact, in extreme versions of such views). And whether the command is given, plus what the command is, is a purely descriptive matter. So there would be a descriptive (though supernatural) respect in which the two cases differ: one includes the command to do X, the other the command to do the opposite.

Much the same may be said of views according to which right and wrong depend on the arbitrary, criterionless choices of an individual human being. On such existentialist views, the fact that a certain choice is made turns out to be the morally relevant descriptive difference. EP, as used in §6.1, remains satisfied. Not surprisingly, then, EP remains satisfied even for normative relativism.[35] Normative relativists allow, as their opponents do not, that the morally relevant differences between two persons can include their merely having adopted different moral first principles in the first place. But whether a certain principle has been adopted, plus what it is, is a purely descriptive difference between the two, in line with EP. Harman does reject a principle that closely resembles EP, but this is a nonformal, substantive principle of universalizability (William Frankena's), according to which (among other things) two persons' merely adopting different first principles is not a morally relevant difference between them.[36]

Is EP true, hence true or false? We need not assume so in the argument for the determinacy of valuation, only that EP is acceptable or warranted (or to be assented to). Thus we avoid begging the question against noncognitivists. Of course, EP might not be a moral principle in the first place, but completely formal or logical. If so, even noncognitivists might see fit to grant it a truth-value. But if EP is a moral principle, then its own truth-value (were it to have one) is also determined by purely natural fact if the conclusion of the argument in §6.1 is correct: namely, that all moral truth is thus determined.

There is no circularity here. We are not assuming the truth of EP in order to deduce EP, or even to deduce that EP is true or false. Instead we are assuming EP's *acceptability*—which, if a sufficiently pragmatic affair, does not require EP to have a truth-value—as a premise in an argument for the acceptability of the conclusion that whether or not the moral judgments (possibly including EP) are true or false, if we pretend they are and distribute those values over them, then there is one and only one such distribution allowed by the facts. If EP happens to be a moral principle, then this conclusion implies that EP's truth-value (if

[35]Such as that espoused by Harman (1978).
[36]Harman (1978), 159.

any) itself is determined. This is very different from concluding that EP is true, or that it is true or false.

Likewise, we need not assume that the second premise—MEA—is strictly true or false. Nor would there be any circularity should MEA happen itself to be a moral principle or at least a normative one (as probably it is), so that its own truth-value would be determined by natural fact. But aside from all this, are we entitled to use MEA in the first place? Doesn't using MEA beg the question against the subjectivist? No. If at this stage of the discussion we were advancing the argument for the determinacy of moral valuation as a non-question-begging proof of objectivism, or as a non-question-begging refutation of subjectivism, then the argument would indeed beg the question; in accepting MEA we would be accepting what the subjectivist denies. But at this stage we are only trying to show that there are intelligible, unqueer premises that jointly entail the determinacy, and therefore that the alternatives listed in the subjectivist's argument from queerness are by no means exhaustive. That is, we are only trying to undermine the argument from queerness by showing that its major premise is false.

The argument for the determinacy does indeed undermine the argument from queerness. It does so first by explicating a simple, familiar relation—determination—which is a clear alternative to those listed, and then by showing that such determinacy follows from a couple of intelligible, unqueer premises: EP and MEA. Since the determinacy does follow, subjectivists must reject at least one of these. Since they themselves accept the unobjectionable EP, they must and do reject MEA.[37] It is *not* the case, they believe, that among all the possible mutually conflicting distributions of truth-values over the moral judgments, just one is correct, meaning that it should be assented to by all parties (whether they know it or not). But subjectivists thereby merely deny what MEA affirms. And the denial or negation of an assertion is itself unintelligible if the assertion is. Thus it might seem that subjectivists cannot be rejecting this premise on the ground that it is unintelligible. Instead, they must be rejecting it as false or incorrect. If so, they must concede that the premises as well as the conclusion of the argument for determinacy are intelligible, even if not both true, and that the relations listed in the argument from queerness do not by any means exhaust the intelligible alternatives as regards what the consequential link might be between facts and values. It would therefore seem that the argument from queerness fails, being based on a false assumption.

[37]On whether rejecting MEA is even coherent, cf. Lyons.

Unfortunately, subjectivists often do not reject MEA for being unintelligible in the sense in which the denial of an unintelligible assertion is itself unintelligible. Rather, they reject it for being unintelligible in the sense of being explanatorily impotent. Their belief that objective values can play no appropriate explanatory role in our accounts of natural events includes the belief that MEA can play no such role either. That is, positing as does MEA that just one member of an exhaustive set of conflicting moral judgments is correct cannot explain or can add nothing to our purely naturalistic explanations of various natural events, including our making the moral judgments we do. All the explanatory work seems to be done by other, nonnormative disciplines such as psychology and anthropology. In this regard, positing uniquely correct judgments independent of the moral principles we happen to hold is like positing witches and is explanatorily unintelligible.[38]

Nevertheless, it seems increasingly clear that positing such correctness does play an important and ineliminable explanatory role and is therefore explanatorily intelligible.[39] There do seem to be real regularities in the world that are identifiable only by appeal to moral properties construed as realized or not, independently of our principles. Such regularities include honesty's engendering trust, justice's commanding allegiance, depravity's arousing condemnation, and so on. In this way the moral virtues and vices figure in many of our best explanations. ("Why does everyone trust him?" "Because he's honest.") Since the moral properties involved evidently are irreducible, the explanations in which they appear evidently are ineliminable. The moral domain therefore enjoys the explanatory autonomy noted earlier for so many others.

This reinforces our verdict that the argument from queerness fails to exhaust the intelligible alternatives as regards what the link or links might be between facts and values. And since the argument fails, it cannot be used to support subjectivism. Nor can it be used to support the rejection of MEA, as so often in effect it has been, and as ultimately it must be.[40] And even if *per absurdum* the argument from queerness succeeded, still it could not be used against MEA. For the argument from queerness would succeed only if the argument for determinacy failed, and the latter would fail only if MEA were false (assuming all parties accept EP). So basing the rejection of MEA on the argument

---

[38]Cf. Sayre-McCord, who articulates the view in order to reject it.

[39]Here I rely heavily on Sturgeon (1985), (1986b); Sayre-McCord; McDowell; Boyd (forthcoming), §§3.1–3.3, 4.2–4.5.

[40]Cf. §6.0, and Brink (1984).

from queerness would beg the question of whether MEA is true. And independent of the arguments from queerness and for determinacy, the weight of the evidence, including various facts about actual moral reasoning and other usage of moral language—including the explanatory— weighs heavily in favor of MEA.[41]

Recall the consequences of undermining the argument from queerness (§6.0). Once the argument is undermined, then not only is the presumption of objectivity undefeated and in full force, but we are free to treat various facts about actual moral reasoning and other usage of moral language, including the explanatory, as powerful independent evidence against subjectivism and in particular against the subjectivist's rejection of MEA. For without some such argument as the one from queerness, the mere fact of moral disagreement does not imply that there are no objective values about which to disagree, and subjectivists have no way of discharging the burden of proving their error thesis (that our normal moral reasoning and usage, entrenched for millennia, are in reality massively in error).

In view of all this—including what I take to be the clear evidence of actual moral reasoning and other usage of moral discourse, again including the explanatory—I shall henceforth assume that MEA is true and therefore (granted EP) that the determinacy of valuation obtains. Thus not only is physicalism consistent with objectivity as regards values, but the objectivity follows from a couple of assumptions the physicalist could easily accept, and it is not after all "hard to see how objective values fit into a physicalist perspective."[42] Indeed it is hard to see how physicalists could reject these two assumptions, given their acceptance of the same assumptions when applied to truth (EPT and MEA, §1.1.1). If 'true' is a value term,[43] then unless there is some relevant difference between truth and other values, acceptance of EP and MEA for truth requires their acceptance for values generally. But since we have conceded that 'true' might not be a full-fledged value term, we cannot go so far as to claim here that the physicalist's minimal theses by themselves do imply or presuppose the objectivity of value. I suspect they do, in virtue of their commitment to a realist notion of truth, but that is another story, too long to tell here, even assuming there is finally a convincing one to tell.

[41]As even Mackie agrees. Again see Sturgeon (1985), (1986b); Sayre-McCord; McDowell; Boyd (forthcoming).
  [42]Contrary to Field (1982), 562.
  [43]Contrary to Field (1982), 563.

6.3. Correspondence with the Facts

> *If there were something in the fabric of the world that validated*
> *certain kinds of concern, then it would be possible to acquire*
> *these merely by finding something out, by letting one's thinking*
> *be controlled by how things were. But . . . there are no*
> *objective values.*

—J. L. MACKIE

"The central problem in moral philosophy is . . . the *is-ought* problem. How is what *is* the case related to what *ought* to be the case?"[44] Central problem or not, does the determinacy of valuation solve it? That depends on what sort of relation we entertained between is and ought. If the relation was an ontological one, of the sort denied in the argument from queerness by Mackie and the tradition he stands for, then the central problem is solved: what *is* the case is related to what *ought* to be the case by nonreductive determination. But if we had an at least partly epistemic relation in mind, whereby ought might be derived from or reduced to or otherwise (immediately) justified by is, then the problem is not solved one way or the other.

Even so, the determinacy of valuation is not without epistemic significance. For we shall see how it guarantees that an important sort of epistemic enterprise is not doomed from the start. The enterprise, roughly, is to discover purely descriptive facts, accessible to unmoved spectators of the actual, which would confirm their value judgments, first principles included. If Quine is right, this sort of enterprise *is* doomed in the case of translation. There is nothing that would confirm the judgment that a given translation is the correct one, since there is no fact of the matter as regards translational correctness. If Quine is right, meanings classically construed are queer entities, related to what there is not by entailment, reduction, causation, supervenience, or even determination. Thus his argument for the indeterminacy of translation is in effect part of an argument from queerness against classical meanings (§1.1.3). But even if an argument from queerness succeeds against meanings, we just saw how it fails against values.

Here we may pause to inquire what might be the difference between values and meanings, in virtue of which values are determinate and meanings allegedly are not. The crucial difference is that EP holds for values but perhaps not for meanings. The principle that there can be no

---

[44]Opening remark of Hudson's Introduction to Hudson, 11. Cf. Nozick, 399–401, 535; and Harman (1985), 29: "The basic issue in moral philosophy is precisely how value and obligation fit into the scientific conception of the world."

moral difference without some relevant descriptive difference is deeply entrenched, near the core of our conceptual scheme, if not exactly analytic. But much of Quine's argument for the indeterminacy of translation aims to show, in effect, that there can be a difference of meaning without any relevant descriptive difference. Thus 'Gavagai' can mean rabbit, rabbit stage, undetached rabbit part, and so on; yet by Quine's lights the circumstances of its utterance could be indistinguishable in all relevant descriptive respects (the relevant ones being the behavioral, for Quine).

Quine could well be wrong about this, as seen in §1.1.3. In any case, the determinacy of valuation shows that even if value judgments are not strictly true or false, there is a fact of the matter as regards the correctness of such a judgment, including a first principle, in the sense at least that one and only one distribution of truth and falsity over it would be correct. We can even define 'correspondence with the facts' for a value judgment J:[45] J corresponds with the facts iff J is true in the one distribution allowed by the purely descriptive facts about the actual world. And the fact with which J corresponds is simply the conjunction of those facts that just suffice to determine J's truth-value in the distribution as true (cf. §1.1.2). More precisely,

> CD. Where J is true in the one distribution allowed by the world but is not a necessary truth, what J corresponds with is the smallest piece of the world to determine J's truth-value.

A *piece* or *subworld* of a world W is simply a subset of W's entities, possibly spatiotemporally scattered, plus their natural properties and relations. W_J is a *smallest* piece (or a least, or just suffices) to determine J's truth-value iff W_J but no proper piece of W_J determines J's truth-value. W_J determines J's truth-value iff given any W relevantly similar to W_J, J is true (false, neuter) in W iff J is true (false, neuter) in W_J. When J is not true in the one distribution allowed by the world, we say J corresponds with nothing.

What of the requirement that J be nonnecessary? If J were necessary, then J would be true in every world W, hence true in every subworld W of any W_J. But then the only subworld that would just suffice to determine J's truth-value would be the empty subworld, and presumably we would have to say that J corresponds with nothing. Thus this notion of correspondence breaks down when applied to value judgments deemed necessary.[46] In view of the trivial determination, remarked in §6.2, of

---

[45]Contrary to many, e.g., Blackburn (1971), 110; and Rorty (1982), xvi, xxxvii.
[46]Here I am indebted to Sosa, in correspondence.

necessary truths by any set of facts whatever, this breakdown is to be expected. There may be ways of revising CD to deflect the difficulty, including the device of stipulating that if J is necessary, then J corresponds with any facts whatever. But we need not inquire, since we have been assuming, with good reason, that even first principles are not true in every P-world (§6.2).

Note also that CD presupposes that there is *the* smallest piece of the world to determine J's truth-value. That there is follows from the argument in §1.1.3 for NMO, the principle that no more than one set of things just suffices to determine a judgment's truth-value. In order for the argument to apply here, we need assume only that moral judgments are about something or other, and that like all judgments their truth-value is determined at bottom only by all of what they are about. The latter principle is AT, a consequence of Tarski's theory and others, defended in §1.1.3.

Philosophers have often questioned what it could mean to say that a value judgment makes a truth-claim, and just what the claim could possibly be (other than one that expresses, say, the speaker's attitudes).[47] There is now a ready reply. The truth-claim J makes is the one that expresses the fact with which J would correspond were J true in the one distribution allowed over the value judgments. J's truth-claim is the class T_J^* of those descriptive truths that would, were J true, just suffice to determine J's truth-value as true. These truths express the descriptive matters in virtue of which J would be correct, even if (or even though) J is not derivable from or reducible to any description, *including* the description expressed by the conjunction of the members of T_J^*. It follows that unmoved spectators of the actual do have something to observe that would confirm J (whether they knew it or not):[48] namely, those phenomena that just suffice to make J correct, or (what comes to the same thing) the purely descriptive facts with which J corresponds. If two people agree on these facts, then (whether they know it or not) they ought to agree on J, even when J is itself a first principle rather than a particular judgment made in light of such a principle. To this not inconsiderable extent, then, moral theory is "observation laden."[49]

Philosophers have also wondered how values could be "part of the fabric of the world," so that a change in the former would require a change in the latter. Here too we have a ready reply. They are part of the fabric in the sense that the correctness of a value judgment is determined

[47]Cf. Nielsen for a review of such questioning.
[48]Contrary to Nielsen, 514.
[49]Sayre-McCord, §1.

by purely natural facts. As seen in §6.1, a world W whose fabric makes various natural facts obtain in W would be one whose fabric thereby makes certain value judgments correct in W; a change in their correctness would require a change in the natural facts.

Thus it seems ever more strained and artificial to withhold strict truth and falsity from value judgments. There is a fact of the matter as regards their correctness; they make truth-claims; they can correspond with certain facts; and they are confirmable by various descriptive phenomena even when we happen not to know which phenomena those are. A distinction between judgments for which all this holds (and more) and judgments which in addition are strictly true or false looks like a distinction without a difference.

How could two people come to agree on what the facts are with which a given value judgment corresponds? Neither the determinacy of valuation nor the argument for it solves or is meant to solve this epistemic problem (because determination is neither reductive nor an implication relation, and EP provides no criteria for what are to count as the relevant similarities). But the determinacy does guarantee there are such facts to be discovered; the epistemic enterprise thus construed is not doomed from the start; correspondence represents an important and intelligible regulative ideal. Because we see how an objective ethics is possible, we need not worry so deeply about irresolvable moral disagreements and the occasional seeming impotence of moral explanations. We are free to apply the logical prerequisites for truth in the spirit of prerequisites for truth-as-correspondence, not for some quasi-realist or internal-realist surrogate.[50] Thus construed, the sevenfold trial by prequisites eases the epistemic problem substantially, by narrowing the scope of a relativism of so many people, so many opinions.

Furthermore, we are free to treat various substantive moral theories—Kantian, utilitarian, contractarian, whatever—as if they were different attempts to discover which moral judgments (principles included) are determined by which facts about what there is, and as attempts to justify their answers to this question, whatever the authors of such theories may themselves have thought. We come to know (or at least justifiably believe) which facts make which moral judgments correct, by means of connective theories (§5.1) whose nonformal principles specify what are to count as the relevant descriptive similarities in virtue of which two persons have the same obligations, two acts have the same worth, or one

[50]If, as seems likely, Blackburn's (1985a) quasi-realism is committed to EP and MEA (as first-order principles), then ironically and inconsistently, it is committed to a realism of the present sort.

principle applies with equal force in distinct circumstances. How such theories are themselves justified, whether foundationally or in terms of wide reflective equilibrium or whatever, we need not here inquire.[51] For in any case it is clear that the moral realist is committed to no "lame analogy" between knowledge of moral properties and knowledge of secondary qualities, according to which the knowledge is to be construed along the lines of some perceptual model.[52]

All this is closely related to the demand that the realist give some positive account of what in the world does determine the truth of a given moral judgment if not warranted assertibility, coherence, or antecedent moral belief. This is equivalent to asking how we are to go about giving truth-conditions for moral judgments. Part of the answer is that what determines a given moral truth J is the piece of the world with which J corresponds, where again a piece of the world is a set of natural entities and their natural properties and relations. But this cannot be the whole answer. The warranted assertibility theorist, for example, could agree with this much, yet go on to claim that the piece of the world which really does the determining—the one that is the smallest to do so—is the one that consists of the evidence that warrants the assertion of J. Likewise, the coherentist could go on to claim that the piece which really does the determining is some appropriate systematic whole of coherent beliefs, including (perhaps) certain moral beliefs or considered judgments in reflective equilibrium. In effect, such antirealists can accept not only the determinacy of moral truth by the world but also its correspondence with the world. But unlike the realist, they hold that every true moral judgment is determined by and corresponds with the same one sort of thing—either long-run evidence, or some coherent set of beliefs in reflective equilibrium, or (in the case of idealists) some aspect of consciousness, or whatever.

The moral realist differs from these theorists not as regards correspondence but as regards *what* the various moral truths correspond with. The point of CD is not to define moral realism or realist truth for moral judgments. Rather, CD defines a word-world relation which true moral judgments can bear to what there is, but which is such that not every moral truth need bear it to the same things or even to the same sorts of things. Yet to the extent that moral realism has been rejected on the ground that no one can make sense of such a relation,[53] CD is of far

[51]But see Thagard (1982), which contains an implicit response to Little. Cf. Copp; Boyd (forthcoming).

[52]Contrary to Blackburn (1985a), 12, 17. Cf. McDowell, 110.

[53]I take it that this is what in their different ways Stevenson, 212–217; Smart (1984), 98; and Blackburn (1984), 243–257, are driving at.

greater use to realists than to antirealists. In this sense, CD is realist in spirit. It enables moral realists to formulate the core of their thesis, even if not all of it. The core is that each true moral judgment corresponds, in a perfectly intelligible sense of 'corresponds', with a specific piece of the world. What realists must add, to distinguish themselves from pragmatists, coherentists, and idealists as regards moral truth, is that by no means does every true moral judgment correspond with long-run evidence, with some belief-system in reflective equilibrium, with some aspect of consciousness, or whatever.

Nevertheless, this is not yet a complete response to the demand for a positive account of what determines the truth of a given moral judgment, if not evidence, coherence, antecedent moral belief, and so on. The response so far is that what does the determining is normally a piece of the world that includes no such things. And we must say *'normally'* here, since some moral judgments may be about evidence, antecedent belief, or the like, by way of being about what attitudes we ought to have toward such things, or what actions we ought to take regarding them. For example, we might decide to hold ourselves morally blameworthy for failing to revise our beliefs in light of certain evidence, or for failing to rid our web of belief of a certain incoherence. But if a moral judgment is to this extent about such things, then obviously its truth-value cannot be determined totally independently of them. So the realist probably should not say that the truth-value of every moral judgment without exception is determined by a piece of the world that includes no evidence, no antecedent moral beliefs, and no beliefs in reflective equilibrium.

Even with this further qualification, the response to the demand for a positive account of what determines the truth of a given moral judgment is incomplete. In order to give a complete response, the moral realist must adopt and defend one or another substantive moral theory. Only such theories attempt to specify in a comprehensive way just what the morally relevant factors are in virtue of which I have the obligations I have, or an act has a certain worth, or a given principle applies. It is only by means of such theories, then, that one can hope to specify what a given moral truth corresponds with, by spelling out what count as the relevant things and natural properties in virtue of which what the judgment is about has the moral status it has.

For example, suppose a moral realist adopts a version of "homeostatic consequentialism," according to which the moral goodness of actions, policies, character traits, and so on, is largely a matter of the extent to which they tend to foster a variety of mutually supporting—hence "homeostatically clustered"—physical and psychological or social human needs, together with the mechanisms that unify them.[54] In such a theory what determines the truth-value of a moral judgment are the various human needs, their clustering, and the mechanisms by which such needs are best unified and fulfilled. And what a true moral judgment corresponds with is some specific subset of these matters which would be spelled out in any eventual detailed development of the theory. Or suppose, instead, that the moral realist adopts (a version of) Rawls's theory. Then what does the determining is the set of things and natural properties that determines what the parties to the original position would choose by way of first principles, conjoined with the natural circumstances in which the principles thus chosen are to be applied. And what a true moral judgment corresponds with is some specific subset of such matters.

In this way does each moral theory "provide whatever reduction is to be had" of moral truth to natural fact,[55] not (or not necessarily) in the sense of reductive definitions of moral terms in natural terms (that is, necessary or even accidental biconditionals that link such terms), but in the sense of specifying what natural things and properties a given true moral judgment corresponds with, hence in effect what its truth-conditions are. Thus nothing need be said about coreferential terms, or indeed about reference at all, but only about the relation of determination between whole sentences and the world, whereby their truth-value is determined by the world even if the reference of their terms is not. Moral realists need not commit themselves to a causal theory of reference and its troubles (§1.1.4).

Harman has complained that "in the absence of a way of reducing moral claims . . . it is obscure how the rightness or wrongness of an action can manifest itself in the world in a way that can affect the sense organs" so that moral judgments are empirically testable.[56] The answer is that even in the absence of reduction—reduction in the sense of (necessarily) coreferential terms—a moral judgment is as testable as is our attribution of various natural properties to the entities in the piece of the world the judgment corresponds with; for what makes the judgment true is just that these entities have those properties. And what the rightness (or wrongness) of an action consists in is certain entities' having certain natural properties: namely, those entities and properties that form the piece of the world with which the judgment that the action is right (or wrong) corresponds. Thus the rightness or wrongness can

---

[54]Boyd (forthcoming), §4.4.
[55]Sturgeon (1985), 61.
[56]Harman (1986).

manifest itself in a way that can affect the sense organs, because the corresponding piece of the world can affect them. It will affect them in one way, eventually, if the entities in that piece have certain natural properties, in another if they have others.

Let us take stock. What the argument for the determinacy of valuation shows is *that* there is something about the natural facts which determines a unique distribution of truth-values over the moral judgments. As to *why* there is something about the facts that does this, the answer lies in the way we use (or ought to use) the moral terms: we use them in line with EP and MEA, from which two principles it follows that the facts determine moral truth. Thus, while it is a scientific or natural fact that, say, secondary qualities are determined by primary, it is instead more of a fact about how we choose to carve up the world by our usage of the moral terms that explains why moral truth is determined by natural fact.[57] As to *what* exactly it is that if known would prevent us from assigning falsity to a really true moral judgment *J*, the answer is, "The facts that just suffice to determine *J*'s truth-value as true—the facts with which *J* corresponds." And as to *how we could ever know*, or at least justifiably believe, that such-and-such are the facts with which *J* corresponds, the answer (in part) is, "By means of appropriate connective theories whose nonformal principles specify what are to count as the relevant natural properties and relations in virtue of which a given item has the moral status it has."

What we see emerging is a new kind of position in meta-ethics—an alternative to the bleak trichotomy entrenched in the aging trivium of naturalism, intuitionism, and emotivism, together with such of their descendants or variants, respectively, as descriptivism, rational intuitionism, and prescriptivism or even Rawls's constructivism.[58] The emerging alternative might be called "determinationism." It differs from naturalism[59] and descriptivism in allowing that ought is not (or need not be) derivable from is, or definable by or reducible to is, so that moral properties are (or can be) nonnatural properties. It differs from intuitionism in not making a mystery of the connection between natural and nonnatural properties but explaining it, via determination; and in making room for (and insisting on) modes of discovery and justification (and explanation) other than a priori intuition or self-evidence. Nor need moral first principles be "given by a moral order prior to and

[57]Cf. Blackburn (1985a), 13–14.

[58]Rawls, 567, 569, 570.

[59]But not necessarily from everything that has been called naturalism; cf. Scott. In fact, determinationism obviously is a naturalism in the sense endorsed by Sturgeon (1985), 58–62, and by Harman (1985), 29–30.

independent from our conception of the person and the social role of morality" (Rawls's phrase for the aspect of intuitionism with which he is most at odds). For the facts that just suffice to determine the principles could easily prove to involve our conception of the person and the social role of morality, rather than some Platonic or other independent moral order known by rational intuition. And finally, determinationism differs from emotivism, prescriptivism, and constructivism in rejecting their noncognitivism and in explicating such matters as fact of the matter, correspondence, truth-claim, confirmability by a class of facts, and being part of the fabric of the world, even for first principles. Thanks to the determinacy, and contrary to Rawls, we can identify objectivity with what Henry Sidgwick called "the point of view of the universe," in the sense that purely descriptive facts about the universe (ourselves included) determine the correctness of moral judgments, even first principles. A determinationist meta-ethics would seem well worth formulating and defending at far greater length than is possible here.

Metaphysicians of every sort, not just physicalists, may take advantage of this meta-ethics. If the truths about the metaphysician's unifiers do suffice to determine all descriptive truth, then automatically they suffice to determine value truth, thanks to the descriptive determinacy of valuation. There is no need to posit two realms of being and knowledge—say, noumenal and phenomenal—in which values and science go their separate ways.

We can therefore achieve an ideal of many philosophers from Plato on: to ground the moral truths in what there is. Yet we can also agree with Sartre and all those we may take him as speaking for, in effect, when he says, "Ontology . . . cannot formulate ethical precepts. It is concerned solely with what is, and we cannot possibly derive imperatives from ontology's indicatives."[60] The reason we can follow both Plato and Sartre is that moral imperatives are grounded in nonmoral fact, in the sense of determination, even if such grounding by itself enables no one to formulate or derive the imperatives from any indicatives.

To this day, physicalist varieties of metaphysics tend to echo the Democritean argument: "In reality there are only atoms and the void; therefore our values are mere conventions." The inference to mere conventions presupposes that values are not determined by physical phenomena. The presupposition is reinforced by the presumed failure of all efforts to show determination via either reduction or derivation, together with the further assumption that there is no other way to do so.

[60]Sartre, 625.

The idea is that since ought can neither be reduced to nor derived from is, "the distinction of vice and virtue is not founded merely on the relations of objects," so that "morality is nothing in the abstract nature of things," if we may use Hume's words to this effect.

Contrary to this whole multistranded tradition, we are entitled to the courage of our conventions. If all descriptive truth is determined by truth at the level of physics, as physicalists contend, then the objective world of matter in motion exhibits an element of value after all, in that the physical truths about the world determine the correct distribution of truth-values over the value judgments. A purely scientific description of us and the world is not ethically neutral, despite long tradition to the contrary, and we are free to regard nature and value as ontologically reunified. Although values seemed banished forever from nature, they were always there. It is we who may now return from long exile, imposed by too-ready acceptance of reducibility and derivability as the only ways to show that the physical world contains an element of value. The moral face of existence can smile as commandingly upon us in this scheme as in any other.

7   The Measure
of All Things

7.0. Introduction

All I've so far written can seem but straw. The problem is not only
that the chapters to date sometimes seem pointless, as when one is grief-
stricken or in love. Even when some mood makes them relevant, they
can seem inadequate. Nor is it just that they fall short of the vision I had
of them. That, after all, was inevitable. Instead, the problem is mostly
with the vision itself, which is limited. It concentrates on domains of
discourse, when there are many other ways for us to be and to represent
and change ourselves and our world or worlds. There are gestures,
caresses, silences, scents, passions, paintings, tastings, concerts, and
many more. Each in its own manner can convey, often better than a
thousand words, a sense of where we are, how our little worlds fit into a
larger one, and what we must do.

Why not broaden the vision? This does occur, to some extent, in the
sections ahead. Even so, there are limits to how broad a philosopher's
vision can be, at least when philosophy's task is defined in certain ways.
Thus suppose that philosophy's "purpose . . . is. . . to discover what is
common to all modes of understanding."[1] If the philosopher's vision is

---

[1]Gadamer, xix.

so broadened as to include everything properly *called* an instance of understanding, then very likely the modes of understanding have nothing distinctive in common. The term 'understanding' is a family-resemblance term like 'game', its various uses related by a series of similarities rather than by a single set of necessary and sufficient conditions. As with games, the only thing common to all instances of understanding might well be that they are a human activity. Nothing distinctive would have been learned about understanding in general (even assuming there is such a thing). Far better to confess to an irreducible multiplicity of ways of understanding.

Of all the ways of understanding and changing ourselves and our worlds, why concentrate on discourse and its domains? Suppose I were to say I am interested in domains of discourse because I am interested in domains of truth, and truth is defined in the first instance for such linguistic items as sentences, statements, or propositions. This is a respectable response, hallowed by long tradition. The trouble is that 'truth' itself is a family-resemblance term, used for many things other than propositional truth. Truth is not really defined "in the first instance" for discourse (or for anything else), and to say so can prevent us from seeing that the strategic choices have already been made when we declare our interest in truth, meaning propositional truth. On the other hand, suppose we are interested not only in the glories of propositional truth but also in its potential evils. Then we need not pretend that 'truth' is not a family-resemblance term, or that we have not already accorded priority to discursive ways of understanding and being. On the contrary, part of what we are interested in is whether nondiscursive ways also enjoy some sort of priority over the discursive.

One of the potential evils of the pursuit of propositional truth is that we may thereby "deny ourselves a place in the world."[2] A reason is that propositional truth usually means objective truth, and objectivity is widely believed to be somehow inimical to authentic human being by omitting the subjective point of view, without which we cannot express or experience death as our own death, time as our time, and our choices as our own. But we see in §7.1 that this *is* a false problem. There are evils attending the unbridled pursuit of propositional truth, but they are not substantially different from those that attend any unbridled pursuit.

A special case of the pursuit of propositional truth is the attempt to unify all things in relation to a particular domain of truth. And physicalism is a special case of this way of unifying all things. But of course there are many other ways of seeing things whole, and some seem far

---

[2]To echo this section's epigraph; Harries (1978a), 88.

more compelling—different ways for different people, and occasionally for the same person at different times. Does one represent the way things are in themselves? The way the world is? The meaning of Being? The ultimate nature of existence? Or are such questions based on false presuppositions? Indeed they are, if we may believe §§7.2–7.3. Hence a traditional aim of philosophers—namely, to "reconstitute the shattered picture of the world"[3]—is misguided to the extent that it presupposes we are to strive for *the* picture, some one all-inclusive portrait, emblematic of the ultimate nature of things.

Still, can't we at least say that "the aim of philosophy . . . is to understand how things in the broadest possible sense of the term hang together in the broadest possible sense of the term"?[4] Not necessarily. Often the aim should be not only to understand things but to change them. Moreover, Sellars thinks the key sort of understanding is a matter of fusing into one vision—into a single stereoscopic view—diverse images or perspectives or conceptions of human-being-in-the-world. But the metaphor of stereoscopic vision will not bear the load. Fusion of two perspectives into a single stereoscopic view occurs only when they are of the same thing, are not too widely separated (about as far as our eyes), and use compatible lenses. In any case we cannot accept Sellars' implicit suggestion that this single stereoscopic, synoptic vision would constitute *the* true, complete account of the world, corresponding presumably with *the* way the world is; there is no such thing.

Sellars is right that philosophical understanding is a matter of "knowing one's way around" with respect to diverse perspectives, conceptual domains, and so on; and that knowing one's way around is mainly a form not of knowing *that* but of knowing *how*. Yet knowing one's way around with respect to the domains is not happily expressed or achieved in terms of stereoscopic vision, and probably not in terms of any visual metaphor. Rather, it is a matter of knowing what discourse to use on what occasion for what purpose, or whether instead to use some nondiscursive way of representing and changing ourselves and our worlds. It is therefore part of the general problem of knowing how best to live and be.

Construed this way, metaphysics and ontology become more a matter of values than of what there is. Traditional metaphysicians aspire to trace what there is, meaning what the ultimate reality is on which everything is dependent. They are convinced that their questions are more fundamental than any others, since they ask about the most basic or real nature of things behind the subject matter of particular inquiries.

[3]Santayana (1910), 214.
[4]Sellars, 1.

The priority supposedly enjoyed by their candidates for the ultimate reality—Substance, Form, Spirit, Matter, whatever—is absolute. But there is no such priority. Our characterizations of what there is reflect prior choices and inventions of (or acquiescence in) particular vocabularies together with entrenched metaphors (§5.3). In this sense "vocabularies acquire their privileges from [those] who use them rather than from their transparency to the real."[5] For there is, to repeat, no such thing as *the* real to which they could be transparent. Characterization of something as the real, or as "reality," reflects a prior choice of vocabulary-cum-metaphor. These choices in turn reflect value judgments, often subconscious. In a sense, therefore, valuing is prior to characterizing something as "real" and thus prior to metaphysics and ontology. Since the values are ours, there is a sense after all in which we are the measure of all things.

These cryptic remarks demand explanation, of course, which the chapter tries to provide. Meanwhile, bear in mind that calling us the measure of all things does not mean that truth is relative or subjective. Nor does calling us the measure conflict with physicalism. In particular, there is no need to revise or retract the physicalist's tough-minded insistence on objectivity as a prerequisite for claiming that certain unifying entities exist. Instead, calling us the measure is a dramatic way of expressing a priority of value over fact. To some it will seem melodramàtic. But this sort of priority might just be what Protagoras had in mind in the first place. The Sophists contributed to the rise of Periclean democracy, and Plato and other aristocrats might well have misrepresented Protagoras' "man the measure" by omitting context and qualifications. In any event, to say that value is prior to fact is not to say that the priority is absolute, as we shall see, but to say that it is conditional. Why bother to dethrone (or defrock) the notion of the way existence is, only to have it reinstated in the guise of talk about value?

Moreover, recall that the correctness of the value judgments is determined by the world. Thus the correctness of our choices of vocabulary-cum-metaphor is no merely relative matter. Which domain of discourse is better to use on what occasion and what our purposes ought to be on that occasion are determined by objective, natural fact. And if all such fact is determined by physical phenomena, as the physicalist believes, then physical reality determines what these choices ought to be. So even though value is prior to fact in one sense, fact is prior to value in another, thanks to the determinacy of valuation. We are the measure of all things, yet reality takes our measure. All too often we fall short, when our words and deeds fail to be what they ought to be.

[5]Rorty (1979), 368.

7.1. Subjective and Objective

Metaphysics lays the foundation of an age by giving it the basis
of its essential form through a particular analysis of the existent
and a particular conception of truth. This basis dominates all
the phenomena which distinguish the age.

—MARTIN HEIDEGGER

Traditional metaphysics tends to be monopolistic. It tends to presume that there is some unique vocabulary, privileged beyond all others in expressing the nature of things or in revealing the only real world. It tends also to presume that whatever cannot be expressed by or reduced to the privileged discourse is either insignificant or nonexistent. This monopolizing or totalizing tendency, not surprisingly, carries over into traditional metaphysicians' notions of truth and existence. Truth and existence, fact and reality, are defined, in effect, only for what fits the metaphysician's scheme. Many aspects of life therefore come to be ignored, repressed, laughed at, distorted, lopped off. Philosophy functions as Procrustes' bed.

An age dominated by Procrustean metaphysics may sense eventually that something is missing and rebel. If the metaphysicians are in the habit of wrapping their claims in the flag of objectivity, then objectivity itself becomes a target for the rebels, who will be in no mood to observe such fine distinctions as the one between objectivity and monopoly, particularly when the metaphysicians themselves fail to observe it.

The distinction between objectivity and monopoly is easy to draw, when objectivity is characterized in terms of invariance through varying perspectives (§1.5[vii]). Recall that we accord objective existence to whatever invariant would provide the simplest explanation for all the otherwise incompatible appearances of a thing. An oil drum's top is said really to be round, because we realize that a round thing would project exactly the sequence of shapes we observe, the ellipses that vary from a minimum (straight as a board) to a maximum (circular). Thus we avoid having to say the top is at once round, elliptical, and straight. Further, we are enabled to say the top is round *period,* rather than round for someone at some time and place, or relative to some way of looking. Equivalently, we can say it is true *period* that the top is round, rather than true for me, or for you, or relative to some perspective of time, place, or eyeglasses. As seen, this objectivity prerequisite for the truth of a sentence amounts to the requirement that the sentence be an eternal one. In practice this usually is achieved by requiring the sentence to contain no indexicals.

Excluding indexicals implies no monopoly, in the sense that some domain enjoys unconditional priority over all others, in virtue of which it expresses "the ultimate nature of existence" or anything of the sort. One reason is that a sentence can be devoid of indexicals yet have the rest of its vocabulary from any of the domains. Another is that even though the requirement expresses a kind of priority for objective discourse, the priority is hardly unconditional. Plainly, what we may say is only that *if* we are interested in truth *period,* or in what there is that is invariant through the perspectives of time, place, culture, and so on, then we had better try to express ourselves by means of eternal sentences.

Furthermore, the requirement to use eternal sentences for expressing truth *period* does not imply that whatever cannot be expressed by objective discourse is insignificant or nonexistent. Subjective phenomena there are which might well be inexpressible in any possible language, let alone in routine objective discourse (§5.4). Yet it can still be true that the objective phenomena—what there are that are invariant through the perspectives of species, times, places, cultures—determine what the subjective phenomena are and what they are like. Moreover, thanks to the determinacy of valuation, we saw how the objective phenomena can manifest themselves in their own occasional insignificance and in the occasionally far greater significance of other things, including any subjective aspects of life that make for authentic human being.

So objectivity is distinct from monopoly in all the senses first listed in §4.0. Failure to observe the distinction can only lead to trouble, whether for champions of objectivity or for rebels against it. Neglect the distinction, and pursuit of purely objective accounts of existence will seem to omit much of what distinguishes us, including what it is like to be the persons we are, experiencing time and choice as we do, and conscience and death. Objectivity will seem to filter us out of existence.

Naturally, we want back in. If objectivity has been pressed on us as monopolistic, we might well decide to "destroy" or "overcome" or "go beyond" the tradition that values objectivity so highly, as did Heidegger. And we might try to do so by showing the ideal of objectivity to be utterly impossible to achieve, or to be incoherent, or itself to presuppose subjectivity anyway. We might try to turn the tables even more completely by arguing that things never have their being or their properties by themselves. We play an essential role, through our language or our "understanding," in determining not only what a thing is but that it is. Thus no object exists or has its properties independently of human being. True authenticity requires that we take responsibility for this selective disclosure or revelation of things.

This way of getting us back into the scheme of things entire is heroic but misdirected. Of course, there *are* notions of objectivity that are monopolistic, and certainly we should direct our fire at them.[6] For example, suppose objectivity means not only (i) invariance, as above, but also that an objectively true sentence must express (ii) something unrelated to any interest of ours, (iii) something abstract (a universal rather than a particular), (iv) something about imperishable existents, and (v) something that excludes all nonequivalent descriptions of (or vocabularies for) whatever the sentence is about. Any such notion is monopolistic, doubly so when conjoined with the doctrine that any talk irreducible to an idiom satisfying (i)–(v) is radically defective. Yet this is a traditional notion of objectivity, perhaps *the* traditional notion, a familiar henchman of Procrustean varieties of metaphysics. Nevertheless, rejecting it does not entail rejecting objectivity in the sense merely of invariance. In order to throw out Procrustean notions of objectivity, it is not at all necessary to throw out the notion of truth *period;* that is, there is no need to throw out realism. To suppose the contrary is to neglect the venerable distinction between the baby and the bath.

Realism becomes monopolistic when (but not only when) it adds that "the primary goal of human thought and discourse is to believe (say) what is true in the realistic sense."[7] This accords primacy, perhaps unconditional, to objective discourse. To the extent that subjective phenomena are inexpressible by objective discourse, much of what distinguishes human being will be omitted, if the goal of discourse is to say only what is true in the realist's sense. Realism is at its most blatantly monopolistic when it implies that I have said something true iff what I have said is the way things are in themselves. The problem is not so much with the phrase 'in themselves', which can be just a potentially misleading way of expressing the independence of how the things are from human thought; the problem is with '*the* way things are', since there is no such thing.

There is a more innocent way of expressing a realist notion of truth: ϕ is true iff the things ϕ is about are the way ϕ says they are. Yet even here trouble lurks, since the phrase '*the* way' appears to imply monopoly, and one might be tempted to conclude that realism can only be monopolistic. But this would misconstrue the role of 'the way' in this sort of truth-schema. The point is not that there is one and only one way the things can be, and ϕ says they are that way. Instead, ϕ says the things are a certain way, and that way is indeed one of the ways they are. Thus even though caution is required in order to formulate realism

[6]As do Dreyfus and Todes, who describe the following notion.
[7]As does Alston (1979), 780.

nonmonopolistically, it can be done. There is no need to go to antirealist extremes simply in order to get subjectivity back into the scheme of things entire, or to reinject the significance of time, conscience, death, and more. From this point of view, a number of modern attacks on objectivity and on realism are gratuitous assaults on innocent bystanders.

Still, don't realist definitions of truth "make objectivity the measure of truth and reality"?[8] In a sense they do. They make objectivity the measure (in the sense of being a logical prerequisite) of *objective* truth—truth *period*—of what there *objectively* is. But this is a mere tautology. What they do *not* do, unlike their monopolistic interpretations, is make objectivity the measure of truth and reality in *other* senses as well—in the sense, say, of truth from a point of view; or of what there relatively is; or of subjective, perspectival truth and reality; or even of truth as subjectivity and truth as disclosure. These other uses of the family-resemblance terms 'true' and 'real' are not co-opted. Nor are we compelled to say that of all the members of the family, propositional truth and objective reality are unconditionally prior to the others, that they are the patriarchs from which all the others are descended and by which they are "grounded." The relations among the members are much more complex than that.

Some paragraphs ago the Heideggerian idea of selective disclosure made yet another appearance (cf. §5.3). Things never have their being or their properties by themselves, so it is said, but only through the cooperation of us and something else (some undisclosed ground). This idea contains some valuable truths, as does the companion idea that we must take responsibility for the disclosure or revelation of things. One such truth is that of all the aspects of a thing, we tend to select only one or a few in terms of which to describe it, know it, enjoy it, use it, and so on. The thing appears to us, becomes part of our world, under certain of its aspects rather than others. Often these others do not even occur to us. All this is reflected in our choice of certain vocabularies and metaphors in talking about the thing. It is reflected also in the idea that all we can ever know is what-there-is-under-a-description.

Another truth here is that we tend to overlook or even repress our prior selective activity. We tend to suppose that the selected aspects in terms of which we now live with the thing are the way it is in itself, what it really or objectively is. Different ways of conceiving the thing are resisted, often dismissed as mere metaphor, despite the fact that (unbeknown to us) other metaphors may well have played a crucial role

[8]Harries (1978a), 88.

in how we ourselves conceived the thing in the first place (§5.3). Yet another truth is that we bear some responsibility for selecting certain aspects under which the thing—or the person—becomes part of our world. After all, we could stir ourselves to heed those poets and others who would disenthrall us from the metaphors by which we habitually understand people and things. What things are like for a bat presumably is fixed. We can plead no such determinism, free as we are to choose or invent alternatives.

Thus these elements of truth in the idea of selective disclosure can readily be accommodated within the present scheme. We might even try assigning the role of the undisclosed ground—or Heidegger's "Being itself" (on one reading)—to the Universe beyond the universe (§3.5). The Universe beyond, after all, is a unity not known through any positive predication; and it is without beginning or end, neither coming to be nor passing away, eternal and immutable. Hence it is hardly a being or a thing in the usual sense but Parmenidean enough for those so inclined,[9] without precluding genuine multiplicity and change (§3.4.1). Also there is mystery aplenty as to its structure. And, prompted in part by its structure, we do selectively carve it (usually unconsciously) into diverse parts or objects, emphasizing certain of its aspects and theirs rather than others, in accordance with our entwined vocabulary and interests. Subsequently, these objects and aspects normally are experienced as presenting themselves to us, or as given and fixed.

What is false in the idea of selective disclosure, according to realists, is that things have their being and their properties never by themselves, but always only in relation to human being. Such a view seems but special pleading for the point of view of our species. Better by far to express the idea of selective disclosure by saying that *for us* things never have their being or their properties by themselves but only through the combined activity of us and something else. This is a tautology, of course, but a valuable one. It reminds us of our role in choosing various vocabularies over others. Vocabularies derive their priorities in part from those who use them, rather than from some alleged transparency to the nature of things themselves. We are the measure of what things are like for us, as is the bat, but we have a choice in the matter and a corresponding responsibility. Nor can we plead on grounds of indeterminacy of valuation that there is no fact of the matter as to what choices we ought to make. Purely descriptive aspects of the Universe beyond the universe (of "Being itself," if we may equate them) determine our obligations here as elsewhere.

[9]Cf. Vick.

7.2. The Very Idea of the Way the World Is

> *If I were asked what is the food for [human beings], I should*
> *have to answer 'none'. For there are many foods. And if I am*
> *asked what is the way the world is, I must likewise answer,*
> *'none'. For the world is many ways.*
>
> —NELSON GOODMAN

What is our place?[10] Traditionally, the question suggests locating us with respect to the way the world is, or to the inmost nature of things. Thus if the world is God's creation, various morals follow as to our place. If instead the world is nothing but matter in motion, certain other morals follow. And if the inmost nature of things is Being itself disclosing itself, still others follow. All such responses to 'What is our place?' seek some ultimate ground, some foundation, relative to which everything else has its place (typically in some implicit hierarchy or chain of being). Of course, the foundations metaphor is now notorious, thanks to various epistemologists' critiques. Yet even if we swallow the metaphor,[11] as I do in this section for the sake of argument, we err if we try to identify the foundation with something that is *the* way the world is.

The general form of the argument that there is no such thing will be "Put up or shut up." Put-up-or-shut-up arguments abound in philosophy, though under politer names. One of the strongest arguments (and the earliest) against the analytic-synthetic distinction proceeds by dismantling all the ways so far put up for maintaining the distinction; it then anticipates some further ways, dismantles them, and concludes that there is no such distinction.[12] Of course, the conclusion does not follow deductively from the failure of only these ways (unless they are the only possible ways). The point is rather that unless some further way of maintaining the distinction is put up, proponents had better shut up about the distinction; for the burden of proof now is overwhelmingly theirs. The argument from queerness against objective values has the same form and was undermined in §§6.1–6.2 by putting up a further way of relating objective values to natural fact. Thus the recipe is clear: examine all the ways so far put up, in effect, for maintaining the very idea of the way the world is, anticipate others, find them all wanting, and conclude that there (probably) is no such thing as the way the world is.[13]

[10]Cf. Harries (1978b).

[11]As does Harries (1978b) in his discussion of Heidegger's (early) search for an ultimate ontological foundation.

[12]Quine (1961).

[13]The argument thus largely expands on N. Goodman's (1960) but without what I take to be his verificationism.

Start with the idea that the way the world is is the way it is to be seen or pictured. The trouble is that there are so many ways of seeing and picturing. I can picture things from front or back, above or below, near or far, in various lights, in motion or at rest, as isolated or as part of this whole or that (which one?), and so on. Nor does it help to grade the various ways of seeing according to their degrees of faithfulness to the way the world is, or absence of distortion. For we require some standard of what is to count as an undistorted seeing. Such a standard is itself either a way of seeing or not. If it is, which one is it? Any answer here begs the question against all the others. Thus consider a popular favorite, seeing all objects as three-dimensional solids obedient to Euclidean laws of perspective. Van Gogh, however, sometimes saw and painted things as obedient to laws of perspective for non-Euclidean space (in particular, for a hyperbolic or Lobachevskian space). And in §3.4.1 we noted, in effect, that one could see things as 4-dimensional. Both this way and van Gogh's are just as much ways of seeing as any favorite. Hence if they are to be condemned or endorsed, it must be by reference to some standard other than a way of seeing.

The standard cannot be the way things are given, for they are given in so many ways, one way to van Gogh, another to Euclideans, and so on; things are not so much given as taken. Further, things more often are given to us (or taken by us) as something to use, like a hammer, as "ready to hand," in Heidegger's phrase, rather than as an isolated *n*-dimensional solid in some spatial perspective. All these and many more are equally ways things are given. One of them can pretend to represent the way the world is only by reference to some standard other than its being the way things are given.

Perhaps the standard of faithfulness should be derived from the way the world is to be described. But there are so very many ways. We describe things in terms of their use to us (we call the hammer a hammer, not a spatiotemporal configuration of constituents). We describe them in terms of their role in a form of life (we call the slabs in Chaco Canyon a solar marker, not a pile of rock). We describe them thereby in terms of their significance or meaning to those engaged in that form of life. Or we describe them instead as ST-sums of basic physical entities. And so on and on.

The field is not appreciably narrowed by requiring the descriptions to be true, not even if 'true' means true *period,* objectively or invariantly true. For we have seen how many distinct, irreducible domains of objectively true discourse there are. To pretend that one domain of truth represents the way the world is either begs the question against all the others or presupposes some standard other than merely being a true description.

Perhaps the standard should be derived instead from the way things are to be understood or explained. But what way is that? Again we confront hopeless variety. Even if we could agree that the explanation should be in terms of efficient causation, how far back in the chain of efficient causes we must go to succeed in explaining an effect is quite arbitrary (§2.6). And anyway, many phenomena seem not to lend themselves to such explanation in the first place. Thus it is that we are compelled to speak of the explanatory autonomy of various domains.

Among continental candidates for the way things are to be understood, a favorite is opening oneself to authentic modes of access to things so as to be attuned possibly to the mystery of Being. That mystery, in part, is supposed to be expressed by the question 'Why is there anything, why not rather nothing?' But this question, according to §§2.1–2.4, expresses no mystery, based as it is on a false presupposition. So in this sense there is no mystery of Being to be attuned to. Even if we waive this embarrassment, plus any that might stem from ambiguities in the notion of an authentic mode of access to things, still the credentials of this way of understanding things, simply as a way of understanding, are no better as regards being *the* way than the physicalist's way. Both are equally ways of understanding, equally comprehensive, coherent, and simple. If one of them crowns itself *the* way to understand things, either the question is begged or some standard is presupposed other than merely being a way of understanding.

The same can be said of those ways of understanding or interpretation (including mysticism) that emphasize context, interrelatedness, and the wholeness of all things rather than things in isolation. So too for those ways that emphasize the significance or meaning of things for our "being towards death" or for any other moods and passions, including those involved in our "average everydayness." Any extra profundity that one of these ways of understanding has over all others as their foundation or ground cannot derive merely from its being a way of understanding. All are ways of unifying the phenomena, ways of relating or mapping them. If one of these ways of mapping and unifying represents *the* way things are, some one ultimate nature, it must be by virtue of some hidden agenda—hidden, possibly, from their authors themselves.

Perhaps the elusive standard should be sought in some universal essence. But even if each thing has something we may call the essence of that thing—a very big 'if'—it hardly follows that all things share a certain essence, let alone share it simply by virtue of their being things or (what is equivalent here) of their existing. But suppose for the sake of argument that they do share one. What would this universal essence be?

It would be some property that all actually existing things not only actually have but have of necessity—a property they have in any possible world in which they exist. Such is the way of essences. Thus we would have to swallow the relevant notion (or notions) of necessity rejected in §2.2, as well as the notion of a property all things share just by virtue of existing.

Even if we swallow them whole, the old dilemma recurs, an irreducible plurality of pretenders. One property all things presumably share in any world in which they exist is the property of instantiating some properties. Another is the property of being determinate, in the sense of instantiating certain properties and not others. Another is the property of bearing various relations to each other. Still another, according to a number of philosophers, is being in time and possibly also in space (hence in either case in spacetime). Yet another, according to some, is being a potential or even actual object of some consciousness. And *if* existence is a property, then existence is a property all things share simply by virtue of existing, though one hesitates to say they exist of necessity.

Of course, all these alleged universal essences are extraordinarily abstract and vacuous, surely a disappointment to anyone seeking the inmost nature of things. But there is a deeper problem. If some such universal essence is singled out as representing the way things are, it cannot be just because it is a universal essence, for each such essence would be as much a universal essence as any other. Hence some further standard would be required. The same goes for any alleged essence of the world, as opposed to the things in it, even assuming we can make sense of the idea of an essence of the world.

So the way the world is cannot be the way it is to be seen, pictured, given, described, described objectively, explained, understood, interpreted, accorded meaning, or accorded an essence. In each case the dilemma is the same: what is advanced as the notion of the way the world is turns out to be many notions, between which no non-question-begging choice can be made without reference to another kind of notion altogether. Unless some further method is put forward for maintaining the very idea of the way the world is, we had better conclude that there is no such thing.

What about taking the sum total, or at least the set, of *all* the ways the world is and calling it *the* way the world is? The trouble is that we would lose the kind of contrast that the phrase 'the way the world is' normally implies. What is implied is a contrast between, say, the way the world is to be objectively described and the way it is to be accorded meaning, whereby the former but not the latter allegedly represents the way the world is. To be told that the sum total of all these alternatives is really the way the world is is to be told nothing to the normal point of the request 'What is the way the world is?'

The conclusion that there is no such thing as the way the world is does not endanger correspondence theories of truth (contrary to both Goodman and at least one of his critics).[14] Granted, such theories often speak of truth as correspondence with the way the world is or with the way things are. And sometimes their intent is indeed monopolistic, as with some (other) objectivist and realist accounts. But more often the point of a correspondence theory is not that there is one and only one way things are, so that a sentence ϕ is true iff what ϕ expresses corresponds with that way. Instead, ϕ says certain things are a certain way, and ϕ is true iff that way corresponds with one of the ways those things indeed are.

What, then, is our place? No one place, surely, but many—at least as many as there are ways the world is. Orientation occurs only in light of some way of representing the terrain—some way of picturing, seeing, describing, understanding, interpreting, feeling, and so on. Each such way is the map, in effect, of a way the world is. Each such map has its own conventions, which help us to inscribe on it 'YOU ARE HERE'. Nor can the philosopher's task be to reconstitute the picture of the world, stereoscopic or otherwise. Thus there is a sense in which our place—or rather, our places—are the places we give ourselves by virtue of our choices of kinds of map or ways of representing people and things. Having chosen a map, we may orient ourselves by means of it, thereby choosing *a* way of orienting ourselves. There is no such thing as *the* way, unless our place has its foundation or ground—assuming the foundations metaphor applies—in something other than the way the world is.

There may indeed be another sort of foundation or ground, one suggested by the following response to the argument of this section. The argument, it may be said, is sound but shallow. It does show there are many ways the world is, yet it fails to note that some ways are more important than others, hence in some sense more fundamental. Their priority has to do with value. When we say ours is the map to use, we need not mean ours is the map of the way the world is. Nor need we deny that what map we should use is a function of our interests and purposes. Instead, we believe that a certain sort of interest or purpose is unconditionally more important or valuable than all others, and that a corresponding priority attaches both to our map and to the way of the world it represents. Thus the hidden agenda, in many a claim as to the

[14]N. Goodman (1978a), ch. 1; Weissman, 208–212.

way the world is, is a claim as to what way has the deepest value. Our place is to be grounded by reference to that way.

There is much truth in this response, including the bit about shallowness. But there is some untruth, too, as we see next.

7.3. The Very Idea of Ultimate Priority

> *There is no single beatific interpretation.*
>
> —F. W. NIETZSCHE

> *Values must from emotional necessity be viewed as absolute by those who use values as compulsive defenses.*
>
> —WESTON LABARRE

Again we encounter the metaphor of foundations. This time there is supposed to be, in virtue of its value, some aspect of existence more basic than all others, the deepest of the ways the world is, the bottom domino of the whole teetering stack. This Atlas of the dominoes lays claim to ultimacy by claiming to be unconditionally the most valuable of them all. In addition, the comparative importance of the others often is defined by some hierarchical relation to Atlas. But this supposition of hierarchy is beside the present point, which is to inquire whether any aspect of existence is unconditionally the most important or valuable in the first place.

Now at least as regards ways of seeing the world, we may readily grant, if only for the sake of argument, that some are intrinsically valuable. That is, they are valuable (beautiful, desirable, good, worthwhile) noninstrumentally, in and of themselves, irrespective of any contribution they may make toward some further end (though they may and often do also make one). For example, van Gogh's ways of seeing and painting presumably enjoy intrinsic worth, as do many another artist's. Nor are examples of intrinsically valuable ways of seeing limited to the arts. Seeing things as all illustrating abstract mathematical relations evidently has some intrinsic value, irrespective of any contribution such seeing might eventually make toward prediction and control of things ("Euclid alone hath looked on beauty bare"). Likewise, we may readily grant that some ways of describing the world are intrinsically valuable; so too for various ways it is given, plus ways of understanding and interpreting it, and of according it a meaning or an essence. Indeed it is hard to think of a way of representing the world that could not have some intrinsic worth. And just as various ways of representing the world have intrinsic value, so presumably do the ways of the world they represent (though the term 'inherent value' might then be better to use).

Yet from the fact that a particular way the world is has intrinsic value or importance, we cannot conclude that it is more valuable than all others, let alone unconditionally so. For some of the others may be not only intrinsically valuable but as intrinsically valuable as it is. Even if they are not, still we cannot conclude that the one intrinsically valuable way is unconditionally or absolutely more valuable. To say one thing is unconditionally more valuable than another is to say either (i) that it is more valuable in every respect, (ii) that it is more valuable everywhere everywhen, (iii) that there is no circumstance in which it may be overridden by the other, or (iv) some combination of (i)–(iii). By contrast, to say it is intrinsically more valuable is to say it has greater value when the two are considered in and of themselves, independent of any consequences they may have. But one thing could be intrinsically more valuable than another, in this sense, without being (intrinsically) more valuable in every respect; one sunset could be intrinsically more beautiful than another—as a whole or on the whole—yet not as regards every hue. Hence (i) does not follow. Also, something could be intrinsically more valuable than something else without being (intrinsically) more valuable everywhere everywhen; chocolate could be intrinsically preferable to strawberry today but not tomorrow. Hence (ii) does not follow. And one thing could be intrinsically more valuable than another when nevertheless there are circumstances in which it would be overridden by the other; preserving another's life is intrinsically better than taking it, yet circumstances of self-defense can justify or even obligate taking it. Hence (iii) does not follow. So the inference from intrinsically greatest value to unconditionally greatest value is unsound.

Is there some other way of showing that one aspect of existence is unconditionally more valuable or important than all others? I think not. Any such aspect would have to be either intrinsically or extrinsically (i.e., nonintrinsically) the most valuable. If it is extrinsically the most valuable, it cannot be unconditionally so. For if it is extrinsically more valuable than the rest, then it is more valuable only in virtue of certain of their consequences. But it can hardly be more valuable in virtue of *all* their consequences. Hence it is more valuable in some respect but not in all. Also, if it is better only in virtue of certain consequences, it will be better only where and so long as those consequences do ensue and are themselves valuable, hence only in certain places and times. And there will be circumstances in which different consequences ensue or are valuable and in which it may be overridden by others.

So any alleged unconditionally most valuable aspect of existence cannot be extrinsically so. But who among us will be so bold as to claim that some aspect we favor is intrinsically more valuable than all others?

And how could such a claim be defended? Here the difficulties resemble those noted in the last section: there are many claimants to the title, and no unproblematic standards for choosing among them. Claimants to the title of the most valuable aspect of existence have included the way it is to be religiously understood (which religion? which version of it?), the way it is to be physicalistically explained (on which version of physicalism?), the way it is disclosed (in which mood?), the way it is to be accorded meaning (which one?), and so on and on.

As to standards, they would have to be standards for something's being intrinsically the most valuable aspect. This excludes any standard for x's being more valuable than y that appeals to consequences or ends. Thus we could not assume that x is intrinsically more important than y on the grounds, say, that x is more conducive than y to a certain sort of understanding, interpreting, seeing, describing, or being in the world. But once we are denied standards that refer to consequences, ends, purposes, or interests, it is hard to see what would count as a standard for the claim that x is intrinsically more valuable than y other than the mere definer of intrinsicality: namely, that x is more valuable than y when considered in themselves, irrespective of consequences and ends.

Still, suppose I were to persuade you, improbably, that a certain aspect of existence is indeed intrinsically the most valuable. If it is to be unconditionally the most valuable, I would need to show it is the most valuable in one or more of senses (i)–(iii). Showing any of these is even more unlikely than showing that some aspect is intrinsically the most valuable. Thus suppose the unconditionally most valuable aspect of existence is one (allegedly) revealed by some particular kind of mystical experience of the oneness of all things. Presumably this aspect is thought to be superior to all others—indeed intrinsically superior—on the whole or as a whole. But (i) it is no better—indeed it is self-avowedly worse— in respect of mathematical expressibility than are the mathematical-physical aspects of existence. Also, (ii) at a later time an aspect revealed by a different kind of mystical experience might be more valuable. And certainly (iii) it could be overridden, as when, in order to save a life, a surgeon (who conceivably if improbably could also be a mystic) temporarily values the person's biomechanical condition over all others.

Of all the ways the world is, therefore, none can pretend to be unconditionally more important or valuable than the rest. A given way can be more important or valuable only in some respect, at some time and place, and in some circumstance in which it is not overridden by another, even if—a very big 'if'—it should prove intrinsically more valuable than the rest. Any primacy one way enjoys over another in virtue of its greater value is thereby at least doubly conditional: on the respect in which it has greater value, and on the circumstances in which nothing overrides it.

So much, then, for priority or primacy in virtue of greater value, or what might be called value priority. What of other notions of priority? Is there some other sense in which one thing might be unconditionally prior to all other? Clearly not. Thus consider explanatory priority. Roughly speaking, x's are explanatorily prior to y's just if y's can be explained (only) by reference to x's, but not vice versa. Obviously, there are as many types of explanatory priority as there are distinct types or notions of explanation. Even waiving this complication, however, it is obvious that unconditional priority of x's over y's does not follow from their explanatory priority. The x's would be prior to the y's with respect to explanatory role but not in every respect.

But aren't we entitled to conclude only that *explanatory* priority is not a sense of priority in which one thing is unconditionally prior to another? For surely there are many other senses. Indeed there are. From time to time philosophers speak of what in effect are causal, evidential, semantic, identificational, ontological, predictional, observational, temporal, conceptual, definitional, logical, experiential, economic, and theological priority, to mention only a few. Yet in each case the presence of the adjective, with its telltale 'al' or 'ic' ending, is the giveaway. It tells us that the priority is in some respect—causal, evidential, conceptual, whatever. Even when the explicit adjective is missing, as it very often is, the context enables us to supply one. What looked like talk of unqualified primacy proves after all to be talk of primacy in some respect, in circumstances where that respect is deemed urgent.

Often the circumstances are those of rebellion against a Procrustean metaphysics that has impressed upon an age its idea of the primary aspect of existence. Some other aspects have been repressed, distorted, lopped off. To restore them, the rebels—who anyway resent being made to feel defensive—resort to strong language. Rhetoric mounts. Soon the hitherto repressed aspects are spoken of as primary, and the qualifying adjectives of their primacy are dropped, even if someone understood and supplied them in the early days. It is easier, after all, to barricade the streets in the name of an ultimate than an ultimate-in-a-respect, or an ultimate-except-in-listed-circumstances. When the Procrustean reaction arrives, it too may have allowed itself to be provoked into the defensive rhetoric of unqualified primacy, even if the rhetoric was not used from the start, or not really meant.

Interests are at stake in these struggles, not merely a group's accumulated self-interest but a self's unselfish interest in certain aspects of things. I may have spent a lifetime searching for the basic structures of what things are like from a human point of view, painstakingly exploring language, mind, meaning, causation, and temporal and other relations among the things under this their "manifest image." If I am told that my interest in such aspects is of little value compared to an interest in some other aspect—in the objective aspect, say, or more narrowly still in the mathematical-physical—then what I feel and what may be intended is an attack not only on my life's work but on my life's worth. Who I am is called into question. No wonder such a threat to my values can provoke an absolutist reaction.

I might well retaliate by claiming priority for my interest. I might claim that human being, by way of intentionality and human understanding, is prior to the objective aspect of things, prior to what there is that is invariant through and independent of various perspectives. Human being, or something disclosed by it, is the ground, the foundation, the primordial source of all else. In such a mood I might well proclaim that truth as disclosure is prior to propositional truth, hence prior to objectivity itself. And of course it *is* prior, as we saw in §§5.3 and 7.1, but only in a respect. Neglecting to say so gives the impression of a claim to unconditional priority.

Or suppose I have spent a lifetime helping to clarify what there is that is invariant through and independent of various perspectives, perhaps by constructing an ideal language (or canonical idiom) purged of every trace of anthropocentrism (tenses, indexicals, subjunctives and related modal expressions, metaphors, and so on). If I am told that my interest in this the objective face of existence is of little import—or worse, that it is the source of inauthenticity, bad faith, rogue technology, and other evils of the age—then my life's worth may seem threatened, assuming I deign to note such attacks in the first place. And again the absolutist reaction is natural.

Thus it is that many a dispute among metaphysicians is more a matter of values than of what there is. Frequently, this fact is disguised by uncritical talk of priority, primacy, ground, foundation, primordiality—by the use of such terms stripped of qualifying adjectives or subscripts to indicate the respect in which something is basic and something else derivative. A couple of metaphysicians can both have their facts right, each knowing intimately a particular aspect of life, yet each believe that the other aspect—if it really is one—is insignificant or derivative. And of course it *will* be insignificant in some respects and in certain circumstances for certain purposes. The question to be addressed by two such metaphysicians, then, is which of their interests is the more valuable in what respect on what occasion. If the comparative value is an extrinsic matter, they should make clear what end is better served by emphasizing one aspect of existence over the other, or by emphasizing a domain of discourse that best expresses that aspect. In particular, we often want to know what domain is better in what respect, on what occasion, and for what purpose.

Assuming we come to know so much, we could record each domain's appropriate conditional value or values. But the values (or at least the valuings) clearly are those of us human beings, as are the choices of domain made in light of them. So a metaphysician may come to suspect that at the center of things are we the measure—the measure by virtue of our valuing and choosing (often unconscious), or by virtue of our deft, unfathomed sense for when to shift from one vocabulary or discourse to another, not merely during the span of a conversation but in one breath. What hidden principles or structures of our language and being govern these shifts? And what can they tell us of the significance or meaning of the aspects of existence our conversations are about? Here surely is a deep matter, prior to all traditional varieties of metaphysics and ontology, something in virtue of which each such philosophy plus the aspect *it* calls basic can be assigned its conditional value and put in its place—if not in the scheme of things entire, then at least in the ongoing conversation we call the history of philosophy in the West. Here surely is the transcendental ground—the province perhaps of "universal hermeneutics"—on the basis of which we can understand, interpret, and locate all particular philosophies, plus all particular modes of experience and domains of truth.

I am willing to concede that the matter may be deep, the exclusive province possibly of hermeneutical disciplines that "precede" the sciences. I would only inquire into the nature of that precedence, and of the priority claimed for our value-laden choosings of vocabulary. Both look to be varieties of explanatory priority, in view of the hermeneuticist's emphasis on modes of understanding or interpretation. In any event, like any variety of priority, each is priority in a respect, in a circumstance, usually for a purpose. So we must not acquiesce in many a hermeneuticist's unqualified talk of precedence, priority, or primacy, lest someone conclude that here finally is *the* ground of all else.

With each new insight into ourselves and our world or worlds there comes a powerful temptation to say, "Here at last is the key to human and other being." Such insights have included reflections on intentionality, will, dread, boredom, hope, becoming, death, caring, and more. Or we may reflect on the "conditions for the possibility" of these and other modes of experience. Or we may be impressed by the significance of means of production, by tool-using, by symbol-using, by language. Or a Freud may alert us to what might otherwise escape notice. But there is no such thing as *the* way we are. We are at least as many ways as there are domains of truth about us.

Is there some scheme, some decision-procedure, to tell us what domain of truth we ought to emphasize, or what vocabulary-cum-metaphor we ought to use, on what occasion for what purpose, if any? Some scheme to tell us whether instead we ought to use some nonverbal way of representing ourselves and our worlds and of orienting ourselves in them? I doubt there is, especially if the scheme is to provide criteria for the correctness of the value judgments involved. All the problems with criteria of truth dwelt on in §1.3 would recur here, no doubt magnified. But the main obstacle is the incredible variety the decision scheme would have to encompass: the variety of occasions on which we choose or acquiesce in a discourse or other mode of representation; the variety of legitimate purposes we might have on a given occasion; the variety of vocabularies and other, often nonverbal, modes of representation we might use to achieve a given purpose; and the variety of aspects of existence that are relevant despite our tendency to sense only a few. Some rules there may be that should influence our choices on these occasions, but in all likelihood they are mostly rules of thumb.

Failing such a scheme, it is consoling to reflect that the correctness of the value judgments involved is determined by purely descriptive truths about what there is (presumably the values all obey EA, §6.1). In that sense, at least, let no one suppose that anything goes—that we may, for example, use the vocabulary of stimulus-response experimenters in circumstances in which we should treat someone as a Thou, not an It. Thus does reality take the measure of the self-styled measure of all things (the measure, of all things). It is consoling also to recall that none of us may hide behind the fact-value distinction to disguise from ourselves either the effects of our choice of vocabulary (on a patient, say) or our responsibility (§§6.0, 7.0). And some will find it consoling even that there is no such scheme, that here is an art, a matter of wisdom, forever safe from attaining the secure path of a science[15]—safe also, one should add, from hierarchical schemes of valuation based on some ultimate face of existence of which the other visages are but masks. For there is no such thing.

[15]Cf. Rorty (1979), 372.

7.4. The Perils of Pluralism

> *Yet after everything has been seen from each dimension's perspective, we still want all these pictures to be woven together into one unified patterning.*
>
> —ROBERT NOZICK

> *A willingness to welcome all worlds builds none . . . awareness of varied ways of seeing paints no pictures. A broad mind is no substitute for hard work.*
>
> —NELSON GOODMAN

Much contemporary pluralism is reactive, if not reactionary. It would lose its punch, if not its point, should the various monopolistic philosophies vanish.[16] What would remain for pluralists to do? What would remain would be important but undramatic. Thus they (and others) could and should catalogue as many as possible of the ways the world is, together with our diverse ways of representing them and of changing ourselves and our worlds, including various ways of seeing, gesturing, picturing, mapping, describing objectively, explaining, understanding, interpreting, intending, according meaning, valuing, and more. It would be important also to analyze and record the various purposes for which we might use a given way of representing and orienting, plus the circumstances in which such purposes would be appropriate. Further, we need careful analyses of the varieties of priority that various ways of representing, valuing, and understanding enjoy over others, in given circumstances for given purposes.

Above all, perhaps, we need analyses of whether there are any sound inferences from a thing's priority over another in one sense to its being prior also in another.[17] Very few such inferences are sound. From the fact that a certain truth ϕ is evidentially prior to another truth ψ (meaning ϕ is part of our evidence for ψ, but not vice versa), we cannot infer that ϕ is explanatorily prior to ψ (meaning ϕ is part of an explanation of why ψ is true). Nor can we infer ontological priority from identificational: from the fact that we cannot identify things of kind y without reference to things of kind x, but not conversely, we cannot infer that y's could not exist unless x's did.[18]

All this cataloguing and analyzing, this botanizing and brush-clear-

---

[16]Rorty (1979), 365–372, makes a similar point about "edifying" versus systematic philosophy.

[17]See Tlumak for a pioneering effort in this direction.

[18]Cf. Moravcsik; Lycan (1970).

ing, would be an enormous task and an important one, often with immediate application to current philosophical debate. For instance, like many before him, Mohanty has rejected the idea that intentionality is (or could be) grounded in the physical order, claiming instead that intentional discourse is prior to all causal discourse, physics included.[19] But Mohanty fails to mention that he uses 'prior' and 'ground' in two senses here. When he says intentional discourse is prior to causal, he means that in using causal discourse or theory, we intend to refer to entities and causal systems of them. Thus the very "sense" of these entities and systems derives from intentionality. In §§5.0 and 5.4 we noted much the same sort of point, to the effect that the very sense or significance of the physical entities depends on truths about our values and interests, hence on intentionality. But when Mohanty says that if physicalism were true, the causal would be prior to (or would ground) the intentional, he means that the latter would be either causally explained by or "captured" (expressed) by the former. Yet clearly, it is logically possible for x to be prior to y in the first sense, while y is prior to x in the second; we cannot infer from x's priority over y in the first sense to y's not being prior to x in the second, or for that matter to x's being prior to y in the second.

Mohanty may be aware of this. His argument against the idea that intentionality is grounded in the natural order is less that intentional discourse is prior to causal than that the latter cannot explain and cannot capture (reduce) the former. But this overlooks the possibility of a nonreductive physicalism compatible with the explanatory autonomy of the domains of discourse, the intentional included. Determination of the intentional by the causal does not imply that the latter sort of discourse can capture (or express or reduce or eliminate) the former. Intentionality is grounded in the physical, in the sense of being nonreductively determined by it (§4.5); at the same time, the physical is grounded in intentionality, in the sense that in using physical discourse, we intend to refer to physical entities in a certain way and thereby give them a "sense." Grounding, like priority, is always in some respect. Failure to specify the respect courts confusion.

Pluralists, then, can warn us against being fooled in this way by a whole class of frequently used philosophical words, words like 'prior', 'ground', 'basic', 'presupposed', 'primordial', 'subordinate', 'primary', 'derivative', and so on. And their warnings will be informed by their presumably increasingly subtle and comprehensive cataloguing and analyzing.

---

[19]Mohanty, 707–708.

Is there anything else pluralists can do, in their role as pluralists? Much depends on just how pluralism is defined. Suppose it is simply the denial, as I have been tacitly assuming, of all forms of monopolistic metaphysics—the denial of any view to the effect either that all legitimate discourse must be reducible to some one privileged discourse or that (reducibility aside) some one discourse enjoys unconditional priority over all others, or that there is such a thing as *the* way existence is for any discourse to describe. In terms of this definition, then, the pluralists' role is to remind us—when we need reminding—of the evils of monopolistic metaphysics, either by repeating their arguments against it, or by presenting us with their rich catalogue of multiplicity, or by satire and parody, or by all these plus calls to the sense of wonder so often dulled by monopolistic philosophies.

Because physicalism is not (or need not be) monopolistic, we pluralists can have no quarrel with it, despite the fact that physicalism involves a monism of entities. For, as we have seen, the monism is combined with a pluralism of properties, of faces of existence, and of irreducible, autonomous, equally privileged ways of representing and changing ourselves and our world or worlds.

The pluralists' peril in all this is that they will be perceived as kibitzing dilettantes by those doing the hard work within a given domain, or the hard work of unifying several. The complaint is not that pluralism bakes no bread but that it paints no pictures, builds no world. Of course, the pluralist can consistently remain a pluralist yet spend a lifetime carefully portraying just one face of existence, or just one way of unifying them all. But the time spent at the portrait, while not inconsistent with pluralism, is not time spent reminding us of the evils of monopoly. When as a painter I put on my pluralist's hat, I leave my painting and become, for a time, a mere esthetician, talking instead of doing. And when as a philosopher I put on my pluralist's hat, I become, for a time, a mere metaphilosopher, talking about the wonderful multiplicity of philosophies but constructing none. I can warn against backsliding into the evil ways of monopoly and against slovenly use of words like 'prior', 'ground', and so on. But this will often seem little more than back-seat driving. And pluralists will appear yet more irresponsible if they should go so far as to insist that unlike their monopolistic foe, they are not even expressing a view or giving arguments.

The real drama in philosophy remains where it has always been, in pairing the rage for order with delight in near chaotic variety. And the highest challenge is to express the two entwined, to express them by a harmony of argument and metaphor, of logic and passion, so that we may understand and respond with all that is best in us. Here the pluralist's refrain—that the rage for order can be satisfied by many different ways of unifying everything—is true but beside the point. What we want is *a* way that will enlighten and ennoble us now, and inform action, along dimensions that our situation and our need make urgent. We also want the wisdom to know just what is urgent, and what philosophical or other vision of unity-in-variety will best serve at just this moment. The great prophets have often been better at this than the great philosophers.

Those who would summon us to a better world, prophets and philosophers alike, often have done so in the name of some alleged ultimate. But surely urgency can be declared without invoking ultimacy, and future prophets must learn to do so. For as seen, there are no ultimates in the sense of absolutely, unconditionally most valuable aspects of things, or overriding goals. Prophecy must therefore be combined with pluralism without degenerating into it. In this the prophet may usefully appeal to the determinacy of valuation, pointing out that even though there are many faces of existence, purely descriptive, objective facts nevertheless determine which one we ought to value most highly on what occasion for what purpose; and that on this occasion, for the given purpose, we ought to follow the prophet in regarding a certain aspect as overriding. Pluralism is no excuse for inaction, nor does the absence of ultimates imply that anything goes.

7.5. Emotions and Secondary Qualities: Faces or Masks?

> *To feel about something may in certain privileged cases be the last, most penetrating way of knowing what the thing is.*
>
> —J. N. FINDLAY

> *This world is but canvas to our imagination.*
>
> —HENRY DAVID THOREAU

Things have effects on us, often in such a way that we mistake a property of the effect for a property of the thing. We attribute to a rainy landscape the somberness we feel on viewing it. We call a bird's song cheery when it is only the male warning others off his territory. We locate redness and other sensible colors in the external object, as if they were dye in cloth. We attribute nowness—or pastness or futurity—to things and events. And the oval appearance of something just glimpsed can make us think the thing elliptical when really it is round, like an oil drum's top.

Objectivists in general and physicalists in particular warn ad nauseam against mistaking a property of an effect on us for a property of the thing. By implication, this is also to warn against confusing a mere mask with a face of existence. Of course, the warnings often are entirely in order. But frequently they are interpreted—and meant—as something deeper and more ominous, as when we are told, in effect, that failure to heed the warnings must inevitably result in "falsification of the way things are" and in the "delusion that the characteristics of the universe tie in closely with the doings of human beings."[20] Often we are further warned against the evils of anthropocentric distortion of reality, and against projecting our idiosyncratic classifications onto a world in which really there is no color, no sound, no fragrance, no flavor, no now, and neither somberness nor cheer.

There is much truth in all this, yet much that is false or misleading. Part of the trouble lies in the talk of *the* way things are, supposedly described by physics. But we have been learning that there is no such thing for physics or anything else to describe. Likewise, we must reject any talk of reality as that which can be described only by physical vocabulary. Further, we should reject any division of vocabularies and the properties they express into primary and secondary, if the alleged primacy is supposed to be unconditional. For again there is no such thing. Vocabularies and the properties or qualities they might express can only be primary or secondary in a respect on an occasion for a purpose. Because it is so difficult to hold such qualifications in mind, we might well forgo all talk of primary and secondary qualities, despite long tradition to the contrary, though in the end I shall not.

Another part of the trouble lies in the presumption that any legitimate map of existence must avoid human projection schemes, and indeed any perspective. Instead, it should be coordinate-free.[21] But a map in polar coordinates centered on us is just as much a map as any other and can be just as comprehensive and accurate. For certain purposes it is clearly superior, much as earth-centered astronomy is superior to Minkowski diagrams for navigation at sea. Only if we treat such a map as coordinate-free would we be guilty of confusing an effect of perspective for a true invariant. So long as we refrain from doing so, and are self-conscious about the legitimate purposes of such maps, we cannot be accused of mistaking a property of a thing's effect on us for a property of the thing. Or if we are so accused, we can retort that either the accusers confuse our interest in man-centered maps with their interest in maps that are coordinate-free, or they fail to see that we are frequently entitled to be interested in other things.

[20]Smart (1963), 71.
[21]Again see Misner, Thorne, and Wheeler, 5–8, on coordinate-free developments of physics and physical geometry.

Still, there remains the unsettling business about a world that is in reality colorless, timeless, and cheerless. What does this mean? If it means there is only one vocabulary to describe the world—the vocabulary of physics, which contains no words for sensible color, nowness, mood and so on—then it is absurd. But generally the intent is different and deeper. The idea is that the so-called secondary qualities would be "really in the world" only if they were "objective properties" of something in the world; because they are not objective properties, nothing in the world has nowness, color, or any other secondary quality.

Implicit in this idea is the identification of a thing's primary qualities with its objective properties. And the relevant way to define an objective property, I think, is as in §1.5(vii). That is, an objective property of a thing is an invariant that would most simply account for certain varying appearances of the thing, as roundness accounts for varying degrees of elliptical appearance of an oil drum's top. Other ways of distinguishing primary from secondary qualities generally fail of their purpose. Suppose that a primary quality of a thing is defined as one of the thing's intrinsic properties. If 'intrinsic' means "definable without reference to any other thing," then some if not all the qualities meant to be primary prove to be secondary. The reason is that many of the relevant physical magnitudes—charge, spin, mass-energy, perhaps even size and shape—are defined in effect in relation to other things. (The first three, at least, are defined in terms of properties of fields, properties which in turn depend on properties of other things in the field.)

On the other hand, suppose 'intrinsic property' means "property without which the thing would cease to be what it is." Here the problem is the inherent ambiguity in the notion of what a thing is. There are many descriptions under which we can define and individuate the thing, many vocabularies relative to which certain of its qualities will be regarded as essential and others not. Only if we have already decided that the vocabulary of physics is somehow privileged as regards expressing what a thing is (or its essence) will the phrase seem useful in defining what a primary quality is. Defining the primary qualities instead as inseparable from the thing and the secondary as separable really amounts to defining them in terms of being intrinsic and extrinsic; the above difficulties recur. Nor does it help to call primary those qualities whose possession could be intersubjectively tested. For routinely, we compare notes when checking the sensible color of a thing, and so too when checking other secondaries.

Sometimes it is said that science can adequately explain and describe the nature of the world solely in terms of the primary qualities; the secondaries therefore are superfluous, and there is no reason to suppose they characterize anything. But as a definition of 'primary' and 'secondary' this fails, for it presupposes a prior inventory of the primaries. Also it is false. Science cannot adequately explain and describe the nature of the world solely in physical terms (even assuming there is such a thing as *the* nature of it to be described). To suppose the contrary overlooks the explanatory autonomy of the domains and presupposes the reducibility of all description to physical description.

We do better to distinguish primary from secondary qualities by identifying the former with the objective properties of a thing, meaning those of its invariants that afford the simplest explanation of certain of its varying appearances. A thing's shape, size, mass, motion, charge, and so on, clearly fall under this heading, even if they prove relational. Probably such invariance-plus-explanatory-import is what traditional philosophers and scientists mainly had in mind all along, however misleadingly they may occasionally have expressed it.

What about colors? That depends on what we mean by a color-word like 'red'. If we mean an energy-state of the surface of the thing, or (perhaps equivalently) an invariant power of the surface whereby light predominantly of certain wavelengths would be absorbed in certain conditions, and others in others, then redness *in this sense* would be an objective property of the thing and hence a primary quality. This explains the tendency in physics to use the color words in much this fashion. But that is hardly their use when they are meant to denote secondary qualities. According to one such use, 'red' means roughly both that the thing literally has the same property as does a certain sensible patch of our visual field when, as we say, we are seeing red, and that the thing has it uniformly, as does the patch. The idea here is partly that just as the thing's being round explains certain varying appearances, including the appearance of roundness itself, so does its literally being red explain certain appearances, including the appearance of redness itself as well as of varying shades in varying lights.

This idea is clear and plausible. Unfortunately, empirical investigation informs us that, unlike the attribution of shape and size, the attribution of this redness to the thing does not yield a sufficiently adequate scheme for explaining and predicting the relevant experiences. Instead, we are driven to explain our color experiences by reference to complex and as yet incompletely understood relations among colorless energy-states and particles of the surface of the thing, together with *contrasting* energy-states of *surrounding* things, plus perhaps their relative motions and other contextual matters.[22] Even when all other normal persons in

---

[22]Cf. Hurvich; Bartelson; Ratliff; Hardin (1984).

normal circumstances agree on the color, it is clear that the color, even if it is in some sense a property of the thing, is not a property that enjoys the explanatory power and simplicity of, say, shape.[23]

Furthermore, put to one side questions about explanatory power and simplicity. Color, in the sense of the selfsame property that a sensible patch of our visual field uniformly has when we are seeing that color, is not an invariant in the first place, let alone one that affords the best explanation. If it were an invariant of the thing said to have that color, then it would be true *period* that it has the color, rather than true relative to some perspective of time, distance, or eyeglasses. Now suppose that two costumes viewed from the back row of an opera house are the same shade of pink, according to all normal percipients. Suppose further that seen up close, or through opera glasses, one indeed is pink but the second resolves into a print of red polka dots on white. We correctly say that the second is not really pink. Seen closer still, through a magnifying glass or microscope, even one of the dots resolves into a skein of multi-colored fibers; closer still, through an electron microscope, it resolves into a multitude of colorless molecules. We cannot say that the dot is red *period*—red in the same uniform way as the patch in our visual field— but only that it is thus uniformly red from a certain distance, at a certain magnification. Its shape, by contrast, does not thus vary. Magnify the dot as you will, it stays round.

Of course, we can still say the dot is red *period, provided* we give the word 'red' a different meaning. For suppose 'red' means "uniformly red to a normal human from a foot away without magnification."[24] Then what happens closer still or under a glass is irrelevant. But even though we might thus restore invariant truth-value, it would not follow that this redness is, in the intended sense, an objective property of the dot. The reason is that being red to a normal human from a foot away without magnification contributes too little toward explaining and pre-dicting our other color experiences of the dot, especially when it is viewed against contrasting energy states of the surfaces of surrounding things, or in other varying contexts.

Much the same is true if 'red' means "could not easily be singled out in a bushel of ripe tomatoes by a normal human at medium distance in sunlight, but could easily be so singled out in a bushel of fresh spin-ach."[25] Because of all this specification of the circumstances and the observer's condition, we could correctly say of a thing that it is, in this

[23]Cf. Hardin (1983).

[24]On some of the problems with this sort of dispositional account, see Averill (1982).

[25]Roughly Smart's (1963) suggestion, 79. Again see Averill (1982) on some of the problems with this sort of analysis. Cf. Averill (1985).

sense of 'red', red *period*. The sentence '*x* is red' would be an eternal one. We could even say that redness in this sense is an invariant—not necessarily an invariant *property* of the thing *x*, since we might well deny it is a property of *x* at all, depending on our criterion of propertyhood,[26] but at least an invariant *relation* among normal human percipients, certain circumstances, and *x*. Yet in any case, redness in this sense contributes too little toward explaining and predicting the full range of our color experiences of *x*. So this redness is not an objective property of *x* in the intended sense.

Because '*x* is red' would be an eternal sentence for suitable senses of 'red', it could be used, in those senses, to express a way *x* is (§1.2). Further, color vocabulary could thereby be used to express a face of existence, provided the vocabulary is similarly used in those senses or used to mean roughly "would be that color to an appropriate human in appropriate conditions." All that is required, in order for a vocabulary to express a face of existence, is the elimination of variable truth-value, by the suitable specification of time, place, conditions of observer, of media, of context, and so on (§§1.1, 4.6, 5.3). The same could be done for vocabulary ordinarily used to express any other secondary qualities.

It is instructive to connect all this with what things are like for a bat. Suppose the bats say, "Things are like *P*," where *P* is a property of their auditory experience. Then they have treated their map of things, erroneously, as though it were coordinate-free. But suppose they say, "Things are like *P* for a bat." Then, since this is an eternal sentence, and assuming it is a true one, they have expressed a way things are: they are like *P* for a bat. Further, assuming they continue to say that things are like such-and-such for a bat, they can use their whole bat-specific vocabulary to express a face of existence—one which, so to speak, smiles only on bats in response to their unique sensory apparatus.

Physicalists occasionally are alarmed that secondary qualities might prove irreducible to primary qualities or relations of objects and events or processes, and thus impossible to fit into a physical account of the world. Hence Armstrong is driven to identify secondary qualities with physical properties of objects or their surfaces, an identification against which he takes "the irreducibility objection" to be "*the* critical one."[27] He need not have worried. Even if they prove irreducible, still the secondaries readily fit into a physical account in the sense that whether a thing has such a quality (or whether several things are related by one) is determined by facts at the level of physics. What things are like for

---

[26]But see Chisholm on "converse intentional properties."
[27]Armstrong, 274.

human beings, as regards color and other secondaries, even if irreducible, is nevertheless determined by primary qualities and relations of things. Once again, irreducibility and inexpressibility are red herrings.

For these reasons, then, we cannot conclude, just because certain predicates express secondary qualities, that in doing so they cannot express a face of existence. Nor can we conclude that "if our philosophical task is, in part, to see the world *sub specie aeternitatis . . .* then we must eschew the concepts of color and other secondary qualities."[28] For to view things under the aspect of eternity is *not* to view them filtered through a particular vocabulary, let alone through some unconditionally privileged one. Rather, it is to view them so as to be able to use sentences about them that are eternal sentences, sentences that if true are true *period*, not true relative to some perspective of time, place, or species. And very many different irreducible vocabularies can be used to frame such sentences.

It is true that predicates for secondary qualities—even when time, place, and state of the percipient are specified—retain an anthropic dimension, if not precisely an anthropocentric one. But this means only that on analysis, such predicates make reference to conditions of human percipients. It does not follow that such predicates cannot be used to express objective truths,[29] faces of existence, or ways things are *sub specie aeternitatis*. It follows only that if our interest is in expressing truths having the kind of comprehensiveness and explanatory power characteristic of physics, then we are well advised to be wary of predicates for secondary qualities. But of course, we remain free to be interested in other things also under the aspect of eternity, as often we ought to be— an ought, as we've seen, that itself is determined by truths at the level of physics. Thus it is irrelevant (and probably false) that beings on a distant planet would have little interest in anthropic predicates, or in what things are like for a human.[30] For we may use our species-specific vocabulary to express a face of existence—one that evidently smiles only on us, in response to our peculiar physiology. And even if distant physicists are not interested, distant psychobiologists presumably would be, much as we are interested on occasion in what it is like to be a bat.

What about somberness, cheer, and all the various moods, emotions, desires, and passions generally? Words that express them can also be used to express faces of existence, provided they are used to mean

[28]Smart (1963), 84.
[29]Cf. McDowell, 119–121.
[30]Contrary to Smart (1963), 150.

roughly "are like that for an appropriate human in appropriate con-
ditons," rather than "are like that." Notice also that a thing to which we
attribute somberness or cheer actually is a thing that has come to play a
certain sort of role, however fleeting, in an individual's life and sometimes in the life of a whole culture. It may play the role simply by virtue
of an association, or constant conjunction, with the feeling. But typically, it plays the role by virtue of being an object of the emotion—
whether of somberness, cheer, anger, love, joy, fear, greed, dread,
anxiety, or whatever. Occasionally, the thing plays a role by virtue of
representing or being a symbol for some emotion.

In whatever way the thing comes to play the role for us, and whatever the precise nature of its role, roles are mostly functional-intentional
affairs, as we called them in §4.5. And we conceded there that the
functional-intentional role of a thing is irreducible not only to the structural-physical state of the thing but also in all likelihood to any natural-
science account of persons and of the thing's role-playing relation to
them. It was because the slabs in Chaco Canyon played such a role that
we called the property of being a solar marker irreducible, hence emergent. And we noted that the same is true of artifacts generally, including
hammers, inscriptions, utterances, artworks, and much more.

We also noted, almost in passing, that even if the slabs had come to
be there by chance, still they would be a solar marker, provided the
Anasazis subsequently used them as such and hence accorded them that
role. That the slabs are a solar marker still would be an objective truth
and still would be determined by truths at the level finally of physics
(§4.5). In like manner, whether certain things are artifacts or products of
chance, still, provided they are accorded appropriate roles, it is an objective truth that they are somber, cheery, offensive, lovable, fearsome,
awesome, nauseating, boring, sickening, inspiring, or whatever;[31] and
this truth about them would be determined by physical truth. For to say
a thing is somber, cheery, offensive, awesome, and so on, is to imply
that it plays a certain functional-intentional role; in that respect it is like
calling something a solar marker.

Now consider the question 'What are the slabs in Chaco Canyon?'
One correct answer is that they are a solar marker. And in the context of
anthropological investigations of the canyon and its former inhabitants,
this clearly is "the last, most penetrating way of knowing what the
thing is."[32] Likewise, in certain appropriate contexts, the correct answer
to the question of what a thing is will be that it is a somber landscape, a

[31]Again see Chisholm on "converse intentional properties."
[32]Findlay, 81; see also 11.

cheery birdcall, an offensive remark, a loved one, a hated enemy, and so on. And in the circumstances this may be the most penetrating way of knowing what the thing is, meaning roughly that in the given context the only pertinent way of classifying the thing is just this way, in terms of emotion.

Our passions probably are not just value judgments,[33] but obviously they involve them heavily. Our emotions, moods, and desires entail certain diverse valuings of things, where the values range from esthetic to prudential to moral, from hypothetical to categorical, from taste to matters of survival, and more. Now let us raise the old philosophical question of whether our emotions have "any correspondence to Reality."[34] What Solomon means here by 'Reality', or what he also calls "*the* world," is the totality of purely descriptive facts, but for our purposes it could even mean the totality only of physical facts. He concludes, as have so many, that the emotions cannot correspond with anything in Reality, nor is it their business to do so. For subjectivity is a standpoint or perspective that is adopted in every emotion, according to Solomon, subjectivity being a matter of what things are like in *my* world not *the* world; and "what *my* world includes that *the* world does not is *value*."[35]

But in view of §6.3, at least the valuational component of an emotion *can* correspond with the facts and hence with something in Reality. Thanks to the determinacy of valuation, we were able to define what it means for a value judgment J to correspond with the facts. And what J corresponds with, we said, is the conjunction T_J of those natural facts that just suffice to determine J's truth-value as true. By the same token, what the valuational component of a passion corresponds with, if it is true, is the conjunction of those natural facts that just suffice to determine, for all the value judgments entailed by the emotion, their truth-value as true. And if, as the physicalist claims, all natural fact is determined by physical fact, then there is likewise something in physical Reality with which the valuational components of emotions can correspond. Not only does *my* world include value; *the* world does too, in the sense that the phenomena admittedly in it determine the value phenomena. And if Solomon is right after all, that the emotions *are* just value judgments (or sets of them), then all this can be said of the emotions themselves, not merely of their valuational components. They too can express faces of existence, via the truth claims they make.

[33]Cf. F. Bergmann.
[34]Solomon, 61.
[35]Solomon, 75, 67.

Whether or not the emotions are just value judgments, we can still raise the question of whether we ought to have a given emotion in a given situation, and which one we ought to have instead (assuming the emotion is controllable in that situation to some appropriate extent).[36] Clearly, we ought not to have a given emotion if the value judgments it entails fail to correspond with Reality in the sense just presented, or are simply false. But suppose there is an ingredient in an emotion over and above its valuational component, perhaps some combination of inner feeling and disturbed state of the body. Then it could happen that the emotion's value judgments are true, and still we ought not to have the emotion (again assuming it is controllable). For example, it could happen that all the value judgments involved in one's hatred of someone are true, yet the hatred is wrong. Thanks to the determinacy of valuation, the truth (or falsity) even of this value judgment—that the hatred is wrong—is determined by natural fact. This world is but canvas to our imagination, as Thoreau says, in the sense that no emotional or other valuation of things in the world is derivable from or reducible to any description. Yet not only are there better and worse ways of spreading our emotions and desires on the canvas, but some ways correspond with the facts and some do not. Contrary to Hume, we need not so thoroughly deplore the mind's "great tendency to spread itself on external objects."[37]

7.6. Whether Existence Is Absurd

> *Say what some poets will, Nature is not so much her own*
> *ever-sweet interpreter, as the mere supplier of that cunning*
> *alphabet, whereby selecting and combining as he pleases, each*
> *man reads his own peculiar lesson according to his own peculiar*
> *mind and mood.*
>   —HERMAN MELVILLE

Is existence absurd? The question is multiply ambiguous. 'Existence' might mean either the activities that make up our lives, or the non-human world, or some aspect of it, or the whole of what there is. Furthermore, 'absurd' has several senses in each of these contexts, senses that must be kept separate. In whatever sense, absurdity of existence often is supposed to be implied by science and by naturalistic philosophy. Thus we hear from a distinguished physicist that "the more the

---

[36]Cf. Sterling.
[37]Hume, I.iii.14, on p. 153 of this edition.

universe seems comprehensible, the more it seems pointless."[38] A distinguished philosopher asks, "Science has helped us to know and understand this world, but what purpose or meaning can it find in it?"[39] He
answers that the scientific world picture robs us of meaning in the sense
of a purpose given us by some nonhuman source. And Hepburn speaks
for many other philosophers when he says that in a naturalistic philosophy, human endeavor viewed *sub specie aeternitatis* must seem to shrivel,
frighteningly, and to be vilified. He asks, "Can the vocabulary of life as
'meaningful' or 'meaningless' still play a role in a naturalistic interpretation of things?"[40]

My own answer is an emphatic "Yes," even when meaning or
purpose is supposed to be something found or discovered rather than
something created by the subject in the very act of deciding which
purpose to pursue. Neither science by itself nor naturalistic or even
physicalistic interpretation of its lessons implies that the universe is
pointless, or that it can supply no purpose or meaning, or that human
endeavor is somehow devalued. Nor is any such thing implied either by
views of things under the aspect of eternity, or by the fact that value and
hence meaning cannot be derived from or reduced to any description.
People sometimes dread philosophy lest it force them to conclude that
existence is meaningless or that our lives ultimately are insignificant,
inconsequential, and absurd. The present philosophy, so far from forc-
ing any such conclusion, entails the opposite. To see why, let us consider one by one the main things that have been thought to imply the
absurdity of existence. In each case we see why it implies no such thing,
at least not when viewed in light of the chapters to date. Thus the
explicit lessons will at first be somewhat negative, but a positive account
will emerge as we go along.

(i) The question 'Why do I exist?' is nearly as ambiguous as the
question 'Is existence absurd?' But when it has the sense of an explanation-seeking why-question (§2.1), the question of why I exist does naturally lead one to wonder finally why the universe exists (§2.0). And it
then seems natural to suppose that if there is no reason for the existence
of the universe, then there can be none for mine. The idea is that if the
existence of the whole of what there is is absurd, then surely my own
existence is absurd; and since there is no explanation, known or unknown, of the existence of the universe, its existence is indeed absurd.

This is a slovenly line of thought almost from start to finish. Sup-

---

[38]Weinberg (1977), 154.
[39]Baier, 103.
[40]Hepburn (1981), 209, 220.

pose there is no explanation of the existence of the universe, in the sense argued in §§2.2–2.4. Does it follow that there is no reason for my own existence? No, neither in the sense that there is no explanation for my existence nor in the sense that my life has no point or purpose, hence no meaning. There would be no explanation of my existence only if an explainer of what explains me must itself have an explanation; that is, only if everything in a parade of explanations itself has an explanation. But this just is or implies a version of the discredited Principle of Sufficient Reason. PSR aside, it is doubtful that the relevant concepts of explanation entail that if x is explained by y, and y has no explanation, then after all x has none either.

As for whether my life would have no point or purpose, hence no meaning, obviously something about the universe could provide such purpose and meaning, even if the existence of the universe has no explanation. Natural facts either about nonhuman nature or about a nonhuman ideal observer could suffice to determine what purpose I ought to adopt, and to that extent what is a meaningful life for me, independent of my actual desires and decisions as to what purpose I will pursue. Thanks to the determinacy of valuation, this meaningfulness would be something to be discovered, not created.

Finally, from the fact that there is no explanation of the universe, it does not follow that it is absurd, as noted in §2.5. In the context of questions about ultimate explanations, to call something absurd, irrational, brute, gratuitous, inconsequential, or an accident is to imply that it fails to satisfy some norm of rationality—in particular, some version of PSR. Hence to call something absurd, on the ground merely that it has no explanation, is to betray an erroneous or obsolete conception of rationality. Also, the absurdity of an explainer, supposing for the moment it is absurd, surely is not automatically inherited by what the explainer explains, nor need any absurdity of the whole be inherited by its parts. But even if it were, we could not conclude that our lives are absurd on the ground merely that the universe has no explanation, for we would still need to establish that the universe is absurd.

(ii) One of Camus' protagonists speaks of the "benign indifference" of the universe.[41] And Santayana speaks of nature's "reptilian indifference."[42] In each case the underlying idea is that reality provides no backing or basis or ground for our values and purposes, hence none for the seeming meaningfulness of our lives. Whether benign or reptilian or neither, reality's alleged indifference to us is thought to be a conse-

[41]Camus, 154.
[42]Santayana (1957), 22.

quence of the supposedly unbridgeable gulf between fact and value, or between *is* and *ought*.[43] Reality is called absurd because it fails to satisfy the human demand that it provide a basis for human values.

Here we need only note that even if reality is identified with the totality of natural fact, the determinacy of valuation shows that reality is not absurd or indifferent (in the foregoing sense of 'indifferent'). Even if (or even though) the totality of natural fact about what there is neither defines nor reduces nor entails any value judgments, including those that validate certain purposes, still reality provides a basis for them in the sense that the facts determine the truths about values. In this sense, reality is laden with value (§6.3), and so too therefore are lives lived in light of values thus determined.

(iii) Perhaps, instead, reality is to be identified only with the natural facts about the nonhuman world. Facts about our wants, needs, and so on are to be excluded. And even though valuation is determined by the totality of fact, it might not be determined by facts about the nonhuman world. That is, the facts that just suffice to determine what our values and purposes ought to be might have to include facts about our wants and needs, so that to this extent and in this sense, meaningfulness is not given by the nonhuman world.

Notice, however, that even if the facts that just suffice to determine this do have to include these facts about us, what our values and purposes ought to be is nevertheless something to be discovered, not a purely subjective matter. For the facts allow one and only one distribution of truth-values over our value judgments, first principles included, and what that distribution is is not something we may choose or create. If it were, then in view of the determinacy, it would follow (by §6.1) that we may choose or create what the distribution is over the purely descriptive judgments, which is absurd (§1.1).

For many the fact that what our purposes ought to be is a matter for discovery will be enough to establish the meaningfulness of existence. For they were troubled not by a seemingly unbridgeable gulf between values and natural facts about nonhuman existence but by the gulf between values and *any* natural facts. They were not troubled by the possibility that in ascertaining what is worthwhile, what we have to go on is partly a matter of what we actually want, approve, or need. Instead, they were troubled that normative judgments about what is worthwhile appear to have no metaphysical or ontological ground in what there is and thereby appear not to be a matter for discovery, because such judgments cannot be derived from or reduced to natural

---

[43]Cf. Hepburn (1981); and Wiggins, 341: "The will itself, taking the inner view, craves objective reasons" for the meaningfulness of life.

facts even about our wants and needs. But the determinacy of valuation puts an end to these particular troubles and therefore to this source of worry about meaninglessness and absurdity.

What about the possibility that the facts that just suffice to determine what our purposes ought to be, and thereby what is worthwhile, must include facts about human wants and needs? This is indeed a possibility but in the present context only a possibility. Neither science nor naturalistic or even physicalistic interpretation of its lessons entails that valuation is not or could not be determined by facts about the nonhuman world. Physical determinacy of valuation is compatible with the claim that nothing has value except in relation to the wants and needs of some imagined ideal observer or spectator of the actual—not an unmoved spectator, of course, but one at least not moved by *our* wants and needs. It is even compatible with the claim that at least some things have value regardless of their relation to the wants and needs of any observer, however unlikely that might seem on other grounds.

In none of these ways, then, does physicalism imply that the world is neutral and cannot endow our lives with meaning. On the contrary, in view of the determinacy of valuation, the world is laden with value and hence with meaning, whether or not we know what the values are and which facts just suffice to determine them.

(iv) If the reason or reasons for our existence are found in ourselves, how can they have the force of truth? And if they do not have the force of truth, how ultimately can they endow our lives with meaning? So we asked, in effect, back in §2.0. But now we are in a position to see that the purposes of our lives do indeed have the force of truth, even if they are "found in ourselves." They have the force of truth in the sense that what they ought to be is determined by the facts, even though—if we assume that our purposes are found in ourselves—the determining facts must include some facts about our wants and needs. Thus the purposes our lives ought to have do correspond with the facts, in the sense of §6.3, and the facts with which they correspond are those that just suffice to determine them. What more by way of having the force of truth could one want?

But there are other senses in which our purposes are perhaps to be found in ourselves. One is that even assuming there is an objective fact of the matter as to what purposes or ends are worthwhile, still we must commit ourselves to them and make them our own. In order for the ends to be effective in our lives, we must in this sense give them their value. Even purposes laid down for us by God would be inert unless we made them our own. So if we want our lives to be meaningful, we cannot discover the meaning; we must provide it.

The trouble here is in the last bit, the suggestion in effect that the meanings are not a matter of discovery and so could not have the force of truth. This does not follow from the obvious fact that in order for ends to be effective we must make them our own. What follows is only that when somehow we discover what the worthwhile ends are, still we have to address the motivational problem of how to commit ourselves to them. A certain end or purpose may have the force of truth (in the above sense of corresponding with certain natural facts), yet we might see that it does and still fail to act on it. Nor need our failure be due to any cynicism. States of depression, for example, often place us in this situation of seeing the truth but not acting. For one in such a state, everything may indeed be meaningless. But *this* meaninglessness is a matter of our being unable to commit ourselves to anything, or being unable to make any purpose our own. It is not a matter of there being no such purposes to be discovered to which we may commit ourselves.

Clearly, certain moods and emotions are better than others for enabling us to make various ends and values our own. Therefore, it is reassuring to recall that the passions themselves can correspond with the facts, or at least their valuational components can, as can the matter of which passion we ought to have (§7.5). Nature may not be, in Melville's words, "her own ever-sweet interpreter," in the sense that the meanings of our lives and of things are derivable from or reducible to descriptions of nature and can therefore be read off from the descriptions. But it does not follow that, selecting as we please, we may read our own peculiar lesson according to our own peculiar mind and mood. For some of our moods correspond with the facts and some do not; so, too, for the meanings or lessons it might please us to draw.

(v) Sometimes absurdity or meaninglessness is identified with endless futility. Sisyphus was condemned by the gods to an existence meaningless in this sense. Each time he heaves the boulder nearly to the top, the gods cause it to roll down. The intended end of the activity—getting the thing to the top—can never be achieved, thanks to a fact about the world. Calling Dial-a-Prayer and arguing theology with the tape is futile in the same sense.

The myth of Sisyphus still moves us because we suspect that our own lives, even the whole career of humankind, might finally be no different. We witness endless cycles of birth and death, rise and decline, struggle and disintegration, all tending toward greater entropy, slowed here and there by enclaves of negative entropy, but sliding inexorably toward ultimate chaos. Yet Sisyphus "would have frustrated the Gods if he could have given worth to his eternal task."[44] And one sure way to do this is to replace the normally intended end of the activity with an

[44]Joske, 260.

end that *can* be achieved, such as the activity itself. Indeed this is the rational thing to do[45] when the activity is inescapable and its normal end unattainable: treat the activity as an end in itself, to be embraced for its own sake or even regarded as just what we were put here to do. Even if the activity is not inescapable, either because suicide is an option or because other activities are, still the morally correct thing to do might well be not merely to reconcile ourselves to the activity but to learn to rejoice in it for its own sake. A reason is that in the circumstances, other people could be depending on us in such a way as to make suicide and the other activities, however tempting, far worse choices from a moral point of view than the Sisyphean activity.

Even when not easier said than done, making the activity itself the end sounds rather subjective. In one sense it is. To a degree, at least, my life would be outwardly unchanged. There I am at the same old routine, rolling boulders up the hill. The change is mostly inward, in my view of things and in my feelings—*mostly* inward, because such a change normally results in outward changes as well: in a lighter step, in a smile, in what I say to others. Still, the overall Sisyphean toil remains unchanged.

Unchanged though it may be, we should not conclude from this that "existence . . . is objectively meaningless"—that "the meaningfulness of life is from within us, it is not bestowed from without"[46]—if this means that there is no objective basis or ground with respect to which value judgments are correct or incorrect, including the judgment that we ought to embrace the Sisyphean activity itself as the end. Thanks to the determinacy of valuation, objective facts determine whether this judgment is correct. And the judgment often is correct, so that on such occasions there are facts for reason to discover that are the facts with which the judgment corresponds.

So long as making the activity itself the end is an option, we cannot say a life filled even with Sisyphean toil is necessarily futile. As defined four paragraphs back, a futile activity is one whose intended end or purpose can never be achieved, thanks to some fact about the world.[47] If the end is the activity, then clearly it can be achieved (so long as the activity can). If much of our life is futile, we ought at least have the grace not to blame reality for failing to provide a basis for human values, but ourselves for failing to adjust our ends. This too human failing, together with the presumption and hubris it involves, is less the stuff of absurdity than of old-fashioned tragedy.

(vi) Still the abyss yawns. Few of us want *all* our activities to be their

[45]Contrary to R. Taylor (1981), 144. Cf. Bennett.
[46]As R. Taylor (1981) concludes, 144, 150.
[47]Cf. Joske, 253.

own ends. And there is always the possibility that those further ends cannot be achieved, the possibility that all such striving will be for nought. Our "incurable desire to cast a shadow across the future"[48] is sure to be frustrated by eventual death and decay. But whether this desire eventually will be frustrated depends on how large a shadow we mean to cast, and how far into the future. If our ambition is radically to change the whole universe forever, then it is likely to be frustrated. Our chances of success are much better if the aim is to benefit, say, a few people as yet unborn, perhaps one's own children or grandchildren. So yes, it is possible that all our striving will be for nought. But this is not much more than a mere logical possibility for many of our strivings and becomes a probability only for the most ambitious ones. How human, and how banal, when ambition proves overweening, to blame something else—even the so-called absurdity of existence—rather than ourselves for absurdly Promethean intent.

Those who nevertheless want an absolute guarantee, not a mere probability, that the ends of their activities will not be frustrated had better learn to make all their activities their own ends. And anyway, who identified meaningfulness with risk-free existence? Those there are who prefer the exhilaration of life on a tightrope, or on the north face of the Eiger, alone, at night, and in winter. One could fall, but better such a fall than the secure, living death some call life. To one in such a mood, it is the risk-free existence that seems absurd.

(vii) For many, even the lessons of (i)–(vi) will not be enough. For we have been talking about "existence" mainly in two senses: existence as the sum of the activities that make up our lives, and existence as the totality of natural fact. But what about existence in the sense of the whole spatiotemporal universe? What meaning could *it* possibly have? If the universe is not the creation of God, or otherwise suitably related to something transcendent, isn't it absurd? And according to scientific naturalism, isn't the universe nothing but a collection of dust, gas, and galaxies wheeling in the void?

Even if the universe proves not to be suitably related to something transcendent, it does not follow that the universe is absurd. The universe might easily have a meaning—or meanings—in virtue of something else. For example, the totality of natural fact might suffice to determine that certain value terms are true of the universe—say, that it is beautiful, terrible, awesome, eerie, intriguing, astonishing, and more. The universe then would have meaning at least in the sense that it objectively has certain value properties.

[48]Joske, 254.

In addition, the universe could have meaning in the sense that it is the appropriate object of certain emotions—not only, on occasion, of terror or awe but of acceptance and even reverence. Even though the appropriateness of these and other emotions could not be read off from a mere description of the universe, in the sense of being derived from or reduced to such a description, still the appropriateness could be non-reductively determined by the description (§7.5). The nonreductive naturalist can even attribute meaning to the universe in the sense of purpose. Not that for naturalists (or many others) it has a purpose in the sense of intent, as do certain organisms. Nor will the naturalistically inclined philosopher say that some transcendent or supernatural being made it for a purpose. But the universe can still have a purpose or point in at least the following ways.

Recall yet again the solar marker in Chaco Canyon. Even if the slabs had been shaped that way by chance, rather than made by an intelligence, still they would have been a solar marker if accorded the role. That would have been their purpose in the Anasazi culture, what they were used for, their point. In like manner, whether or not the universe is made, it can be accorded the role of, say, (a) the symbol and source of truth, beauty, and goodness, if only because facts about its aspects or its parts determine such matters. We may go further and recall that by Chapter 3 the universe is also (b) the eternal, immutable, uncreated, independent, self-existent, explanatorily necessary First Cause of all that is. For many, (a) and (b) will be more than enough to justify according the universe the role of divinity—of such divinity, at any rate, as we were ever entitled to believe in or ever will be. Indeed, many would see (a) and (b) as more than enough to justify asserting that the universe *is* the divine, that it is all the divinity we need or ever really needed. And if we conclude that only the True Universe, not the manifest, is strictly the bearer of these properties of divinity, then we may treat the manifest universe as related after all to something transcendent, with respect to which we must refrain from positive predication (§3.5). In rough analogy with a solar marker, we could treat the manifest universe as a kind of God-marker, representing our present best attempt to limn certain aspects of the Universe beyond the universe. That then would be the purpose or point of the universe.

The next chapter develops these speculations further and explores the prospects of some other theisms, including the Judeo-Christian. Here we need only note that naturalism in general and physicalism in particular, so far from implying that the universe is nothing but a collection of motes in the void, can treat it as divinity—in the spirit at least of Spinoza—or as a marker of such divinity, and possibly in other ways as well. The hackneyed objection that no such religious value terms are found in or are reducible to scientific discourse about the universe is irrelevant. True, if we insist on comprehending the universe solely in terms reducible to the scientific, then, as Weinberg says, the more the universe seems comprehensible, the more it will seem pointless; and, as Baier says, science will be unable to find meaning or purpose in it. But the determinacy of valuation licenses comprehending the universe in irreducible value terms, in which we rightly express the meanings and purposes of and in the universe.

Viewing things *sub specie aeternitatis,* unless it just means abjuring any irreducible discourse (contrary to §7.5), does not vilify human endeavor or eliminate meaning. On the contrary, the description of things under the aspect of eternity determines meaning, value, purpose, and point. It determines these dimensions of "order in the drama of Time."[49] And if viewing ourselves *sub specie aeternitatis* means viewing humanity from some remote point in space or time, from which we seem but busy ants or flies of a summer, then we may reply that the correctness or incorrectness of the decision so to view ourselves is itself determined by natural fact. No doubt on occasion such a view is entirely appropriate, if only to deflate overweening pretension. But on other occasions it is completely inappropriate, as when it renders us incapable of making certain ends or purposes our own even though they are objectively worthwhile. Taking the measure of the measure of all things is no one-sided affair. The mood that comes over us when we view everything from afar does not always correspond with the facts, any more than does blinkered preoccupation with our petty aims.

[49]Wisdom, 207.

8 God

*If the atheist denies that God exists, he does so on the basis
of his own apprenticeship in the school of the transcendent.
He is almost obsessively preoccupied with what there is and
with the implications of . . . objectivity.*

—D. M. MacKinnon

8.0. Introduction

By now the present philosophy may seem physicalist in name only,
rejecting as it does virtually everything traditionally associated with
such views. Gone is the Democritean refrain, "Nothing but atoms and
the void exist, therefore our values are mere conventions." For we have
seen how the physical phenomena determine and thereby are laden with
value, so that in important senses existence is anything but meaningless.
Gone also is the notion that the nature of reality is material in the first
place. For we have rejected the very idea of *the* nature of things, emphasizing instead the irreducible plurality of faces of existence, none of
which enjoys unconditional priority over any other. Indeed we noted a
sense in which valuing is prior to characterizing some realm of phenomena as real, the material included, plus a sense in which the physical
phenomena manifest themselves in their own occasional insignificance
and in the occasionally far greater significance of other things.

Gone too is the belittling of secondary qualities and of emotions.
The latter can correspond with the facts, and the former, suitably construed, represent ways things are. We even admitted ineffable subjective
states, such as what it is like to be a bat, or to be the persons we are,
experiencing time and death as we do, and conscience and mystery. For
we were able to reject the view that everything real must be brought
under an objective description, just as we rejected any other doctrine of
universal reducibility. In this spirit we confirmed metaphor as among
the indispensable ways of expressing faces of existence; reduction to

literal discourse, let alone to aseptic precision, proved needless. Thus was each domain seen to enjoy its appropriate antonomy; there was no need to commit monopoly in any of its forms.

Gone finally is the idea that "all is becoming, all is changing, all is in passage out of the past and into the future, and so all causes and effects come and go—and all is mortal—and nothing else is real" (§3.4.5). Whatever may be the case with the familiar 3-world of common sense, the 4-universe—the whole of spacetime—is eternal in a fivefold sense: (i) it is not subject to becoming, to change, to process, or to corruption and decay; (ii) it is not in time and thus not to be dated as past, present, or future; (iii) it is a "tenseless" existent; (iv) its parts are not distinguished by being transiently past, present, future, or still to come, relative to one another; and (v) it is of such "duration" that it neither ceases to be nor comes into existence. In addition, it is the uncreated, explanatorily independent, metaphysically necessary, self-existent First Cause of all that is.

In these and other ways, then, did few things if any prove to be nothing but material things. Yet even though we can thus tighten our belts without narrowing our minds, the fact is that we have tightened our belts. That is, we have tightened our inventory of what there is to include only the mathematical-physical. Not everything is nothing but a physical or even a natural thing, yet everything is either a spatiotemporal sum of basic physical entities or (if sets exist) a set in some rank of the hierarchy of sets (INV, §4.1). Further, we have endorsed the physical discernibility of all discernibles (MND, §4.2), and the determination of all truth by physical truth (TT, §4.3).

When conjoined with a realism of the sort explained in §1.1, these three principles are the minimal theses characteristic of all versions of physicalism properly so-called. The present philosophy therefore is physicalist not in name only but in principle. And this means that despite rejecting so much traditionally associated with physicalism, the present view appears to threaten belief in the existence of God, for God seems nowhere to be found in its inventory of what there is. Indeed the present view could well be a *greater* threat to theism than traditional physicalisms, not despite rejecting so much but because of rejecting it. For so long as physicalism is reductive, monopolistic, antagonistic to much that is human, and so on, it will seem an obviously inadequate account; theists may well remain correspondingly undisturbed by what such a view would imply. But a nonreductive, nonmonopolistic physicalism of the present sort is not so easily dismissed; the usual objections—typically antireductive—are blocked.

Of course, there are nonphysicalist varieties of metaphysics that

might also succeed in avoiding reductive and other monopolistic pretensions, but they are likely to prove cold comfort to the theist. The
unifying entities posited by such a metaphysics must exist, yet in many
instances the claim that they do flunks a prerequisite for truth, typically
the objectivity prerequisite. Nor is it at all clear that the spirit of such a
metaphysics could be retained in any revision that does take full account
of contemporary knowledge of spacetime (§§1.5[vii], 3.4, 5.0). Even if
the prerequisites for truth happen to be satisfied, there are further hurdles. For one thing, the metaphysics must be able to unify all the domains of discourse, by means of its alleged unifying entities, in such a
way that truths about the latter determine the truths in the former. A
necessary condition of doing so is to unify the sciences. But it is exceedingly difficult, if not impossible, to argue persuasively that truths in the
various sciences are determined ultimately by anything other than physical truth. This is especially clear in the case of the natural sciences. What
is it that determines, say, the truths of chemistry, if not truths of physics? And as regards the latter, it is even more difficult to argue, in
anything approaching convincing detail, that such truths themselves are
determined by further truths. In detail, what connective theory (or
happy family of such theories) would enable one to infer that and how
the specifics of quantum physics or of general relativity are determined
by particular truths about the alleged unifying nonphysical entity or
entities? And what particular truths are these?

At every step of the way, the theist will be haunted by the realization
that nonreductive physicalism very likely has already succeeded in unifying the sciences. The theist must therefore argue extra hard for the
extra entities, on pain of violating Occam's injunction against multiplying them beyond necessity. One such argument might be that the extras
are required for unifying the domains beyond the sciences. But if we
have learned anything in this essay, it is that they are not required.
Meaning, metaphor, emotions, values, ineffable subjective states, and
more were all appropriately accounted for. Indeed religious discourse
might prove to consist in the expression of such matters. If so, there is
no reason why religious truth could not itself be determined by physical
truth. The only question would be which religious sentences are true,
and in particular whether they include 'God exists'.

Suppose, however impossible it may seem, that some nonphysicalist
theory clears all these hurdles. There remains another. Unless God can
be found somewhere in its inventory of what there is, such a theory
would appear to be of little use to theists. Of course, this presupposes
that the existence of God is at least in part a matter of what there is, and
that belief in God's existence is warranted only to the extent that God

appears in some warranted inventory. Yet this is a false presupposition, according to certain theists. Their idea is that theism is a matter not of what there is but of how we ought to talk about it and how we ought to see it. The idea thus has affinities with the point in §§7.0–7.4 that metaphysics often is more a matter of values than of what there is, and that metaphysical disputes often are disputes about what discourse ought to take what sort of priority on what occasion for what purpose. Theists believe that their discourse about God often ought to take precedence and in any case is true, though as lately noted, its truth need not have implications for what there is but rather for how to value it. If so, looking for God in any inventory is misguided, as is supposing that Occam's razor has very much to do with ascertaining the truth of God-talk.

We return to this idea in §8.2 and explore it further. Meanwhile, let us assume that a metaphysics is of direct use to the theist only if God can be found somewhere in its inventory. The problem then is not only that there is no guarantee that the inventory will include God, but that many theists themselves deny that any plausible contemporary metaphysics presents an inventory in which God can be found. Such theists include those who reject *any* God of the philosophers. Yet they also include those who base their rejection not on blanket condemnation of the relevance of metaphysics to theology but on particular problems involved in construing the alleged existent as God. It is in this spirit that many theologians emphasize the particular problems involved in construing something in Whitehead's inventory as God, or in so construing Heideggerian Being, or whatever.

On the other hand, suppose God is explicitly mentioned in the inventory. Then we must ask how God got there. What line of reasoning could warrant such a posit? It cannot be any of the traditional arguments for the existence of God. They are too flawed, individually and taken together. The cosmological or first-cause argument presupposes the Principle of Sufficient Reason, among other things. But PSR is fatally vulnerable to the criticisms in §2.4 if not also to others, and the remaining presuppositions too are flawed. The design argument, on behalf of a divine explanation for the order and adaptation we see around us, presumes that there is no equally good alternative explanation in purely natural terms, though of course there is; and some of the argument's other assumptions are just as problematic (in particular, the assumption that the alleged designer is identical with God). The ontological argument involves the notion of a being that exists by the necessity of its own nature; the argument therefore falls prey to objections of the sort sketched in §2.2 against this notion and against the kind of necessity it presupposes, and to others as well. If God is posited as the ground of morality, then to the usual objections we may add that morality already has an adequate ground, in the sense that moral truth is determined by natural fact. Likewise, if God is wanted for injecting meaning and purpose into an otherwise absurd world, we may add to the usual objections the fact that meaning and purpose were there all along, contained in the world in the sense of being determined by facts about it.

But suppose the line of reasoning for explicitly listing God in the inventory is none of these. Suppose instead that certain aspects of existence have so far found no explanation and that God is invoked to fill the explanatory gap. Here the trouble is threefold at least. PSR seems once again presupposed in the presumption that there must always be some explanation to be found. In addition, such a God-of-the-gaps typically has been vulnerable to unexpected advances in the relevant fields of knowledge as they fill the gaps with some nonsupernatural explanation, as so often they have.[1] Finally, in light of such advances and of the dynamic consilience of certain varieties of naturalism (the present one included), the inductive evidence favors the presumption that where there is indeed an explanation to be found, it will be in natural terms.

At this point, some theists concede that no line of reasoning warrants including God explicitly in any list of what there is. They then make a virtue of necessity: here is a matter not of mere reason but of faith. But we saw in §1.5 how one's faith, if it is to be true, must satisfy the logical prerequisites for truth. Defenders of the idea of certification of a belief by faith alone might well be right to the extent that there need be no positive line of reasoning sufficient to establish the belief's truth, or even to make it only probable. And they might rightly be encouraged in this view by the difficulties (if not downright failures) in all proposed criteria of truth (or at least in criteria of truth for religious assertions)—difficulties rehearsed in §1.3.[2] But they are wrong if they think we may be indifferent to the line or lines of reasoning involved in checking to see whether a belief satisfies the prerequisites. One's faith, however fervent, must be well-formed, be nonempty, have no false presuppositions, be self-consistent, be consistent with all other truths, have no false implications, and satisfy the objectivity or invariance prerequisite. Otherwise, it is not true.

For each of these prerequisites there are powerful arguments to the

---

[1]For an accessible account of how the gaps in physics may now all have been closed, see Davies.

[2]See also Popkin.

effect that theism flunks it. Even if theists can counter the arguments one by one, in the course of doing so their view gets revised, often in the direction of emptiness, as we noted in §1.5(iv) in connection with the problem of evil. The result is an increasingly complex, ad hoc set of defensive assumptions. One is reminded of nothing so much as the proliferation of epicycles and eccentrics in the waning days of Ptolemaic astronomy. Of course, staggering complexity may be tolerated in a view so long as no better is available. Yet for at least a century theism has been increasingly on the defensive, intellectually and philosophically, mainly because so many reflective people have come to suspect that there are better accounts of what there is.

Faced with all these difficulties, how might theists respond? They have four alternatives, logically speaking. Where theism conflicts with naturalism in general or physicalism in particular, they may (1) reject theism. Alternatively, they may (2) reject naturalism; probably this is the instinctive first choice of most theists. Their next choice usually is to try to show that there is no real conflict in the first place by (3) showing that naturalism and theism are not logically inconsistent with each other. Often this is attempted, in effect, when theists argue that there is no inconsistency between science and religion, and when they (or some of them) insist that the question of God is not a question to which Occam's razor could apply. But there is a more fruitful way of trying to show that there is no conflict, not by showing merely that the two views are not inconsistent but by (4) attempting a synthesis of the two, in which each enriches the other while correcting the other's occasional extremes.

Obstacles aplenty confront this fourth way, quite possibly insurmountable. All the same, theologians would be well advised to pursue it, for the very good reason that the other alternatives are so bleak. Alternative (1) is the bleakest of all, for theists. But even nontheists perhaps should concede that a wise and tolerant theism, if true, would be invaluable—or valuable enough, at any rate, that its rejection should be a matter of bitter regret for all concerned, however dull their sense of loss may have become with the passage of time. As regards (2), we have just been reviewing the strengths of nonreductive physicalism, plus corresponding weaknesses in other views. If these chapters do not establish the truth of some such naturalism, they nevertheless show how costly its rejection would be; few will have read this far only to turn back. As regards (3), all of us ought ultimately to be dissatisfied with the conclusion merely that there is no logical inconsistency between naturalism and theism. For we would want to know *why* they are consistent, despite so many appearances to the contrary, and we would want to know the nature of this deeper compatibility. We crave coherence and unity, a craving that can never be satisfied by mere logical consistency but ultimately only by some sort of synthesis, however uneasy and tentative.

What if the theologians believe no variety of naturalism to be true, including the present nonreductive, tolerant sort? Even then they ought to explore how far theism might incorporate such a metaphysics. The reason is that, true or not, naturalism is so widespread and deeply entrenched among philosophers and reflective laymen. For better or worse, it is the dominant view in some of the most influential parts of our culture. If theists hope even to gain a hearing for their view in an increasingly secular world, let alone persuade others, what better course than to explain and justify themselves in terms consistent with the naturalism they too assume (if only for the sake of argument)? Whatever the spiritual, emotional, and cultural sources of their beliefs—and whatever their justification in *theists'* eyes—theists need to present a rational apologetic that incorporates an austere contemporary naturalism. For it is late in the day, and theists may have no other hope of restoring their views to the influence which, if true, they so richly deserve. To decline the attempt would be as though Aquinas had proceeded without the Aristotelian-Ptolemaic system of the world.

Indeed our situation in many ways resembles that of the thirteenth century, when translation of the Aristotelian corpus presented theists with a science and philosophy evidently superior to anything yet at hand and threatened to shatter their picture of the world. In effect they too confronted the four alternatives above. Averroists adopted an analogue of the first: where scripture conflicts with Aristotelian-Ptolemaic science and philosophy—that is, with the naturalism of the day—scripture must yield. Bonaventure adopted an analogue of the second: in case of conflict the naturalism must go. Aquinas adopted what amounted to a middle path: evidently dissatisfied with such extremes and also with declarations of mere consistency, he strove to show how his theism could incorporate the seemingly hostile, newly translated world view. The result was the powerful synthesis we call Thomism.

Our own picture of the world, descended from the medieval, has been shattered not by recovery of ancient text but by discovery in our own sciences from Copernicus to Darwin and beyond, and by related blows from philosophy. One by one, religious claims have had to be abandoned or qualified, until it is unclear whether such claims have any content left at all. The impression often is of a series of rearguard actions in a losing battle, delaying the inevitable, perhaps, but little more. And beyond the matter of particular advances in particular sciences that conflict with particular religious claims, there looms the matter of the general explanatory power of scientific naturalism, as outlined and extended in these chapters—a power which, in view of Occam's principle, seems to leave no room for God in any plausible inventory of what there is. The sciences may well have no peer in ascertaining what there is, because of the organized and systematic way they hunt for the invariants in our perspectives, in line with the objectivity prerequisite. If so, then those who care about what there is and about the implications of objectivity have little choice, in their "apprenticeship in the school of the transcendent,"[3] but to absorb the teachings of an austere naturalism.

The moral seems clear. What the theologian requires above all is a simple, compelling theory of God, world, and us that does full justice to scientific naturalism—full justice in the sense of assuming that it is true and of living with its full implications. Far easier said than done, of course, but the obligation merely to try and, failing, to try again and again has been neglected for so long that it is no longer seen as an obligation, only as a quixotic ideal to which one might reasonably have aspired in the Middle Ages. Yet there is no more powerful way for the theologian to proceed, and a faith that seeks understanding would be well advised to seek its understanding, in this day and age, within some such framework of science and philosophy. Even the true believer probably should be satisfied with no less. The reason is that the most illuminating and long-lasting theologies of the past—Augustine's, say, or Aquinas's—were achieved not by denouncing or ignoring the best science and philosophy of their day, or even by presenting a theology merely not inconsistent with it, but by incorporating it into their rational theology as a framework within whose confines they could interpret and support the central theistic claims.

It would be absurd to suggest that the waning pages of this or any other book might rival the great theologies. What §§8.2–8.3 suggest are mere possibilities, though a true theologian might see fit some day to exploit them in full. The possibilities are connective theories, or rather sketches of them, presented in the same spirit as are theories in physics, a field in which it is not at all surprising to learn, for example, that "Bohr . . . doubted the [Heisenberg-Pauli] theory would be the great new revolution in physics because it was not sufficiently 'crazy.'"[4] Or consider the spirit in which Georgi and Glashow advance SU(5) as "the gauge group of the world" in an effort to unify all elementary-particle forces: "Our hypotheses may be wrong and our speculations idle, but

---

[3]MacKinnon, 168–169.
[4]Weinberg (1976), 13.

the uniqueness and simplicity of our scheme are reasons enough that it be taken seriously."[5] The speculations of §§8.2–8.3 are presented in the same spirit and are likewise revisionary rather than descriptive.[6] In any case, they have as their aim to beg no question against physicalists, other naturalists, or nominalists, but to accept their terms of the debate, if only for the sake of argument; and to show how, strictly within such limits, one might conceivably build a sound theism.[7] And what better basis is there for this sort of apologetics than physicalism? It can hardly be accused of multiplying entities beyond necessity, or of any other tender-minded loading of the dice in favor of theism. In this respect its minimal theses are uncompromising.

Despite the efforts of the chapters so far, to say nothing of what a whole pantheon of naturalists might add, many theists will remain doubtful not only about the truth of naturalism in general and its severe physicalist versions in particular but also about the truth of *any* "scientific image" of the world. Further, some will doubt not only the correctness of these views but whether it is advisable even to contemplate expressing theism within such a framework, for purposes of rational apologetics or any other purpose, however widespread or influential naturalism may be and however responsible for the intellectual component of rampant secularism. Let those who share these doubts read on.[8] For they can still enjoy the spectacle of seeing an (alleged) archenemy having to open the rear door to what he threw out the front. Or, to change the figure, little is so entertaining as seeing the devil quoted to scripture's purpose.

Atheists will voice the opposite extreme of reaction to the hypotheses and speculations of §§8.2–8.3. One of them, a distinguished professional philosopher, writes, "What happened to the sound judgment that has pervaded the book till now? Is there a crowd of theologians somewhere who need to be placated?" Another regards my treatment of theism as a reduction to absurdity of the idea that we currently understand either the relation of determination or the physicalism that presupposes it. Still another insists that it can only be illusory to believe that physicalism might allow for objective values, let alone for God, and

---

[5]Georgi and Glashow, 438.

[6]Strawson, xiii.

[7]In this regard the present chapter is a remote descendant of Post (1974).

[8]And also read Ross, 86–90, esp. 88: "In the light of the new scientific knowledge, the formulations of belief are reexamined [by the religious person] and found to convey elements which were given undue emphasis, elements not central to the belief required and guaranteed. . . . Gradually those elements are abandoned or rephrased and the original belief is recast. . . . That the expression of faith should occasionally adjust itself to the achievements of science is neither unexpected nor scandalous."

doubts that such values and God have anything more to be said for them than does phlogiston.

When one encounters this sort of reflex hostility, which is fairly widespread among professional philosophers and other intellectuals, it sometimes helps to be candid about one's motives. Mine are mixed, perhaps beyond unraveling. But one motive I do not have is the desire to defend theism at all costs. I have no such irreversible commitment. Instead, I have a detached stance that horrifies many of my theist friends. For among my motives the overriding one is, as I like to think, a dispassionate curiosity about what the best evidence, argument, and theory construction might allow us to believe. This is a philosopher's motive, not a theologian's (perhaps because "curiosity is insubordination in its purest form.")[9] Further, I believe that if the enterprise sketched in §8.2 does not succeed, or if no related attempt at a synthesis of theism and an austere naturalism succeeds, then the only alternative is atheism. The reason is that the other attempts to articulate and support theism, ranging from the classical arguments to various contemporary theologies, cannot survive the withering scrutiny of what I take to be the best of today's science and philosophy, a best that includes a minimal physicalist version of naturalism. Thus the failure, if it comes to that, of the contemplated synthesis of theism and physicalism, so far from being a reduction to absurdity of the latter, I would regard as a reduction to absurdity of the former.

Note in this connection that the theism entertained in §8.2, even if it were itself patently absurd, would be a *reductio* of the determination relation, and of the physicalism that presupposes the relation, only if the theism followed from the minimal physicalist theses. But it does not. In this respect there is a parallel with objectivism as regards values. The objectivism, we saw, does not follow from the minimal physicalist theses (unless it follows indirectly from realism as regards truth-value; §§6.2–6.3). Instead, it follows from them in conjunction with the assumption of Meta-Ethical Antirelativism—an assumption which in context is non-question-begging and for which there is sufficient independent evidence, as noted in §6.2.

Similarly, the theism entertained below follows from the minimal theses only in conjunction with a further assumption. But unlike MEA, this further assumption is problematic. It is a normative assumption to the effect that the objectively correct values include certain theistic values, as they are called in §8.2, together with the theistic ways of seeing and experiencing that they give rise to. For some forms of theism—

[9]Nabokov, 42.

some nontraditional ones—the assumption is perhaps not too difficult to defend (as we see in effect toward the end of §8.2). For traditional forms, including the Judeo-Christian, the assumption is very difficult to defend; §8.2 lists some of the possibly insuperable objections to it.

Thus in the end I leave open the question of whether the crucial normative assumption can even survive the trial by prerequisites, let alone be proved true, much as theoretical physicists generally leave the testing of their theories to their experimental brethren. But at least the crucial assumption is a normative one, requiring normative argument to the effect that the objectively true value judgments include the theistic ones. Complex and controversial though such argument is, it is objective in principle, thanks to the determinacy of valuation. Just as important, it is not a matter of what should be included in our inventory of what there is; hence in that sense it is not a matter of metaphysics or ontology, and not a matter to which Occam's razor could apply. The crucial normative assumption is perfectly consistent with the minimal physicalist theses and, when conjoined with them, forms a synthesis of physicalism and theism in which each enriches the other while correcting the other's occasional extremes. Provided, of course, the assumption is true.

8.1. Renaming the Whirlwind

> *Matter is the invisible wind which, sweeping for no reason over the field of essences, raises some of them into a cloud of dust: and that whirlwind we call existence.*
> —GEORGE SANTAYANA

> *Then the Lord answered Job out of the whirlwind, and said, Who is this that darkeneth counsel by words without knowledge?*
> —JOB 38:1–2

Traditions there are, or at least times and places, in which the name 'God' would be given, unhesitatingly, to the eternal, self-existent First Cause, whatever it should turn out to be—especially if in addition we must refrain from positive predications of it and if, nonetheless, truths about it or its aspects determine all value and meaning. In any such view the Universe beyond the universe is God (§§3.5, 7.6). Nor can materialists or other secular philosophers object that the name 'God', which among other things is a value term, reduces to no stretch of scientific discourse. For as repeatedly seen, reducibility is a red herring.

Many theists will raise the opposite sort of objection, to the effect that no such God is God enough. Missing, they will say, is God the personal Creator *ex nihilo,* utterly transcendent, who yet acts and is revealed in history and who in other ways differs from the gods of monists and pantheists. Let such theists hold their peace for the duration of this section, while we probe how far religious discourse about what there is might be warranted within an austere naturalistic framework, whether or not such discourse expresses what amounts to some favored version of Judeo-Christian theism. In effect we shall also be exploring ideas and methods that theologians might profitably lift from the previous chapters, whether or not they accept a naturalist's inventory of what there is. Even if the present philosophy ultimately threatens theism, it suggests promising new tools for philosophical theology.

First and foremost, perhaps, is the idea that there is no one way to name the whirlwind.[10] That is, there is no one vocabulary to which all others must or can be reduced, and none that enjoys unconditional primacy. Thus in particular there is nothing unconditionally prior about scientific description of things. Religious discourse about them can take precedence, on occasion, rather as there are times when "to feel about something may be the most penetrating way of knowing what a thing is" (§7.5). From the fact that on analysis a predicate proves to contain some reference to human emotions, it does not follow that the predicate cannot express an objective truth, or a way things are, or a face of existence.

For example, predicates that express the holiness of certain places and events, or the blessedness of certain persons and acts, or buoyant confidence in the goodness of creaturely existence despite all suffering, or the redeeming power of *agape*—all these predicates and more, if construed in the manner proposed in §7.5 for predicates for secondary qualities and for what things are like for a particular subject, could be true and could express a face of existence, one that smiles only on religious persons in response to their training in these ways of seeing and feeling. Such predicates may be construed roughly as of the subjunctive form "would be that way (or would be like that) for an appropriately religious person in appropriate circumstances." Often the things to which such predicates apply play a certain role in the life of a religious community, not unlike the solar marker in Chaco Canyon. Even if the things are not made or created, literally, but come to be only by chance (so far as any science is concerned), nevertheless, they satisfy the predicates if accorded the appropriate role. Even if everything is identical with some mathematical-physical entity or other—as the physicalist

---

[10]Gilkey (1969) is titled *Naming the Whirlwind.*

contends—nevertheless, everything is describable by some subjunctive religious predicate, and in that sense is a religious entity.

Why use religious predicates, subjunctive or otherwise? Evidently because there are purposes for which they are wanted that other kinds of discourse do not adequately serve. We can get some idea of these purposes by listing dimensions of meaning that religious discourse can have, occasionally perhaps all in one utterance. Such discourse—which includes parable, prayer, creeds, poetry, and more—may (i) suggest ways of interpreting certain experiences in light of a vision of meaningful existence; (ii) express ideals which, if lived up to, will save humankind; (iii) express answers to 'Why am I here?'; (iv) provide patterns for human action—not just abstract ideals, but vivid, actual exemplars; (v) use compelling, unforgettable imagery; (vi) arrest our attention by their strangeness, leaving us in sufficient doubt about their precise application to tease us into active thought, and also into active commitment and works; and so on. Particular religions tend to believe that their particular religious discourse, in their scripture or descended from it, serves these purposes better than any other.

The judgment that some particular religious discourse is the one called for on a given occasion clearly is in large part a value judgment. But theologians need no longer be bullied into holding that the decision to use or continue in some such language game or form of life is a matter ultimately of subjective preference or "faith," on the ground, say, that the decision is neither derivable from nor reducible to any totality of natural fact. Instead, they can borrow the idea of the determinacy of valuation and argue that this decision corresponds with the facts in the sense of §6.3, as indeed it might. In so doing they are presupposing, harmlessly, that the value terms involved obey both EP (no normative difference without some relevant natural difference) and MEA (only one distribution of truth-values over the normative judgments is correct; §6.1–6.2). For to the extent that their religion is a "historical" one, theists have always held that their values are relevant to this particular world, so that God's existence makes a difference to what this world is like, whereby a change in truth-value of a religious claim would change the truth-values of some nonreligious claims about the world.[11]

The determinacy of valuation has other theological applications.

---

[11]Cf. Bambrough, 89: "[Theists] must conceive the existence of God in such a way that it makes a difference to what *this* world is like, just as the beauty of a picture must be conceived in such a way that the beauty cannot be present or absent independently of any other properties of the picture." Also Hick (1983), 106: "The meaning of 'God exists' will be indicated by spelling out the past, present, and future difference which God's existence is alleged to make within human experience."

Thus consider the enduring problem of the relation between something's being God's command and the obligation we presumably have to obey it. In what way is this *ought* consequential upon the divine *is*?[12] The obligation evidently cannot be derived from or reduced to the fact that such-and-such is God's command; hence theologians usually have been driven to some form of intuitionism. They no longer need be, for they could try to show that such facts about God nonreductively determine the obligation. And they could try to argue further that the obligation obtains because of God's command, not the other way round, by trying to argue that the determination goes only in the one direction. If they succeed, they will have a solution to the Euthyphro problem of whether an action is right because it is loved by the gods, or vice versa.[13]

But the most striking theological application of determinacy might well be the following. If Quine is right, translation suffers indeterminacy, and there is no fact of the matter as regards translation. Many have wondered whether there is likewise no fact of the matter as regards religious assertions, if not exactly because of indeterminacy, then because of closely related failures. Theologians may now reply that in view of the determinacy of valuation, and in view of their own commitment only to religious claims whose terms obey EP and MEA, religious language thus construed suffers no such indeterminacy, whatever the fate of translation, since EP and MEA jointly entail determinacy.

Theologians could even afford to endorse the idea that all religious truths, not just those whose terms obey EP and MEA, are determined by physical truth. For they need not fear that God-talk must then be reducible at least in principle to physics or even to psychology, or to anything else. Further, having assumed the physical determination of religious truth, the theologian could about-ship and accord religious truth its appropriate sort of priority over the physical, however that priority might best be defined. Determination is not the only relation of priority or grounding, and not the only way to unify the domains. By no means is it always the most important. Relating things in terms of their value or meaning or purpose often takes precedence (§§7.0–7.3), and religious ways of so relating them are no exception. Religious ways of unifying the domains are to this extent as legitimate as any others.

Nor does the assumption that all religious truth is determined by physical truth preclude theologians from arguing that the latter is also determined by the former. That is, they could argue for codetermina-

---

[12]Cf. Rowe (1980), 637.
[13]Cf. Quinn, ch. 2.

tion, even though any such argument seems unlikely to succeed, in view of the challenge from §§5.0 and 8.0. The challenge is to present in detail the connective theory (or other argument) which would enable us to infer that and how the specifics of, say, quantum theory or general relativity are determined by particular religious truths. And what particular truths are these? Mere promissory notes will not do, and references to God's creating the world so as to obey these specific physical laws are too pat, even if they survive other criticism (such as presupposing PSR, or violating Occam's principle, or flunking a prerequisite, or whatever; §8.0). Nevertheless, unlikely though it seems that any argument will succeed in showing determination of physical truth by religious truth, stranger things have happened in philosophy, and theologians should not be deterred from trying.

The assumption that all religious truth is determined by physical truth is, by itself, consistent with an even more dramatic possibility. It is conceivable (if unlikely) that in the one distribution of truth-values over the religious sentences allowed by the distribution over the physical, truth gets assigned to a sentence that entails the existence of an entity not identical with any physical entity. If so, physical truth would determine that the physicalist's inventory is incomplete. It is in this spirit, perhaps, that traditional a posteriori arguments for the existence of God were conducted—such as cosmological arguments, which proceed from assumptions deemed true by medieval natural science to the conclusion that there is a being beyond those the science is about. Even though the traditional arguments fail, some other strategy might succeed in increasing our inventory of what there is by showing how physical truth itself determines that the expanded inventory is right. Physicalists believe that no such strategy will succeed, and for very good reason. Nevertheless, they should not close their minds to the possibility that there are more things in heaven and earth than are dreamt of in their philosophy.

Suppose theologians are warranted in assuming that all religious truth is determined by physical truth. Then not only can they absolve theology of the indeterminacy that translation allegedly suffers; they also gain the right to claim objectivity, or invariance, for religious truth. For if religious truth is determined by physical truth, which is a paradigm of the sort of objectivity here at issue, then religious truth is automatically determined by objective truth. Further, each religious truth thereby corresponds with a definite set of objective facts; namely, those that just suffice to determine the truth-value of the religious claim as true, even when we have (or can have) no idea just what facts those are. This world may be but canvas to the religious imagination, in the sense that no religious assertion about it is derivable from or reducible to physics or any other admittedly objective discourse. Nevertheless, there are better and worse ways of spreading such imagination on external objects, and some ways correspond with the facts, while others do not (§7.5). Religious names for the whirlwind ultimately are no arbitrary affair.

But is anyone warranted in assuming to begin with that all religious truth is physically determined? Physicalists are compelled to assume so, in view of what they see as the overwhelming evidence for their principle that *all* truth is thus determined. For them the real question, therefore, is whether religious sentences are strictly true-or-false in the first place, and if so, which ones are true. Mostly, physicalists have tended to agree that the key creedal sentences are true or false, and that those which imply there is a God are false.

Some physicalists, however, unduly impressed with the irreducibility of much if not all religious discourse, would reject such discourse as meaningless. Others, impressed by the fact that such discourse is value-laden and that values cannot be derived from facts, would likewise consign it to the flames. Still others are dismayed by the highly imprecise and metaphorical nature of much religious discourse, and by any mention of ineffable subjective states. In all these cases, the conclusion drawn usually is atheism, even if the relevant discourse (including 'God exists') is supposed to be strictly neither true nor false, and there is supposed to be no fact of the matter that the discourse could express.

And in all these cases the opening gambit is a mistake. Irreducibility is beside the point; valuation is physically determinate; metaphorical truth is also thus determinate, as is the factual ground of any metaphorical sentences that are strictly neither true nor false (§5.3); imprecision is no bar to truth or to determination (§4.4); and ineffable subjective states fit quite respectably into the overall program (§5.4). The physicalist therefore is better off conceding truth-or-falsity to religious assertions, and along with it their determinacy. The only question then is which ones are true, and in particular whether they include 'God exists'.

Theologians, of course, are not compelled to assume that religious truth is physically determined. That is, they are not compelled to do so if they are entitled to reject the principle that *all* truth is so determined. In §8.0 we reviewed some of the obstacles to rejecting it. Here we have been listing the advantages to theologians of accepting it, plus other ways it need not be so stifling to their enterprise as one might have thought. If the principle is true, then all we are and all we can hope to be we owe to the disposition of physical entities. Yet little of what we are and can hope to be is physically or even scientifically expressible; much of it can be named only with the help of discourse that we must confess is religious.

There are other ideas that theologians could borrow from earlier chapters. If attacked for their talk of eternity, of self-existence, of first causes, or of unexplained explainers, they could reply *"Tu quoque"*: such talk turns up in the enemy's camp as well (Chapters 2–3). If chided for their talk of mystery, of transcendence, of things beyond, or of a *via negativa,* again they could point to parallels in the hostile camp (§§3.2, 3.5) that flow from the transcendent notion of truth celebrated in Chapter 1. And if charged with committing monopoly in some form, they could reply that yes, some of their more traditional colleagues are guilty, just as many traditional metaphysicians are (§§5.0, 7.1), but that they themselves need not be; there is, in their view, no such thing as *the* way God is but many ways, and each domain of true discourse about God, including what is sound in each religion, expresses a way God is. Tolerance and ecumenism would therefore have a solid basis in metaphysics (§§7.3–7.4), as well as in epistemology (§§1.3–1.4).

Moreover, there are important senses in which theologians and some philosophers are right when they conclude that we may properly condemn a "total vision of the world" if its moral implications are unacceptable.[14] This runs counter to the modern temper, according to which we ought first to establish a satisfactory world-view, then read off its moral implications, if any. We are supposed to attend first to neutral fact, then to values, let the chips fall where they may.

The facts, however, are not neutral but laden with value. Whatever our subjective response to the facts may be, and whatever our interpretations of or projections onto them, they determine that certain values are correct instead of others. And this means that in principle, at least, normative arguments can count against world-views. For if the facts are as the world-view describes, then certain value judgments J_i correspond with those facts, and others do not (§6.3). Hence a normative argument to the effect that one or more of the J_i must be false would impugn the world-view's claim to describe the facts. In this sort of case, values would enjoy a sort of evidential priority over facts.

Which domain of truth—which vision of the world—ought we to employ if we are to see each other from a correct and sufficiently rich moral point of view? The theologian believes that only a theistic vision of the world and us can do justice to the uniqueness and sanctity of each individual life, to the tensions between duty or virtue and the pursuit of

[14]Cf. Mitchell, 120, 158.

one's own happiness, to the necessity of love and forgiveness, and to much more, including not least the felt objectivity of these and other imperatives.[15] A correct and sufficiently subtle morality requires a certain sort of "seeing-as," according to the theologian, a seeing-as that involves, among other things, seeing us and the world as created, for a purpose, by a loving and transcendent God. Persons, the world, and morality thus become a kind of "God-marker" (§7.6). They are not nothing but natural and secular phenomena.

This line of thought resembles certain arguments from morality for the existence of God. Yet there are crucial differences. Theologians would not here be inferring from the requirements or presuppositions of morality to the existence of some being not already included in a rationally warranted inventory of what there is. Instead of thus inflating ontology to save morality, theologians would be inferring from what they believe are the requirements of a correct and fully adequate morality to the correctness of a certain way of seeing and talking. Then they could rightly point out that the truth of the theist's discourse, and the correctness of the theist's seeing-as, would not be a matter of extra entities (no more than seeing a person as having inalienable rights compels us to look for entities—the rights—over and above persons and their nonnormative properties and relations). Hence there is no question of entities to which Occam's razor might apply.

But how would theologians be entitled to infer in the first place that their seeing-as is correct or true? Insofar as it is based on values, isn't it *merely* a seeing-as, with no basis in reality? This objection is nearly unstoppable so long as values cannot be appropriately grounded in facts. If they cannot, then morals will always arguably be incapable of objective truth, and we cannot safely infer from them to the objective truth of whatever they presuppose or require. But moral values *are* appropriately grounded, via their determinacy. There is a fact of the matter about them, and we may speak of the particular facts with which a moral judgment corresponds. And this quality of there being a fact of the matter is inherited by whatever the moral values entail.

Hence, *if* theologians are right about what is the correct morality and about what it entails, then their seeing-as is correct, and much of their God-talk is true and forms a domain of truth. Its truth would be determined by natural fact, and ultimately by physical fact, if physicalism holds. Yet the correctness of their seeing-as, and its involvement with the moral point of view, would mean that a mathematical-physical seeing-as cannot be monopolistically true (as we know anyway, from §§4.6, 7.3). There would be many occasions on which religious dis-

---

[15]Cf. Mitchell.

course and seeing or experiencing take priority—at least those occasions when we ought to adopt a fully adequate moral point of view. Social creatures that we are, such occasions may be expected vastly to out-number those in which a purely mathematical-physical seeing-as would be appropriate and often to outweigh them in other ways as well. Physicalism, therefore, conjoined with a certain view of morality and of what it requires, would direct us on many occasions to use religious names for the whirlwind. The trouble, of course, is that this view of morality and of what it requires could very well be wrong.

8.2. God as Not the Value of a Variable

Do we have in theistic experience mere *projection? Or do we have a projection matched by an objectively existing God?*
—R. W. HEPBURN

To be is to be the value of a variable.
—W. V. QUINE

Either God is the value of a variable or not. This is to say, nearly enough, that either God is in the complete, correct inventory of what there is or not. If God is supposed to be in the inventory, then automati-cally Occam's razor is relevant, and theists encounter all the probably insuperable difficulties rehearsed in §8.0, both in arguing for God's existence and—more significantly—in defeating arguments against God's existence, especially the argument from evil and arguments to the effect that the hypothesis is explanatorily impotent or at least super-fluous. On the other hand, if God is not in the inventory, hence not the value of a variable, then we seem compelled to conclude that there is no God.

This is the thinking theist's basic dilemma. Another way to put it is that either 'God' refers or it does not. If we suppose it refers, then Occam's razor is very keen. But if it does not refer, how could talk of God be true? The price we pay for denying that Occam's razor has anything to do with ascertaining the truth of God-talk, hence for deny-ing that theism is in this way a matter of what there is, is to deprive 'God' not merely of any clear referent but of any referent at all. It then seems impossible for assertions like 'God is the maker of heaven and earth' to be true, since their subject-term fails to refer. Such would-be assertions appear to be in the same boat as 'The present king of France is bald'.

Despite the disaster that such reference failure seems to entail, it is understandable why some theologians insist, though not always ex-plicitly, that the question of God is not a question to which Occam's razor could apply, indeed not strictly a question of extra entities at all. For the insistence does justice to the theist's tendency to declaim, "God is not this, not that, indeed not any*thing*—not any mere being, entity or existent." It is also thereby a powerful bulwark against idolatry, or the identification of God with some limited being or aspect of existence. It thus emphasizes in perhaps the strongest possible way God's transcendence, as opposed to the status of mere beings, or even as opposed to the status of the Gods of the philosophers. And it helps account for what theists often see as a deep difference between science and religion, in virtue of which there really is no conflict between them: science asks questions to which Occam's principle is relevant; religion does not.

In addition, the denial that theism is in this way a matter of what there is enables theologians to steer clear of abstract metaphysical disputes, including the traditional arguments for and against the existence of God, and to concentrate instead on articulating and practicing the form of life to which they belong. This will involve, among other things, doing kerygmatic theology, or explaining the group's religious language-game, replete with its metaphors, myths, models, and paradigms, which not only express but give rise to certain ways of acting and of seeing-as.

Normally, the latter include seeing heaven and earth as made by God. But how could this seeing-as be correct, or based on fact, if it is not *true* that God made heaven and earth? And to repeat, how can the latter be true if 'God' fails to refer? If theists have no answer, they are stuck with a form-of-life relativism—unless they retreat to the other horn of their basic dilemma and suppose after all that 'God' does refer, hence that God is the value of a variable, even if it is an incompletely describable value, perhaps to the extent of being describable only via negative predication.

Is there some way a theologian might try to argue that God-talk *is* objectively true, even though 'God' not only has no clear referent but has no referent at all? Indeed there is. Toward the end of §8.1 we saw what in effect are its outlines. To begin with, no law of logic requires an assertion's subject-term to refer, even when the assertion is to be true (or false). Counterexamples abound. There are no point-masses, frictionless surfaces, objects free of all perturbing influences, or other ideal objects.[16] Yet many a truth in physics mentions such things, as do textbook paradigms like "A perfectly smooth elephant of negligible girth is rolling down an inclined plane. . . ." Nor need there be any entities called duties, rights, virtues, or the Good, over and above persons and

---

[16]Quine (1960), 249.

their natural properties and relations. Yet it can be true that a certain duty is painful, or a certain right inalienable, or the Good unattainable, and so on. Hence God-talk could be true even if its subject-term fails to refer. Its surface grammar could be one thing, its depth grammar quite another.

But in what could the truth of God-talk consist, if not in a subject's possession of a property? One answer, perhaps the only one, is that ultimately its truth consists in or at least is based on the objective correctness of certain values and of a way of life. The God-talk, or much of it, could be a way of expressing the objectively correct values (as we see further below). Or it could be a way of expressing a vision of ourselves and the world which the values require us to preserve, a vision without which the way of life would disintegrate (roughly as morals disintegrate when we see each other always as an It, not a Thou). Thus the God-talk could express a unified complex of seeings-as, whose objective correctness is based on the objective correctness of the values and of the way.

So long as the fact-value gap is held to be unbridgeable, the values and the way of life will seem in the last analysis to be arbitrary. But the gap is bridged, granted EP, MEA, and the consequent determinacy of valuation. There is a fact of the matter as regards values and forms of life and, therefore, a fact of the matter as regards the kinds of seeing-as entailed by them. By so much would our theologian's task be made easier. Something else would make it nearly as hard as ever. One would still have to argue that the theistic values and form of life are indeed among the true ones. And one would still have to show that they require a theistic complex of experiencing and seeing-as— not at all easy to do if the values allegedly requiring the theistic experiencing and seeings-as are supposed to be strictly moral values (§8.1). It is not at all clear that theistic seeings-as are required in order to do justice to the uniqueness of each individual life, to the tensions between duty and happiness, to love and forgiveness, to the felt objectivity of these and other imperatives, and so on. And this is unclear even though the moral language in question evolved within the Judeo-Christian theism present at the creation of much of our culture.

Suppose it is indeed impossible to show that strictly moral values commit us to theistic experiencing or seeings-as. Even so, the theologian could try to show that there are further kinds of objectively correct values that do so commit us—values of a more nearly religious sort. If there are, then the God-talk could be true even though 'God' fails to refer. For the talk could express either these further correct values or a vision of things required by the values and by the way of life based on them. In either case, the theologian would be engaged not in covert metaphysics, inflating ontology to save the way, but in a variety of normative argument—complex and controversial, yet no less objective in principle for all that.

Still, what about the very assertion that God *exists?* Or that *there is* a God? How could such assertions be true if 'God' fails to refer? Any theism worthy of the name must assert or at least presuppose that God exists, that there is a God. Yet to believe God exists is surely to believe something about what there is. It is to believe God is, hence in effect that God is the value of a variable.

Our theologian would have but one reply here. We must consistently treat 'God exists' or 'There is a God' as something other than an assertion to the effect that 'God' refers or that God is in the complete, correct inventory of what there is. One possibility, probably the strongest, is to treat 'God exists' ('There is a God', 'God is', etc.) as a kind of *meta*-assertion, to the effect that the theist's God-talk *is true*—namely, the God-talk that expresses the experiencing, seeings-as, and values required by the form of life to which the theist belongs. And as noted, provided the form of life and its values are correct, the God-talk is indeed true, and objectively so.

But doesn't treating 'God exists' this way amount to conferring truth on 'God exists' on the dubious ground that even though there is no such thing as God, still the sentence is true because all it means is that it is good or useful for people to see the world as if there were? This objection is beside the point on at least two counts. First, the contemplated theory does not use or imply the clause 'even though there is no such thing as God'. The reason it does not is contained in the parenthetical in the previous paragraph: the sentences 'There is a God', 'God is', and so on, are all to be treated the same way as 'God exists': namely, as meta-assertions to the effect that the theist's God-talk—including this selfsame God-talk, such as 'There is a God', 'God exists', etc.—is true. They are not to be treated as assertions to the effect that God is in the inventory, and (equivalently) not to be translated by the Quinean objectual existential quantifier. Thus the contemplated theory does not say 'Even though there is no such thing as God' but says rather 'Even though God is not in the inventory of what there is, hence not the value of a variable and not a matter to which Occam's razor could apply, the God-talk is true'. This is just like saying, correctly, that even though duties, rights, and the like are not entities, hence not values of variables and not things to which Occam's razor could apply, still talk about such things is true, as when we assert that we have certain duties and rights, or even that there are such duties and rights (§6.0).

Second, even within the theory, 'God exists' does not mean it is good or useful for people to see the world as if there were a God (no more than 'There are rights' means it is good for us to see the world as if there were). Instead, it means the God-talk is *true,* meaning true *period,* objectively true, as 'true' has meant ever since §1.1. And such truth could easily be independent of, hence transcend, what is useful or "good for us," in the usual sense of this phrase. The theory treats 'God exists' not as a meta-assertion to the effect that it is good for us to see the world as if there were a God, but rather as a meta-assertion that the God-talk is true, hence that it is objectively correct to see the world as appropriately related to God—whether or not doing so is perceived to be in our self-interest (even our long-term self-interest) and, perception aside, whether or not it is in our self-interest. Thus the theory does not amount to a "philosophy as if," according to which viewing the world as if there were a God is a pragmatic fiction; the God-talk need not be pragmatic and is no fiction. Nor does the theory force us to ask, "Why on earth is it objectively good for people to see the world according to a theistic mythology?" But it clearly does force us to ask whether theistic seeings-as and values are objectively correct, and how we could ever know. The assumption that they are is the problematic normative assumption mentioned in §8.0. We return to it and its troubles below.

Meanwhile, note that if the assumption is true, then there is a sense in which a theologian could plausibly argue that in theistic experience we do not have *mere* projection. Rather, "we have a projection matched by an objectively existing God." True, in all valuation and seeing-as we have projection, just as we do in emotion (§7.5), if only in the sense that what the correct values are, and the correct seeings-as, cannot be reduced to or derived from natural fact, hence not read off from it. But thanks to the determinacy of valuation, some of the values and seeings-as (and emotions) are objectively correct and some are *mere* projections. *If* the theologian can make good on the complex normative argument just mentioned, then the theistic values and seeings-as—the theistic experience—are not mere projections, but are matched by an objectively existing God, in the sense that the God-talk is true and indeed objectively so, via the determinacy of valuation.

Unfortunately, some of the required seeings-as seem inconsistent with the lessons of an austere naturalism. For example, how is it possible to see the universe as created when §3.2 tells us that it is not? The argument there was that since there is nothing not part of the universe, and since a creator would have to be something not part of the universe, the universe is not even the sort of thing that could have a creator. However, to deny that the universe is created, in this sense, is to deny that there is any being outside the universe who stands in the causal relation "creator of" to the universe, on the ground that there is nothing outside (§3.2). Hence *this* idea of creation presupposes that a creator must be in the inventory of what there is. But this is just what our imagined theologian denies. Therefore, the account of creation, whatever precisely it comes to, does not imply that the universe is created in the sense rejected in §3.2. Hence there is at least no inconsistency between the two. Our theologian's intended account of creation involves no extra entities but is valuational through and through. Presumably, to see the universe as created *ex nihilo* is, among other things, to see what there is as essentially good, not as meaningless or absurd, and to see our lives as having a certain meaning and destiny dependent not on our transient purposes but on invariant and irreducible if sometimes mysterious imperatives about faith, hope, and love.[17] Or so our theologian may hope to make clear.

Reconstructions of religion in naturalistic terms are nothing new. Mostly, they do not pretend to be versions of theism. When they do, their strategy has been to identify God with nature or one of its aspects. Julian Huxley, for example, identifies God with the forces of nonhuman nature.[18] Huxley is therefore vulnerable to the charge that 'God' is just another name for something with few or none of the properties of true divinity. And any such view is reductive, as are all identity theories properly so-called (§4.0). We would have to say that God is nothing but the forces of nonhuman nature.

The theology we have been imagining is open to no such charge. In it, 'God' is not just another name for some aspect of nature, or for anything else. For 'God' does not refer, is not in that sense a name, and God therefore could not be nothing but such-and-such. By the same token, the theology is neither pantheist nor monist. For it does not identify God with anything, not even with the universe as a whole. And it accords truth to 'God is the maker of heaven and earth', which is incompatible with pantheism and with monism (where both are taken to entail that it is never correct to value or see what there is as created, on the ground that doing so would imply a dualism). Because the theology assigns truth to the theist's characteristic creedal sentences and falsity to the pantheist's, it is a version of theism, not pantheism.

This is so despite the fact that the theology is to be constructed within a naturalistic framework, and indeed within a physicalistic one. For nowhere need we multiply entities beyond the physical or deny that

---

[17]Cf. Gilkey (1965), 23, 35, 72, 77–78, 150, 190, 204.
[18]Huxley.

all truth is determined by physical truth. On the contrary, we would be entitled to say that such truth determines that the theist's God-talk also is true *and frequently takes precedence.* Or rather, we would be entitled to say this *provided* the difficult normative argument mentioned above is sound—the argument to the effect that certain values and ways of life of a moral and religious sort are among the true ones, and that their pursuit requires a theistic complex of seeings-as, in which the universe is seen as created *ex nihilo* by a being at once personal yet transcendent, and in which certain events are experienced as revelatory, as miraculous, and so on.

Isn't there high tension between such God-talk and a purely naturalistic account of the world? Indeed there is, but again no inconsistency. The tension derives mainly from two sources. One is the habit of supposing that a naturalistic metaphysics (or indeed any metaphysics), if true, must be monopolistically or exclusively true. But no discourse enjoys monopoly over another (in any of the senses from §§4.0, 4.6). So naturalistic metaphysics is not exclusively true, true though it is. Religious domains of truth not only can coexist with it but can and frequently do take precedence. Yet entrenched habits die hard, especially the habit of supposing there is such a thing as *the* way things are, some one ultimate face of existence. So we continue to feel a tension between naturalism and assertions about God. In due course the tension will disappear, with the disappearance of monopolistic metaphysics and the rise of pluralism, or so our theologian may hope.

The second source of tension, and much the more intractable, is the habit of supposing that God-talk can be true only if 'God' refers to a being beyond any naturalist's inventory of what there is. The habit is so strong that many may never be able to break it. For it is rooted in the very grammar of much God-talk—in the surface grammar, subject-predicate in form, according to which to assert something about God is to ascribe a property to a subject, if not exactly to what the tradition called a substance or for that matter to what was called an essence. Construing God-talk in this subject-predicate manner may fairly be called a form of literalism. An analogue in morals would be to construe talk about virtues, duties, and rights as talk literally about entities. An analogue in physics would be to search for a perfectly smooth elephant of negligible girth.

The advantages of outgrowing such subject-predicate literalism in theology are plain. To repeat, doing so would accord with the theist's tendency to resist identifying God with this or that, would thereby help thwart idolatry, would thus emphasize powerfully the divine transcendence, would help account for key differences between science and religion, would bypass abstract metaphysical disputes about what must be in the inventory of what there is, and would thereby pave the way for theologians to argue for the objective truth of God-talk in the manner sketched above—all without violating the physicalist's account of what there is. It therefore seems well worth the sustained effort it would take to break the habit of subject-predicate literalism via repeated exercises in self-conscious intellectual tact. "Habit is habit," as Mark Twain says, "and not to be flung out of the window by any man, but coaxed downstairs a step at a time."

Theologians and others have worried that the alternative to construing God-talk literally is vague abstraction and ultimately emptiness. But at least as regards subject-predicate literalism, according to which 'God' must refer, we need not worry. As seen, God-talk could well be objectively, solidly true even when 'God' refers to nothing. But if it is thus true, then the nonemptiness prerequisite is satisfied (§1.5[ii]). And if the truth of the God-talk consists in expressing certain objectively correct values (including the value of certain seeings-as), then, roughly speaking, the content of such talk is the content of those values. Since the values in question are widely acknowledged to have implications that are specific and concrete, the content of the God-talk ultimately would be anything but abstract and vague. In some sense it would be at least as rich and detailed as the form of community it is meant both to reflect and to sustain.

Some other kinds of literalism depend on this one; if it goes, they go. For example, just as creation is commonly thought of as a causal relation between God and world, miracles are thought to be the result of God's causal intervention in the world. A certain event is seen as specially related to God's activity and plan, hidden though the latter may be. The believer may say of the event, "Here God made the world" or "Here God acted to save a life (or the Israelites, or the true church, or . . .)," or "Here God acted to authenticate the Commandments," and so on. Construed literally, this implies that there is a being referred to by 'God' who stands in a causal relation with the event in question. And the further presumption is that the laws of nature were thereby created and later momentarily broken, suspended, or otherwise overridden. Who created and assures the regularity of events can also interrupt.

There is little doubt that the surface grammar of assertions about creation and divine miracles implies some such standard account of both. And on any such account, belief in miracles must seem mere superstition from the point of view of naturalism and, naturalism aside, from the point of view of modern theories of rational evidence (as Hume in effect argued long ago). But if 'God' does not refer, then it does not refer to a supernatural being who creates and overrides natural laws via some mysterious causal activity. The theologian is free to give a different account of the miraculous.

At this point it is customary to object that if miracles are not literally violations or suspensions of natural laws or regularities, then to call something a miracle is merely to report one's response to it as astounding, wondrous, or a sign, and perhaps to urge others so to respond as well. Since this is a subjective matter, the objection continues, we cannot say that a miracle is a miracle regardless of whatever anyone happens to believe about it; nor can we say of the miraculous event that it somehow transcends nature. So much for the "demythologizing" of miracle-talk.

Once more the determinacy of valuation is strategic. Here it allows us to deny that subjectivism is the only alternative to an account of miracles as violations of lawlike regularities. For we could argue that calling an event a miracle is to engage in a certain kind of seeing-as required by the theist's form of life, and that seeing the event this way is objectively correct, determined by natural fact. Thus a miracle would be a miracle regardless of what anyone happens to believe about it, since there would be a fact of the matter as regards the value judgments involved when the believer says, "Here the living God of faith acted in the world." And because calling something a miracle would be a matter of values and seeings-as, then whether the miraculous event could be explained by the sciences, as perhaps typically it can be, would be irrelevant. Miracle-talk would be not a kind of inverse physics, not even metaphysics, but valuational through and through.

The miraculous event would "transcend nature," on this account, at least in the twofold sense that its property of miraculousness would be expressible by no scientific description and that no discoveries in the sciences could tell us whether or not it is a miracle. Instead, we would have to engage in a kind of religious normative inquiry, complex and controversial but objective in principle nonetheless, thanks to the determinacy of valuation. Hume's doubts about miracles would thus have been met, not as one might have expected, but by overcoming his seemingly unrelated doubts about determining *ought* from *is*.

Other kinds of literalism that depend on subject-predicate literalism are not far to seek. Like literalism with respect to miracle-talk and creation, they mostly presuppose that there is a being who stands in a supernatural causal relation with the rest of what there is. Thus talk of God's power—which bears on the problem of evil—usually is construed as implying (among other things) that there is a being referred to by 'God' who stands outside the natural order but who could intervene to prevent pain and suffering if and when appropriate. But if 'God' does not refer, then it does not refer to a being who, by suspending the regular course of events, could intervene to prevent pain and suffering, whatever the surface grammar suggests. Talk of God's power would have to be construed in some other way, as were creation and miracle-talk, and probably along roughly similar lines. Whether this eventually would yield a solution to the problem of evil (as I suspect) is a matter we may leave to any theologian so bold as to undertake completing the strategy outlined in this section, according to which God is not the value of a variable, and the truth of God-talk is a matter of the objective correctness of certain values and seeings-as.

The main problem for this strategy is to make good on the difficult, controversial, normative argument to the effect that the theistic values and seeings-as are among the true ones, and that they frequently take precedence over others. There are at least three major potential objections to any such argument.

The first is that any normative justification for a theistic complex of seeings-as is heavily outweighed by various side effects of such seeings-as. The God-talk involved, some say, implies an authoritarian, patriarchal morality, fit at best for the early stages of child-rearing; implied also are an archaic sexism, tribal arrogance, and species chauvinism, among other evils. Even if the God-talk implies or encourages no such things, the habit of subject-predicate literalism is too ingrained to be broken even by the utmost self-conscious intellectual tact, which the ordinary believer cannot achieve anyway. Hence continued use of God-talk must inevitably encourage the wrong sort of supernaturalism, in talk of creation, miracles, power, and more. And since such supernaturalism not only has no evidence for it but has the bulk of evidence against it, it seduces the believer into irrationalism and superstition. The evils of such side effects outweigh whatever normative support there might be for the God-talk at issue and show that the theistic values cannot be among the true ones.

The second sort of objection is that *other* religious varieties of seeing-as might well be normatively justified too, or instead. What, if anything, is normatively superior about Western theism (Jewish, Christian, Islamic)? Why not some Far Eastern variety of theism? Why not some nontheistic variety of a Far Eastern religion? All these alternatives represent forms of life and complexes of seeings-as that rival the best of ours and indeed seem superior in some respects, as for example in the attitudes they encourage toward animals, plants, and the environment as a whole.

The third is simply that the normative argument will lead away from any traditional variety of religious seeing-as, including Oriental, perhaps because the bad side effects of any such religious discourse—laden as it is with supernaturalism—must always outweigh whatever normative evidence there might be for the truth of such discourse.

These objections and others may or may not succeed. They merely indicate that our theologian has work to do, either by way of arguing that the foregoing implications and side effects are not so bad, or that they really do not follow from theism properly understood or properly revised. The point here is that the work would be work in value theory or axiology, not in metaphysics or ontology, let alone in cosmogony. And as seen, the axiological work can go on entirely within a physicalist metaphysics.

Suppose the normative argument does indeed lead away from traditional forms of religious seeing-as, away from those that are more or less sufficient from the point of view of one (or more) of the great world religions. Even then, not all God-talk is out. For example, suppose we construe 'God exists' as a meta-assertion to the effect both that there is a truth of the matter in morals, first principles included, and that we will to be governed by the principles, whatever they are and come what may. According to the determinacy of valuation, there is indeed a truth of the matter in morals. So the first part of this assertion that God exists is true. The rest is a matter of our will, a matter of resolve or commitment, hence in that sense a matter of faith.

What exactly is involved in the meta-assertion that there is a truth of the matter in morals? To the extent that this meta-assertion is supposed to rest on the determinacy of valuation, it involves whatever the argument for the determinacy involves (§6.1). That argument rests on two stated premises, EP and MEA. It follows that to assert 'God exists' is, on this account at least, to assert EP and MEA. It follows further that if one rejects EP, by being unwilling to treat like cases alike, then one is an atheist. Likewise, to be a meta-ethical relativist is to be an atheist. In short, if in either sense everything is permitted, then God does not exist.

What Dostoevsky's character actually said was the converse: "If God does not exist, then everything is permitted." Suppose, not implausibly, that Ivan meant there would be no truth of the matter in morals. Then what he said is true, on any account according to which 'God exists' is implied by the meta-assertion that there is a truth of the matter in morals. This meta-assertion, however, is not equivalent merely to the conjunction of EP and MEA, though it does involve them to the extent that the argument for there being a truth of the matter rests in part on EP and MEA.

What else does it rest on? Not surprisingly, it rests also on the assumption that there is a truth of the matter as regards description, a point taken for granted ever since §1.1. To see that this further assumption is needed, recall that the conjunction of EP and MEA entails that the world's entities and their natural properties allow one and only one distribution of truth-values over the moral judgments (§6.1). Hence there is a truth of the matter as to which such distribution is correct only if there is a truth of the matter as to what the natural properties are. That is, there is a truth of the matter in morals only if there is a truth of the matter in description. Moral realism presupposes descriptive realism.

It follows that to be an antirealist is to be an atheist. This is true not only when 'God exists' is *equivalent* to the meta-assertion that there is a truth of the matter in morals but also when it only *implies* it, as it does in all traditional varieties of theism, East and West. If what there is does not determine the descriptive truths irrespective of our capacity to know them—if in this deep sense everything is permitted, and we are the measure—then again God does not exist.

We argued in §1.1 that what there is does determine the descriptive truths. The argument assumed that the (value) term 'true' is to be used in such a way that (i) we allow no difference in a distribution of truth-values over a set of judgments without some relevant difference in the phenomena, and (ii) only one distribution of truth-values over the descriptive judgments is correct. It follows that committing ourselves to use 'true' in this way is to take a step in the direction of theism. Conversely, those theists ill serve their cause who abandon this objective notion of truth when their faith is threatened by the trial by prerequisites. Rejecting talk of objective truth in favor of talk of truth as subjectivity, in the manner of Kierkegaard or at least his theological descendants, is not merely to talk about truth in a changed sense but, ironically, to become an atheist. Indeed those atheists who do commit themselves to this objectivist-realist notion of truth thereby embrace notions of transcendence and mystery unavailable to antirealists who *call* themselves theists. For according to realists, there can be truths that transcend humans' capacity ever to know them even in principle, and there can thus be mysteries aplenty, even unfathomable mysteries, expressed by questions to which there is a true answer but none known or perhaps knowable by us. Faith in a God beyond our full comprehension has a precise secular counterpart in realists' commitment to use the term 'true' as they do. This should come as no surprise if we recall the historical background, which includes St. Augustine's virtually identifying God with Truth.

8.3. God as Partly the Value of a Variable

The divine substance transcends every form which our intellect attains.

— AQUINAS

Before and after Aquinas the tradition presumed that there must be some sort of divine substance or being to which 'God' could refer. Aquinas held that Aristotle, in showing that there is a first cause, had shown that the divine substance exists, though of course Aristotle could not have anticipated identifying such divinity with the God of Christian revelation. In §3.3, without any Aristotelian assumptions, we reached the Aristotelian conclusion that the First Cause or Unmoved Mover, suitably defined, does exist. By the end of Chapter 3 we had further concluded that this First Cause is eternal, immutable, independent, explanatorily necessary, and self-existent. And by the end of Chapter 7 we had seen that the First Cause determines all meaning and value.

Is it possible, contrary perhaps to all expectation, that a theologian could do in the twentieth century roughly what Aquinas did in the thirteenth? In particular, is it possible to construct a theology within which 'God', at least in certain crucial uses, refers to the First Cause as defined within an austere contemporary naturalism? Is it even desirable? Perhaps not. For we have lately noted the advantages of a theology in which 'God' does not refer. Each such advantage translates into a disadvantage for a theology in which it does. In the latter, the theologian would risk identifying God with some limited being or aspect of existence, making it more difficult to thwart idolatry, emphasize God's transcendence, account for certain differences between science and religion, and bypass abstract quarrels in metaphysics en route to the really urgent questions about values, vision, action, and community.

Even so, theologians probably should pursue referential alternatives as well. For one thing, referential alternatives would be more continuous with the tradition, which often presumes in effect that God is the value of a variable. For another, such alternatives might reassure theists made uneasy by total rejection of subject-predicate literalism: the surface grammar of God-talk cannot be *quite* so misleading, they may say; there must be *some* such talk in which a subject is ascribed a property; it cannot *all* be a matter of values and seeings-as, however objectively grounded these may be in what there is; some *further* anchor in reality is needed, via reference.

Moreover, even if the noun 'God' refers, it need not (and cannot) refer at its every occurrence but only in certain favored cases. In effect the tradition often insisted on as much, when it insisted that positive predications of God are analogical at best and that only (some of) the negative predications are unequivocally or literally true. For to call a sentence like 'God is noncorporeal' unequivocally true is to imply that in this sentence 'God' can refer to God the divine substance even when the sentence's predicate is construed literally, giving 'corporeal' the same sense it has when applied to creatures. And to call 'God is the loving creator' only analogically true is to imply that in this sentence 'God' *cannot* refer to the divine substance when the predicate is construed literally, giving 'loving' and 'creator' the same sense they have when applied to us. If 'God' is to refer to God in this and other positive predications, and if they are to be true, then the predicates must be construed nonliterally, as expressing some sort of analogy or perhaps some sort of metaphor, myth, or symbol. It follows that if the predicates are to be taken literally, or if there is no adequate account of the intended notion of analogy, metaphor, or whatever, then if the positive predication is to be true, 'God' cannot refer in it.

Doctrines of analogy are notoriously inadequate. So too are attempts to specify what underlies the metaphors, the myths, the symbols. All such doctrines and attempts encounter the same general difficulty: if the positive predication is true and 'God' refers to God, then there must be some underlying relation between God and world in virtue of which God may truly if nonliterally be called, say, the loving Creator of the world (and/or good, knowing, mighty, etc.). But what precisely is this relation (or what are the relations)? To say for example that it is "causal" is merely to use another analogy or metaphor. For it is clear that causation *ex nihilo* is not the same as any sort of causation by or among creatures. Suppose one says instead that causation *ex nihilo* is a matter of God's merely thinking and willing things into existence. Then, because such thinking and willing are radically distinct from anything in our experience, again we have been offered nothing but further analogy or metaphor. "We are hopelessly floundering in a sea of 'extended meanings' with no lifeline to the dry ground of ordinary meaning."[19]

The simplest way out—perhaps the only way—is to stipulate that in no positive predication is 'God' to refer. Hence there need be no direct relation of the expected sort between the divine substance and the world, in virtue of which the predication would be true. As to how the positive predication could be true when its subject term fails to refer, we need only recall §8.2. Such a sentence could express objectively true values limned but scarcely exhausted by the sentence's manifest or sur-

[19]Preller, 21. Cf. Hepburn (1955).

face content, values that sustain and are sustained by the experiences and seeings-as of the community of the faithful. And the objective correctness of this form of life and its values would be determined by truths about the divine substance.

Thus theologians need not indulge in murky talk of analogy, metaphor, myth, and symbol as ways of saying something true about the divine substance. Since the subject term of a positive predication does not refer to the divine substance, the predication is not strictly about the divine substance, not even analogically or metaphorically about it. If we must say the predication is about something, then the theologian had better say it is about abiding theistic values or a theistic vision of us and the world that the values require believers to preserve. In negative predications, by contrast, 'God' may be allowed to refer, and indeed to refer to one and the same being in all of them—to God the divine substance. An exception would have to be made of course for some negative predications, including any that appear within referentially opaque contexts. In this referential sort of theology, God would be the value of a variable but only partly so, in the sense that not every occurrence of the variable's intended substituend 'God' refers, even in referentially transparent contexts.

Perhaps the most important consequence of this double standard toward occurrences of 'God' is that it blocks unrestricted substitutivity of identity even in many referentially transparent contexts, such as 'God is the loving Creator'. For if a term t does not refer in a sentence ϕ, then substitution of t^* for t in ϕ, where t^* *does* refer, cannot be relied on to preserve ϕ's truth value. This is so even if in some context outside ϕ we must assert that $t = t^*$. In the latter case, however, instead of saying that substitutivity of identity breaks down even in many referentially transparent contexts, it might be clearer to say that what we had treated as transparent contexts are henceforth to be treated as opaque. If so, then the erstwhile transparent (or seemingly transparent) positive predications, such as 'God is the loving creator', would henceforth be construed as referentially opaque. Such opacity would be but a consequence of the *via negativa*, according to which only negative predications of God can be unequivocally true. More precisely, it would be a consequence if, as is surely the case, no doctrine of analogical or metaphorical or symbolic predication can overcome the general objection lately sketched, plus other objections one could raise.

Suppose a philosophical theologian decides that in certain negative predications 'God' refers to the First Cause. In any such view it follows that God is identical with the First Cause. Throughout history, with stupefying monotony, one then hears a certain blunt retort against this or any other identification of God with some God of the philosophers: if God is indeed identical with, say, the First Cause, then since God is supposed to love, understand, answer prayers, and so on, it follows (by substitutivity of identity) that the First Cause loves, understands, answers prayers, and so on. Since this is absurd, the proposed identification must be rejected. No philosopher's abstraction can possibly be the living God of faith.

At the heart of this sort of objection is literalism—in particular, subject-predicate literalism about positive predications. This explains why the objection often appears more than a little obtuse. Once one understands that the positive predications are not to be taken literally, it is fairly easy to see that their subject term 'God' need not refer to the divine substance, and should not refer to it if the positive predicates are to be construed as having at all their ordinary senses, in which they apply to creatures. In any case, to stop the objection cold, our theologian need only stipulate that 'God' is not to refer in positive predications (and probably not even in some negative ones). For if 'God' does not refer in ϕ, then substitutivity of identity cannot be relied on to preserve ϕ's truth-value, as seen. Hence our theologian would not be forced to say that the First Cause, or whatever, loves, understands, answers prayers, and so on, even analogically or metaphorically.

Our theologian could even agree—indeed insist—that no philosopher's abstraction can possibly be the living God of faith. The predicate 'is the living God of faith' is a positive one, along with the host of others it carries in its train. Having stipulated that 'God' never refers in a positive predicate, our theologian could further stipulate the following. While, for example, 'The God of Abraham, Isaac and Jacob is the living God of faith' is to be true, not only can substitution not be relied on to preserve its truth, but every substitution that does refer is to be counted as yielding a falsehood. Thus, in particular, where 'a' refers to some philosopher's abstraction, 'a is the living God of faith' is never true. No such abstraction can be the living God of faith. Doctrines of analogical or metaphorical predication are supposed to achieve the same result. But our theologian could achieve it without shouldering their notorious burdens. So too, but rather more simply, could a theologian who adopts the completely nonreferential approach outlined in §8.2.

What reasons might a contemporary theologian give for identifying the divine substance with the First Cause as defined in §3.3? First, one must be able to defeat the usual objections against identifying the divine substance with *any* God of the philosophers. The objections are mostly to the effect that key positive predications cannot be true of any such abstraction, not even analogically true. No such x can love, answer prayer, be what the believer means to pray to, perform miracles, redeem, and so on and on. But we have seen how this sort of objection can be blocked. 'God' is not to refer in any such predication, whatever the surface grammar may suggest, so that in particular 'God' is not to refer to x; further, every referring substitution for 'God' in a positive predication is to be counted as yielding a falsehood; hence x cannot be the living God of faith.

Next, with regard to what the relation is between the divine substance and the facts about the world in virtue of which these positive predications would be true, our theologian could reply, "Determination." One would not have to appeal to mystifying doctrines of analogy, metaphor, myth, symbol, or whatever. As to what the truth of the positive predications could consist in, if not in the ascription of a property to a substance, one could reply that they are true in virtue of expressing objectively correct values and seeings-as at the heart of the theist's form of life. Provided the complex normative argument mentioned in §8.2 is sound, the First Cause would indeed determine that these things are true.

How could our theologian defend against the charge that identifying the divine substance with the First Cause commits us to pantheism or to monism? The First Cause, after all, turned out to be identical with the Universe as a whole (§3.3). And even though this is meant to be the true universe—the Universe beyond the universe—identifying the divine substance with it seems to entail pantheism. This is so despite the fact that the First Cause, or the Universe beyond, satisfies the key negative predications, as seen in §3.5, in virtue of being immutable, not in time, tenseless, without beginning or end, not created, not explanatorily dependent on any being, and such that we must refrain from any positive physical predications about it—plus other positive descriptions as well—so that in this sense it "transcends every form which our intellect attains."

Our theologian would have a twofold defense. First, as pointed out in §8.2, the theology would accord truth to such sentences as 'God is the maker of heaven and earth', 'God acts and is revealed in history', 'No philosopher's abstraction is the living God of faith', and so on. All such assertions are incompatible with pantheism and monism (where both are construed as entailing that it is never correct to value or see what there is as created, as filled with miracle, as containing genuinely revelatory events, and so on, on the ground that doing so would imply a dualism). Because the theology would thus assign truth to the conjunction of the theist's key creedal sentences and falsity to the conjunction of the pantheist's, the theology would be a version of theism, not pantheism.

Unfortunately, there is a pantheist sentence—namely, 'God = the Universe'—to which truth would be assigned, precisely because the present, referential theology would identify the divine substance with the First Cause. Having to assign truth to this sentence would seem an embarrassment. Showing that it would not be is the second part of our referential theologian's defense. One must explain why merely assigning truth to this sentence would not suffice to make anyone a pantheist. Pantheism not only identifies God with the Universe but holds that therefore all and only the positive predications that can be true of God are those that can be true of the Universe. In short, the pantheist presupposes unrestricted substitutivity of identity in at least some positive predications, including 'God is the proper object of our worship, reverence, and awe'. This sentence remains true for the pantheist when 'the Universe' is substituted for 'God'. For the theist, such substitution does not preserve truth. Our referential theologian would differ from the pantheologian, then, not in the truth-value assigned to 'God = the Universe' but in adopting the double standard according to which, in positive predications but not in negative, 'God' does not refer, and substitutivity fails. Roughly speaking, what is referentially transparent according to the pantheist would be referentially opaque according to the theist. The double standard would distinguish the theist's dualism from the pantheist's monism. Perhaps in a sense the double standard would *be* the theist's dualism.

How could our theologian respond to the charge that identifying the divine substance with the First Cause is an instance of physical reduction? After all, mind-body identity theories were called reductive in §4.0, as was any theory according to which a term from a domain ψ is coextensive (of necessity or at least accidentally) with some ϕ-term. In the present instance, it is a religious term—'the divine substance' or 'God'—which is supposed to refer to the same entity as the physicalistic (or at least naturalistic) term 'the First Cause' or 'the Universe beyond the universe'.

A likely response here would be to point out that the negation of a physical or other natural predicate is not in general itself a physical or natural predicate (§4.2). The terms 'the First Cause' and 'the Universe beyond' were characterized by means of the negations of physical or natural predicates, even where strictly physical or natural predicates were used at all. Thus the Universe beyond was characterized as a certain *un*known or *in*completely known "whole," where even the spacetime by reference to which this notion of a whole or ST-sum could be clarified was itself unknown (§3.5). The First Cause too was characterized as a certain ST-sum, where again the spacetime presupposed is unknown (so it proved in §3.5). Further, the sum in this case was of all the *un*explained explainers, plus anything else with no explanation, known or unknown (FC, §3.3). Thus in some such fashion our theologian might try to argue that 'the First Cause' and 'the Universe beyond' are not physicalistic or naturalistic terms in the first place, so that the theology is not committed to any physicalist or naturalist reduction.

The difficulties for a referential theology, in which God is identified with the First Cause, seem to be multiplying, as do the contortions required to escape them. If so, we have further reason to suspect that a wholly nonreferential approach eventually would prove superior. But let us press on, if only to honor and possibly to illuminate the tradition, with which a partly referential approach would be more continuous.

The Universe beyond was characterized in §3.5 as the unknown or incompletely known whole that *physics* attempts to describe. Even if this does not suffice to make 'the Universe beyond' a strictly physical or natural term, doesn't it mean that the Universe beyond is physical in all but name? How then could the Universe be called the divine substance? Our theologian might reply first that even though physics attempts to describe this unknown or incompletely known whole, so do many other disciplines, theology included. What the theologian is interested in, unlike the physicist, are largely those aspects of the whole that determine meaning and value, and just what the meanings and values are that are thus determined. If we must call "the Universe beyond" a physical thing on the ground that physics takes a certain interest in it, then we must also call it a theological thing on the ground that theology takes an interest in it. Neither characterization would represent *the* nature of the beyond or otherwise take priority over the other. Indeed the word 'Universe', which through long usage tends to have strong naturalistic or even physicalistic connotations, looks like a monopolistic name. Hence a case could be made that on many occasions this name ought not be used of the beyond, implying as it may that there is some one vocabulary, mainly mathematical-physical, that is uniquely privileged in expressing the most fundamental aspect of the beyond.

Instead, our theologian could argue that 'God' and 'the divine substance' are names of the beyond that on occasion ought to take precedence; the beyond is not nothing but a mathematical-physical abstraction. The argument might be not only that the beyond satisfies the negative predications and determines all meaning and value, and not only that truths about it determine that the theist's key creedal sentences are objectively true, but also that there is additional normative value in thinking of the beyond as identical with God the divine substance, a value that outweighs any negative side effects such thinking may have. According to such a theology, the assertion that God exists would amount to the assertion that (i) the beyond exists (and 'the beyond' may be substituted for 'God' only in certain negative predications), and that (ii) the appropriate positive predications are true. Clause (ii) is essentially the meta-assertion discussed in §8.2 and would require the same sort of normative warrant.

So we are back to the difficult, controversial, normative argument the theologian must construct to show that the theistic seeings-as and values are among the true ones and that they frequently take precedence over others. If we are talking about Judeo-Christian theism, then neither a theology in which God is the value of a variable nor one in which God is not can quite succeed, even within the present, tolerant sort of non-reductive naturalism, unless that normative argument can be made. Otherwise the theologian has no real defense for talk of creation *ex nihilo,* of miracles, of power, of revelation, and so on (§§8.0–8.2).

I do not know whether the normative argument ultimately can be made and successfully defended. The potential objections sketched in §8.2 are not easily dismissed, at least not when properly spelled out and vigorously pursued. Those objections are, once again, that continued use of orthodox God-talk encourages not only an authoritarian, infantile morality but archaic sexism, tribal arrogance, and species chauvinism; that even if it encourages none of these, it encourages supernaturalism and hence superstition in talk of miracles, creation, power, and more; that other religious varieties of seeing-as may be superior; and that in any case no traditional variety of seeing-as in any of the great world religions is sufficiently valuable to outweigh its negative side effects, such as superstition, irrationality, fanaticism, otherworldly distraction from the social tasks at hand, or whatever.

Clearly, the theologian has work to do. But it is work in value theory, not in metaphysics. Physicalism and theism can both be true, enriching each other while correcting the other's occasional extremes. Both can express faces of the beyond. And even if the normative arguments prove someday to undercut all traditional forms of religious seeing-as—those that are more or less sufficient from the point of view of one of the great world religions—still not all God-talk is excluded, as we saw toward the end of §8.2. The assertion that God exists could amount to the assertion that there is an objective truth of the matter in morals, first principles included, and that we will to be governed by the principles, whatever they are and come what may. Thanks to the determinacy of valuation, the first part of this assertion is true, regardless of what is in the inventory of what there is. The second part is a matter of our will, a matter of resolve or commitment. Our resolve ought not be inhibited, then, by worries about what exactly is in the inventory. Freed of worries about what there is, we may concentrate instead on bringing about what there ought to be.

Bibliography

ACHINSTEIN, PETER. The Object of Explanation. In S. Korner, ed., *Explanation* (New Haven: Yale University Press, 1975), 1–45.

ALSTON, WILLIAM. (1978). Meta-Ethics and Meta-Epistemology. In A. J. Goldman and J. Kim, eds., *Values and Morals* (Dordrecht: Reidel), 275–297.

ALSTON, WILLIAM. (1979). Yes, Virginia, There Is a Real World. *Proceedings and Addresses of the American Philosophical Association,* 52, 779–808.

ANNIS, DAVID B. Epistemic Justification. *Philosophia,* 6 (1976), 259–266.

ARMSTRONG, DAVID M. *A Materialist Theory of Mind.* London: Routledge and Kegan Paul, 1968.

AVERILL, EDWARD W. (1982). The Primary-Secondary Quality Distinction. *Philosophical Review,* 91, 843–861.

AVERILL, EDWARD W. (1985). Color and the Anthropocentrism Problem. *Journal of Philosophy,* 82, 281–304.

BAIER, KURT. The Meaning of Life. In E. D. Klemke, ed., *The Meaning of Life* (New York: Oxford University Press, 1981), 81–117.

BAKER, LYNNE RUDDER. Temporal Becoming: The Argument from Physics. *Philosophical Forum,* 6 (1974), 218–236.

BAMBROUGH, RENFORD. *Reason, Truth and God.* London: Methuen, 1969.

BARTELSON, C. J. BROWN. *Color Research and Application,* 1 (1976), 181–191.

BELNAP, NUEL D. Questions: Their Presuppositions, and How They Can Fail to Arise. In Karel Lambert, ed., *The Logical Way of Doing Things* (New Haven; Yale University Press, 1969), 23–39.

BENACERRAF, PAUL. What Numbers Could Not Be. *Philosophical Review,* 74 (1965), 47–73.

BENNETT, JAMES O. 'The Meaning of Life': A Qualitative Perspective. *Canadian Journal of Philosophy,* 14 (1984), 581–592.

BERGMANN, FRITHJOF. (1985). Review of R. Solomon's *The Passions. Journal of Philosophy,* 75, 200–208.

BERGMANN, MERRIE. (1982). Metaphorical Assertions. *Philosophical Review,* 91, 229–245.

BERGSON, HENRI. *Creative Evolution.* London: Macmillan, 1911.

BLACK, MAX. (1962). *Models and Metaphors.* Ithaca: Cornell University Press.

BLACK, MAX. (1979). More about Metaphors. In A. Ortony, ed., *Metaphor and Thought* (Cambridge: Cambridge University Press), 19–43.

BLACKBURN, SIMON. (1971). Moral Realism. In J. Casey, ed., *Morality and Moral Reasoning* (London: Methuen), 106–124.

BLACKBURN, SIMON. (1984). *Spreading the Word.* Oxford: Clarendon Press.

BLACKBURN, SIMON. (1985a). Errors and the Phenomenology of Value. In T. Honderich, ed., *Morality and Objectivity* (London: Routledge and Kegan Paul), 1–22.

BLACKBURN, SIMON. (1985b). Supervenience Revisited. In I. Hacking, ed., *Exercises in Analysis: Essays by Students of Casimir Lewy* (Cambridge: Cambridge University Press), 47–67.

BLOCK, NED. What Is Functionalism? In Ned Block, ed., *Readings in the Philosophy of Psychology,* vol. 1 (Cambridge: Harvard University Press, 1980), 67–106.

BONEVAC, DANIEL A. Mathematics and Metalogic. *Monist,* 67 (1984), 56–71.

BORN, MAX. Physical Reality. *Philosophical Quarterly,* 3 (1953), 139–194.

BOYD, RICHARD. (1979). Metaphor and Theory Change. In A. Ortony, ed., *Metaphor and Thought* (Cambridge: Cambridge University Press), 356–408.

BOYD, RICHARD. (1980). Materialism without Reductionism: What Physicalism Does Not Entail. In Ned Block, ed., *Readings in the Philosophy of Psychology,* vol. 1 (Cambridge: Harvard University Press), 67–106.

BOYD, RICHARD. (1982). Scientific Realism and Naturalistic Epistemology. In P. D. Asquith and R. N. Giere, eds., *PSA 1980,* vol. 2 (East Lansing, Mich.: Philosophy of Science Association).

BOYD, RICHARD. (Forthcoming). How to Be a Moral Realist. In G. Sayre-McCord, ed., *Moral Realism* (Ithaca: Cornell University Press).

BRINK, DAVID. (1984). Moral Realism and the Skeptical Arguments from Disagreement and Queerness. *Australasian Journal of Philosophy,* 62, 111–125.

BRINK, DAVID. (1986). Externalist Moral Realism. *Southern Journal of Philosophy,* 24, Supplement, 23–41.

BROMBERGER, SYLVAIN. Why-Questions. In Robert G. Colodny, ed., *Mind and Cosmos* (Pittsburgh: University of Pittsburgh Press, 1966), 86–111.

BROOKE-ROSE, C. *A Grammar of Metaphor.* London: Secker and Warburg, 1958.

BURGE, TYLER. Semantical Paradox. *Journal of Philosophy,* 76 (1979), 169–198.

BURRILL, DONALD P., ed. *The Cosmological Arguments.* Garden City, N.Y.: Anchor Books, 1967.

CAMPBELL, KEITH. Materialism. In P. Edwards, ed., *Encyclopedia of Philosophy,* vol. 5 (New York: Macmillan, 1967), 179–188.

CAMUS, ALBERT. *The Stranger.* New York: Vintage. 1946. Translated by Stuart Gilbert.

CARR, CRAIG L. The Concept of Formal Justice. *Philosophical Studies,* 39 (1981), 211–226.

CARTWRIGHT, RICHARD. Scattered Objects. In K. Lehrer, ed., *Analysis and Meta-*

physics: Essays in Honor of Roderick Chisholm (Dordrecht: Reidel, 1975), 153–171.

CASTAÑEDA, HECTOR-NERI. (1973). On the Conceptual Autonomy of Morality. *Nôus*, 7, 67–77.

CASTAÑEDA, HECTOR-NERI. (1975). *Thinking and Doing*. Dordrecht: Reidel.

CAUSEY, ROBERT. (1972a). Attribute Identities in Microreductions. *Journal of Philosophy*, 69, 407–422.

CAUSEY, ROBERT. (1972b). Uniform Microreduction. *Synthese*, 25, 176–218.

CHEN, EDWIN. Michigan's PBB Disaster. *Atlantic*, 244 (1979), 16–26.

CHIHARA, CHARLES S. *Ontology and the Vicious Circle Principle*. Ithaca: Cornell University Press, 1973.

CHISHOLM, RODERICK. Converse Intentional Properties. *Journal of Philosophy*, 79 (1982), 537–545.

CHRISTIAN, WILLIAM A. Domains of Truth. *American Philosophical Quarterly*, 12 (1975), 61–68.

CHURCHLAND, PAUL. (1979). *Scientific Realism and the Plasticity of Mind*. Cambridge: Cambridge University Press.

CHURCHLAND, PAUL. (1981). Eliminative Materialism and Propositional Attitudes. *Journal of Philosophy*, 78, 67–90.

CHURCHLAND, PAUL. (1985). Reduction, Qualia, and the Direct Introspection of Brain States. *Journal of Philosophy*, 82, 8–28.

COLLINGWOOD, R. G. *An Essay on Metaphysics*. Oxford: Clarendon Press, 1940.

COPP, DAVID. Considered Judgments and Moral Justification: Conservatism in Moral Theory. In D. Copp and D. Zimmerman, eds., *Morality, Reason and Truth* (Totowa, N.J.: Rowman and Allanheld, 1985), 141–168.

CORNMAN, JAMES. Foundational versus Nonfoundational Theories of Empirical Justification. *American Philosophical Quarterly*, 17 (1977), 287–297.

CRESSWELL, M. J. The World Is Everything That Is the Case. *Australasian Journal of Philosophy*, 50 (1972), 1–13.

DAHER, ADEL. God and Factual Necessity. *Religious Studies*, 6 (1970), 23–40.

DANCY, JONATHAN. On Moral Properties. *Mind*, 90 (1981), 367–385.

DAVIDSON, DONALD. (1970). Mental Events. In L. Foster and J. W. Swanson, eds., *Experience and Theory* (Amherst: University of Massachusetts Press), 79–101.

DAVIDSON, DONALD. (1977). Reality without Reference. *Dialectica*, 31, 247–258.

DAVIDSON, DONALD. (1978). What Metaphors Mean. *Critical Inquiry*, 5, 31–47.

DAVIES, PAUL. *God and the New Physics*. New York: Simon and Schuster, 1983.

DRETSKE, FRED. Laws of Nature. *Philosophy of Science*, 44 (1977), 248–268.

DREYFUS, HUBERT, AND SAMUEL TODES. The Existential Critique of Objectivity. In J. M. Edie and F. H. Parker, eds., *Patterns in the Life World: Essays in Honor of John Wild* (Evanston: Northwestern University Press, 1970), 346–387.

EARMAN, JOHN. (1972). Some Aspects of General Relativity and Geometrodynamics. *Journal of Philosophy*, 69, 634–647.

EARMAN, JOHN. (1977). Till the End of Time. In J. Earman, C. Glymour, and J. Stachel, eds., *Foundations of Space-Time Theories* (Minneapolis: University of Minnesota Press), 109–133.

EARMAN, JOHN. (1978). The Universality of Laws. Philosophy of Science, 45, 173–181.

EBERLE, ROLF. (1970a). Nominalistic Systems. Dordrecht: Reidel.

EBERLE, ROLF. (1970b). Models, Metaphors, and Interpretations. Appendix to C. Turbayne's The Myth of Metaphor, rev. ed. (Columbia: University of South Carolina Press), 219–233.

EDWARDS, PAUL. (1967a). Why? In P. Edwards, ed., Encyclopedia of Philosophy, vol. 8 (New York: Macmillan), 296–302.

EDWARDS, PAUL. (1967b). The Cosmological Argument. In D. P. Burrill, ed., The Cosmological Arguments (Garden City, N.Y.: Anchor Books), 101–123.

ELLIS, BRIAN. Truth as a Mode of Evaluation. Pacific Philosophical Quarterly, 61 (1980), 85–99.

EWING, A. C. The Fundamental Questions of Philosophy. New York: Macmillan, 1951.

FEINBERG, GERALD. Physics and the Thales Problem. Journal of Philosophy, 63 (1966), 5–17.

FEYERABEND, PAUL. Materialism and the Mind-Body Problem. Review of Metaphysics, 17 (1963), 49–66.

FIELD, HARTRY. (1973). Theory Change and the Indeterminacy of Reference. Journal of Philosophy, 70, 462–481.

FIELD, HARTRY. (1974). Quine and the Correspondence Theory. Philosophical Review, 83, 200–228.

FIELD, HARTRY. (1980). Science without Numbers. Princeton: Princeton University Press.

FIELD, HARTRY. (1982). Realism and Relativism. Journal of Philosophy, 79, 553–567.

FINDLAY, JOHN N. Axiological Ethics. London: Macmillan, 1970.

FRANKLIN, R. L. Necessary Being. Australasian Journal of Philosophy, 35 (1957), 97–110.

FRIEDMAN, MICHAEL. (1975). Physicalism and the Indeterminacy of Translation. Noûs, 9, 353–374.

FRIEDMAN, MICHAEL. (1979). Review of van Fraassen's The Scientific Image. Journal of Philosophy, 79, 274–283.

FRIEDMAN, MICHAEL. (1983). Foundations of Space-Time Theories. Cambridge, Mass.: Harvard University Press.

FUMERTON, R. A. Inferential Justification and Empiricism. Journal of Philosophy, 73 (1976), 557–569.

GADAMER, HANS-GEORG. Truth and Method. New York: Seabury, 1975.

GEACH, PETER T. Commentary on Aquinas. In D. P. Burrill, ed., The Cosmological Arguments (Garden City, N.Y.: Anchor Books, 1967), 58–82.

GEORGI, HOWARD, AND S. L. GLASHOW. Unity of All Elementary Particle Forces. Physical Review Letters, 32 (1974), 438–441.

GEROCH, ROBERT. Space-Time Structure from a Global Viewpoint. In R. K. Sachs, ed., General Relativity and Cosmology (New York: Academic Press, 1971), 71–103.

GEWIRTH, ALAN. Ethics. Encyclopaedia Britannica, vol. 6 (15th ed., 1974) 976–998.

GILKEY, LANGDON. (1965). *Maker of Heaven and Earth: A Study of the Christian Doctrine of Creation*. Garden City, N.Y.: Doubleday.

GILKEY, LANGDON. (1969). *Naming the Whirlwind: The Renewal of God-Language*. New York: Bobbs-Merrill.

GLYMOUR, CLARK. (1977). Indistinguishable Space-Times and the Fundamental Group. In J. Earman, C. Glymour, and J. Stachel, eds., *Foundations of Space-Time Theories* (Minneapolis: University of Minnesota Press), 50–60.

GLYMOUR, CLARK. (1978). Two Flagpoles Are More Paradoxical than One. *Philosophy of Science*, 45, 118–119.

GOODMAN, FELICITAS D. (1972). *Speaking in Tongues*. Chicago: University of Chicago Press.

GOODMAN, NELSON. (1960). The Way the World Is. *Review of Metaphysics*, 14, 48–56.

GOODMAN, NELSON. (1966). *The Structure of Appearance*. New York: Bobbs-Merrill.

GOODMAN, NELSON. (1978a). *Ways of Worldmaking*. Indianapolis: Hackett.

GOODMAN, NELSON. (1978b). Reply to Hellman. *Erkenntnis*, 12, 285–288.

GRAVES, JOHN. *The Conceptual Foundations of Contemporary Relativity Theory*. Cambridge, Mass.: MIT Press, 1971.

GRIM, PATRICK. There Is No Set of All Truths. *Analysis*, 44 (1984), 206–208.

GRÜNBAUM, ADOLF. (1967a). The Status of Temporal Becoming. In R. M. Gale, ed., *The Philosophy of Time* (Garden City, N.Y.: Doubleday), 322–353.

GRÜNBAUM, ADOLF. (1967b). *Modern Science and Zeno's Paradoxes*. Middletown, Conn.: Wesleyan University Press.

GRÜNBAUM, ADOLF. (1968). *Geometry and Chronometry in Philosophical Perspective*. Minneapolis: University of Minnesota Press.

GRÜNBAUM, ADOLF. (1971). The Meaning of Time. In E. Freeman, ed., *Basic Issues in the Philosophy of Time* (Lasalle, Ill.: Open Court), 195–228.

GRÜNBAUM, ADOLF. (1973). Geometry and Ontology. *Journal of Philosophy*, 70, 775–800.

GRÜNBAUM, ADOLF. (1977). Absolute and Relational Theories of Space and Space-Time. In J. Earman, C. Glymour, and J. Stachel, eds., *Foundations of Space-Time Theories* (Minneapolis: University of Minnesota Press), 303–373.

HARDIN, CLYDE L. (1983). Colors, Normal Observers and Standard Conditions. *Journal of Philosophy*, 80, 806–813.

HARDIN, CLYDE L. (1984). A New Look at Color. *American Philosophical Quarterly*, 21, 123–133.

HARE, R. M. (1952). *The Language of Morals*. Oxford: Clarendon Press.

HARE, R. M. (1957). Nothing Matters. In his *Applications of Moral Philosophy* (Berkeley: University of California Press, 1972), 32–47.

HARE, R. M. (1963). *Freedom and Reason*. Oxford: Clarendon Press.

HARE, R. M. (1985). Ontology in Ethics. In T. Honderich, ed., *Morality and Objectivity* (London: Routledge and Kegan Paul), 39–53.

HARMAN, GILBERT. (1965). The Inference to Best Explanation. *Philosophical Review*, 74, 88–95.

HARMAN, GILBERT. (1976). Inferential Justification. *Journal of Philosophy*, 73, 570–571.

HARMAN, GILBERT. (1977). *The Nature of Morality: An Introduction to Ethics.* New York: Oxford University Press.

HARMAN, GILBERT. (1978). What is Moral Relativism? In A. J. Goldman and J. Kim, eds., *Values and Morals* (Dordrecht: Reidel), 143–161.

HARMAN, GILBERT. (1985). Is There a Single True Morality? In D. Copp and D. Zimmerman, eds., *Morality, Reason and Truth* (Totowa, N.J.: Rowman and Allanheld), 27–48.

HARMAN, GILBERT. (1986). Moral Explanations of Natural Facts—Can Moral Claims Be Tested against Moral Reality? *Southern Journal of Philosophy,* 24, Supplement, 57–68.

HARRIES, KARSTEN. (1978a). Metaphor and Transcendence. *Critical Inquiry,* 5, 73–90.

HARRIES, KARSTEN. (1978b). Fundamental Ontology and the Search for Man's Place. In M. Murray, ed., *Heidegger and Modern Philosophy: Critical Essays* (New Haven: Yale University Press), 65–79.

HARRIS, J. H. Popper's Definitions of Verisimilitude. *British Journal for the Philosophy of Science,* 25 (1974), 160–166.

HAUGELAND, JOHN. Weak Supervenience. *American Philosophical Quarterly,* 19 (1982), 93–103.

HAWKING, S. W., AND G. F. R. ELLIS. *The Large Scale Structure of Space-Time.* Cambridge: Cambridge University Press, 1973.

HEIDEGGER, MARTIN. (1959). *An Introduction to Metaphysics.* New Haven, Conn.: Yale University Press. This is Ralph Manheim's translation of *Einführung in die Metaphysik* (Tubingen, 1953).

HEIDEGGER, MARTIN. (1971). *Poetry, Language, Thought.* New York: Harper and Row. Translated by Albert Hofstadter.

HELLMAN, GEOFFREY. (1978). Accuracy and Actuality. *Erkenntnis,* 12, 209–228.

HELLMAN, GEOFFREY. (1983). Realist Principles. *Philosophy of Science,* 50, 227–249.

HELLMAN, GEOFFREY. (1985). Determination and Logical Truth. *Journal of Philosophy,* 82, 607–616.

HELLMAN, GEOFFREY, AND F. W. THOMPSON. (1975). Physicalism: Ontology, Determination, Reduction. *Journal of Philosophy,* 72, 551–564.

HELLMAN, GEOFFREY, AND F. W. THOMPSON. (1977). Physicalist Materialism. *Nôus,* 11, 309–345.

HEMPEL, CARL G. *Philosophy of Natural Science.* Englewood Cliffs, N.J.: Prentice-Hall, 1966.

HEPBURN, R. W. (1955). Demythologizing and the Problem of Validity. In A. Flew and A. MacIntyre, eds., *New Essays in Philosophical Theology* (London: Macmillan), 227–242.

HEPBURN, R. W. (1981). Questions about the Meaning of Life. In E. D. Klemke, ed., *The Meaning of Life* (New York: Oxford University Press), 209–226.

HETHERINGTON, STEPHEN C. Tooley's Theory of Laws of Nature. *Canadian Journal of Philosophy,* 13 (1983), 101–106.

HICK, JOHN. (1960). God as Necessary Being. *Journal of Philosophy,* 57, 725–734.

HICK, JOHN. (1983). *Philosophy of Religion,* 3rd ed. Englewood Cliffs, N.J.: Prentice-Hall.

HORGAN, TERENCE. (1982). Supervenience and Microphysics. *Pacific Philosophical Quarterly,* 63, 29–43.

HORGAN, TERENCE. (1984). Supervenience and Cosmic Hermeneutics. *Southern Journal of Philosophy,* 22, Supplement, 19–38.

HUDSON, W. D., ed. *The Is-Ought Question.* London: Macmillan, 1969.

HULL, DAVID L. *Philosophy of Biological Science.* Englewood Cliffs, N.J.: Prentice-Hall, 1974.

HUME, DAVID. *A Treatise of Human Nature.* Garden City, N.Y.: Doubleday, 1961.

HURVICH, LEO M. *Color Vision.* Sunderland, Minn.: Sinauer, 1981.

HUXLEY, JULIAN. *Religion without Revelation.* New York: Harper, 1958.

ISHAM, C. J., R. PENROSE, AND D. W. SCIAMA, eds. *Quantum Gravity 2: A Second Oxford Symposium.* Oxford: Clarendon Press, 1981.

JACKSON, FRANK, ROBERT PARGETTER, AND ELIZABETH W. PRIOR. Functionalism and Type-Type Identity Theories. *Philosophical Studies,* 42 (1982), 209–225.

JOSKE, W. D. Philosophy and the Meaning of Life. In E. D. Klemke, ed., *The Meaning of Life* (New York: Oxford University Press, 1981), 248–261.

KEUTH, HERBERT. Verisimilitude or the Approach to the Whole Truth. *Philosophy of Science,* 43 (1976), 311–336.

KILDAHL, JOHN P. *The Psychology of Speaking in Tongues.* New York: Harper and Row, 1972.

KIM, JAEGWON. (1978). Supervenience and Nomological Incommensurables. *American Philosophical Quarterly,* 15, 149–158.

KIM, JAEGWON. (1979). Causality, Identity and Supervenience in the Mind-Body Problem. *Midwest Studies in Philosophy,* 4, 31–49.

KIM, JAEGWON. (1982). Psychophysical Supervenience. *Philosophical Studies,* 41, 51–70.

KIM, JAEGWON. (1984a). Supervenience and Supervenient Causation. *Southern Journal of Philosophy,* 22, Supplement, 45–56.

KIM, JAEGWON. (1984b). Concepts of Supervenience. *Philosophy and Phenomenological Research,* 45, 153–176.

KIMBROUGH, STEVEN O. On the Reduction of Genetics to Molecular Biology. *Philosophy of Science,* 46 (1979), 389–406.

KLEE, ROBERT L. Micro-Determinism and Concepts of Emergence. *Philosophy of Science,* 51 (1984), 44–63.

KNEALE, WILLIAM C. (1960). Time and Eternity. *Proceedings of the Aristotelian Society,* 61, 87–108.

KNEALE, WILLIAM C. (1967). Eternity. In P. Edwards, ed., *Encyclopedia of Philosophy,* vol. 3 (New York: Macmillan), 63–66.

KRIPKE, SAUL. (1975). Outline of a Theory of Truth. *Journal of Philosophy,* 72, 690–716.

KRIPKE, SAUL. (1982). *Wittgenstein on Rules and Private Language.* Cambridge, Mass.: Harvard University Press.

KUHN, THOMAS. (1979). Metaphor in Science. In A. Ortony, ed., *Metaphor and Thought* (Cambridge: Cambridge University Press), 409–419.

KYBURG, HENRY. Conjunctivitis. In M. Swain, ed., *Induction, Acceptance, and Rational Belief* (Dordrecht: Reidel, 1970), 55–82.

LAKOFF, GEORGE, AND MARK JOHNSON. (1980a). Conceptual Metaphor in Everyday Language. *Journal of Philosophy*, 77, 453–486.

LAKOFF, GEORGE, AND MARK JOHNSON. (1980b). *Metaphors We Live By*. Chicago: University of Chicago Press.

LEATHERDALE, W. H. *The Role of Analogy, Model and Metaphor in Science*. New York: American Elsevier, 1974.

LEVIN, MICHAEL. *Metaphysics and the Mind-Body Problem*. Oxford: Clarendon Press, 1979.

LEWIS, DAVID. (1983a). New Work for a Theory of Universals. *Australasian Journal of Philosophy*, 61, 343–377.

LEWIS, DAVID. (1983b). *Philosophical Papers*. Oxford: Oxford University Press.

LEWIS, DAVID. (1984). Putnam's Paradox. *Australasian Journal of Philosophy*, 62, 221–236.

LICHTENBERG, JUDITH. Subjectivism as Moral Weakness Projected. *Philosophical Quarterly*, 33 (1984), 378–385.

LITTLE, DANIEL. Reflective Equilibrium and Justification. *Southern Journal of Philosophy*, 22 (1984), 373–387.

LYCAN, WILLIAM G. (1969). Hare, Singer and Gewirth on Universalizability. *Philosophical Quarterly*, 19, 135–144.

LYCAN, WILLIAM G. (1970). Identifiability-Dependence and Ontological Priority. *Personalist*, 51, 503–513.

LYCAN, WILLIAM G. (1979). The Trouble with Possible Worlds. In Michael Loux, ed., *The Possible and the Actual* (Ithaca: Cornell University Press), 274–316.

LYCAN, WILLIAM G. (1981). Form, Function, and Feel. *Journal of Philosophy*, 78, 24–50.

LYONS, DAVID. Ethical Relativism and the Problem of Incoherence. *Ethics*, 86 (1976), 107–121.

McCALL, STORRS. Objective Time Flow. *Philosophy of Science*, 43 (1976), 337–362.

McDOWELL, JOHN. Values and Secondary Qualities. In T. Honderich, ed., *Morality and Objectivity* (London: Routledge and Kegan Paul, 1985), 110–129.

McFETRIDGE, I. G. Supervenience, Realism, Necessity. *Philosophical Quarterly*, 35 (1985), 245–258.

MACKENZIE, J. C. Moral Scepticism and Moral Conduct. *Philosophy*, 59 (1984), 473–479.

MACKIE, J. L. *Ethics: Inventing Right and Wrong*. New York: Penguin Books, 1977.

MACKINNON, D. M. *The Problem of Metaphysics*. Cambridge: Cambridge University Press, 1974.

MADDY, PENELOPE. Sets and Numbers. *Nôus*, 15 (1981), 495–511.

MALAMENT, DAVID. Observationally Indistinguishable Space-Times: Comment on Glymour's Paper. In J. Earman, C. Glymour, and J. Stachel, eds., *Foundations of Space-Time Theories* (Minneapolis: University of Minnesota Press, 1977), 61–80.

MARGOLIS, JOSEPH. (1978). *Persons and Minds: The Prospects of Nonreductive Materialism.* Dordrecht: Reidel.

MARGOLIS, JOSEPH. (1984). *Philosophy of Psychology.* Englewood Cliffs, N.J.: Prentice-Hall.

MENDELSON, ELLIOTT. *Introduction to Mathematical Logic,* 2d ed. New York: Van Nostrand, 1979.

MERRILL, G. H. The Model-Theoretic Argument against Realism. *Philosophy of Science,* 47 (1980), 69–81.

MILLER, BARRY. (1974). Making Sense of Necessary Existence. *American Philosophical Quarterly,* 11, 47–54.

MILLER, DAVID (1974a). Popper's Qualitative Theory of Similitude. *British Journal for the Philosophy of Science,* 25, 166–177.

MILLER, DAVID (1974b). On the Comparison of False Theories by their Bases. *British Journal for the Philosophy of Science,* 25, 178–188.

MISNER, C., K. THORNE, AND J. A. WHEELER. *Gravitation.* San Francisco: W. H. Freeman, 1973.

MITCHELL, BASIL. *Morality: Religious and Secular.* Oxford: Oxford University Press, 1980.

MOHANTY, J. N. Intentionality and Noema. *Journal of Philosophy,* 78 (1981), 706–717.

MONDADORI, FABRIZIO, AND ADAM MORTON. Modal Realism: The Poisoned Pawn. *Philosophical Review,* 85 (1976), 3–20.

MOORE, A. W. (1984). Possible Worlds and Diagonalization. *Analysis,* 44, 21–22.

MOORE, G. E. (1922). *Philosophical Studies.* London: Routledge and Kegan Paul.

MORAVCSIK, J. M. E. Strawson and Ontological Priority. In R. J. Butler, ed., *Analytical Philosophy: Second Series* (New York: Barnes and Noble, 1965), 106–119.

MUNITZ, MILTON. *The Mystery of Existence.* New York: Appleton-Century-Crofts, 1965.

NABOKOV, VLADIMIR. *Bend Sinister.* New York: Holt, 1947.

NAGEL, THOMAS. *Mortal Questions.* Cambridge: Cambridge University Press, 1979.

NERLICH, GRAHAM. (1979a). Is Curvature Intrinsic to Physical Space? *Philosophy of Science,* 46, 439–458.

NERLICH, GRAHAM. (1979b). What Can Geometry Explain? *British Journal for the Philosophy of Science,* 30, 69–83.

NIELSEN, KAI. On Deriving an Ought from an Is: A Retrospective Look. *Review of Metaphysics,* 32 (1979), 487–514.

NOVITZ, DAVID. Another Look at Metaphorical Meaning. *Philosophia,* 15 (1985), 325–328.

NOZICK, ROBERT. *Philosophical Explanations.* Cambridge, Mass.: Harvard University Press, 1981.

OAKLEY, I. T. An Argument for Scepticism concerning Justified Beliefs. *American Philosophical Quarterly,* 13 (1976), 226–237.

PEACOCKE, CHRISTOPHER. Review of Lewis's *Philosophical Papers. Journal of Philosophy,* 82 (1985), 42–45.

PENELHUM, TERENCE M. Divine Necessity. In D. P. Burrill, ed., *The Cosmological Arguments* (Garden City, N.Y.: Anchor Books, 1967), 143–161.

PETERSON, SANDRA. Remarks on Three Formulations of Ethical Relativism. *Ethics,* 95 (1985), 887–908.

PLACE, U. T. Is Consciousness a Brain Process? *British Journal of Psychology,* 47 (1956), 44–50.

PLANTINGA, ALVIN. (1967a). Necessary Being. In D. P. Burrill, ed., *The Cosmological Arguments* (Garden City, N.Y.: Anchor Books, 1967), 125–141.

PLANTINGA, ALVIN. (1967b). *God and Other Minds.* Ithaca: Cornell University Press.

POLAKOW, AVRON. *Tense and Performance.* Amsterdam: Rodopi, 1981.

POLLOCK, JOHN. *Knowledge and Justification.* Princeton: Princeton University Press, 1974.

POPKIN, RICHARD H. *The History of Skepticism from Erasmus to Spinoza.* Berkeley: University of California Press, 1979.

POST, JOHN F. (1971). Paradox in Critical Rationalism and Related Theories. *Philosophical Forum,* 3, 27–61.

POST, JOHN F. (1974). New Foundations for Philosophical Theology: Quine with God. *Journal of Philosophy,* 71, 736–748.

POST, JOHN F. (1978). Review of M. Fisk's *Nature and Necessity. British Journal for the Philosophy of Science,* 19, 189–195.

POST, JOHN F. (1979). Presupposition, Bivalence and the Possible Liar. *Philosophia,* 8, 645–650.

POST, JOHN F. (1980). Infinite Regresses of Justification and of Explanation. *Philosophical Studies,* 38, 31–52.

POST, JOHN F. (1983). A Gödelian Theorem for Theories of Rationality. *Proceedings of the 11th International Conference on the Unity of the Sciences,* vol. 2 (New York, ICF Press), 1071–1086. Reprinted in W. W. Bartley and G. Radnitzky, eds., *Evolutionary Epistemology and Theories of Rationality* (LaSalle, Ill.: Open Court, 1986).

POST, JOHN F. (1984a). On the Determinacy of Valuation. *Philosophical Studies,* 45, 315–333.

POST, JOHN F. (1984b). On the Determinacy of Truth and Translation. *Southern Journal of Philosophy,* 22, Supplement, 117–135.

POST, JOHN F. (1984c). Comment on Teller. *Southern Journal of Philosophy,* 22, Supplement, 163–167.

PRELLER, VICTOR. *Divine Science and the Science of God: A Reformulation of Thomas Aquinas.* Princeton: Princeton University Press, 1967.

PUTNAM, HILARY. (1977). Realism and Reason. *Proceedings and Addresses of the American Philosophical Association,* 50, 483–498.

PUTNAM, HILARY. (1979). Reflections on Goodman's *Ways of Worldmaking. Journal of Philosophy,* 76, 603–618.

QUINE, W. V. (1960). *Word and Object.* Cambridge, Mass.: MIT Press.

QUINE, W. V. (1961). Two Dogmas of Empiricism. In his *From a Logical Point of View* (New York: Harper and Row), 20–46.

QUINE, W. V. (1969). *Ontological Relativity and Other Essays.* New York: Columbia University Press.

QUINE, W. V. (1970a). *Philosophy of Logic.* Englewood Cliffs, N.J.: Prentice-Hall.

QUINE, W. V. (1970b). On the Reasons for the Indeterminacy of Translation. *Journal of Philosophy,* 67, 178–183.

QUINE, W. V. (1972). *Methods of Logic,* 3rd ed. New York: Holt, Rinehart and Winston.

QUINE, W. V. (1976). *Ways of Paradox,* rev. ed. Cambridge, Mass.: Harvard University Press.

QUINE, W. V. (1978a). Goodman's *Ways of Worldmaking. New York Review of Books,* 25, 25. Reprinted in his *Theories and Things* (Cambridge: Harvard University Press, 1981), 96–99.

QUINE, W. V. (1978b). Facts of the Matter. *Southwestern Journal of Philosophy,* 9, 155–169.

QUINE, W. V. (1978c). On the Nature of Moral Values. In A. J. Goldman and J. Kim, eds., *Values and Morals* (Dordrecht: Reidel), 37–45.

QUINN, PHILIP L. *Divine Commands and Moral Requirements.* Oxford: Clarendon Press, 1978.

RATLIFF, FLOYD. On the Psychophysiological Bases of Universal Color Terms. *Proceedings of the American Philosophical Society,* 120 (1976), 311–330.

RAWLS, JOHN. Kantian Constructivism in Moral Theory: The Dewey Lectures 1980. *Journal of Philosophy,* 77 (1980), 515–572.

RESCHER, NICHOLAS. *The Coherence Theory of Truth.* London: Oxford University Press, 1973.

REYMAN, J. E. An Anasazi Solar Marker? *Science,* 209 (1980), 858–860.

RICHARDSON, ROBERT C. Functionalism and Reductionism. *Philosophy of Science,* 46 (1979), 533–558.

RORTY, RICHARD. (1965). Mind-Body Identity, Privacy, and Categories. *Review of Metaphysics,* 19, 24–54.

RORTY, RICHARD. (1970). In Defense of Eliminative Materialism. *Review of Metaphysics,* 24, 112–121.

RORTY, RICHARD. (1979). *Philosophy and the Mirror of Nature.* Princeton: Princeton University Press.

RORTY, RICHARD. (1982). *The Consequences of Pragmatism.* Minneapolis: University of Minnesota Press.

ROSENBERG, ALEXANDER. Fitness. *Journal of Philosophy,* 80 (1983), 457–473.

ROSENBERG, ALEXANDER, AND MARY B. WILLIAMS. 'Fitness' in Fact and Fiction: A Rejoinder to Sober. *Journal of Philosophy,* 82 (1985), 343–385.

ROSS, JAMES F. *Introduction to the Philosophy of Religion.* London: Macmillan, 1969.

ROTHBART, DANIEL R. The Semantics of Metaphor and the Structure of Science. *Philosophy of Science,* 51 (1984), 595–615.

ROWE, WILLIAM L. (1975). *The Cosmological Argument.* Princeton: Princeton University Press.

ROWE, WILLIAM L. (1978). *Philosophy of Religion.* Belmont, Calif.: Wadsworth.

ROWE, WILLIAM L. (1980). Review of Quinn's *Divine Commands and Moral Requirements. Philosophical Review,* 89, 637–639.

SALMON, NATHAN U. (1981). *Reference and Essence.* Princeton: Princeton University Press.

SALMON, WESLEY. (1978). Why Ask, 'Why?'? An Inquiry concerning Scientific Explanation. *Proceedings and Addresses of the American Philosophical Association,* 51, 683–705.

SAMARIN, W. J. *Tongues of Men and Angels.* New York: Macmillan, 1972.

SANTAYANA, GEORGE. (1910). *Three Philosophical Poets: Lucretius, Dante, and Goethe.* Cambridge: Harvard University Press.

SANTAYANA, GEORGE. (1957). *Dialogues in Limbo.* Ann Arbor: University of Michigan Press.

SARTRE, JEAN-PAUL. *Being and Nothingness.* New York: Philosophical Library, 1956. Translated by Hazel Barnes.

SAYRE-MCCORD, GEOFFREY. Moral Theory and Explanatory Impotence. In G. Sayre-McCord, ed., *Moral Realism* (Ithaca: Cornell University Press, forthcoming).

SCHEFFLER, ISRAEL. *Beyond the Letter.* London: Routledge and Kegan Paul, 1979.

SCHICK, F. Three Logics of Belief. In M. Swain, ed., *Induction, Acceptance, and Rational Belief* (Dordrecht: Reidel, 1970).

SCOTT, ROBERT B., JR. Five Types of Ethical Naturalism. *American Philosophical Quarterly,* 17 (1980), 261–270.

SELLARS, WILFRID. Philosophy and the Scientific Image of Man. Two lectures given at the University of Pittsburgh, December, 1960. Reprinted in his *Science, Perception and Reality* (London: Routledge and Kegan Paul, 1963).

SHOPE, ROBERT K. Eliminating Mistakes about Eliminative Materialism. *Philosophy of Science,* 46 (1979), 590–612.

SINGH, JAGJIT. *Great Ideas and Theories in Modern Cosmology.* New York: Dover, 1966.

SMART, J. J. C. (1963). *Philosophy and Scientific Realism.* London: Routledge and Kegan Paul.

SMART, J. J. C. (1972). Space-Time and Individuals. In R. Rudner and I. Scheffler, eds., *Logic and Art: Essays in Honor of Nelson Goodman* (New York: Bobbs-Merrill), 3–20.

SMART, J. J. C. (1984). *Ethics, Persuasion and Truth.* London: Routledge and Kegan Paul.

SNEED, JOSEPH D. *The Logical Structure of Mathematical Physics.* Dordrecht: Reidel, 1971.

SOAMES, SCOTT. What Is a Theory of Truth? *Journal of Philosophy,* 81 (1984), 411–429.

SOBER, ELLIOTT. Realism and Independence. *Nôus,* 16 (1982), 369–385.

SOFAER, A., V. ZINSER, AND R. M. SINCLAIR. A Unique Solar Marking Construct. *Science,* 206 (1979), 283–291.

SOLOMON, ROBERT. *The Passions.* Garden City, N.Y.: Anchor Books, 1976.

SOSA, ERNEST. (1979). The Status of Temporal Becoming: What Is Happening Now? *Journal of Philosophy,* 76, 26–42.

SOSA, ERNEST. (1980). The Raft and the Pyramid: Coherence versus Foundations in the Theory of Knowledge. In P. A. French, T. E. Uehling, and H. K. Wettstein, eds., *Minnesota Studies in Philosophy, Vol. 5—Studies in Epistemology* (Minneapolis: University of Minnesota Press, 1980), 3–25.

SOSA, ERNEST. (1983). Nature Unmirrored, Epistemology Naturalized. *Synthese,* 52, 49–72.

SPECTOR, MARSHALL. *Concepts of Reduction in Physical Science.* Philadelphia: Temple University Press, 1978.

STEGMULLER, WOLFGANG. *Collected Papers on Epistemology, Philosophy of Science and History of Philosophy.* Dordrecht: Reidel, 1977.

STERLING, MARVIN C. The Cognitive Theory of Emotions. *Southwest Journal of Philosophy,* 10 (1979), 165–176.

STERN, JOSEPH. (1983). Metaphor and Grammatical Deviance. *Nôus,* 17, 577–599.

STERN, JOSEPH. (1985). Metaphor as Demonstrative. *Journal of Philosophy,* 82, 677–710.

STEVENSON, CHARLES. Ethical Fallibility. In R. T. DeGeorge, ed., *Ethics and Society: Original Essays on Contemporary Problems* (New York: Doubleday, 1966).

STRAWSON, PETER. *Individuals: An Essay in Descriptive Metaphysics.* Garden City, N.Y.: Doubleday, 1963.

STUMP, ELEONORE, AND NORMAN KRETZMANN. Eternity. *Journal of Philosophy,* 78 (1981), 429–458.

STURGEON, NICHOLAS. (1985). Moral Explanations. In D. Copp and D. Zimmerman, eds., *Morality, Reason and Truth* (Totowa, N.J.: Rowman and Allanheld), 49–78.

STURGEON, NICHOLAS. (1986a). What Difference Does It Make Whether Moral Realism Is True? *Southern Journal of Philosophy,* 24, Supplement, 115–141.

STURGEON, NICHOLAS. (1986b). Harman on Moral Explanations of Natural Facts. *Southern Journal of Philosophy,* 24, Supplement, 69–78.

TARSKI, ALFRED. The Concept of Truth in Formalized Languages. In *Logic, Semantics, Metamathematics* (Oxford: Clarendon Press, 1956), now in a second edition, edited by John Corcoran (Indianapolis: Hackett, 1983), 152–278.

TAYLOR, CHARLES. (1971). Interpretation and the Sciences of Man. *Review of Metaphysics,* 25, 3–51.

TAYLOR, EDWIN F., AND JOHN A. WHEELER. *Spacetime Physics.* San Francisco: W. H. Freeman, 1963.

TAYLOR, RICHARD. (1963). *Metaphysics.* Englewood Cliffs, N.J.: Prentice-Hall.

TAYLOR, RICHARD. (1981). The Meaning of Life. In E. D. Klemke, ed., *The Meaning of Life* (New York: Oxford University Press), 141–150.

TELLER, PAUL. (1984). A Poor Man's Guide to Supervenience and Determination. *Southern Journal of Philosophy,* 22, Supplement, 137–162.

TELLER, PAUL. (1985). Is Supervenience Just Disguised Reduction? *Southern Journal of Philosophy,* 23, 93–99.

THAGARD, PAUL. (1978). The Best Explanation: Criteria for Theory Choice. *Journal of Philosophy,* 75, 76–92.

THAGARD, PAUL. (1982). From the Descriptive to the Normative in Psychology and Logic. *Philosophy of Science,* 49, 24–42.

TICHY, PAVEL. On Popper's Definition of Verisimilitude. *British Journal for the Philosophy of Science,* 25 (1974), 155–160.

TLUMAK, JEFFREY. Cross-Categorial Priority Arguments. *Metaphilosophy,* 14 (1983), 32–39.

TOOLEY, MICHAEL. The Nature of Laws. *Canadian Journal of Philosophy,* 7 (1977), 667–698.

TUANA, NANCY. Quine's Hidden Premises. *Southern Journal of Philosophy*, 21 (1983), 123–135.

UNGER, PETER. The Causal Theory of Reference. *Philosophical Studies*, 43 (1983), 1–45.

VAN FRAASSEN, BAS C. (1977). The Pragmatics of Explanation. *American Philosophical Quarterly*, 14, 143–150.

VAN FRAASSEN, BAS C. (1985). Salmon on Explanation. *Journal of Philosophy*, 82, 639–651.

VAN INWAGEN, PETER. The Doctrine of Arbitrary Undetached Parts. *Pacific Philosophical Quarterly*, 62 (1981), 123–127.

VICK, GEORGE. Heidegger's Linguistic Rehabilitation of Parmenides' 'Being'. In M. Murray, ed., *Heidegger and Modern Philosophy: Critical Essays* (New Haven: Yale University Press, 1978), 203–221.

WALLACE, JOHN. Only in the Context of a Sentence Do Words Have Any Meaning. *Midwest Studies in Philosophy*, 2 (1977), 144–164.

WARNOCK, G. J. Every Event Has a Cause. In Antony Flew, ed., *Logic and Language II* (Garden City, N.Y.: Anchor Books, 1965), 312–330.

WEINBERG, STEVEN. (1972). *Gravitation and Cosmology*. New York: Wiley.

WEINBERG, STEVEN. (1976). The Forces of Nature. *Bulletin of the American Academy of Arts and Sciences*, 29, 13–29.

WEINBERG, STEVEN. (1977). *The First Three Minutes: A Modern View of the Origin of the Universe*. New York: Basic Books.

WEISSMAN, DAVID. *Eternal Possibilities: A Neutral Ground for Meaning and Existence*. Carbondale: Southern Illinois University Press, 1977.

WENGART, R. G. The Logic of Essentially Ordered Causes. *Notre Dame Journal of Formal Logic*, 12 (1971), 406–422.

WHEELER, JOHN A. *Geometrodynamics*. New York: Academic Press, 1962.

WHITEHEAD, A. N. (1925). *Science and the Modern World*. New York: Macmillan.

WHITEHEAD, A. N. (1929). *Process and Reality*. New York: Macmillan.

WIGGINS, DAVID. Truth, Invention and the Meaning of Life. *Proceedings of the British Academy*, 62 (1976), 331–378.

WILLIAMS, BERNARD. (1985). Ethics and the Fabric of the World. In T. Honderich, ed., *Morality and Objectivity* (London: Routledge and Kegan Paul), 203–214.

WILLIAMS, DONALD C. (1951). The Myth of Passage. Reprinted in R. M. Gale, ed., *The Philosophy of Time* (Garden City, N.Y.: Doubleday, 1967), 98–116.

WILLIAMS, MARY B. (1970). Deducing the Consequences of Evolution. *Journal of Theoretical Biology*, 29, 343–385.

WILSON, GEORGE. (1979). Cheap Materialism. *Midwest Studies in Philosophy*, 4, 51–72.

WILSON, MARK. (1980). The Observational Uniqueness of Some Theories. *Journal of Philosophy*, 77, 208–233.

WISDOM, JOHN. The Meanings of the Question of Life. In E. D. Klemke, ed., *The Meaning of Life* (New York: Oxford University Press, 1981), 205–208.

WONG, DAVID. *Moral Relativity*. Berkeley: University of California Press, 1984.

WOODWARD, JAMES. Explanatory Asymmetries. *Philosophy of Science*, 51 (1984), 421–442.

YOUNG, J. MICHAEL. The Ontological Argument and the Concept of Substance. *American Philosophical Quarterly,* 11 (1974), 181–191.

ZIMMERMAN, DAVID. Moral Realism and Explanatory Necessity. In D. Copp and D. Zimmerman, eds., *Morality, Reason and Truth* (Totowa, N.J.: Rowman and Allanheld, 1985), 79–103.

Index

Library of Congress Cataloging-in-Publication Data

Post, John F., 1936–
    The faces of existence.

    Bibliography: p.
    Includes index.
    1. Metaphysics.   I. Title.
BD111.P65   1987   110   86-19894
ISBN 0-8014-1968-9 (alk. paper)